SPARES DIVISION

SPARE PARTS CATALOGUE

for

JAGUAR 'E' TYPE

3.8 SERIES 1
GRAND TOURING MODELS

ENGINE NUMBERS

R.1001 Onwards

RA.1001 Onwards

NOTE: Suffix /8 or /9 to the Engine Number denotes the Compression Ratio.

CHASSIS NUMBERS

Open	Right-Hand Drive	850001 Onwards
Open	Left-Hand Drive	875001 Onwards
Fixed Head Coupé	Right-Hand Drive	860001 Onwards
Fixed Head Coupé	Left-Hand Drive	885001 Onwards

JAGUAR CARS LIMITED, COVENTRY, ENGLAND

Telephone:
Coventry 27677 (P.B.X.)

PUBLICATION J.30
Code: Bentley's 2nd

Telegraphic Address:
"JAGUAR" COVENTRY

INDEX TO SECTIONS

Part No.	Description	Plate No.	No. per Unit	Remarks
C.16758	**IGNITION TIMING POINTER ON OIL SUMP**	1–68	1	
UCS.125/4R	**Screw**, Set, securing Timing Pointer to front of Oil Sump		2	
C.724	**Washer**, Shakeproof, on Setscrews		2	
FW.104/T	**Washer**, Plain, under Shakeproof Washers		2	
C.15849	**BRACKET ASSEMBLY FOR LEFT-HAND FRONT ENGINE MOUNTING**	1–69	1	
C.15850	**BRACKET ASSEMBLY FOR RIGHT-HAND FRONT ENGINE MOUNTING**	1–70	1	
UFS.143/6R	**Screw**, Set, securing Engine Mounting Brackets to Cylinder Block		6	
C.727	**Washer**, Shakeproof, on Setscrews		6	
C.18556	**FRONT ENGINE MOUNTING (RUBBER)**	1–71	2	
UFS.150/7R	**Screw**, Set, securing Engine to Rubber Mounting		2	
FW.108T	**Washer**, Plain, on Setscrews		2	
FG.108/X	**Washer**, Spring, on Setscrews		2	
C.18242	**Packing Plate**, under Rubber Mountings	1–72	As req'd	
UFS.131/6R	**Screw**, Set, securing Rubber Mountings to Flange Support Brackets		4	
C.8667/2	**Nut**, Self-Locking, on Setscrews		4	
C.12890	**STABILISING LINK AT REAR OF CYLINDER BLOCK**	1–73	1	
C.10940	**Bush**, in Stabilising Link	1–74	1	
UFB.143/14R	**Bolt**, securing Stabilising Link to Bearing Brackets		1	
C.8737/4	**Nut**, Self-Locking, on Bolt		1	
C.11607	**Stepped Washer**, on Stabilising Link, at top of Rubber Mounting	1–75	1	
C.11688	**Stepped Washer**, on Stabilising Link, at bottom of Rubber Mounting	1–76	1	
C.8667/3	**Nut**, Self-Locking, securing Stabilising Link to Rubber Mounting		1	
C.18441	**RUBBER MOUNTING FOR STABILISING LINK AT TOP**	1–77	1	⎫ SUPERSEDED BY C.20217 AND C.20201 IN SETS.
UFS.131/6R	**Screw**, Set, securing Rubber Mounting to Dash		2	
C.19267	**Tapped Plate**, for fixing of Rubber Mounting		1	
C.725	**Washer**, Shakeproof, on Setscrews		2	
FW.105/T	**Washer**, Plain, under Shakeproof Washers		2	⎭
C.20217	**RUBBER MOUNTING FOR STABILISING LINK AT TOP**		1	⎫ SUPERSEDES C.18441 AND C.19267 IN SETS.
UFS.131/6R	**Screw**, Set, securing Rubber Mounting to Dash		2	
C.20201	**Tapped Plate**, for fixing of Rubber Mounting		1	
C.725	**Washer**, Shakeproof, on Setscrews		2	
FW.105T	**Washer**, Plain, under Shakeproof Washers		2	⎭

CYLINDER BLOCK

Part No.	Description	Plate No.	No. per Unit	Remarks
C.14922	**BEARING BRACKET, L.H., ON CLUTCH HOUSING, FOR MOUNTING OF STABILISING LINK AT BOTTOM**	1–78	1	
C.14923	**BEARING BRACKET, R.H., ON CLUTCH HOUSING, FOR MOUNTING OF STABILISING LINK AT BOTTOM**	1–79	1	
UCS.131/6R	**Screw**, Set, securing Bearing Brackets to Clutch Housing		4	
C.725	**Washer**, Shakeproof, on Setscrews		4	
C.17769	**SUPPORT BRACKET ASSEMBLY FOR REAR ENGINE MOUNTING (UNDER GEARBOX)**	1–80	1	Fitted from Chassis No. 850001 to 850168. 875001 to 875590. 860001 to 860009. 885001 to 885050. **USE C.19430 FOR ALL REPLACEMENTS.**
C.19430	**SUPPORT BRACKET ASSEMBLY FOR REAR ENGINE MOUNTING (UNDER GEARBOX)**		1	Fitted from Chassis No. 850169 to 850648. 875591 to 878888. 860010 to 861061. 885051 to 888081.
UFS.131/5R	**Screw**, Set, securing Support Bracket to Body Floor		5	
FG.105/X	**Washer**, Spring, on Setscrews		5	
C.12677	**RUBBER MOUNTING UNDER GEARBOX**	1–81	2	Fitted from Chassis No. 850001 to 850648. 875001 to 878888. 860001 to 861061. 885001 to 888081.
C.8737/3	**Nut**, Self-Locking, securing Rubber Mountings to Gearbox and Support Bracket		4	
FW.106/T	**Washer**, Plain, under Nuts		4	
C.21333	**SUPPORT BRACKET ASSEMBLY FOR REAR ENGINE MOUNTING (UNDER GEARBOX)**		1	Fitted to Chassis No. 850649 and subs. 878889 and subs. 861062 and subs. 888082 and subs. **(See note below)**
C.12335	**Spring Seat** (Rubber) inside Bracket		1	
C.12265	**Centre Bush** (Rubber)		1	
C.12299	**COIL SPRING FOR REAR ENGINE MOUNTING**		1	Fitted to Chassis No. 850649 and subs. 878889 and subs. 861062 and subs. 888082 and subs. **(See note below)**
C.19119	**Retainer**, at top of Coil Spring		1	
C.21336	**Pin Assembly**, securing Retainer to Gearbox and locating Support Bracket		1	
8668	**GASKETS PACKAGE FOR COMPLETE ENGINE OVERHAUL (SD.1111)**		1	

NOTE : The following cars were fitted with Support Bracket C.19430 and Rubber Mountings C.12677:
Open R.H. Drive 850653, 850654.
Open L.H. Drive 878895, 878900, 878907, 878908, 878913, 878914, 878915, 878926, 878936, 878937, 878939, 878958, 878986, 879005, 879024, 879049.
Fixed Head R.H. Drive 861087.
Fixed Head L.H. Drive 888086, 888096, 888101, 888103, 888109, 888113, 888117, 888118, 888120, 888134, 888157, 888178, 888238.

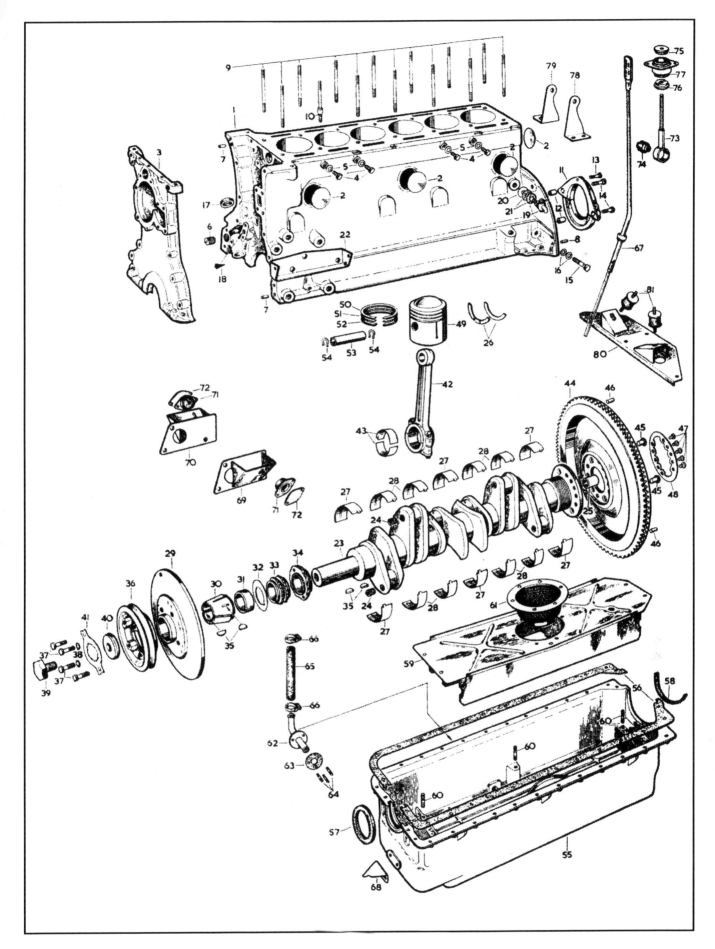

PLATE 1

OIL PUMP

Part No.	Description	Plate No.	No. per Unit	Remarks
C.17655	**OIL PUMP COMPLETE (HE.4707)**		1	
C.17656	**Body only** (HE.4708)	2– 1	1	
C.17665	**Rotor Assembly** (HE.4723) (comprising Inner Rotor, Outer Rotor, Driving Shaft and Locking Pin)	2– 2	1	**SUPPLIED ONLY AS A COMPLETE ASSEMBLY.**
C.17657	**Cover,** at bottom of Pump (HE.4709)	2– 3	1	
UCS.131/6R	**Screw,** Set, securing Cover	2– 4	2	
UCS.131/14R	**Screw,** Set, securing Cover	2– 5	2	
FG.105/X	**Washer,** Spring, on Setscrews	2– 6	4	
C.8649	**'O' Ring,** in Oil Pump Body and Cover	2– 7	2	
C.8646	**Drive Shaft,** between Distributor and Coupling Shaft	2– 8	1	
C.8647	**Bush,** on Drive Shaft	2– 9	1	
C.2393	**Washer,** on Drive Shaft (at bottom of Bush)	2–10	1	
C.2152	**Helical Gear,** driving Oil Pump and Distributor	2–11	1	
C.753	**Key,** locking Helical Gear on Drive Shaft	2–12	1	
UFN.256/L	**Nut,** at bottom of Drive Shaft	2–13	1	
C.2151	**Special Washer,** locking Nut	2–14	1	
C.8648	**Shaft,** coupling Driving Gear in Pump and Drive Shaft for Distributor	2–15	1	
C.9294	**Dowel Bolt,** securing Oil Pump to Bearing Cap	2–16	3	
C.7263	**Tab Washer,** on Bolts	2–17	3	
C.8608	**OIL DELIVERY PIPE FROM PUMP TO CYLINDER BLOCK**	2–18	1	
C.2220	**Gasket,** between Flange of Delivery Pipe and Cylinder Block	2–19	1	
UFB.131/6R	**Bolt,** securing Delivery Pipe to Cylinder Block		2	
C.7263	**Tab Washer,** locking Bolts		2	
C.16760	**OIL SUCTION PIPE FROM OIL SUMP TO PUMP**	2–20	1	
C.6824	**Clip,** securing Suction Pipe to Struts	2–21	2	
C.8665	**Strut,** on Pump, supporting Suction Pipe	2–22	1	
C.16761	**Strut,** on Bearing Cap, supporting Suction Pipe	2–23	1	
UFS.125/5R	**Screw,** Set, securing Clips to Struts		2	
FW.104/T	**Washer,** Plain, on Setscrews		2	
C.3968/1	**Nut,** Self-Locking, on Setscrews		2	
C.6829	**Plate,** sealing bottom of Suction Pipe	2–24	1	
C.6828	**Spring,** compressing Plate	2–25	1	
C.1221/4	**Split Pin,** retaining Plate and Spring on Suction Pipe	2–26	1	

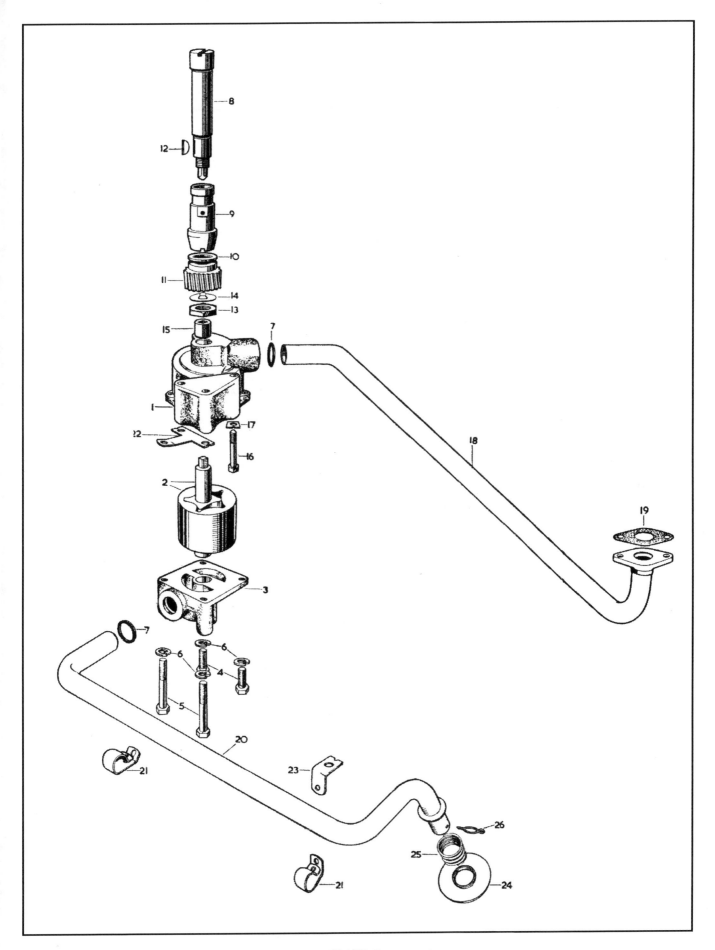

PLATE 2

OIL CLEANER

Part No.	Description	Plate No.	No. per Unit	Remarks
C.15839	**OIL CLEANER COMPLETE (FA.2746)**	3– 1	1	
7984	**Canister Assembly** (125429)	3– 2	1	
6159	**Spring**, at bottom of Canister (160441)	3– 3	1	
6160	**Washer**, Plain, at top of Spring (174660)	3– 4	1	
6161	**Washer**, Felt, under Pressure Plate (141251)	3– 5	1	
6886	**Pressure Plate** (134477)	3– 6	1	
8705	**Bolt**, through Canister (46387)	3– 7	1	
6158	**Washer** (Rubber) under Head of Bolt (137574)	3– 8	1	
6163	**Spring Clip**, on Bolt (174966)	3– 9	1	
1526	**Element** (FG.2306)	3–10	1	
6883	**Sealing Ring**, between Filter Head and Canister (137493)	3–11	1	
8750	**Filter Head** (41077/101)	3–12	1	
8104	**Balance Valve Assembly**, in Filter Head (50011)	3–13	1	
8103	**Washer**, under Head of Valve (27612)	3–14	1	
2714	**Relief Valve** (118261)	3–15	1	
8105	**Spring**, for Relief Valve (160698)	3–16	1	
8106	**Spider and Pin Assembly**, under Spring (44128)	3–17	1	
8108	**Adaptor**, retaining Relief Valve and for connection of Hose to Oil Sump (104702)	3–18	1	
8107	**Washer**, under Adaptor (140150)	3–19	1	
8751	**Drain Plug**, at bottom of Filter Head (21665-281)	3–20	1	
8752	**Washer**, on Drain Plug (140085)	3–21	1	
C.15962	**Gasket**, between Cylinder Block and Oil Cleaner	3–22	1	
UFB.131/21R	**Bolt**, securing Oil Cleaner to Cylinder Block		4	
FW.105/E	**Washer** (Copper) on Bolts		4	
FW.105/T	**Washer** (Steel) on Bolts		4	
C.15949	**HOSE, BETWEEN OIL CLEANER AND SUMP**	3–23	1	
C.2905/2	**Clip**, securing Hose	3–24	2	

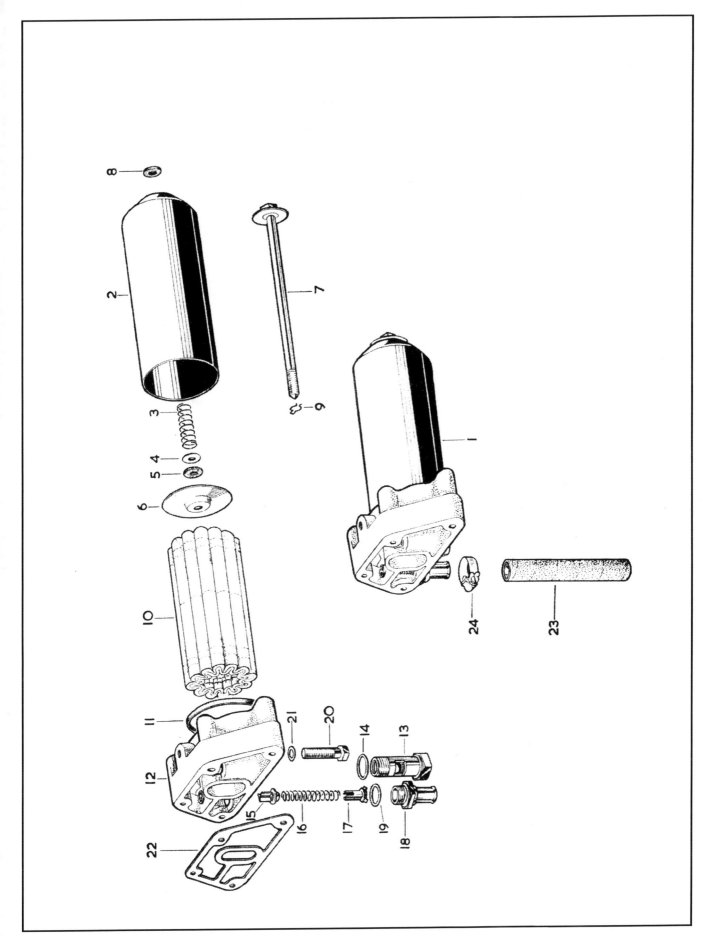

PLATE 3

13

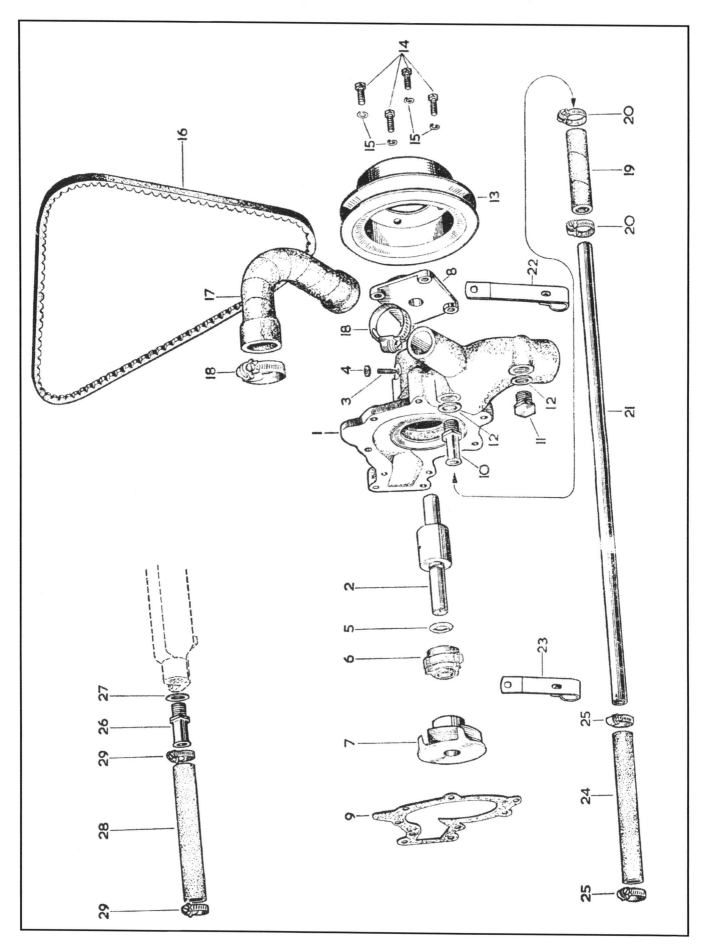

PLATE 4

Part No.	Description	Plate No.	No. per Unit	Remarks
C.15694	**WATER PUMP, COMPLETE**		1	
C.14944	**Body only**	4– 1	1	
C.8167	**Spindle,** complete with Bearing	4– 2	1	
C.8011	**Screw** (Allen Head) retaining Bearing in Pump Body	4– 3	1	
UFN.225/L	**Nut,** locking Screw	4– 4	1	
C.8256	**Thrower,** on long end of Spindle, adjacent to Bearing	4– 5	1	
C.6773	**Seal,** on long end of Spindle, adjacent to Thrower	4– 6	1	
C.7675	**Impeller**	4– 7	1	
C.17654	**Carrier,** for Pulley, on short end of Spindle	4– 8	1	
C.2303	**Gasket,** between Water Pump and Cylinder Block	4– 9	1	
C.17421	**Adaptor,** on Water Pump, for Heater Hose connection	4–10	1	
C.799	**Plug,** sealing redundant aperture in Pump Body	4–11	1	
C.2296/1	**Washer** (Copper) on Adaptor and Plug	4–12	2	
C.14588	**PULLEY FOR WATER PUMP**	4–13	1	Fitted from Engine No. R.1001 to R.5249.
C.20176	**PULLEY FOR WATER PUMP**		1	Fitted to Engine No. R.5250 to R.9999. RA.1001 and subs.
UFS.131/5R	**Screw,** Set, securing Pulley to Carrier	4–14	4	
FG.105/X	**Washer,** Spring, on Setscrews	4–15	4	
C.15840	**BELT, DRIVING PULLEY**	4–16	1	Fitted from Engine No. R.1001 to R.5249.
C.19524	**BELT, DRIVING PULLEY**		1	Fitted to Engine No. R.5250 to R.9999. RA.1001 and subs.
C.7548	**BY-PASS WATER HOSE**	4–17	1	
C.2905/12	**Clip,** securing By-pass Hose	4–18	2	
	THE ITEMS LISTED BELOW ARE THE HEATER CONNECTIONS FROM THE WATER PUMP AND INLET MANIFOLD.			
C.14999/1	**HOSE, BETWEEN ADAPTOR ON WATER PUMP AND FRONT RETURN PIPE**	4–19	1	
C.2905/2	**Clip,** securing Hose	4–20	2	

WATER PUMP

Part No.	Description	Plate No.	No. per Unit	Remarks
C.16871	**FRONT RETURN PIPE ALONG SIDE OF CYLINDER BLOCK**	4–21	1	
C.16964	**Clip,** front, securing Front Return Pipe to Cylinder Block	4–22	1	
C.16963	**Clip,** rear, securing Front Return Pipe to Cylinder Block	4–23	1	
UFS.119/8R	**Screw,** Set, securing clips to Front Return Pipe		2	
UFN.119/L	**Nut,** on Setscrews		2	
C.723/A	**Washer,** Shakeproof, under Nuts		2	
C.4399	**HOSE, BETWEEN FRONT AND REAR RETURN PIPES**	4–24	1	
C.2905/2	**Clip,** securing Hose to Return Pipes	4–25	2	
C.17421	**ADAPTOR, IN INLET MANIFOLD, FOR WATER FEED TO HEATER UNIT**	4–26	1	
C.2296/1	**Washer** (Copper) on Adaptor	4–27	1	
C.18987	**HOSE, BETWEEN ADAPTOR AND R.H. FEED PIPE BEHIND DASH PANEL**	4–28	1	
C.2905/2	**Clip,** securing Hose to Adaptor and R.H. Feed Pipe	4–29	2	

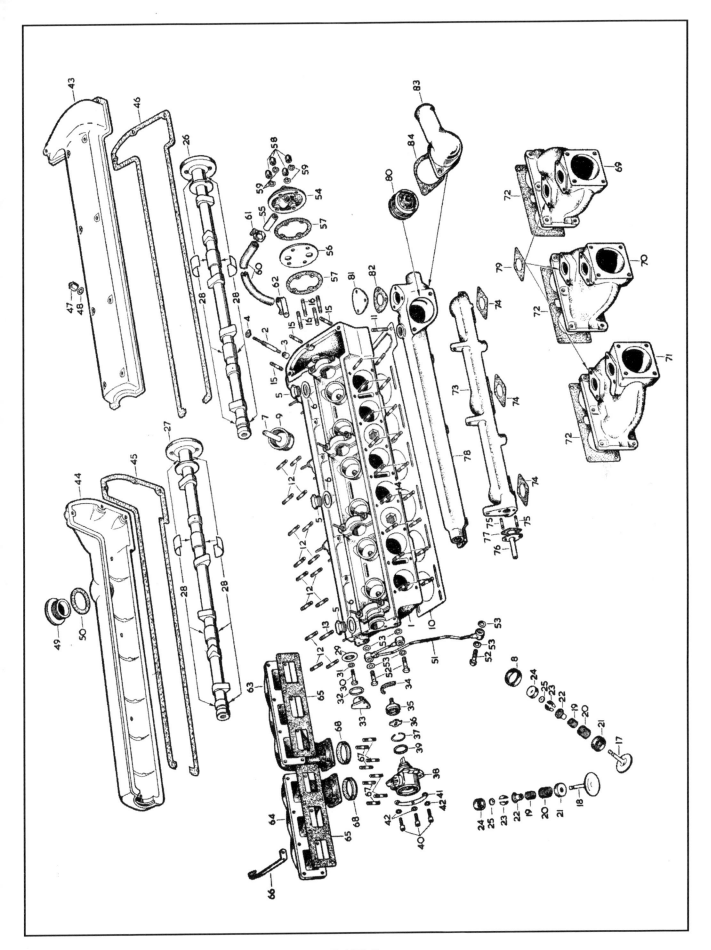

PLATE 5

CYLINDER HEAD

Part No.	Description	Plate No.	No. per Unit	Remarks
8377	**CYLINDER HEAD ASSEMBLY, COMPLETE (SD.1105)**		1	
	(Comprising Cylinder Head, Valves, Valve Inserts, Guides, Springs, Tappets, Tappet Guides, Adjusting Pads, Camshafts, Camshaft Covers, Filler Cap, Rev. Counter Generator, Breather Cover, etc.)			
C.14957	**CYLINDER HEAD**	5– 1	1	
C.2326	**Stud**, in Cylinder Head, for fixing of Camshaft Bearing Caps and Covers	5– 2	16	
C.2373	**Ring Dowel**, on Studs	5– 3	16	
C.2323	**'D' Washer**, on Studs	5– 4	16	
UFN.131/L	**Nut**, securing Bearing Caps		16	
FG.105/X	**Washer**, Spring, under Nuts		16	
C.2157	**Core Plug** (headed) on top of Cylinder Head	5– 5	3	
C.2296/2	**Washer** (Copper) under Headed Core Plug	5– 6	3	
C.15509	**Guide**, for Inlet Valve	5– 7	6	
C.15506	**Guide**, for Exhaust Valve		6	
C.12507	**Insert**, for Inlet Valve	5– 8	6	
C.9865	**Insert**, for Exhaust Valve		6	
C.7262	**Guide**, for Tappets	5– 9	12	
C.11530	**Core Plug**, on Inlet Face of Cylinder Head		2	
C.11531	**Washer** (Copper) on Core Plugs		2	
C.13795	**Gasket**, between Cylinder Head and Cylinder Block	5–10	1	**SUPERSEDED BY C.19113.**
C.19113	**Gasket**, between Cylinder Head and Cylinder Block		1	
C.2189	**Stud** (Short) for fixing of Cylinder Head to Timing Cover and Cylinder Block	5–11	4	
UFN.131/L	**Nut**, on Studs		4	
FG.105/X	**Washer**, Spring, under Nuts at Cylinder Head		2	
FW.105/E	**Washer** (Copper) under Nuts at Timing Cover		2	
C.2325	**Stud**, in Cylinder Head, for fixing of Exhaust Manifolds	5–12	15	
C.7624	**Stud**, in Cylinder Head, for fixing of Exhaust Manifolds and Dipstick Retaining Clip	5–13	1	
UFN.131/Q	**Nut** (Bronze) for Exhaust Manifold Studs		16	
FG.105/X	**Washer**, Spring, under Nuts		16	
C.11761	**Stud**, in Cylinder Head, for fixing of Inlet Manifolds	5–14	18	
C.4202/2	**Nut**, on Inlet Manifold Studs		18	
FG.105/X	**Washer**, Spring, under Nuts		18	
C.6727/1	**Stud**, in front end of Cylinder Head, for fixing of Camshaft Covers	5–15	6	
C.6727	**Stud**, in front face of Cylinder Head, for fixing of Breather Housing	5–16	4	
C.317	**Core Plug** for Exhaust face of Cylinder Head		2	
C.2328	**Dome Nut**, securing Cylinder Head to Cylinder Block		14	
C.2385	**'D' Washer**, under Dome Nuts		10	
FW.207/T	**Washer**, Plain, under Dome Nuts		4	
8667	**GASKETS PACKAGE FOR DECARBONISING ENGINE (SD.1110)**		1	

Part No.	Description	Plate No.	No. per Unit	Remarks
C.12444	**INLET VALVE**	5–17	6	
C.7708	**EXHAUST VALVE**	5–18	6	
C.7137	**VALVE SPRING, INNER**	5–19	12	
C.7136	**VALVE SPRING, OUTER**	5–20	12	
C.2181	**Seat,** for Valve Springs	5–21	12	
C.2159	**Collar,** at top of Valve Seats	5–22	12	
C.430	**Cotter,** retaining Collar to Valve Seats	5–23	24	
C.7213/1	**TAPPET**	5–24	12	

VALVE ADJUSTING PADS

Part No.	Description	Plate No.	No. per Unit	Remarks
C.2243/A	**Adjusting Pad** (.085″ thick)	5–25	12	
C.2243/B	**Adjusting Pad** (.086″ thick)	5–25	12	
C.2243/C	**Adjusting Pad** (.087″ thick)	5–25	12	
C.2243/D	**Adjusting Pad** (.088″ thick)	5–25	12	
C.2243/E	**Adjusting Pad** (.089″ thick)	5–25	12	
C.2243/F	**Adjusting Pad** (.090″ thick)	5–25	12	
C.2243/G	**Adjusting Pad** (.091″ thick)	5–25	12	
C.2243/H	**Adjusting Pad** (.092″ thick)	5–25	12	
C.2243/I	**Adjusting Pad** (.093″ thick)	5–25	12	
C.2243/J	**Adjusting Pad** (.094″ thick)	5–25	12	
C.2243/K	**Adjusting Pad** (.095″ thick)	5–25	12	
C.2243/L	**Adjusting Pad** (.096″ thick)	5–25	12	**SELECTIVE SIZES.**
C.2243/M	**Adjusting Pad** (.097″ thick)	5–25	12	
C.2243/N	**Adjusting Pad** (.098″ thick)	5–25	12	Choose the Pad of the desired thickness.
C.2243/O	**Adjusting Pad** (.099″ thick)	5–25	12	
C.2243/P	**Adjusting Pad** (.100″ thick)	5–25	12	
C.2243/Q	**Adjusting Pad** (.101″ thick)	5–25	12	
C.2243/R	**Adjusting Pad** (.102″ thick)	5–25	12	
C.2243/S	**Adjusting Pad** (.103″ thick)	5–25	12	
C.2243/T	**Adjusting Pad** (.104″ thick)	5–25	12	
C.2243/U	**Adjusting Pad** (.105″ thick)	5–25	12	
C.2243/V	**Adjusting Pad** (.106″ thick)	5–25	12	
C.2243/W	**Adjusting Pad** (.107″ thick)	5–25	12	
C.2243/X	**Adjusting Pad** (.108″ thick)	5–25	12	
C.2243/Y	**Adjusting Pad** (.109″ thick)	5–25	12	
C.2243/Z	**Adjusting Pad** (.110″ thick)	5–25	12	

CYLINDER HEAD

Part No.	Description	Plate No.	No. per Unit	Remarks
C.14985	**INLET CAMSHAFT**	5–26	1	Fitted from Engine No. R.1001 to R.1216 R.5001 and subs.
C.17138	**INLET CAMSHAFT**		1	Fitted from Engine No. R.1217 to R.5000.
C.13081	**EXHAUST CAMSHAFT**	5–27	1	
C.2288	**Bearing,** for Camshafts	5–28	16 halves	
C.2324	**OIL THROWER, AT REAR END OF EXHAUST CAMSHAFT**	5–29	1	
UFS.137/4R	**Screw,** Set, securing Oil Thrower to Exhaust Camshaft	5–30	1	
FW.106/E	**Washer** (Copper) on Setscrew	5–31	1	
C.2312	**Sealing Ring,** at rear end, between Exhaust Camshaft Cover and Cylinder Head	5–32	1	⎫ Fitted from Engine No. R.1001 to R.2599.
C.2312/1	**Sealing Ring** (Oversize) at rear end, between Exhaust Camshaft Cover and Cylinder Head	5–32	1	⎬ **Fit C.2312/1 only if necessary to prevent oil leak.**
C.19044	**Sealing Ring,** at rear end, between Exhaust Camshaft Cover and Cylinder Head		1	Fitted to Engine No. R.2600 and subs.
C.2154/1	**FLANGED SEALING PLUG AT LEFT-HAND REAR OF CYLINDER HEAD**	5–33	1	Fitted from Engine No. R.1001 to R.2599.
C.19043	**FLANGED SEALING PLUG AT LEFT-HAND REAR OF CYLINDER HEAD**		1	Fitted to Engine No. R.2600 and subs.
C.7134/2	**Screw,** Set, securing Flanged Plug to Cylinder Head		2	
FW.105/E	**Washer** (Copper) on Setscrews		2	
C.14991	**SEAL, BETWEEN REAR BEARING CAP AND R.H. (INLET) CAMSHAFT, FOR ELECTRIC REV. COUNTER GENERATOR**	5–34	1	

Part No.	Description	Plate No.	No. per Unit	Remarks
C.16771	**ADAPTOR, AT END OF R.H. (INLET) CAMSHAFT, FOR ELECTRIC REV. COUNTER GENERATOR**	5–35	1	
C.16772	**DRIVING DOG, COUPLING ADAPTOR TO ELECTRIC REV. COUNTER GENERATOR**	5–36	1	
C.16773	**Circlip,** securing Driving Dog to Adaptor	5–37	1	
C.14996	**GENERATOR, ON INLET CAMSHAFT, FOR ELECTRIC REV. COUNTER**	5–38	1	
9993	**Connector Moulding Assembly** (41-161-105-00)		1	
9994	**Gasket,** under Moulding (31-754-707)		1	
AS.306/2.5H	**Screw,** Set, securing Moulding (30-232-089-11)		2	
AG.106/X	**Washer,** Spring, on Setscrews (30-282-010-11)		2	
C.14990	**'O' Ring** on Generator	5–39	1	
C.14992	**Screw** (Allen Head) securing Generator to Cylinder Head	5–40	3	
C.15918	**Plate Washer,** on Screws, adjacent to Cylinder Head	5–41	1	
C.15919	**Lock Washer,** between head of Screws and Plate Washer	5–42	3	
C.14987/1	**COVER FOR R.H. (INLET) CAMSHAFT**	5–43	1	
C.7186/1	**COVER FOR L.H. (EXHAUST) CAMSHAFT**	5–44	1	Fitted from Engine No. R.1001 to R.2599.
C.19042	**COVER FOR L.H. (EXHAUST) CAMSHAFT**		1	Fitted to Engine No. R.2600 and subs.
C.6735	**Gasket,** between L.H. Camshaft Cover and Cylinder Head	5–45	1	
C.14988	**Gasket,** between R.H. Camshaft Cover and Cylinder Head	5–46	1	
C.2327	**Dome Nut,** securing Camshaft Covers to Cylinder Head	5–47	22	
FW.104/E	**Washer** (Copper) under Dome Nuts	5–48	22	
C.1022	**OIL FILLER CAP ON LEFT-HAND CAMSHAFT COVER**	5–49	1	
C.419	**Washer** (Fibre) on Filler Cap	5–50	1	

CYLINDER HEAD

Part No.	Description	Plate No.	No. per Unit	Remarks
C.5849	**OIL PIPE FROM CYLINDER BLOCK TO REAR OF CYLINDER HEAD**	5–51	1	
C.5846	**Banjo Bolt,** securing Oil Pipe to Cylinder Head and Block	5–52	3	
C.4146	**Washer** (Copper) at each side of Banjos	5–53	6	
C.8048	**FRONT COVER AND BREATHER HOUSING**	5–54	1	Fitted from Chassis No. 850001 to 850091. 875001 to 875385. 860001 to 860004. 885001 to 885020.
C.2391	**Pipe,** in Cover	5–55	1	
C.2390	**Baffle,** behind Cover	5–56	1	
C.2227	**Gasket,** at front and rear of Baffle	5–57	2	
C.2327	**Dome Nut,** securing Cover to Cylinder Head	5–58	4	
FG.104/X	**Washer,** Spring, under Dome Nuts	5–59	4	
C.2485/1	**FLEXIBLE PIPE FOR BREATHER ON FRONT COVER (27″ LONG)**	5–60	1	Fitted from Chassis No. 850001 to 850091. 875001 to 875385. 860001 to 860004. 885001 to 885020.
C.2905/3	**Clip,** securing Flexible Pipe to Front Cover	5–61	1	
C.1040/21	**Clip,** securing Flexible Pipe to L.H. Undershield	5–62	1	
UFS.125/4R	**Screw,** Set, securing Clip to L.H. Undershield		1	
UFN.125/L	**Nut,** on Setscrew		1	
C.724	**Washer,** Shakeproof, under Nut		1	
C.18584	**FRONT COVER AND BREATHER HOUSING ASSEMBLY**		1	
C.18604/1	**Gauze Filter Assembly,** behind Front Cover		1	
C.2227	**Gasket,** at front and rear of Filter		2	
C.2327	**Dome Nut,** securing Cover to Cylinder Head		4	
FG.104/X	**Washer,** Spring, under Dome Nuts		4	Fitted to Chassis No. 850092 and subs. 875386 and subs. 860005 and subs. 885021 and subs.
C.18591	**ELBOW HOSE, BETWEEN TOP OF BREATHER HOUSING AND BREATHER PIPE**		1	
C.15886/8	**Clip,** securing Elbow Hose		2	

Part No.	Description	Plate No.	No. per Unit	Remarks
C.19002	**BREATHER PIPE FROM ELBOW HOSE TO ADAPTOR ON AIR BOX BASE**		1	
C.19007	**Clip**, on Inlet Manifold Stud, securing Pipe		1	
UFS.119/4R	**Screw**, Set, through Clip		1	
UFN.119/L	**Nut**, on Setscrew		1	
C.723/A	**Washer**, Shakeproof, under Nut		1	
C.18589	**HOSE, BETWEEN BREATHER PIPE AND ADAPTOR ON AIR BOX BASE**		1	Fitted to Chassis No. 850092 and subs. 875386 and subs. 860005 and subs. 885021 and subs.
C.15886/8	**Clip**, securing Hose		2	
C.19003	**ADAPTOR, ON AIR BOX BASE, FOR CONNECTION OF HOSE FROM BREATHER**		1	
C.19006	**Gasket**, under Adaptor		1	
UFN.125/L	**Nut**, securing Adaptor		2	
FG.104/X	**Washer**, Spring, under Nuts		2	
C.18396	**EXHAUST MANIFOLD, FRONT**	5–63	1	
C.18397	**EXHAUST MANIFOLD, REAR**	5–64	1	
C.2318	**Gasket**, between Exhaust Manifolds and Cylinder Head	5–65	2	
C.15848	**Clip**, under Manifold nut, retaining Dipstick	5–66	1	
C.11583	**Distance Piece**, under Clip		1	
C.2369	**Stud**, in outlet flanges of Exhaust Manifolds, for attachment of Exhaust Down Pipes	5–67	8	
C.17916	**Nut**, securing Exhaust Pipes to Manifold		8	
FG.106/X	**Washer**, Spring, under Nuts		8	
C.18405/1	**Sealing Ring**, between outlet flanges of Manifolds and Exhaust Down Pipes	5–68	2	
C.15831	**INLET MANIFOLD, FRONT**	5–69	1	
C.15832	**INLET MANIFOLD, CENTRE**	5–70	1	

CYLINDER HEAD

Part No.	Description	Plate No.	No. per Unit	Remarks
C.15833	**INLET MANIFOLD, REAR**	5–71	1	
C.14127	**Gasket,** between Inlet Manifolds and Cylinder Head	5–72	3	
C.2496	**Stud,** in Inlet Manifold, for attachment of Water Outlet and Air Balance Pipes		12	
C.6570	**Stud,** in Inlet Manifold, for attachment of Carburetters		12	
C.4202/2	**Nut,** on Studs		24	
FG.105/X	**Washer,** Spring, under Nuts		24	
C.14918	**AIR BALANCE PIPE**	5–73	1	Fitted from Engine No. R.1001 to R.2933.
C.18945	**AIR BALANCE PIPE**		1	Fitted to Engine No. R.2934 and subs.
C.11577	**Gasket,** between Air Balance Pipe and Inlet Manifolds	5–74	3	
C.12472	**Stud,** in Balance Pipe, for attachment of Brake Servo Adaptor	5–75	2	
C.14746	**ADAPTOR, AT REAR OF AIR BALANCE PIPE, FOR CONNECTION OF BRAKE SERVO VACUUM HOSE**	5–76	1	
C.14089	**Gasket,** between Adaptor and Balance Pipe	5–77	1	
UFN.125/L	**Nut,** securing Adaptor		2	
FG.104/X	**Washer,** Spring, under Nuts		2	
C.15905	**WATER OUTLET PIPE**	5–78	1	
C.11577	**Gasket** for Water Outlet Pipe	5–79	3	
C.2496	**Stud,** in Water Outlet Pipe, for attachment of Outlet Elbow		2	
C.12867/2	**THERMOSTAT IN WATER OUTLET PIPE (OPENING TEMPERATURE 159° TO 168° F)**	5–80	1	Fitted from Engine No. R.1001 to R.8299.
C.20766/2	**THERMOSTAT IN WATER OUTLET PIPE (OPENING TEMPERATURE 159° TO 168° F)**	5–80	1	Fitted to Engine No. R.8300 and subs.

Part No.	Description	Plate No.	No. per Unit	Remarks
C.17345	**BLANKING PLATE, IN WATER OUT-LET PIPE, SEALING REDUNDANT CHOKE THERMOSTAT APERTURE**	5–81	1	
C.2475	**Gasket,** between Blanking Plate and Water Outlet Pipe	5–82	1	
C.7134/1	**Screw,** Set, securing Blanking Plate to Water Outlet Pipe		3	
C.723/A	**Washer,** Shakeproof, on Setscrews		3	
C.12422	**WATER OUTLET ELBOW**	5–83	1	
C.4985	**Gasket** for Water Outlet Elbow	5–84	1	
C.4202/2	**Nut,** securing Water Outlet Elbow to Outlet Pipe		2	
FG.105/X	**Washer,** Spring, under Nuts		2	
UN.12Y	**SPARKING PLUG (CHAMPION)**		6	
	HIGH TENSION SPARKING PLUG LEADS			
C.4976	**Lead** to No. 1 Sparking Plug		1	Fitted from Engine No. R.1001 to R.3854.
C.4977	**Lead** to No. 2 Sparking Plug		1	
C.4978	**Lead** to No. 3 Sparking Plug		1	
C.4979	**Lead** to No. 4 Sparking Plug		1	**USE 5520/1 FOR ALL REPLACEMENTS.**
C.4980	**Lead** to No. 5 Sparking Plug		1	
C.4981	**Lead** to No. 6 Sparking Plug		1	
C.4741	**Lead** to Ignition Coil		1	
5520/1	**HIGH TENSION CABLE TO SPARKING PLUGS AND COIL (21'-0" LONG)**		1	Fitted to Engine No. R.3855 and subs.
C.16979	**TERMINAL FOR SPARKING PLUG LEADS (INCORPORATING SUPPRESSOR)**		6	
C.17456	**TERMINAL FOR SPARKING PLUG LEADS**		6	**FOR EXPORT ONLY.**

CYLINDER HEAD

Part No.	Description	Plate No.	No. per Unit	Remarks
C.18285	**RUBBER SLEEVE FOR SPARKING PLUG TERMINALS**		6	
C.2451	**CONDUIT, ALONG CENTRE OF CYLINDER HEAD, ENCLOSING SPARKING PLUG LEADS**		1	
C.4983	**SPACER FOR SPARKING PLUG LEADS (THICK)**		2	
C.4984	**SPACER FOR SPARKING PLUG LEADS (THIN)**		3	Fitted from Engine No. R.1001 to R.3854.
C.4982	**CLIP AROUND THICK SPACER**		1	
C.19890	**CLIP, ON TIMING COVER BOLT, RETAINING SPARKING PLUG LEADS**		1	
3204	**Grommet,** in Clip		1	
UFB.131/15R	**Bolt,** securing Clip		1	
C.2155	**Distance Piece,** on Bolt		1	Fitted to Engine No. R.3855 and subs. **MAY BE USED TO REPLACE C.4983, C.4984 and C.4982.**
C.19889	**SLEEVE (P.V.C.) FOR SPARKING PLUG AT FRONT OF CYLINDER HEAD**		1	

Part No.	Description	Plate No.	No. per Unit	Remarks
C.2169	**SPROCKET FOR CAMSHAFTS**	6– 1	2	
C.2329	**Adjusting Plate,** inside Camshaft Sprockets	6– 2	2	⎫ **SUPPLIED ONLY AS AN ASSEMBLY**
C.2191	**Clamping Plate,** on Adjusting Plates	6– 2	2	⎭ **TO PART No. 1003.**
C.2193	**Circlip,** retaining Adjusting Plates in Sprockets	6– 3	2	
C.2178	**Guide Pin,** through Adjusting Plates	6– 4	2	
C.2194	**Star Washer,** on Guide Pin, behind Adjusting Plates	6– 5	2	
C.2261	**Circlip,** retaining Guide Pins	6– 6	2	
C.2310	**Screw,** Set, securing Adjusting Plates and Sprockets to Camshafts		4	
C.4128/1	**FRONT MOUNTING BRACKET FOR TIMING GEAR**	6– 7	1	
C.4129	**REAR MOUNTING BRACKET FOR TIMING GEAR**	6– 8	1	
C.2182	**Stud,** for fixing of front and rear Mounting Brackets		4	
UFN.125/L	**Nut,** securing Brackets on Studs		4	
C.724	**Washer,** Shakeproof, under Nuts		4	
C.7424	**Bolt** (Long) securing Mounting Bracket to Cylinder Block		4	
C.740	**Washer,** Shakeproof, on Bolts		4	
C.2166	**Bolt** (Short) securing rear Mounting Bracket and Intermediate Chain Damper to Cylinder Block		2	
C.16831	**Tab Washer,** retaining Bolts		1	
C.2308	**IDLER SPROCKET (21 TEETH) BETWEEN MOUNTING BRACKETS**	6– 9	1	
C.2319	**Bush,** for Idler Sprocket		1	
C.2177	**ECCENTRIC SHAFT, THROUGH IDLER SPROCKET, FOR ADJUSTMENT OF UPPER TIMING CHAIN**	6–10	1	
C.2282	**Plug,** in end of Eccentric Shaft	6–11	1	
C.4404	**ADJUSTMENT PLATE, ON FACE OF FRONT MOUNTING BRACKET, FOR MICRO ADJUSTMENT OF UPPER TIMING CHAIN**	6–12	1	
C.3338/4	**Nut,** securing Adjustment Plate to Eccentric Shaft		1	
C.742	**Washer,** Shakeproof, under Nut		1	
C.4405	**Plunger Pin,** in front Mounting Bracket, holding Adjustment Plate in tension	6–13	1	
C.2297	**Spring,** behind Plunger Pin	6–14	1	

TIMING GEAR

Part No.	Description	Plate No.	No. per Unit	Remarks
C.2309	**INTERMEDIATE SPROCKET (20 TEETH) AT BOTTOM OF UPPER TIMING CHAIN**		1	SUPERSEDED BY C.17154. USE C.17154 FOR ALL REPLACEMENTS.
C.2320	**Bush,** for Sprocket		1	
C.2307	**INTERMEDIATE SPROCKET (28 TEETH) AT TOP OF LOWER TIMING GEAR**		1	SUPERSEDED BY C.17154. USE C.17154 FOR ALL REPLACEMENTS.
C.926	**Key,** locking Intermediate Sprockets together		1	
C.17154	**INTERMEDIATE SPROCKET ASSEMBLY AT TOP OF LOWER TIMING CHAIN**	6–15	1	SUPERSEDES C.2309 AND C.2307.
C.2320	**Bush,** for Sprocket		1	
C.2161	**SHAFT, HOLDING INTERMEDIATE SPROCKETS**	6–16	1	
C.2335	**Circlip,** retaining Shaft	6–17	1	
C.2256	**TOP TIMING CHAIN**	6–18	1	
C.13616	**L.H. DAMPER ASSEMBLY FOR UPPER TIMING CHAIN**	6–19	1	
C.13617	**R.H. DAMPER ASSEMBLY FOR UPPER TIMING CHAIN**	6–20	1	
C.13660	**Distance Piece,** for Upper Dampers	6–21	4	
C.13615	**INTERMEDIATE DAMPER ASSEMBLY FOR UPPER TIMING CHAIN**		1	SUPERSEDED BY C.13615/1. USE C.13615/1 FOR ALL REPLACEMENTS
C.13615/1	**INTERMEDIATE DAMPER ASSEMBLY FOR UPPER TIMING CHAIN**	6–22	1	SUPERSEDES C.13615 at Engine No. R.5533.
C.2255	**BOTTOM TIMING CHAIN**	6–23	1	
C.13614	**VIBRATION DAMPER FOR LOWER TIMING CHAIN**		1	Fitted from Engine No. R.1001 to R.8138.
UFS.131/5R	**Screw,** Set, securing Damper to Cylinder Block		2	
C.7436	**Tab Washer,** on Setscrews		1	

Part No.	Description	Plate No.	No. per Unit	Remarks
C.13614/1	**VIBRATION DAMPER FOR LOWER TIMING CHAIN**	6–24	1	⎫ Fitted to Engine No. R.8139 and subs.
UFS.131/5R	**Screw**, Set, securing Damper to Cylinder Block		2	
C.20397	**Tab Washer**, locking Setscrews		1	⎭
C.10332	**HYDRAULIC CHAIN TENSIONER ASSEMBLY**	6–25	1	
6029	**Tab Washer**, securing Adjuster Plug		1	
C.9766	**Shim**, for adjustment of Hydraulic Chain Tensioner	6–26	As req'd	
UFB.125/11R	**Bolt**, securing Hydraulic Chain Tensioner to Cylinder Block		2	
C.10333	**Tab Washer**, retaining Bolts		1	
6265	**REPAIR KIT FOR HYDRAULIC CHAIN TENSIONER (SD.1042)**		1	
	(Comprising Cylinder Barrel, Spring, Plug and Tab Washer)			
C.13457	**FILTER GAUZE, IN CYLINDER BLOCK, BEHIND HYDRAULIC CHAIN TENSIONER**	6–27	1	
C.8614/1	**FRONT TIMING COVER**	6–28	1	
C.8615	**Gasket**, between Timing Cover and Cylinder Block	6–29	2 halves	
C.8593	**Oil Seal**, between Timing Cover and Crankshaft	6–30	1	
C.2183	**Stud**, in Front Timing Cover, for fixing of Cylinder Head		2	
C.2184	**Stud**, in Front Timing Cover, for fixing of Water Pump		3	
C.2325	**Stud**, in Front Timing Cover, for fixing of Oil Sump		4	
UFN.131/L	**Nut**, on Studs		9	
FG.105/X	**Washer**, Spring, under Nuts		5	
C.725	**Washer**, Shakeproof, at Oil Sump fixing		4	
UFB.131/9R	**Bolt**, securing Timing Cover to Cylinder Block		1	
UFB.131/26R	**Bolt**, securing Timing Cover and Water Pump to Cylinder Block		2	
UFB.131/14R	**Bolt**, securing Timing Cover to Cylinder Block		2	1 required after Engine No. R.1509.
UFB.131/21R	**Bolt**, securing Timing Cover and Water Pump to Cylinder Block		3	4 required after Engine No. R.1509.
UFB.131/22R	**Bolt**, securing Timing Cover, Water Pump and Dynamo Adjusting Link to Cylinder Block		1	Up to Engine No. R.1509.
FG.105/X	**Washer**, Spring, on Bolts		9	
UFB.137/11R	**Bolt**, securing Timing Cover to Cylinder Block		5	3 required after Engine No. R.1845.
FG.106/X	**Washer**, Spring, on Bolts		5	3 required after Engine No. R.1845.
UFB.131/15R	**Bolt**, securing Timing Cover to Cylinder Block		1	For Engine No. R.1845 and subs.
C.14924	**DYNAMO ADJUSTING LINK**		1	⎫ Fitted from Engine No. R.1001 to R.1509.
FW.105/T	**Washer**, Plain, for Adjusting Link		1	⎭

TIMING GEAR

Part No.	Description	Plate No.	No. per Unit	Remarks
C.2286	**DYNAMO ADJUSTING LINK**		1	Fitted from Engine No. R.1510 to R.1844.
C.18307	**Distance Piece,** behind Adjusting Link		1	
UFB.131/20R	**Bolt,** for Adjusting Link		1	
C.18850	**DYNAMO LINK**	6–31	1	Fitted to Engine No. R.1845 to R.9999. RA.1001 and subs.
C.18307	**Distance Piece,** behind Link	6–32	1	
UFB.131/20R	**Bolt,** securing Link		1	
C.18732	**BRACKET ASSEMBLY MOUNTING AUTOMATIC FAN BELT TENSIONER**	6–33	1	
UFB.137/13R	**Bolt,** securing Bracket and Timing Cover to Cylinder Block		1	
UFB.137/14R	**Bolt,** securing Bracket and Timing Cover to Cylinder Block		1	Fitted to Engine No. R.1845 to R.9999. RA.1001 and subs.
FG.106/X	**Washer,** Spring, on Bolts		2	
C.18447	**TORSION SPRING AUTOMATICALLY ADJUSTING TENSION ON FAN BELT**	6–34	1	
C.18835	**CARRIER FOR JOCKEY PULLEY**	6–35	1	Fitted from Engine No. R.1845 to R.9999. RA.1001 to RA.1099.
C.8737/2	**Nut,** Self-Locking, securing Carrier to Bracket		1	
C.18454	**Thrust Washer,** under Nut		1	
C.21330	**CARRIER FOR JOCKEY PULLEY**		1	Fitted to Engine No. RA.1100 and subs.
C.8737/2	**Nut,** Self-Locking, securing Carrier to Bracket		1	**May be used IN PAIRS to replace C.18835 and C.18454.**
C.21326	**Thrust Washer and Stop,** under Nut		1	
C.18733	**JOCKEY PULLEY ASSEMBLY FOR FAN BELT**		1	Fitted from Engine No. R.1845 to R.5249.
C.3968/2	**Nut,** Self-Locking, securing Pulley to Carrier		1	
C.19521	**JOCKEY PULLEY ASSEMBLY FOR FAN BELT**	6–36	1	Fitted to Engine No. R.5250 to R.9999. RA.1001 and subs.
C.3968/2	**Nut,** Self-Locking, securing Pulley to Carrier		1	

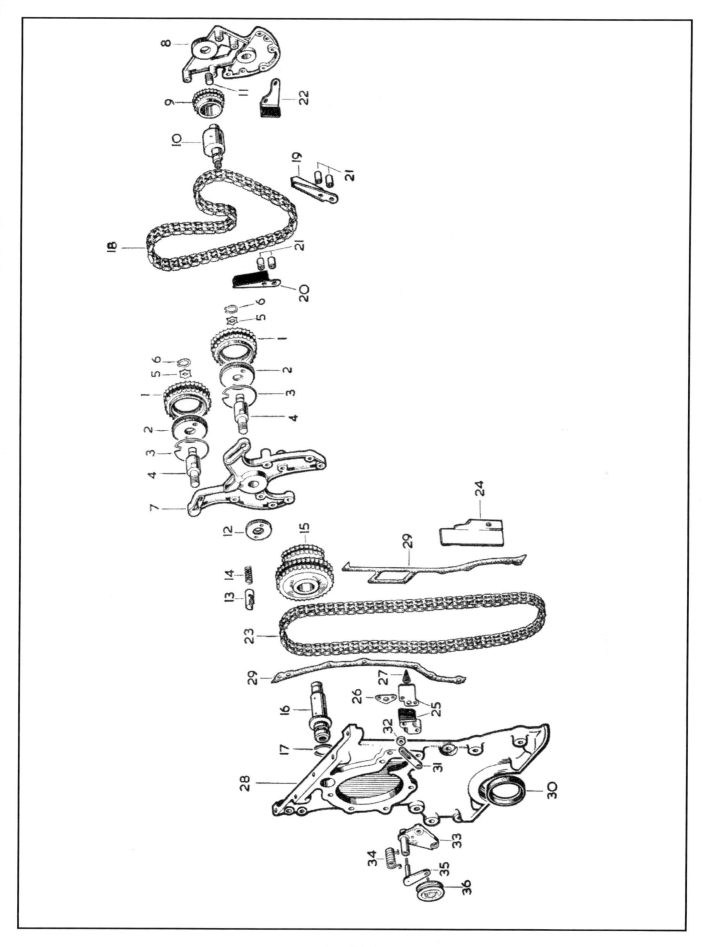

PLATE 6

31

CARBURETTERS AND PETROL FILTER

Part No.	Description	Plate No.	No. per Unit	Remarks
C.15835	**FRONT CARBURETTER ASSEMBLY (HD.8)**	7– 1	1	
8762	**Body only** (AUC.8271)	7– 2	1	
7090	**Adaptor,** for Ignition Union (AUC.2044)	7– 3	1	
7091	**Gasket,** under Adaptor (AUC.2014)	7– 4	1	
5618	**Screw,** securing Adaptor (AUC.2175)		2	
C.723	**Washer,** Shakeproof, on Screws (AUA.4643)		2	
7106	**Ignition Union** (AUC.4490)	7– 5	1	
8763	**Suction Chamber and Piston Assembly** (AUC.8063)	7– 6	1	
7093	**Screw,** holding Jet Needle in position (AUC.2057)		1	
8764	**Damper Assembly** in Suction Chamber (AUC.8115)	7– 7	1	
7095	**Washer,** for Damper (AUC.4900)	7– 8	1	
7871	**Spring,** assisting return of Piston (AUC.2107)	7– 9	1	
7872	**Skid Washer,** under Spring, at bottom of Piston (AUC.1048)	7–10	1	
5618	**Screw,** securing Suction Chamber to Carburetter Body (AUC.2175)		4	
C.18439	**Jet Needle** (UM)	7–11	1	
7860	**Jet Assembly** (AUC.8156) (comprising Jet Unit, with Diaphragm and Cup)	7–12	1	
6958	**Jet Bearing** (AUC.2001)	7–13	1	
6959	**Nut,** locking Jet Bearing (AUC.2002)	7–14	1	
8765	**Spring,** under Jet Diaphragm (AUD.2093)	7–15	1	
8766	**Jet Housing Assembly** (AUC.8655)	7–16	1	
8759	**Shoe and Rod Assembly,** for operation of Throttle during Cold Starting (AUC.8962)	7–17	1	
8760	**Return Spring** for Shoe and Rod Assembly (AUC.2020)	7–18	1	
8761	**Plate,** at top of Shoe and Rod Assembly (AUC.2019)	7–19	1	
7879	**Screw,** securing Plate (AUC.4790)		1	
C.723	**Washer,** Shakeproof, on Screw (AUA.4643)		1	
7048	**Screw,** in Plate, for operation of Choke/Throttle opening (AUC.2521)	7–20	1	
7049	**Spring,** on screw (AUC.2451)	7–21	1	
6993	**Float Chamber Assembly** (AUC.2009)	7–22	1	
7115	**Bolt,** securing Float Chamber to Carburetter Body (AUC.2110)		4	
C.723	**Washer,** Shakeproof, on Bolts		4	
7117	**Lid** for Float Chamber (AUC.4261)	7–23	1	
1090	**Float** (AUC.1123)	7–24	1	
6970	**Needle and Seat,** controlling Petrol Flow to Float Chamber (AUC.8170)	7–25	1	
7118	**Lever,** operating Float Needle (AUC.1980)	7–26	1	
1153	**Pin,** securing Lever to Float Chamber Lid (AUC.1152)	7–27	1	
7119	**Gasket,** under Float Chamber Lid (AUC.1147)	7–28	1	
5832	**Cap Nut,** securing Lid (AUC.1867)	7–29	1	
1298	**Serrated Washer** (Fibre) on Cap Nut adjacent to Lid (AUC.1928)	7–30	1	
7120	**Alum Washer,** on Cap Nut (AUC.1557)	7–31	1	
479	**Filter,** in Inlet Connection on Float Chamber Lid (AUC.2139)	7–32	1	
C.11488	**Banjo Bolt,** securing Feed Pipe to Float Chamber (AUC.2698)	7–33	1	
C.11489	**Fibre Washer,** on Banjo Bolt (AUC.2141)	7–34	2	
6967	**Valve,** for slow-running adjustment (AUC.2028)	7–35	1	
6966	**Spring,** for slow-run Valve (AUC.2027)	7–36	1	
6968	**Gland Washer,** for slow-run Valve (AUC.2029)	7–37	1	
6969	**Dished Washer** (Brass) at top of Gland Washer (AUC.2030)	7–38	1	

Part No.	Description	Plate No.	No. per Unit	Remarks
C.15836	**CENTRE CARBURETTER ASSEMBLY (HD.8)**	7–39	1	
8767	**Body only** (AUC.8272)		1	
8763	**Suction Chamber and Piston Assembly** (AUC.8063)		1	
7093	**Screw,** holding Jet Needle in position (AUC.2057)		1	
8764	**Damper Assembly,** in Suction Chamber (AUC.8115)		1	
7095	**Washer,** for Damper (AUC.4900)		1	
7871	**Spring,** assisting return of Piston (AUC.2107)		1	
7872	**Skid Washer,** under Spring, at bottom of Piston (AUC.1048)		1	
5618	**Screw,** securing Suction Chamber to Carburetter (AUC.2175)		4	
C.18439	**Jet Needle** (UM)		1	
7860	**Jet Assembly** (AUC.8156) (comprising Jet Unit, with Diaphragm and Cup)		1	
6958	**Jet Bearing** (AUC.2001)		1	
6959	**Nut,** locking Jet Bearing (AUC.2002)		1	
8765	**Spring,** under Jet Diaphragm (AUD.2093)		1	
8768	**Jet Housing Assembly** (AUC.8654)		1	
8759	**Shoe and Rod Assembly,** for operation of Throttle during cold starting (AUC.8962)		1	
8760	**Return Spring,** for Shoe and Rod Assembly (AUC.2020)		1	
8761	**Plate,** at top of Shoe and Rod Assembly (AUC.2019)		1	
7879	**Screw,** securing Plate (AUC.4790)		1	
C.723	**Washer,** Shakeproof, on Screw (AUA.4643)		1	
7048	**Screw,** in Plate, for operation of Choke/Throttle opening (AUC.2521)		1	
7049	**Spring,** on Screw (AUC.2451)		1	
8756	**Abutment Bracket,** for Choke Control Outer Cable (AUC.1288)		1	
8757	**Cable Clamp,** for Abutment Bracket (AUC.2102)		1	
5803	**Bolt,** securing Cable Clamp (AUC.2694)		1	
AN.102/L	**Nut,** on Bolt		1	
5648	**Washer,** Spring, under Nut (AUC.2246)		1	
7114	**Float Chamber Assembly** (AUC.2088)		1	
7115	**Bolt,** securing Float Chamber to Carburetter Body (AUC.2110)		4	
C.723	**Washer,** Shakeproof, on Bolts		4	
7117	**Lid,** for Float Chamber (AUC.4261)		1	
1090	**Float** (AUC.1123)		1	
6970	**Needle and Seat,** controlling Petrol Flow to Float Chamber (AUC.8170)		1	
7118	**Lever,** operating Float Needle (AUC.1980)		1	
1153	**Pin,** securing Lever to Float Chamber Lid (AUC.1152)		1	
7119	**Gasket,** under Float Chamber Lid (AUC.1147)		1	
5832	**Cap Nut,** securing Lid (AUC.1867)		1	
1298	**Serrated Washer** (Fibre) on Cap Nut adjacent to Lid (AUC.1928)		1	
7120	**Alum Washer,** on Cap Nut (AUC.1557)		1	
479	**Filter,** in Inlet Connection on Float Chamber (AUC.2139)		1	
C.11488	**Banjo Bolt,** securing Feed Pipe to Float Chamber Lid (AUC.2698)		1	
C.11489	**Fibre Washer,** on Banjo Bolt (AUC.2141)		2	
6967	**Valve,** for slow-running adjustment (AUC.2028)		1	
6966	**Spring,** for slow-run Valve (AUC.2027)		1	
6968	**Gland Washer,** for slow-run Valve (AUC.2029)		1	
6969	**Dished Washer** (Brass) at top of Gland Washer (AUC.2030)		1	

CARBURETTERS AND PETROL FILTER

Part No.	Description	Plate No.	No. per Unit	Remarks
C.16650	**REAR CARBURETTER ASSEMBLY (HD.8)**	7–40	1	
8766	Jet Housing Assembly (AUC.8655)		1	
7116	Lid, for Float Chamber (AUC.4260)		1	
	All other items for Rear Carburetter are as for Centre Carburetter C.15836, except that Abutment Bracket (8756) and Cable Clamp (8757) are not fitted.			
8762	**BODY FOR FRONT CARBURETTER (AUC.8271)**	7–2	1	
8767	**BODY FOR CENTRE AND REAR CARBURETTERS (AUC.8272)**		2	
7862	Piston Lift Pin (AUC.2065)		3	
7863	Spring, for Lift Pin (AUC.2066)		3	
6964	Seating Washer, for Lift Pin (AUC.2098)		3	
7865	Brass Washer at top of Seating Washer (AUC.4944)		3	
7866	Circlip, securing Washers and Spring on Lift Pin (AUC.1250)		3	
8758	**CHOKE CONNECTING ROD, BETWEEN REAR AND CENTRE CARBURETTERS (AUC.1427)**	7–41	1	
C.10700	**CHOKE CONNECTING ROD, BETWEEN CENTRE AND FRONT CARBURETTERS (AUC.2872)**	7–42	1	
8755	**FORK END, FOR FIXING OF CONNECTING RODS TO CARBURETTERS (AUC.2256)**	7–43	3	
AN.102/L	Nut, securing Fork Ends on Rods (AUC.2156)		3	
5511	Clevis Pin, retaining Fork Ends to Front and Rear Carburetters (AUC.2108)	7–44	2	
AW.102/T	Washer, on Clevis Pins		2	
L.102/5U	Split Pin, retaining Clevis Pins, and for retention of Connecting Rod to centre Fork End		4	

Part No.	Description	Plate No.	No. per Unit	Remarks
C.18832	**ADAPTOR, SECURING CHOKE CONTROL CABLE TO CENTRE CARBURETTER (AUC.5058)**	7—45	1	
C.18833	**Special Screw,** securing Cable in Adaptor (AJD.7026)	7—46	1	
C.14371	**LEVER, ON CARBURETTER SPINDLES, FOR CONNECTION OF THROTTLE RETURN SPRINGS (AUC.8405)**	7—47	3	
5803	**Bolt,** through Levers (AUC.2694)		3	
5614	**Nut,** on Bolts (AUC.2156)		3	
7966	**Washer,** under Nuts (AUC.8396)		3	
C.14366	**THROTTLE RETURN SPRING**	7—48	3	
C.15963	**BRACKET ASSEMBLY, UNDER FRONT AND REAR CARBURETTERS, ANCHORING RETURN SPRING**	7—49	2	
C.15844	**BRACKET ASSEMBLY, UNDER CENTRE CARBURETTER, ANCHORING RETURN SPRING**	7—50	1	
C.17631	**LEVER ASSEMBLY, ON CARBURETTER SPINDLES, FOR CONNECTION OF THROTTLE CONTROL RODS**	7—51	3	

CARBURETTERS AND PETROL FILTER

Part No.	Description	Plate No.	No. per Unit	Remarks
C.17635	**CONTROL ROD, LINKING CARBURETTER LEVERS WITH SLAVE SHAFTS**	7–52	3	
C.13824	**Clip,** securing Control Rods	7–53	6	
C.14103	**LEVER, ON SLAVE SHAFTS, FOR CONNECTION OF CONTROL RODS (AUC.4054)**	7–54	3	
5803	**Bolt,** through Levers		3	
5614	**Nut,** on Bolts		3	
7966	**Washer,** under Nuts		3	
C.14145	**THROTTLE SLAVE SHAFT ASSEMBLY, FRONT**	7–55	1	
C.18537	**THROTTLE SLAVE SHAFT ASSEMBLY, CENTRE**	7–56	1	
C.18443	**Distance Piece,** on Centre Slave Shaft, adjacent to Lever for Centre Carburetter	7–57	1	
4833	**COUPLING, BETWEEN FRONT AND CENTRE SLAVE SHAFTS (AUC.4334)**	7–58	1	
5801	**Bolt,** through Coupling (AUC.2669)		2	
673	**Nut,** on Bolts (AUC.2673)		2	
4812	**Washer,** under Nuts (AUC.4612)		2	
C.18905	**THROTTLE SLAVE SHAFT ASSEMBLY, REAR**	7–59	1	R.H. DRIVE CARS ONLY.

Part No.	Description	Plate No.	No. per Unit	Remarks
C.18540	**THROTTLE SLAVE SHAFT ASSEMBLY, REAR**		1	**L.H. DRIVE CARS ONLY.**
C.17413	**INSULATOR BETWEEN CARBURETTERS AND INLET MANIFOLDS**	7–60	3	
C.7221	**Gasket** at each side of Insulators	7–61	6	
C.16873	**OVERFLOW PIPE FOR FRONT CARBURETTER**	7–62	1	
C.16874	**OVERFLOW PIPE FOR CENTRE CARBURETTER**	7–63	1	
C.16875	**OVERFLOW PIPE FOR REAR CARBURETTER**	7–64	1	
C.14090	**Clip,** on Oil Cleaner Bolt, securing Overflow Pipes	7–65	1	
C.12336	**SUCTION PIPE FROM FRONT CARBURETTER TO DISTRIBUTOR VACUUM CONTROL**	7–66	1	
C.15823	**PETROL FEED PIPE ASSEMBLY LINKING CARBURETTERS**	7–67	1	

CARBURETTERS AND PETROL FILTER

Part No.	Description	Plate No.	No. per Unit	Remarks
C.17335	**PETROL PIPE ASSEMBLY, BETWEEN FEED PIPE AND FILTER**	7–68	1	
C.13681	**PETROL FILTER ASSEMBLY (AC.7950001)**	7–69	1	
7297	**Filter Casting**	7–70	1	
7298	**Sealing Washer** between Filter Casting and Glass Bowl	7–71	1	
7299	**Filter Gauze**	7–72	1	
7300	**Glass Bowl**	7–73	1	
7301	**Retaining Strap Assembly**	7–74	1	
C.13705	**Banjo Bolt,** securing Petrol Pipes to Filter	7–75	2	
C.784	**Fibre Washer,** at each side of Banjos	7–76	4	
C.17354	**BRACKET, ON FRONT FRAME FIXING BOLT, FOR MOUNTING OF PETROL FILTER**	7–77	1	
UFS.131/6R	**Screw,** Set, securing Filter to Bracket		2	
UFN.131/L	**Nut,** on Setscrews		2	
FG.105/X	**Washer,** Spring, under Nuts		2	

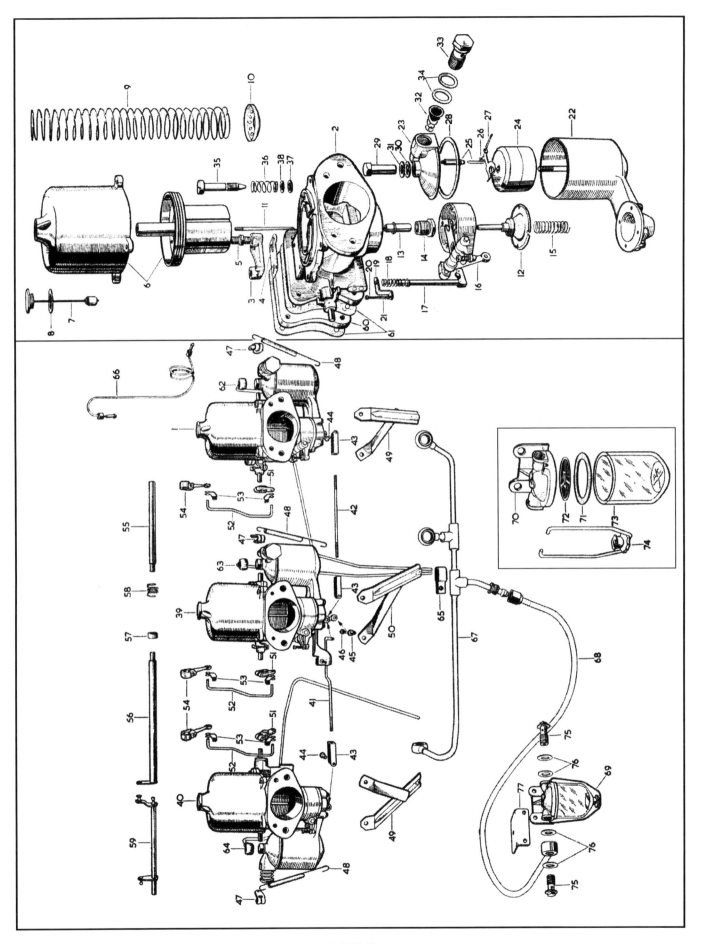

PLATE 7

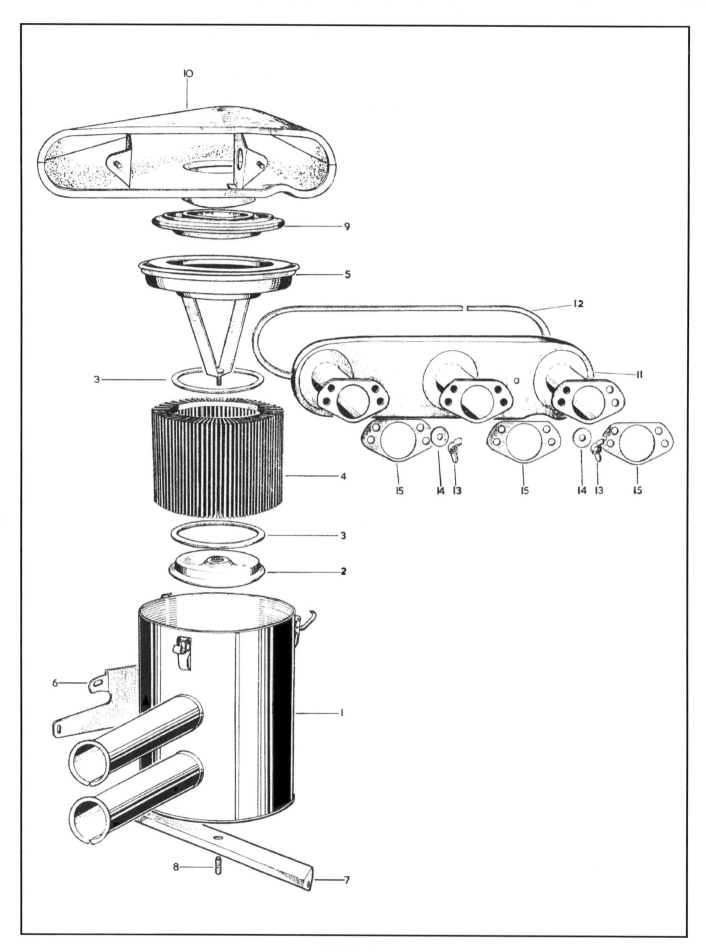

PLATE 8

Part No.	Description	Plate No.	No. per Unit	Remarks
C.17545	**AIR CLEANER ASSEMBLY (AC.7955780)**		1	
8420	**Shell Assembly,** for Air Cleaner (7955783)	8– 1	1	
8419	**Retaining Plate Assembly,** for Element (7955782)	8– 2	1	
8417	**Gasket,** at top and bottom of Element (7955504)	8– 3	2	
8416	**Element** (A.4847)	8– 4	1	
8418	**Top Plate Assembly** (7955781)	8– 5	1	
C.17651	**BRACKET, MOUNTING AIR CLEANER**	8– 6	1	
UFS.131/4R	**Screw,** Set, securing Bracket to Air Cleaner		2	
C.725	**Washer,** Shakeproof, on Setscrews		2	
FW.105/T	**Washer,** Plain, under Shakeproof Washers		2	
UFS.125/4R	**Screw,** Set, securing Bracket to Body		2	
C.724	**Washer,** Shakeproof, on Setscrews		2	
FW.104/T	**Washer,** Plain, under Shakeproof Washers		2	
C.17652	**SUPPORT BRACKET FOR AIR CLEANER**	8– 7	1	
C.12705	**Stud,** for fixing of Support Bracket to Air Cleaner	8– 8	1	
UFN.131/L	**Nut,** on Stud		1	
C.725	**Washer,** Shakeproof, under Nut		1	
FW.105/T	**Washer,** Plain, under Shakeproof Washer		1	
UFS.131/3R	**Screw,** Set, securing Support Bracket to Body		2	
C.725	**Washer,** Shakeproof, on Setscrews		2	
C.17546	**RUBBER GROMMET, BETWEEN AIR CLEANER AND AIR INTAKE BOX**	8– 9	1	
C.17533	**AIR INTAKE BOX ASSEMBLY**	8–10	1	

AIR CLEANER INSTALLATION

Part No.	Description	Plate No.	No. per Unit	Remarks
C.17540	**BASE ASSEMBLY FOR AIR INTAKE BOX (COMPLETE WITH TRUMPETS)**	8–11	1	Fitted from Chassis No. 850001 to 850091. 875001 to 875385. 860001 to 860004. 885001 to 885020.
C.19012	**BASE ASSEMBLY FOR AIR INTAKE BOX (COMPLETE WITH TRUMPETS)**		1	Fitted to Chassis No. 850092 and subs. 875386 and subs. 860005 and subs. 885021 and subs.
C.17539	**Gasket** (Neoprene) between Base and Air Intake Box	8–12	1	
C.12734	**Wing Nut,** securing Air Intake Box to Base	8–13	2	
C.17544	**Special Washer,** under Wing Nuts	8–14	2	
C.7164	**Gasket,** between Base and Carburetters	8–15	3	
C.4202/2	**Nut,** securing Base to Carburetters		6	
FG.105/X	**Washer,** Spring, under Nuts		6	

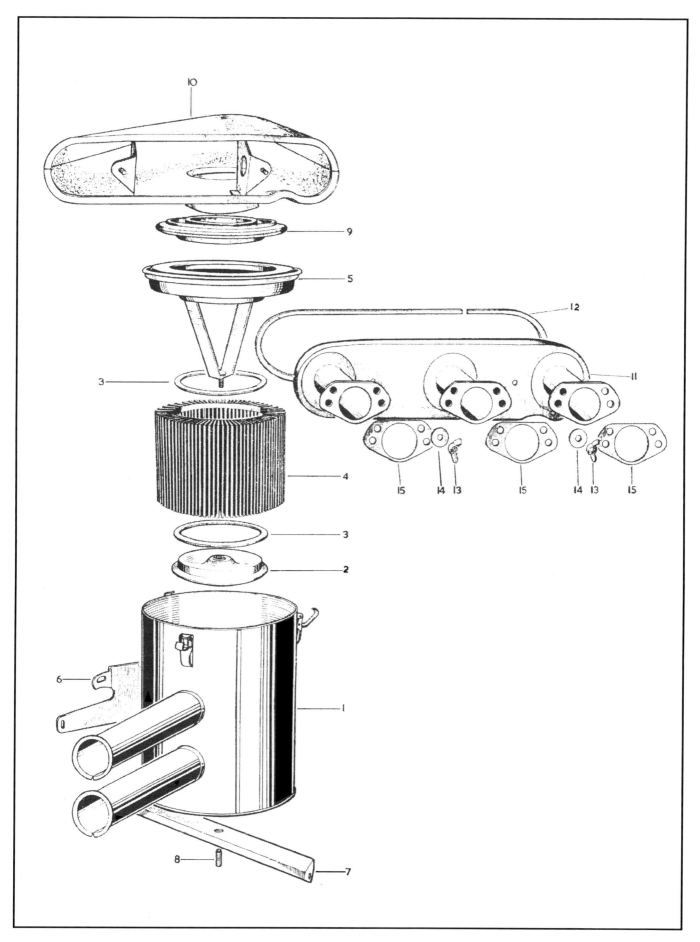

PLATE 8

ACCELERATOR CONTROLS
(R.H. DRIVE CARS ONLY)

Part No.	Description	Plate No.	No. per Unit	Remarks
C.17840	**ACCELERATOR PEDAL ASSEMBLY**		1	Fitted from Chassis No. 850001 to 850474. 860001 to 860374 except 860365.
C.20223	**ACCELERATOR PEDAL ASSEMBLY**	9– 1	1	Fitted to Chassis No. 850475 and subs. 860375 and subs., also 860365.
C.14366	**Return Spring,** for Accelerator Pedal	9– 2	1	
C.17844	**HOUSING ASSEMBLY FOR ACCELERATOR PEDAL**	9– 3	1	
C.17851	**Pivot Bush,** at each side of Housing		2	
C.17848	**Stud,** for fixing of Housing to Scuttle	9– 4	3	
C.18721	**Stop Plate,** on Studs, for pedal travel adjustment		1	Fitted from Chassis No. 850001 to 850474. 860001 to 860375 except 860365.
C.20639	**Stop Plate,** on Studs, for pedal travel adjustment	9– 5	1	Fitted to Chassis No. 850475 and subs. 860375 and subs., also 860365.
C.8667/1	**Nut,** Self-Locking, securing Housing to Scuttle		3	
FW.104/T	**Washer,** Plain, under Nuts		3	
BD.19706	**Gasket,** under Accelerator Pedal Housing		1	
C.18302	**ACCELERATOR PEDAL LEVER ASSEMBLY**	9– 6	1	
C.3767	**Ball Pin,** in end of Lever		1	
UFB.137/16R	**Bolt,** securing Pedal and Lever in Housing		1	
C.410	**Special Washer,** under head of Bolt		1	
C.18273	**Spacing Collar,** on Bolt		1	Fitted from Chassis No. 850001 to 850248. 860001 to 860020.
C.989	**Special Washer,** on Boss of Pedal Lever		1	
C.19915	**Spacing Collar,** on Pivot Bolt		1	Fitted to Chassis No. 850249 and subs. 860021 and subs. **MAY BE USED TOGETHER TO REPLACE C.18273 AND C.989.**
C.19914	**Special Washer,** on Boss of Pedal Lever		1	
C.8737/3	**Nut,** Self-Locking, on Bolt		1	
C.17867	**CONTROL ROD, BETWEEN PEDAL LEVER AND FULCRUM LEVER**	9– 7	1	
C.17858	**FULCRUM LEVER ASSEMBLY**	9– 8	1	
C.3767	**Ball Pin,** in ends of Lever		2	
C.18292	**Bracket Assembly,** on Brake Servo fixing Studs, for mounting of Fulcrum Lever	9– 9	1	
L.102.5/8U	**Split Pin,** retaining Fulcrum Lever on Bracket		1	
BD.1708/5	**Washer,** D.C. Spring, under Split Pin		1	
FW.104/T	**Washer,** Plain, under D.C. Spring Washer		1	
C.18275	**Eccentric Sleeve,** for Fulcrum Lever Stop Adjustment	9–10	1	
UFB.125/10R	**Bolt.** securing Sleeve to Fulcrum Mounting Bracket		1	
C.724	**Washer,** Shakeproof, on Bolt		1	
FW.104/T	**Washer,** Plain, under Shakeproof Washer		1	

Part No.	Description	Plate No.	No. per Unit	Remarks
C.17868	**CONTROL ROD, BETWEEN FULCRUM LEVER AND THROTTLE REAR SLAVE SHAFT**	9–11	1	
C.18905	**REAR SHAFT SLAVE ASSEMBLY FOR THROTTLE OPERATION**		1	Fitted from Engine No. R.1001 to R.2933.
C.3767	**Ball Pin,** in Lever of Rear Slave Shaft		1	
C.18938	**REAR SLAVE SHAFT ASSEMBLY FOR THROTTLE OPERATION**	9–12	1	Fitted to Engine No. R.2934 and subs.
C.3767	**Ball Pin,** in Lever of Rear Slave Shaft		1	
C.13605	**BUSH ASSEMBLY, SUPPORTING END OF REAR SLAVE SHAFT**	9–13	1	
C.18545	**Housing Assembly,** for Bush	9–14	1	
UFS.125/5R	**Screw,** Set, securing Housing to Mounting Bracket		2	
C.724	**Washer,** Shakeproof, on Setscrews		2	
C.18548	**BRACKET ASSEMBLY, MOUNTING HOUSING TO DASH**	9–15	1	
UFS.125/5R	**Screw,** Set, securing Bracket to Dash		2	
C.724	**Washer,** Shakeproof, on Setscrews		2	
FW.104/T	**Washer,** Plain, under Shakeproof Washers		2	
C.18537	**CENTRE SLAVE SHAFT ASSEMBLY FOR THROTTLE OPERATION**		1	Fitted from Engine No. R.1001 to R.2933.
C.18443	**Distance Piece,** on Centre Slave Shaft, adjacent to boss on Air Balance Pipe		1	
C.14145	**FRONT SLAVE SHAFT ASSEMBLY FOR THROTTLE OPERATION**		1	Fitted from Engine No. R.1001 to R.2933.
C.18935	**FRONT SLAVE SHAFT ASSEMBLY FOR THROTTLE OPERATION**	9–16	1	Fitted to Engine No. R.2934 and subs.

ACCELERATOR CONTROLS
(R.H. DRIVE CARS ONLY)

Part No.	Description	Plate No.	No. per Unit	Remarks
C.18941	**ADAPTOR, IN FRONT BOSS ON AIR BALANCE PIPE, SUPPORTING FRONT SLAVE SHAFT**	9–17	1	
C.18942	**ADAPTOR, IN REAR BOSS ON AIR BALANCE PIPE, SUPPORTING FRONT AND REAR SLAVE SHAFTS**	9–18	1	Fitted to Engine No. R.2934 and subs.
C.18943	**Tab Washer**, securing Adaptors	9–19	2	
4833	**FLEXIBLE COUPLING LINKING FRONT AND CENTRE SLAVE SHAFTS (AUC.4334)**		1	
5803	**Bolt**, through Coupling		2	Fitted from Engine No. R.1001 to R.2933.
5614	**Nut**, on Bolts		2	
7966	**Washer**, Spring, under Nuts		2	
C.14103	**LEVER, ON FRONT AND CENTRE SLAVE SHAFTS, FOR CONNECTION OF CONTROL RODS TO CARBURETTERS (AUC.4054)**		3	
5803	**Bolt**, securing Levers to Slave Shafts		3	Fitted from Engine No. R.1001 to R.2933.
5614	**Nut**, on Bolts		3	
7966	**Washer**, Spring, under Nuts		3	
C.17635	**CONTROL ROD, LINKING LEVERS ON SLAVE SHAFTS WITH CARBURETTERS**		3	Fitted from Engine No. R.1001 to R.2933.
C.14104	**CONTROL ROD, LINKING LEVERS ON SLAVE SHAFTS WITH CARBURETTERS**	9–20	3	Fitted to Engine No. R.2934 and subs.
C.13824	**Clip**, securing Control Rods	9–21	6	

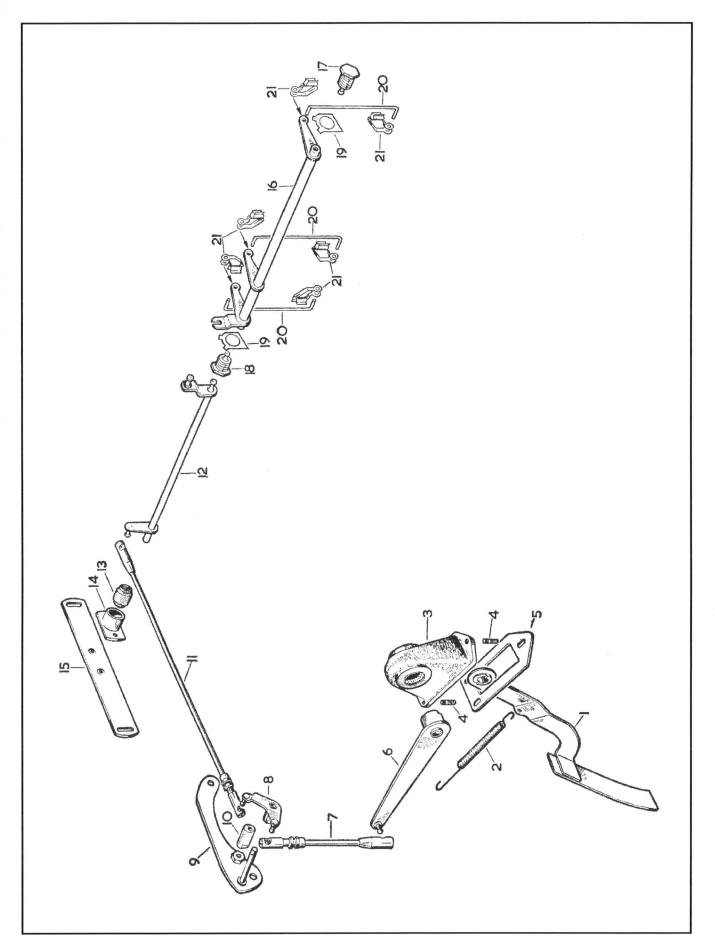

PLATE 9

ACCELERATOR CONTROLS
(L.H. DRIVE CARS ONLY)

Part No.	Description	Plate No.	No. per Unit	Remarks
C.18467	**ACCELERATOR PEDAL ASSEMBLY**	10– 1	1	
UFS.125/4R	**Screw,** Set, securing Accelerator Pedal to Floor		2	
C.724	**Washer,** Shakeproof, on Setscrews		2	
C.18478	**LINK ASSEMBLY, BETWEEN PEDAL AND ACCELERATOR DROP ARM**	10– 2	1	
C.18482	**Retainer,** for Link	10– 3	1	
C.8667/17	**Nut,** Self-Locking, securing Retainer to Link		1	
C.18476	**ACCELERATOR DROP ARM ASSEMBLY**	10– 4	1	
C.14366	**Return Spring,** for Drop Arm	10– 5	1	
C.17845	**HOUSING ASSEMBLY FOR DROP ARM**	10– 6	1	
C.17851	**Pivot Bush,** at each side of Housing		2	
C.17848	**Stud,** for fixing of Housing to Scuttle	10– 7	4	
C.8667/1	**Nut,** Self-Locking, securing Housing to Scuttle		4	
FW.104/T	**Washer,** Plain, under Nuts		4	
BD.19708	**Gasket,** under Accelerator Pedal Housing		1	
C.18270	**CONNECTING LEVER BETWEEN DROP ARM AND CONTROL ROD**	10– 8	1	
C.3767	**Ball Pin,** in Connecting Lever		1	
UFB.137/16R	**Bolt,** securing Drop Arm and Connecting Lever in Housing		1	
C.410	**Special Washer,** under head of Bolt		1	
C.18273	**Spacing Collar,** on Bolt		1	Fitted from Chassis No.
C.989	**Special Washer,** on Boss of Connecting Lever		1	875001 to 875910. 885001 to 885124.
C.19915	**Spacing Washer,** on Bolt		1	Fitted to Chassis No.
C.19914	**Special Washer,** on Boss of Connecting Lever		1	875911 and subs. 885125 and subs. **MAY BE USED TOGETHER TO REPLACE C.18273 AND C.989.**
C.8737/3	**Nut,** Self-Locking, on Bolt		1	
C.19053	**CONTROL ROD BETWEEN CONNECT-ING LEVER AND FULCRUM LEVER**	10– 9	1	

Part No.	Description	Plate No.	No. per Unit	Remarks
C.17859	**FULCRUM LEVER ASSEMBLY**	10–10	1	
C.3767	**Ball Pin,** in ends of Fulcrum Lever		2	
C.18276	**Pivot Pin,** for Fulcrum Lever	10–11	1	
C.18275	**Eccentric Sleeve,** for Fulcrum Lever stop adjustment	10–12	2	
UFB.125/11R	**Bolt,** securing Eccentric Sleeves to Dash		2	
C.18274	**Stiffening Plate,** on Pivot Pin and Setscrews	10–13	1	
C.18483	**Tab Washer,** locking Pivot Pin and Setscrews	10–14	1	
C.17870	**CONTROL ROD BETWEEN FULCRUM LEVER AND THROTTLE REAR SLAVE SHAFT**	10–15	1	
C.18540	**REAR SLAVE SHAFT ASSEMBLY FOR THROTTLE OPERATION**		1	Fitted from Engine No. R.1001 to R.2933.
C.3767	**Ball Pin,** in Lever of Rear Slave Shaft		1	
C.18937	**REAR SLAVE SHAFT ASSEMBLY FOR THROTTLE OPERATION**	10–16	1	Fitted to Engine No. R.2934 and subs.
C.3767	**Ball Pin,** in Lever of Rear Slave Shaft		1	
C.13605	**BUSH ASSEMBLY SUPPORTING END OF REAR SLAVE SHAFT**	10–17	1	
C.18545	**Housing Assembly,** for Bush	10–18	1	
UFS.125/5R	**Screw,** Set, securing Housing to Mounting Bracket		2	
C.724	**Washer,** Shakeproof, on Setscrews		2	
C.18548	**BRACKET ASSEMBLY, MOUNTING HOUSING TO DASH**	10–19	1	
UFS.125/5R	**Screw,** Set, securing Bracket to Dash		2	
C.724	**Washer,** Shakeproof, on Setscrews		2	
FW.104/T	**Washer,** Plain, under Shakeproof Washers		2	
C.18537	**CENTRE SLAVE SHAFT ASSEMBLY FOR THROTTLE OPERATION**		1	Fitted from Engine No. R.1001 to R.2933.
C.18443	**Distance Piece,** on Centre Slave Shaft, adjacent to boss on Air Balance Pipe		1	

ACCELERATOR CONTROLS
(L.H. DRIVE CARS ONLY)

Part No.	Description	Plate No.	No. per Unit	Remarks
C.14145	**FRONT SLAVE SHAFT ASSEMBLY FOR THROTTLE OPERATION**		1	Fitted from Engine No. R.1001 to R.2933.
C.18935	**FRONT SLAVE SHAFT ASSEMBLY FOR THROTTLE OPERATION**	10–20	1	Fitted to Engine No. R.2934 and subs.
C.18941	**ADAPTOR, IN FRONT BOSS ON AIR BALANCE PIPE, SUPPORTING FRONT SLAVE SHAFTS**	10–21	1	
C.18942	**ADAPTOR, IN REAR BOSS ON AIR BALANCE PIPE, SUPPORTING FRONT AND REAR SLAVE SHAFTS**	10–22	1	Fitted to Engine No. R.2934 and subs.
C.18943	**Tab Washer,** securing Adaptors	10–23	2	
4833	**FLEXIBLE COUPLING LINKING FRONT AND CENTRE SLAVE SHAFTS (AUC.4334)**		1	
5803	**Bolt,** through Coupling		2	Fitted from Engine No. R.1001 to R.2933.
5614	**Nut,** on Bolts		2	
7966	**Washer,** Spring, under Nuts		2	
C.14103	**LEVER, ON FRONT AND CENTRE SLAVE SHAFTS FOR CONNECTION OF CONTROL RODS TO CARBURETTERS (AUC.4054)**		3	
5803	**Bolt,** securing Levers to Slave Shafts		3	Fitted from Engine No. R.1001 to R.2933.
5614	**Nut,** on Bolts		3	
7966	**Washer,** Spring, under Nuts		3	
C.17635	**CONTROL ROD, LINKING LEVERS ON SLAVE SHAFTS WITH CARBURETTERS**		3	Fitted from Engine No. R.1001 to R.2933.
C.14104	**CONTROL ROD, LINKING LEVERS ON SLAVE SHAFTS WITH CARBURETTERS**	10–24	3	Fitted to Engine No. R.2934 and subs.
C.13824	**Clip,** securing Control Rods	10–25	6	

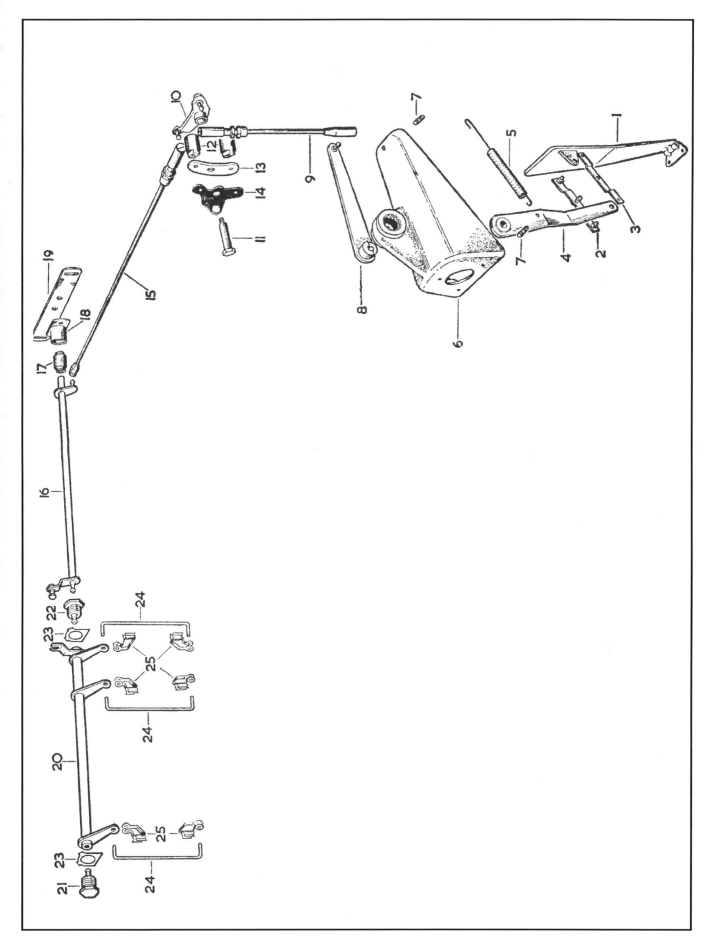

PLATE 10

CLUTCH UNIT
NOT SUITABLE FOR RACING OR COMPETITION PURPOSES

Part No.	Description	Plate No.	No. per Unit	Remarks
C.16172	**CLUTCH UNIT, COMPLETE** (BB.10/160/A)	11– 1	1	
C.16173	**CLUTCH COVER ASSEMBLY** (BB.45696/106)		1	
2546	**Cover only** (45616)	11– 2	1	
8769	**Thrust Spring** (Violet) (49970)	11– 3	12	
8097	**Pressure Plate** (50401)	11– 4	1	
6839	**Release Lever** (48992)	11– 5	3	
2472	**Plate,** Release Lever (40968)	11– 6	1	
2395	**Retainer,** Release Lever (40015)	11– 7	3	
2527	**Strut,** Release Lever (42606)	11– 8	3	
2588	**Eyebolt,** Release Lever (48243)	11– 9	3	
2523	**Pin,** through Eyebolt (42604)	11–10	3	
5086	**Nut,** on Eyebolt (48132)	11–11	3	
2545	**Anti-Rattle Spring** (45577)	11–12	3	
6840	**RELEASE BEARING ASSEMBLY (48444)**		1	
2590	**Release Bearing and Cup** (48443)	11–13	1	
4163	**Retainer,** securing Cup to Clutch Operating Fork (41628)	11–14	2	
7643	**DRIVE PLATE ASSEMBLY (47627/124)**		1	
2561	**Facings Package** (consisting of Clutch Linings and Rivets) (46663)		1	**FOR RENEWAL OF DRIVEN PLATE LININGS.**
C.1782	**Dowel,** for location of Clutch Unit to Flywheel		2	
C.20311	**Bolt,** securing Clutch Unit to Flywheel	11–15	6	
C.8737/3	**Nut,** Nylon, on Bolts	11–16	6	

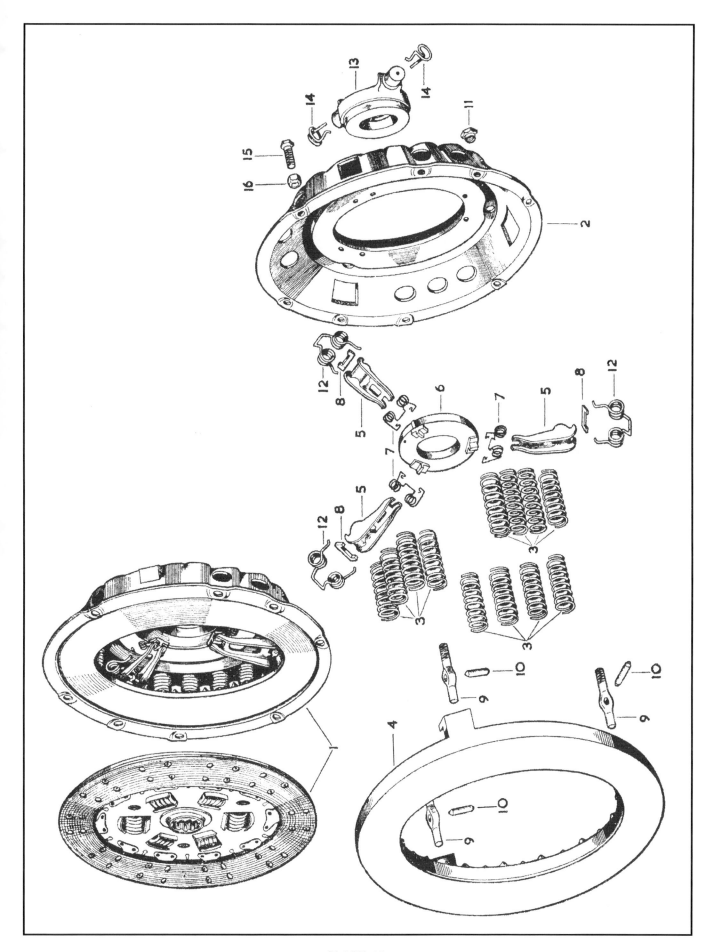

PLATE 11

CLUTCH UNIT
FOR RACING OR COMPETITION USE

Part No.	Description	Plate No.	No. per Unit	Remarks
C.16174	**CLUTCH UNIT, COMPLETE (BB.10/161)**	12– 1	1	**SUPERSEDED BY C.19951**
C.19951	**CLUTCH UNIT, COMPLETE (BB.10/161A)**		1	
C.16175	**CLUTCH COVER ASSEMBLY (BB.45696/107)**		1	**SUPERSEDED BY C.19952**
2546	**Cover only** (45616)	12– 2	1	
8769	**Thrust Spring** (Violet) (49970)	12– 3	12	
8780	**Pressure Plate** (48575)	12– 4	1	
6839	**Release Lever** (48992)	12– 5	3	
2472	**Plate,** Release Lever (40968)	12– 6	1	
2395	**Retainer,** Release Lever (40015)	12– 7	3	
2527	**Strut,** Release Lever (42606)	12– 8	3	
2588	**Eyebolt,** Release Lever (48243)	12– 9	3	
2523	**Pin,** through Eyebolt (42604)	12–10	3	
5086	**Nut,** on Eyebolt (48132)	12–11	3	
2545	**Anti-Rattle Spring** (45577)	12–12	3	
C.19952	**CLUTCH COVER ASSEMBLY (BB.45696/112)**		1	
10022	**Thrust Spring** (Buff with Black) (51448A)		12	

All other items as for C.16175.

Part No.	Description	Plate No.	No. per Unit	Remarks
6840	**RELEASE BEARING ASSEMBLY (48444)**		1	
2590	**Release Bearing and Cup** (48443)	12–13	1	
4163	**Retainer,** securing Cup to Clutch Operating Fork (41628)	12–14	2	
C.16215	**DRIVEN PLATE ASSEMBLY (46093/42)**		1	
C.1782	**Dowel,** for location of Clutch Unit to Flywheel		2	
C.20311	**Bolt,** securing Clutch Unit to Flywheel	12–15	6	
C.8737/3	**Nut,** Nyloc, on Bolt	12–16	6	

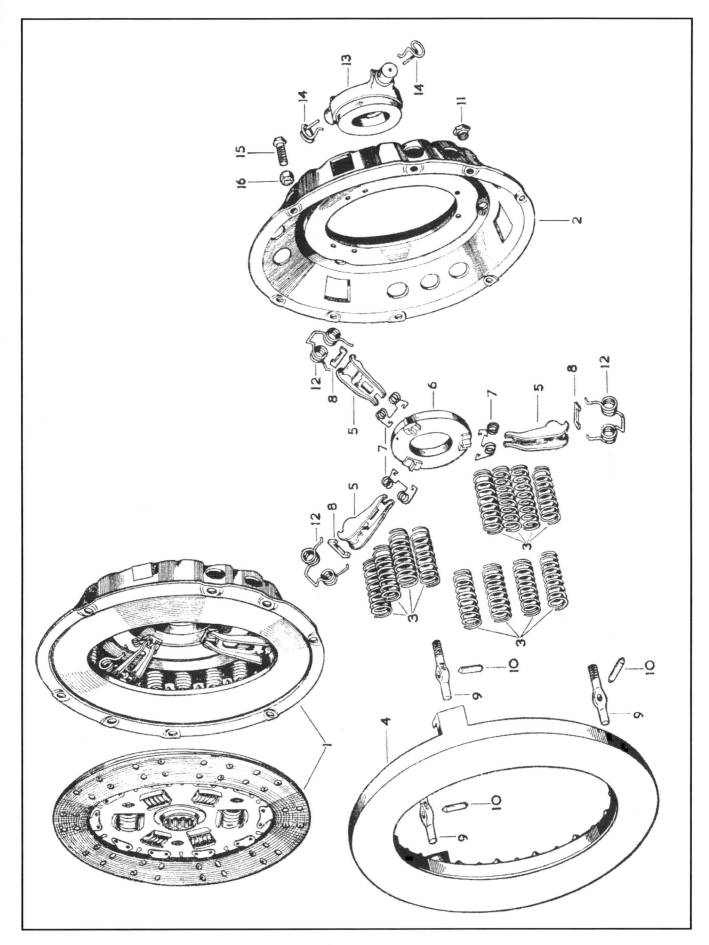

PLATE 12

CLUTCH CONTROLS

Part No.	Description	Plate No.	No. per Unit	Remarks
C.14494	**CLUTCH HOUSING** (COMPLETE WITH BUSHES)	13- 1	1	FITTED TO GEARBOX WITH SHAVED GEARS.
C.14494/G	**CLUTCH HOUSING** (COMPLETE WITH BUSHES)		1	FITTED TO GEARBOX WITH CLOSE RATIO GROUND GEARS.
C.10025	**Bush,** for Throw-out Shaft		2	
FB.107/13D	**Bolt,** securing Clutch Housing to Gearbox		6	
C.9859	**Bolt,** securing Clutch Housing to Gearbox		1	
C.9860	**Bolt,** securing Clutch Housing to Gearbox		1	
FW.107/T	**Washer,** Plain, on Bolts		2	
C.587	**Plate,** locking Bolts	13- 2	2	
C.5073	**Plate,** locking Bolts	13- 3	1	
UFB.137/23R	**Bolt,** securing Clutch Housing to Cylinder Block		11	
C.726	**Washer,** Shakeproof, on Bolts		11	
UFB.137/23R	**Bolt,** securing Clutch Housing and Support Brackets to Cylinder Block		2	
UFN.137/L	**Nut,** on Bolts		2	
C.726	**Washer,** Spring, under Nuts		2	
C.1221/1	**Split Pin,** in Oil Drain Hole, at bottom of Clutch Housing		1	
C.11910	**Cover,** over Timing aperture at bottom of Clutch Housing	13- 4	1	
BD.524/2	**Rivet,** securing Cover to Clutch Housing		1	
C.18739	**OIL SEAL, AT REAR OF CLUTCH HOUSING, FOR GEARBOX PRIMARY SHAFT**	13- 5	1	FITTED TO GEARBOX WITH SHAVED GEARS.
C.6738	**OIL SEAL, AT REAR OF CLUTCH HOUSING, FOR GEARBOX PRIMARY SHAFT**		1	FITTED TO GEARBOX WITH CLOSE RATIO GROUND GEARS.
C.5072	**COVER PLATE, AT BACK OF CLUTCH HOUSING**	13- 6	1	
UCS.125/4R	**Screw,** Set, securing Cover Plate		4	
C.724	**Washer,** Shakeproof, on Setscrews		4	
C.19207	**SUPPORT BRACKET AT R.H. SIDE OF CLUTCH HOUSING**	13- 7	1	
C.19206	**SUPPORT BRACKET AT L.H. SIDE OF CLUTCH HOUSING**	13- 8	1	
UFB.131/10R	**Bolt,** securing Support Brackets to Cylinder Block		3	
UFB.131/12R	**Bolt,** securing Support Brackets to Cylinder Block		1	
UFN.131/L	**Nut,** on Bolts		4	
FG.105/X	**Washer,** Spring, under Nuts		4	
UFB.137/11R	**Bolt,** securing Support Brackets to Clutch Housing		4	
UFN.137/L	**Nut,** on Bolts		4	
C.726	**Washer,** Shakeproof, under Nuts		4	

Part No.	Description	Plate No.	No. per Unit	Remarks
C.9857	**SHAFT, HOLDING OPERATING FORK TO CLUTCH HOUSING**	13–9	1	
C.9797	**FORK, ON SHAFT, OPERATING RELEASE BEARING**	13–10	1	
C.8011	**Screw** (Allen Head) securing Clutch Operating Fork to Shaft		1	
UFN.125/L	**Nut,** locking Screw		1	
C.5120	**RETURN SPRING FOR CLUTCH OPERATING FORK**	13–11	1	
C.5178	**Plate,** anchoring Return Spring	13–12	1	
C.16989	**SLAVE CYLINDER FOR CLUTCH OPERATION (110272)**	13–13	1	
8335	**Body only** (110271)	13–14	1	
8336	**Spring** (89500)	13–15	1	
6139	**Cup Filler,** at top of Spring (87575)	13–16	1	
8591	**Seal,** behind Piston (27526)	13–17	1	
8592	**Piston** (103439)	13–18	1	
8337	**Circlip,** retaining Piston in Slave Cylinder Body (K.19714)	13–19	1	
6142	**Rubber Boot,** over end of Slave Cylinder (33427)	13–20	1	
6096	**Bleeder Screw,** in Slave Cylinder (28696)	13–21	1	
C.9858	**Stud,** for mounting of Slave Cylinder to Clutch Housing	13–22	2	
UFN.137/L	**Nut,** on Studs		2	
FG.106/X	**Washer,** Spring, under Nut		1	
C.726	**Washer,** Shakeproof, under Nut		1	
8593	**REPAIR KIT FOR SERVICING CLUTCH SLAVE CYLINDER (SSB.601)**		1	
C.9798	**OPERATING ROD BETWEEN SLAVE CYLINDER AND CLUTCH FORK**	13–23	1	
C.10360	**ADJUSTER ASSEMBLY FOR OPERATING ROD**	13–24	1	
C.9800	**Bush,** for Adjuster		1	
UFN.231/L	**Nut,** locking Adjuster to Operating Rod		1	
C.9801	**Pivot Pin,** securing Adjuster to Clutch Operating Fork	13–25	1	
L.103/7U	**Split Pin,** securing Pivot Pin		1	
FW.105/T	**Washer,** Plain, behind Split Pin		1	
BD.1708/1	**Washer,** Double Coil Spring, behind Plain Washer		1	
C.17827	**PIPE ASSEMBLY BETWEEN SLAVE CYLINDER AND FLEXIBLE HOSE (VBO.7664)**	13–26	1	

CLUTCH CONTROLS

Part No.	Description	Plate No.	No. per Unit	Remarks
C.11603	**FLEXIBLE HOSE, BETWEEN HYDRAULIC PIPES (KL.93475)**	13–27	1	
UFN.237/L	**Nut,** securing Flexible Hose		2	
C.741	**Washer,** Shakeproof, under Nuts		2	
C.17826	**Bracket,** on Scuttle, receiving outboard end of Hose	13–28	1	
C.17828	**Bracket,** at R.H. side of Cylinder Block, receiving inboard end of Hose	13–29	1	
C.2155	**Distance Piece,** under Bracket	13–30	1	
C.17831	**PIPE ASSEMBLY BETWEEN FLEXIBLE HOSE AND CLUTCH MASTER CYLINDER (VBO.7666)**	13–31	1	R.H. DRIVE CARS ONLY.
C.17833	**PIPE ASSEMBLY BETWEEN FLEXIBLE HOSE AND PIPE CONNECTOR (VBO.7662)**		1	L.H. DRIVE CARS ONLY.
C.13187	**PIPE CONNECTOR (VBO.1766)**		1	L.H. DRIVE CARS ONLY.
C.17832	**PIPE ASSEMBLY BETWEEN CONNECTOR AND CLUTCH MASTER CYLINDER (VBO.7663)**		1	⎫
C.1040/8	**Clip,** securing Pipe to Scuttle		2	⎬ L.H. DRIVE CARS ONLY. ⎭
C.17643	**CLUTCH MASTER CYLINDER ASSEMBLY (VBM.4044)**	13–32	1	⎫
8543	**Body only (VBM.3261)**	13–33	1	
8296	**Seal,** on Valve (VBO.4842)	13–34	1	
8545	**Valve (VBO.7465)**	13–35	1	
6943	**Spring,** on Valve (VBO.1410)	13–36	1	
8546	**Spring Support,** Forward (VBO.7552)	13–37	1	Fitted from Chassis No.
8548	**Main Spring (VBO.7551)**	13–38	1	850001 to 850547.
8547	**Spring Support,** Rear (VBO.4451)	13–39	1	875001 to 877488.
8549	**Cup Seal,** on Piston (VBO.8206)	13–40	1	860001 to 860646.
8544	**Piston (VBO.7550)**	13–41	1	885001 to 886218.
8550	**Static Seal,** on Piston (VBO.7554)	13–42	1	
8551	**Push Rod Assembly (VBO.7625)**	13–43	1	
6948	**Circlip,** retaining Push Rod in Cylinder Body (VBO.2048)	13–44	1	
6945	**Dust Excluder,** over end of Cylinder Body (VBO.1869)	13–45	1	⎭

Part No.	Description	Plate No.	No. per Unit	Remarks
C.20775	**CLUTCH MASTER CYLINDER ASSEMBLY (VBM.4044/1)**		1	Fitted to Chassis No. 850548 and subs. 877489 and subs. 860647 and subs. 886219 and subs.
9314	**Spring Support,** Forward (VBO.8885)		1	
	All other items are as for Clutch Master Cylinder Assembly C.17643.			
C.18203	**Stud,** for mounting of Clutch Master Cylinder	13–46	2	
UFN.131/L	**Nut,** on Studs		2	
C.725	**Washer,** Shakeproof, under Nuts		2	
J.105/12S	**Clevis Pin,** securing Clutch Pedal to Master Cylinder Push Rod	13–47	1	
L.102.5/6U	**Split Pin,** retaining Clevis Pin		1	
FW.105/T	**Washer,** Plain, behind Split Pin		1	
8552	**REPAIR KIT FOR SERVICING OF CLUTCH MASTER CYLINDER (VBM.8063) (COMPRISING CUP SEAL, STATIC SEAL, VALVE SEAL, DUST EXCLUDER AND TUBE OF RUBBER GREASE)**		1	
C.17829	**PIPE ASSEMBLY BETWEEN CLUTCH MASTER CYLINDER AND LOW PRESSURE HOSE (VBO.7599)**	13–48	1	R.H. DRIVE CARS ONLY.
C.18716	**PIPE ASSEMBLY BETWEEN CLUTCH MASTER CYLINDER AND LOW PRESSURE HOSE**		1	L.H. DRIVE CARS ONLY.
C.6854	**LOW PRESSURE HOSE BETWEEN PIPE AND FLUID RESERVOIR**	13–49	1	R.H. DRIVE CARS ONLY.
C.18717	**LOW PRESSURE HOSE BETWEEN PIPE AND FLUID RESERVOIR**		1	L.H. DRIVE CARS ONLY.
C.15886/4	**Clip,** securing Hose on Pipe	13–50	1	
C.15886/5	**Clip,** securing Hose to Fluid Reservoir	13–51	1	
C.18616	**RESERVOIR ASSEMBLY FOR CLUTCH FLUID**		1	Fitted from Chassis No. 850001 to 850555. 875001 to 877556. 860001 to 860677. 885001 to 886282.
1578	**Cap,** on Reservoir		1	
1193	**Washer,** under Cap		1	

CLUTCH CONTROLS

Part No.	Description	Plate No.	No. per Unit	Remarks
C.19646	**RESERVOIR ASSEMBLY FOR CLUTCH FLUID**	13–52	1	Fitted to Chassis No. 850556 and subs.
C.19515	**Cap,** on Reservoir		1	877557 and subs. 860678 and subs. 886283 and subs.
C.17476	**BRACKET ASSEMBLY FOR MOUNTING OF FLUID RESERVOIRS**		1	**R.H. DRIVE CARS ONLY.**
UFS.125/4R	**Screw,** Set, clamping Reservoir Clips		3	Fitted from Chassis No.
C.8667/1	**Nut,** Self-locking, on Setscrews		3	850001 to 850555.
UFS.131/4R	**Screw,** Set, securing Bracket to Dash		2	860001 to 860677.
C.725	**Washer,** Shakeproof, on Setscrews		2	
C.20232	**BRACKET FOR MOUNTING OF FLUID RESERVOIRS**	13–53	1	**R.H. DRIVE CARS ONLY.** Fitted to Chassis No.
UFS.131/4R	**Screw,** Set, securing Bracket to Dash		2	850556 and subs.
C.725	**Washer,** Shakeproof, on Setscrews		2	860678 and subs.
C.18693	**BRACKET ASSEMBLY FOR MOUNTING OF FLUID RESERVOIRS**		1	**L.H. DRIVE CARS ONLY.** Fitted from Chassis No.
UFS.125/4R	**Screw,** Set, clamping Reservoir Clips		3	875001 to 877556.
C.8667/1	**Nut,** Self-locking, on Setscrews		3	885001 to 886282.
C.20234	**BRACKET FOR MOUNTING OF FLUID RESERVOIRS**		1	**L.H. DRIVE CARS ONLY.** Fitted to Chassis No. 877557 and subs. 886283 and subs.
C.19497	**CLAMP, SECURING RESERVOIR TO BRACKET**	13–53A	2	Fitted to Chassis No. 850556 and subs.
C.20235	**Stud,** securing Clamp		2	860678 and subs. 877557 and subs.
C.8737/1	**Nut,** Self-Locking, on Studs		4	886283 and subs.
C.17812	**BRACKET ASSEMBLY, FOR FIXING OF RESERVOIR BRACKET TO L.H. SIDE MEMBER**		2	
C.17811	**Clamping Piece,** for Brackets		2	**L.H. DRIVE CARS ONLY.**
UFS.125/9R	**Screw,** Set, through Clamps		2	
UFN.125/L	**Nut,** on Setscrews		2	
C.724	**Washer,** Shakeproof, under Nuts		2	

Part No.	Description	Plate No.	No. per Unit	Remarks
C.18695	**SHIELD ASSEMBLY, PROTECTING RESERVOIRS FROM EXHAUST HEAT**		1	
UFS.131/7R	**Screw**, Set, securing Shield and Reservoir Bracket to Fixing Bracket		4	**L.H. DRIVE CARS ONLY.**
C.18698	**Spacer**, on Setscrews		4	
FW.105/T	**Washer**, Plain, on Setscrews		8	**L.H. DRIVE CARS ONLY** From Chassis No.
UFN.131/L	**Nut**, on Setscrews		4	875001 to 877556.
C.725	**Washer**, Shakeproof, under Nuts		4	885001 to 886282.
FW.105/T	**Washer**, Plain, on Setscrews		6	**L.H. DRIVE CARS ONLY**
UFN.131/L	**Nut**, on Setscrews		2	For Chassis No.
C.725	**Washer**, Shakeproof, on Setscrews		4	877557 and subs.
C.21255	**Clip**, retaining Nuts		2	886283 and subs.
C.17253	**HOUSING FOR CLUTCH PEDAL**		1	
C.18203	**Stud**, for mounting of Clutch Master Cylinder and for fixing of Housing to Scuttle		6	
C.12473	**Stud**, for mounting of Brake Master Cylinders and for fixing of Servo Bracket to Housing		9	Fitted from Chassis No. 850001 to 850232. 875001 to 875858.
C.17260	**Bush**, in Housing, for Clutch Pedal		1	860001 to 860020.
UCS.125/3R	**Screw**, Set, retaining Bush		1	885001 to 885104.
C.21755	**Washer** (Tufnol) between Brake and Clutch Pedals		1	
C.17256	**Shaft**, through Bush, for mounting of Brake Pedal		1	
C.17485	**Circlip**, retaining Shaft		1	
C.17481	**Washer**, under Circlip		1	
C.19666	**HOUSING FOR CLUTCH PEDAL**	13–54	1	
C.18203	**Stud**, for mounting of Clutch Master Cylinder and for fixing of Housing to Scuttle		6	
C.12473	**Stud**, for mounting of Brake Master Cylinder and for fixing of Servo Bracket to Housing		9	Fitted to Chassis No. 850233 and subs.
C.19613	**Flanged Bearing Tube**, at side of Pedal Housing	13–55	1	875859 and subs.
UCS.125/4R	**Screw**, Set, securing Bearing Tube	13–56	2	860021 and subs.
C.724	**Washer**, Shakeproof, on Setscrews	13–57	2	885105 and subs.
C.19623	**Bush**, in Bearing Tube, for Brake Pedal Shaft	13–58	1	
C.21755	**Washer** (Tufnol) between Brake and Clutch Pedals	13–59	1	
C.17256	**Shaft**, through Bush, for Mounting of Brake Pedal	13–60	1	
C.17485	**Circlip**, retaining Shaft	13–61	1	
C.18262	**Gasket**, between Housing and Scuttle	13–62	1	
C.8667/2	**Nut**, Self-locking, securing Housing to Scuttle		5	
FW.105/T	**Washer**, Plain, under Nuts		5	
C.18831	**CLUTCH PEDAL**		1	**R.H. DRIVE CARS ONLY.** Fitted from Chassis No. 850001 to 850232. 860001 to 860020.
C.19673	**CLUTCH PEDAL**	13–63	1	**R.H. DRIVE CARS ONLY.** Fitted to Chassis No.
C.19154	**Bush**, in boss of Clutch Pedal	13–64	2	850233 and subs. 860021 and subs.
C.18830	**CLUTCH PEDAL**		1	**L.H. DRIVE CARS ONLY.** Fitted from Chassis No.
C.19010	**Return Spring**, for Clutch Pedal		1	875001 to 875858. 885001 to 885104.

CLUTCH CONTROLS

Part No.	Description	Plate No.	No. per Unit	Remarks
C.19672	**CLUTCH PEDAL**		1	**L.H. DRIVE CARS ONLY.** Fitted to Chassis No.
C.19154	**Bush,** in boss of Clutch Pedal		2	875859 and subs. 885105 and subs.
C.15245	**STEEL PAD FOR CLUTCH PEDAL**		1	Fitted from Chassis No. 850001 to 850474. 875001 to 876998. 860001 to 860374 except 860365. 885001 to 885870.
C.20221	**STEEL PAD FOR CLUTCH PEDAL**	13–65	1	Fitted to Chassis No. 850475 and subs. 876999 and subs. 860375 and subs, also 860365. 885871 and subs.
C.8667/2	**Nut,** Self-locking, securing Pad to Pedal		1	
C.9934	**RUBBER PAD FOR CLUTCH PEDAL**	13–66	1	

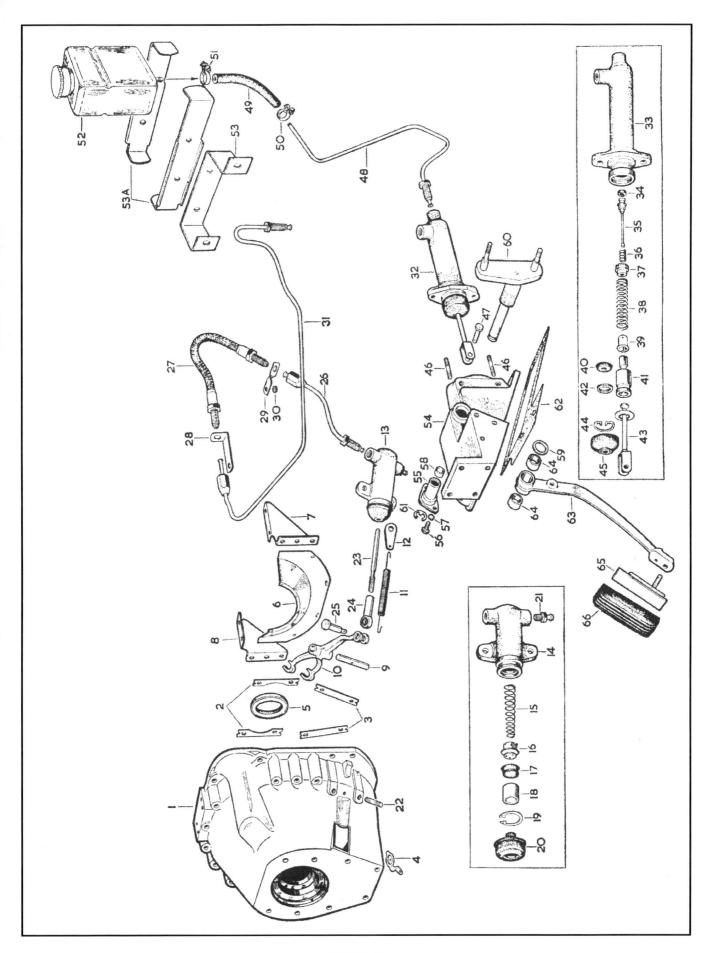

PLATE 13

GEARBOX
SHAVED GEARS

Part No.	Description	Plate No.	No. per Unit	Remarks
C.17600	**GEARBOX ASSEMBLY**		1	NOTE.—This Gearbox may be identified by the prefix letters "EB" and suffix letters "JS" to the Serial number on the Gearbox.
C.19208	**GEARBOX CASE**	14— 1	1	
C.799	**Plug,** Oil Drain, at bottom of Casing	14— 2	1	
C.799	**Plug,** Oil Level, at side of Casing	14— 2	1	
C.785	**Washer** (Fibre) on Drain Plugs	14— 3	2	
C.857	**Plate,** on Casing, locking Counter and Reverse Shafts	14— 4	1	
FS.205/7D	**Screw,** Set, securing Locking Plate	14— 5	1	
FG.105/X	**Washer,** Spring, on Setscrews	14— 6	1	
C.1845	**Ball Bearing,** for Mainshaft (Hoff.MS.12½KV3)	14— 7	1	
C.1855	**Circlip,** securing Mainshaft Bearing	14— 8	1	
C.1838	**Ball Bearing,** for Constant Pinion Shaft (Hoff.340KV3)	14— 9	1	
C.12195	**Collar,** between Casing and Circlip	14—10	1	
C.1840	**Circlip,** on Ball Bearing, behind Collar	14—11	1	
C.920	**Washer** (Fibre) in Casing, at front end of Countershaft	14—12	1	
C.1834	**Gasket,** between Gearbox Case and Clutch Housing	14—13	1	
C.18959	**REAR END COVER**	14—14	1	Fitted up to and including Gearbox Serial No. EB.245 JS
C.19041	**REAR END COVER**	14—14	1	Fitted from Gearbox Serial No. EB.246 JS to EB.8858 JS.
C.21415	**REAR END COVER**	14—14	1	Fitted to Gearbox Serial No. EB.8859 JS and subs. **See note below.**
C.19209	**Gasket,** between Rear End Cover and Casing	14—15	1	
FS.105/9D	**Screw,** Set, securing Rear End Cover to Casing		7	
FG.105/X	**Washer,** Spring, on Setscrews		7	
C.859	**Seal,** Oil, in Rear End Cover	14—16	1	

NOTE : The following cars were fitted with Rear End Cover C.19041 :
      Open R.H. Drive : 850653, 850654.
      Open L.H. Drive : 878895, 878900, 878907, 878908, 878913, 878914, 878915, 878926, 878936, 878937, 878939, 878958, 878986, 879005, 879024, 879049.
  Fixed Head R.H. Drive : 861087.
  Fixed Head L.H. Drive : 888086, 888096, 888101, 888103, 888109, 888113, 888117, 888118, 888120, 888134, 888157, 888178, 888238.

Part No.	Description	Plate No.	No. per Unit	Remarks
C.15847	**SPEEDOMETER DRIVEN GEAR ASSEMBLY IN REAR END COVER**	14–17	1	Fitted up to and including Gearbox Serial No. EB.245 JS.
C.19024	**SPEEDOMETER DRIVEN GEAR ASSEMBLY IN REAR END COVER**	14–17	1	Fitted to Gearbox Serial No. EB.246 JS and subs.
C.846	**Screw,** locking Speedo Driven Gear in Cover	14–18	1	
FG.105/X	**Washer,** Spring, on Locking Screw	14–19	1	
C.9177	**Sealing Ring** (Rubber) for Speedometer Driven Gear	14–20	1	
8779	**GEARBOX REMOTE CONTROL ASSEMBLY (SD.1112)** (COMPRISING TOP COVER, CHANGE-SPEED LEVER, CHANGE-SPEED FORKS, SELECTORS, ETC.)	14–21	1	
C.13332	**TOP COVER**	14–22	1	
C.1083	**Switch,** for Top Cover, operating Reversing Light	14–23	1	
C.4531	**Gasket,** for Switch	14–24	1	
C.860	**Gasket,** between Top Cover and Gearbox Case	14–25	1	
FS.105/7D	**Screw,** Set, securing Top Cover to Gearbox Case		6	
FB.105/11D	**Bolt,** securing Top Cover to Gearbox Case		2	
FB.105/15D	**Bolt,** securing Top Cover to Gearbox Case		2	
FG.105/X	**Washer,** Spring, on Bolts and Setscrews		10	
OD.105/6H	**Dowel,** positioning Top Cover to Casing	14–26	2	
C.1319	**Ball,** engaging Striking Rods	14–27	3	
C.13334	**Plunger,** holding Balls in position	14–28	3	
C.845	**Spring,** at top of Plungers	14–29	3	
C.13333	**Shim,** for Spring Tension	14–30	As req'd.	
C.18442	**Plug,** sealing redundant Breather aperture	14–31	1	
C.930	**Washer** (Fibre) for Plug	14–32	1	
C.7426	**Stud,** in Top Cover, for fixing of Change-Speed Lever Housing	14–33	4	
UFN.131/L	**Nut,** on Studs		4	
FG.105/X	**Washer,** Spring, under Nuts		4	
C.9840	**Welch Washer,** $\frac{7}{16}''$ diameter, at L.H. side of Top Cover	14–34	2	
787	**Welch Washer,** $\frac{5}{8}''$ diameter, at front and rear of Top Cover (ends of Striking Rods)	14–35	6	
C.799	**Plug,** in Dipstick aperture	14–36	1	
C.785	**Washer** (Fibre) on Plug	14–37	1	
C.7379	**Plug,** sealing redundant hole for Overdrive Switch in Top Cover	14–38	1	
C.2296/1	**Washer** (Copper) on Plug	14–39	1	

GEARBOX
SHAVED GEARS

Part No.	Description	Plate No.	No. per Unit	Remarks
	STRIKING GEAR			
C.9841	**Striking Rod Assembly,** 1st/2nd Gears (complete with Interlock Rollers)	14–40	1	
C.9846	**Striking Rod,** 3rd/Top Gears	14–41	1	
C.9845	**Striking Rod,** Reverse Gear	14–42	1	
C.9854	**Stop** for 1st/2nd Speed Striking Rod	14–43	1	
C.9851	**Change-Speed Fork,** 1st/2nd Gears	14–44	1	
C.9852	**Change-Speed Fork,** 3rd/Top Gears	14–45	1	
C.9847	**Change-Speed Fork,** Reverse Gear	14–46	1	
C.9853	**Selector,** 3rd/Top Gears	14–47	1	
C.9848	**Plunger,** in Change-Speed Fork, for Reverse Selection	14–48	1	
C.9849	**Spring,** tensioning Reverse Plunger	14–49	1	
C.1319	**Ball,** locking Reverse Plunger	14–50	1	
C.14704	**Spring,** loading Locating Ball	14–51	1	
C.19772	**Dowel Screw,** locating Change-Speed Forks, Selector and 2nd Speed Stop, on Striking Rods	14–52	5	
C.837	**Wire,** locking Dowel Screws		As req'd	
C.922	**Ball,** between Striking Rods, for Interlock	14–53	2	
C.14468	**HOUSING, ON TOP COVER, FOR CHANGE-SPEED LEVER**	14–54	1	
C.1907	**Bush,** inside Housing, for Pivot Jaw	14–55	1	
C.13338	**Gasket,** under Housing	14–56	1	
C.841	**Breather,** at R.H. side of Housing	14–57	1	
C.930	**Washer** (Fibre) for Breather	14–58	1	
C.12454	**'O' RING, IN HOUSING, FOR REMOTE CONTROL SHAFT**	14–59	1	
C.13335	**Retaining Cup,** for 'O' Ring	14–60	1	
C.14305	**REMOTE CONTROL SHAFT**	14–61	1	
C.13341	**SELECTOR FINGER, ON REMOTE CONTROL SHAFT**	14–62	1	
C.19772	**Dowel Screw,** securing Selector Finger to Remote Control Shaft	14–63	1	
C.837	**Wire,** locking Dowel Screw		As req'd	
787	**Welch Washer,** ⅝" diameter, at rear of Housing	14–64	1	

Part No.	Description	Plate No.	No. per Unit	Remarks
C.14470	**PIVOT JAW, HOUSING SELECTOR LEVER**	14–65	1	
C.1894	**Washer**, (Tufnol) at each side of Housing Turret	14–66	2	
C.1905	**Washer**, Double Coil Spring, between 'D' Washer and Tufnol Washer	14–67	1	
C.1914	**'D' Washer** on Pivot Jaw, adjacent to Nut	14–68	1	
FN.407/L	**Slotted Nut**, securing Pivot Jaw to Housing		1	
L.103/8U	**Split Pin**, retaining Nut		1	
C.14829	**SELECTOR LEVER ON END OF CHANGE-SPEED LEVER**	14–69	1	
C.1906	**Bush**, inside Selector Lever	14–70	1	
C.1908	**Washer** (Tufnol) at each side of Selector Lever	14–71	2	
C.1929	**Washer**, Double Coil Spring, between Tufnol Washer and Selector Lever	14–72	1	
C.1912	**Pivot Pin**, mounting Selector Lever in Pivot Jaw	14–73	1	
FN.407/L	**Slotted Nut**, securing Pivot Pin		1	
L.103/8U	**Split Pin**, retaining Slotted Nut		1	
C.4054	**CHANGE-SPEED LEVER**	14–74	1	
C.16154	**Knob**, for Change-Speed Lever	14–75	1	
C.1928	**Nut**, locking Knob to Change-Speed Lever	14–76	1	
C.1915	**RUBBER BUSH, HOUSING CHANGE-SPEED LEVER IN SELECTOR LEVER**	14–77	2	
C.1919	**Washer**, at top of Rubber Bush	14–78	1	
C.1904	**Washer**, at bottom of Rubber Bush	14–79	1	
FN.405/L	**Slotted Nut**, securing Change-Speed Lever to Selector Lever		1	
L.103/8U	**Split Pin**, retaining Slotted Nut		1	

GEARBOX
SHAVED GEARS

Part No.	Description	Plate No.	No. per Unit	Remarks
C.885	**FLANGE, ON MAINSHAFT, FOR UNIVERSAL JOINT**	15– 1	1	
C.840	**Nut,** Slotted, securing Flange to Mainshaft	15– 2	1	
C.925	**Washer,** Plain, under Slotted Nut	15– 3	1	
L.104/12U	**Pin,** Split, securing Slotted Nut	15– 4	1	
C.4994	**MAINSHAFT**	15– 5	1	
C.14932	**Gear,** Speedometer Driving	15– 6	1	⎰ Fitted up to and including Gearbox Serial
C.909	**Distance Piece,** behind Speedometer Driving Gear	15– 7	1	⎱ No. EB.245 JS.
C.19026	**Gear,** Speedometer Driving	15– 6	1	⎰ Fitted to Gearbox Serial No. EB.246 JS and
C.19286	**Distance Piece,** behind Speedometer Driving Gear	15– 7	1	⎱ subs.
C.10209	**Sleeve,** Synchronising Assembly, 2nd Speed	15– 8	1	
C.900	**Spring,** in 2nd and 3rd/Top Synchro Sleeves	15– 9	12	
C.922	**Ball,** in 2nd and 3rd/Top Synchro Sleeves at top of Springs and Plungers	15–10	15	
C.901	**Plunger** in 2nd and 3rd/Top Synchro Sleeves (.490″ long)	15–11	3	⎱ **SELECTIVE SIZES.** Choose the Plunger
C.901/1	**Plunger** in 2nd and 3rd/Top Synchro Sleeves (.495″ long)	15–11	3	⎰ of the desired length.
C.901/2	**Plunger** in 2nd and 3rd/Top Synchro Sleeves (.500″ long)	15–11	3	
C.10201	**Gear,** 1st Speed	15–12	1	
C.10202	**Gear,** 2nd Speed	15–13	1	
C.10203	**Gear,** 3rd Speed	15–14	1	
C.1850	**Roller,** Needle, in 2nd and 3rd Speed Gears	15–15	82	
C.1849	**Plunger,** in Mainshaft, locking 2nd and 3rd Speed Gears	15–16	2	
C.1324	**Spring,** under Plungers	15–17	2	
C.10206/1	**Washer,** Thrust, front and rear of 2nd and 3rd Speed Gears (.471″/.472″ thick)	15–18	2	
C.10206/2	**Washer,** Thrust, front and rear of 2nd and 3rd Speed Gears (.473″/.474″ thick)	15–18	2	**SELECTIVE SIZES.** Choose the Washer of the desired thickness.
C.10206/3	**Washer,** Thrust, front and rear of 2nd and 3rd Speed Gears (.475″/.476″ thick)	15–18	2	
C.10208	**Sleeve,** Synchronising 3rd/Top Speeds	15–19	1	
C.4049/1	**Sleeve,** Operating 3rd/Top Speeds	15–20	1	
C.903	**Shim,** for Synchro Sleeve (.006″ thick)	15–21	As req'd	
C.914	**Shim,** for Synchro Sleeve (.028″ thick)	15–21	As req'd	
C.10200	**CONSTANT PINION SHAFT ASSEMBLY**	15–22	1	
C.1843	**Bearing,** Roller, inside Constant Pinion Shaft	15–23	1	
C.2121	**Oil Thrower,** on Constant Pinion Shaft	15–24	1	
C.11932	**Locknut,** on Constant Pinion Shaft, securing Front Bearing	15–25	2	
C.11933	**Tab Washer,** retaining Locknut	15–26	1	

Part No.	Description	Plate No.	No. per Unit	Remarks
C.10205/1	**REVERSE GEAR (COMPLETE WITH BUSHES)**	15–27	1	
C.2070	**Reverse Spindle**	15–28	1	
C.1893	**Lever,** operating Reverse Gear	15–29	1	
C.1899	**Fulcrum Pin,** for Operating Lever	15–30	1	
C.777	**Nut,** Slotted, securing Fulcrum Pin	15–31	1	
FW.106/T	**Washer,** Plain, under Slotted Nut	15–32	1	
L.103/8U	**Pin,** Split, retaining Slotted Nut and Reverse Slipper	15–33	2	
C.866	**Reverse Slipper**	15–34	1	
C.4284	**Sealing Ring,** on Reverse Spindle	15–35	1	
C.1856	**COUNTERSHAFT**	15–36	1	
C.10204	**GEAR UNIT (CLUSTER) ON COUNTERSHAFT**	15–37	1	
C.1864	**Retaining Ring,** at rear of Needle Rollers	15–38	2	
C.918	**Needle Roller**	15–39	58	
C.1861	**Thrust Washer,** Inner, at rear of Counter adjacent to Needle Rollers	15–40	1	
C.1862	**Thrust Washer,** Outer, at rear of Counter (.156″ thick)	15–41	1	To eliminate end float on Countershaft, select Washer which has the desired thickness.
C.1862/1	**Thrust Washer,** Outer, at rear of Counter (.159″ thick)	15–41	1	
C.1862/2	**Thrust Washer,** Outer, at rear of Counter (.162″ thick)	15–41	1	
C.1862/3	**Thrust Washer,** Outer, at rear of Counter (.152″ thick)	15–41	1	
C.1862/4	**Thrust Washer,** Outer, at rear of Counter (.164″ thick)	15–41	1	
C.10210	**Retaining Ring,** at outer end of Front Needle Rollers	15–42	1	
C.8835	**Thrust Washer,** Inner, at front end of Counter	15–43	1	
C.1859	**Thrust Washer,** Outer Assembly, at front end of Counter	15–44	1	
C.4285	**Sealing Ring,** on Countershaft	15–45	1	

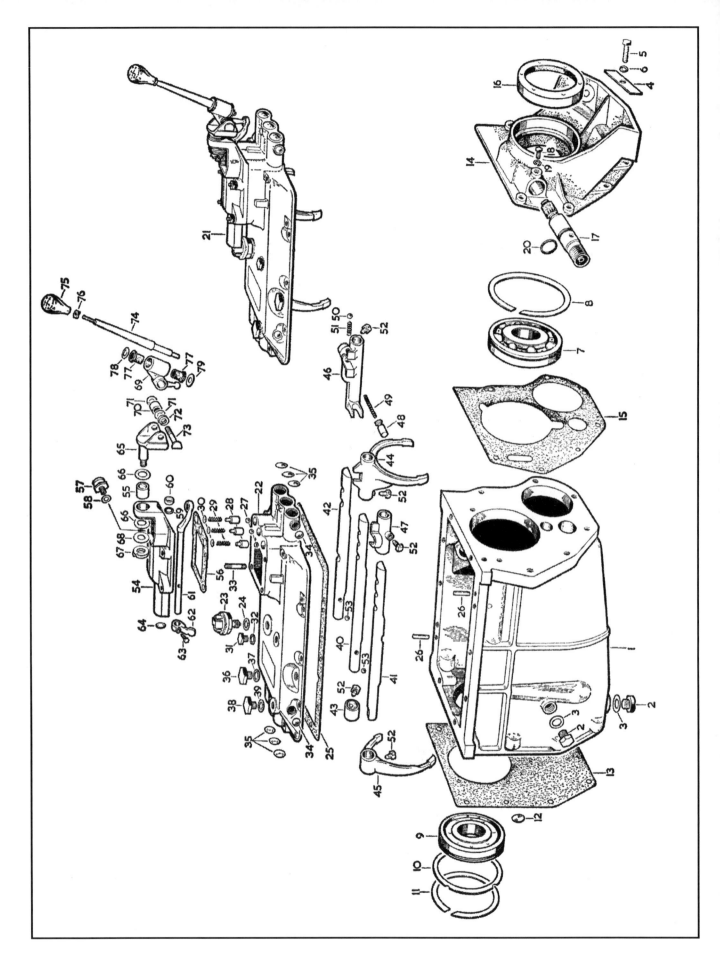

PLATE 14

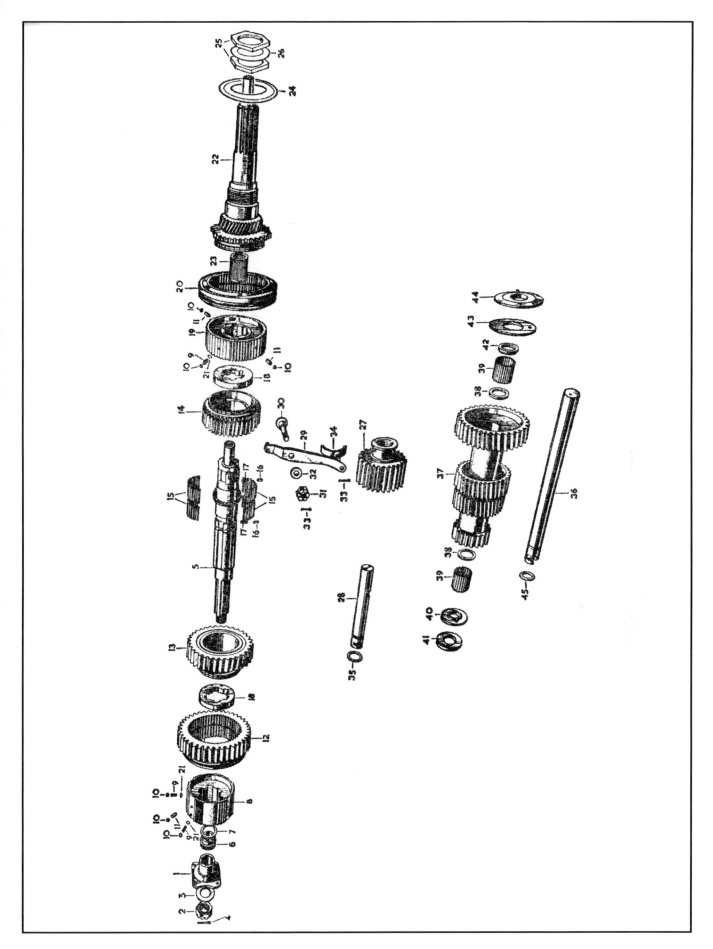

PLATE 15

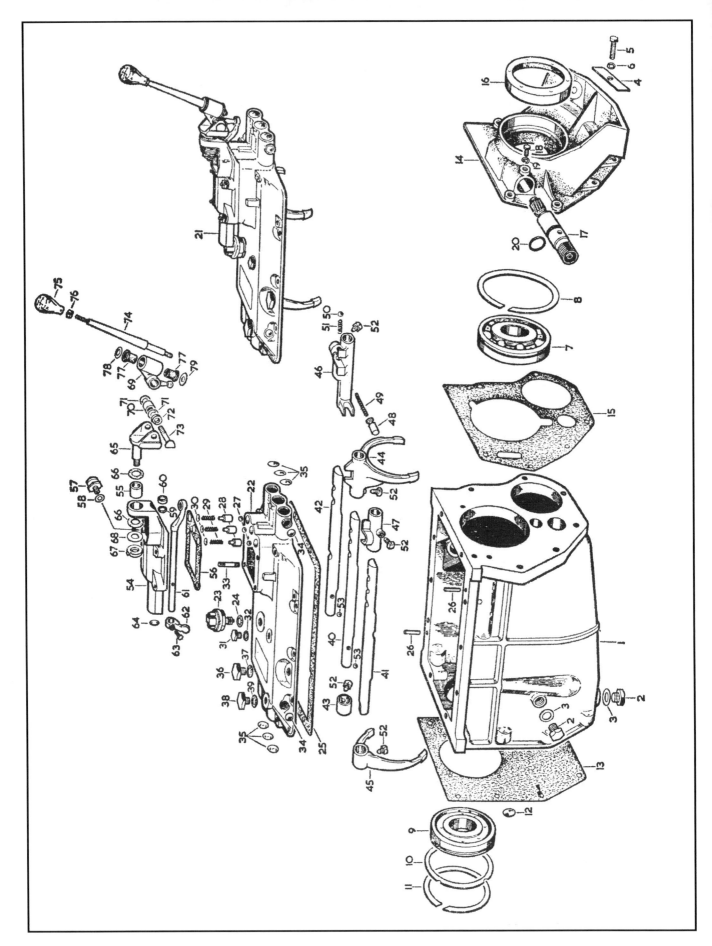

PLATE 16

Part No.	Description	Plate No.	No. per Unit	Remarks
C.19280	**GEARBOX ASSEMBLY**		1	NOTE.—This Gearbox may be identified by the prefix letters "EB" and suffix letters "CR" to the Serial number on the Gearbox.
C.9815	**GEARBOX CASE**	16– 1	1	
C.799	**Plug,** Oil Drain, at bottom of Casing	16– 2	1	
C.799	**Plug,** Oil Level, at side of Casing	16– 2	1	
C.785	**Washer** (Fibre) on Drain Plugs	16– 3	2	
C.857	**Plate,** on Casing, locking Counter and Reverse Shafts	16– 4	1	
FS.205/7D	**Screw,** Set, securing Locking Plate	16– 5	1	
FG.105/X	**Washer,** Spring, on Setscrew	16– 6	1	
C.1845	**Ball Bearing,** for Mainshaft (Hoff.MS.12½V.3)	16– 7	1	
C.1855	**Circlip,** securing Mainshaft Bearing	16– 8	1	
C.1838	**Ball Bearing,** for Constant Pinion Shaft (Hoff.340V.3)	16– 9	1	
C.1841	**Collar,** between Casing and Circlip	16–10	1	
C.1840	**Circlip,** on Ball Bearing, behind Collar	16–11	1	
C.920	**Washer** (Fibre) in Casing, at front end of Countershaft	16–12	1	
C.1834	**Gasket,** between Gearbox Case and Clutch Housing	16–13	1	
C.18959	**REAR END COVER**	16–14	1	Fitted up to and including Gearbox Serial No. EB.8858 CR.
C.21415	**REAR END COVER**	16–14	1	Fitted to Gearbox Serial No. EB.8859 CR and subs. **See note below.**
C.1866	**Gasket,** between Rear End Cover and Casing	16–15	1	
FS.105/9D	**Screw,** Set, securing Rear End Cover to Casing		7	
FG.105/X	**Washer,** Spring, on Setscrews		7	
C.859	**Seal,** Oil, in Rear End Cover	16–16	1	
C.15847	**SPEEDOMETER DRIVEN GEAR ASSEMBLY IN REAR END COVER**	16–17	1	
C.846	**Screw,** locking Speedo Driven Gear in Cover	16–18	1	
FG.105/X	**Washer,** Spring, on Locking Screw	16–19	1	
C.9177	**Sealing Ring** (Rubber) for Speedometer Driven Gear	16–20	1	
8779	**GEARBOX REMOTE CONTROL ASSEMBLY (SD.1112)**	16–21	1	
	(COMPRISING TOP COVER, CHANGE-SPEED LEVER, CHANGE-SPEED FORKS, SELECTORS, ETC.)			

NOTE : The following cars were fitted with Rear End Cover C.18959 :
     Open R.H. Drive : 850653, 850654.
     Open L.H. Drive : 878895, 878900, 878907, 878908, 878913, 878914, 878915, 878926, 878936, 878937, 878939, 878958, 878986, 879005, 879024, 879049.
  Fixed Head R.H. Drive : 861087.
  Fixed Head L.H. Drive : 888086, 888096, 888101, 888103, 888109, 888113, 888117, 888118, 888120, 888134, 889157, 888178, 888238.

GEARBOX
(CLOSE RATIO GROUND GEARS)

Part No.	Description	Plate No.	No. per Unit	Remarks
C.13332	**TOP COVER**	16–22	1	
C.1083	**Switch**, for Top Cover, operating Reversing Light	16–23	1	
C.4531	**Gasket**, for Switch	16–24	1	
C.860	**Gasket**, between Top Cover and Gearbox Case	16–25	1	
FS.105/7D	**Screw**, Set, securing Top Cover to Gearbox Case		6	
FB.105/11D	**Bolt**, securing Top Cover to Gearbox Case		2	
FB.105/15D	**Bolt**, securing Top Cover to Gearbox Case		2	
FG.105/X	**Washer**, Spring, on Bolts and Setscrews		10	
OD.105/6H	**Dowel**, positioning Top Cover to Casing	16–26	2	
C.1319	**Ball**, engaging Striking Rods	16–27	3	
C.13334	**Plunger**, holding Balls in position	16–28	3	
C.845	**Spring**, at top of Plungers	16–29	3	
C.13333	**Shim**, for Spring Tension	16–30	As req'd	
C.18442	**Plug**, sealing redundant Breather aperture	16–31	1	
C.930	**Washer** (Fibre) for Plug	16–32	1	
C.7426	**Stud**, in Top Cover, for fixing of Change-Speed Lever Housing	16–33	4	
UFN.131/L	**Nut**, on Studs		4	
FG.105/X	**Washer**, Spring, under Nuts		4	
C.9840	**Welch Washer**, $\frac{7}{16}$" diameter, at L.H. side of Top Cover	16–34	2	
787	**Welch Washer**, $\frac{5}{8}$" diameter, at front and rear of Top Cover (ends of Striking Rods)	16–35	6	
C.799	**Plug**, in Dipstick Aperture	16–36	1	
C.785	**Washer** (Fibre) on Plug	16–37	1	
C.7379	**Plug**, sealing redundant hole for Overdrive Switch in Top Cover	16–38	1	
C.2296/1	**Washer** (Copper) on Plug	16–39	1	

Part No.	Description	Plate No.	No. per Unit	Remarks
	STRIKING GEAR			
C.9841	**Striking Rod Assembly**, 1st/2nd Gears (complete with Interlock Rollers)	16–40	1	
C.9846	**Striking Rod**, 3rd/Top Gears	16–41	1	
C.9845	**Striking Rod**, Reverse Gear	16–42	1	
C.9854	**Stop**, for 1st/2nd Speed Striking Rod	16–43	1	
C.9851	**Change-Speed Fork**, 1st/2nd Gears	16–44	1	
C.9852	**Change-Speed Fork**, 3rd/Top Gears	16–45	1	
C.9847	**Change-Speed Fork**, Reverse Gear	16–46	1	
C.9853	**Selector**, 3rd/Top Gears	16–47	1	
C.9848	**Plunger**, in Change-Speed Fork, for Reverse Selection	16–48	1	
C.9849	**Spring**, tensioning Reverse Plunger	16–49	1	
C.1319	**Ball**, locking Reverse Plunger	16–50	1	
C.14704	**Spring**, loading Locating Ball	16–51	1	
C.19772	**Dowel Screw**, locating Change-Speed Forks, Selector and 2nd Speed Stop, on Striking Rods	16–52	5	
C.837	**Wire**, locking Dowel Screws		As req'd	
C.922	**Ball**, between Striking Rods, for Interlock	16–53	2	

Part No.	Description	Plate No.	No. per Unit	Remarks
C.14468	**HOUSING, ON TOP COVER, FOR CHANGE-SPEED LEVER**	16–54	1	
C.1907	**Bush**, inside Housing, for Pivot Jaw	16–55	1	
C.13338	**Gasket**, under Housing	16–56	1	
C.841	**Breather**, at R.H. side of Housing	16–57	1	
C.930	**Washer** (Fibre) for Breather	16–58	1	

Part No.	Description	Plate No.	No. per Unit	Remarks
C.12454	**'O' RING, IN HOUSING, FOR REMOTE CONTROL SHAFT**	16–59	1	
C.13335	**Retaining Cup,** for 'O' Ring	16–60	1	
C.14305	**REMOTE CONTROL SHAFT**	16–61	1	
C.13341	**SELECTOR FINGER, ON REMOTE CONTROL SHAFT**	16–62	1	
C.19772	**Dowel Screw,** securing Selector Finger to Remote Control Shaft	16–63	1	
C.837	**Wire,** locking Dowel Screw		As req'd	
787	**Welch Washer,** ⅝" diameter, at rear of Housing	16–64	1	
C.14470	**PIVOT JAW HOUSING SELECTOR LEVER**	16–65	1	
C.1894	**Washer** (Tufnol) at each side of Housing Turret	16–66	2	
C.1905	**Washer,** Double Coil Spring, between 'D' Washer and Tufnol Washer	16–67	1	
C.1914	**'D' Washer,** on Pivot Jaw, adjacent to Nut	16–68	1	
FN.407/L	**Slotted Nut,** securing Pivot Jaw to Housing		1	
L.103/8U	**Split Pin,** retaining Nut		1	
C.14829	**SELECTOR LEVER ON END OF CHANGE-SPEED LEVER**	16–69	1	
C.1906	**Bush,** inside Selector Lever	16–70	1	
C.1908	**Washer** (Tufnol) at each side of Selector Lever	16–71	2	
C.1929	**Washer,** Double Coil Spring, between Tufnol Washer and Selector Lever	16–72	1	
C.1912	**Pivot Pin,** mounting Selector Lever in Pivot Jaw	16–73	1	
FN.407/L	**Slotted Nut,** securing Pivot Pin		1	
L.103/8U	**Split Pin,** retaining Slotted Nut		1	

GEARBOX
(CLOSE RATIO GROUND GEARS)

Part No.	Description	Plate No.	No. per Unit	Remarks
C.4054	**CHANGE-SPEED LEVER**	16–74	1	
C.16154	**Knob,** for Change-Speed Lever	16–75	1	
C.1928	**Nut,** locking Knob to Change-Speed Lever	16–76	1	
C.1915	**RUBBER BUSH, HOUSING CHANGE-SPEED LEVER IN SELECTOR LEVER**	16–77	2	
C.1919	**Washer,** at top of Rubber Bush	16–78	1	
C.1904	**Washer,** at bottom of Rubber Bush	16–79	1	
FN.405/L	**Slotted Nut,** securing Change-Speed Lever to Selector Lever		1	
L.103/8U	**Split Pin,** retaining Slotted Nut		1	
C.885	**FLANGE, ON MAINSHAFT, FOR UNIVERSAL JOINT**	17–1	1	
C.840	**Nut,** Slotted, securing Flange to Mainshaft	17– 2	1	
C.925	**Washer,** Plain, under Slotted Nut	17– 3	1	
L.104/12U	**Pin,** Split, securing Slotted Nut	17– 4	1	
C.4994	**MAINSHAFT**	17– 5	1	
C.14932	**Gear,** Speedometer Driving	17– 6	1	
C.909	**Distance Piece,** behind Speedometer Driving Gear	17– 7	1	
C.7480	**Sleeve,** Synchronising Assembly, 2nd Speed	17– 8	1	
C.900	**Spring,** in 2nd and 3rd/Top Synchro Sleeves	17– 9	12	
C.922	**Ball,** in 2nd and 3rd/Top Synchro Sleeves at top of Springs and Plungers	17–10	15	
C.901	**Plunger** in 2nd and 3rd/Top Synchro Sleeves (.490″ long)	17–11	3	SELECTIVE SIZES. Choose the Plunger of the desired length.
C.901/1	**Plunger** in 2nd and 3rd/Top Synchro Sleeves (.495″ long)	17–11	3	
C.901/2	**Plunger** in 2nd and 3rd/Top Synchro Sleeves (.500″ long)	17–11	3	
C.2040	**Gear, 1st Speed**	17–12	1	
C.4125	**Gear, 2nd Speed**	17–13	1	
C.4123	**Gear Assembly,** 3rd Speed	17–14	1	
C.1850	**Roller,** Needle, in 2nd and 3rd Speed Gears	17–15	82	
C.1849	**Plunger,** in Mainshaft, locking 2nd and 3rd Speed Gears	17–16	2	
C.1324	**Spring,** under Plungers	17–17	2	
C.2678/1	**Washer,** Thrust, front and rear of 2nd and 3rd Speed Gears (.471″/.472″ thick)	17–18	2	SELECTIVE SIZES. Choose the Washer of the desired thickness.
C.2678/2	**Washer,** Thrust, front and rear of 2nd and 3rd Speed Gears (.473″/.474″ thick)	17–18	2	
C.2678/3	**Washer,** Thrust, front and rear of 2nd and 3rd Speed Gears (.475″/.476″ thick)	17–18	2	
C.4122	**Sleeve,** Synchronising, 3rd/Top Speeds	17–19	1	
C.4049	**Sleeve,** Operating, 3rd/Top Speeds	17–20	1	
C.903	**Shim,** for Synchro Sleeve (.006″ thick)	17–21	As req'd	
C.914	**Shim,** for Synchro Sleeve (.028″ thick)	17–21	As req'd	

Part No.	Description	Plate No.	No. per Unit	Remarks
C.9252	**CONSTANT PINION SHAFT ASSEMBLY**	17–22	1	
C.1843	**Bearing,** Roller, inside Constant Pinion Shaft	17–23	1	
C.2121	**Oil Thrower,** on Constant Pinion Shaft	17–24	1	
C.1838/1	**Circlip,** retaining Ball Bearing on Constant Pinion Shaft	17–25	1	
C.2109	**Washer,** for Constant Pinion	17–26	1	
C.2110	**Shim,** for Constant Pinion	17–27	As req'd	
C.2111	**Shim,** for Constant Pinion	17–28	As req'd	
C.2044/2	**REVERSE GEAR (COMPLETE WITH BUSHES)**	17–29	1	
C.2070	**Reverse Spindle**	17–30	1	
C.1893	**Lever,** operating Reverse Gear	17–31	1	
C.1899	**Fulcrum Pin,** for Operating Lever	17–32	1	
C.777	**Nut,** Slotted, securing Fulcrum Pin	17–33	1	
FW.106/T	**Washer,** Plain, under Slotted Nut	17–34	1	
L.103/6U	**Pin,** Split, retaining Slotted Nut and Reverse Slipper	17–35	2	
C.866	**Reverse Slipper**	17–36	1	
C.4284	**Sealing Ring,** on Reverse Spindle	17–37	1	
C.1856	**COUNTERSHAFT**	17–38	1	
C.2041	**Gear,** 1st Speed, on Counter	17–39	1	
C.1864	**Retaining Ring,** at rear of Needle Rollers	17–40	2	
C.918	**Needle Roller,** inside each end of Countershaft	17–41	58	
C.1861	**Thrust Washer Assembly,** Inner, at rear end of Counter adjacent to Needle Rollers	17–42	1	
C.1862	**Thrust Washer,** Outer, at rear of Counter (.156" thick)	17–43	1	⎫
C.1862/1	**Thrust Washer,** Outer, at rear of Counter (.159" thick)	17–43	1	⎪ **SELECTIVE SIZES.** Choose Washer of desired thickness.
C.1862/2	**Thrust Washer,** Outer, at rear of Counter (.162" thick)	17–43	1	⎬
C.1862/3	**Thrust Washer,** Outer, at rear of Counter (.152" thick)	17–43	1	⎪
C.1862/4	**Thrust Washer,** Outer, at rear of Counter (.164" thick)	17–43	1	⎭
C.2043	**Retaining Ring,** at outer end of Front Needle Rollers	17–44	1	
C.8835	**Thrust Washer,** Inner, at front end of Counter	17–45	1	
C.1859	**Thrust Washer Assembly,** Outer, at end of Counter	17–46	1	
C.5826	**Constant Wheel**	17–47	1	
C.2046	**Gear,** 3rd Speed, on Countershaft	17–48	1	
C.2047	**Gear,** 2nd Speed, on Countershaft	17–49	1	
C.2048	**Split Ring,** locating Constant Wheel	17–50	2 halves	
C.2072	**Circlip,** positioning 3rd Speed Gear and Constant Wheel	17–51	2	
C.4285	**Sealing Ring,** on Countershaft	17–52	1	

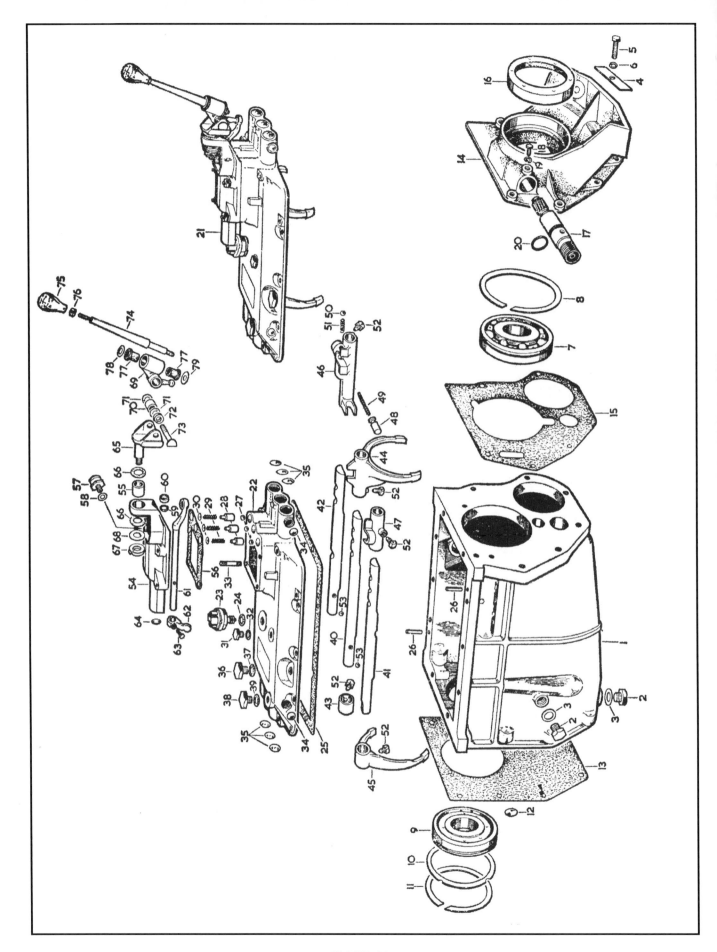

PLATE 16

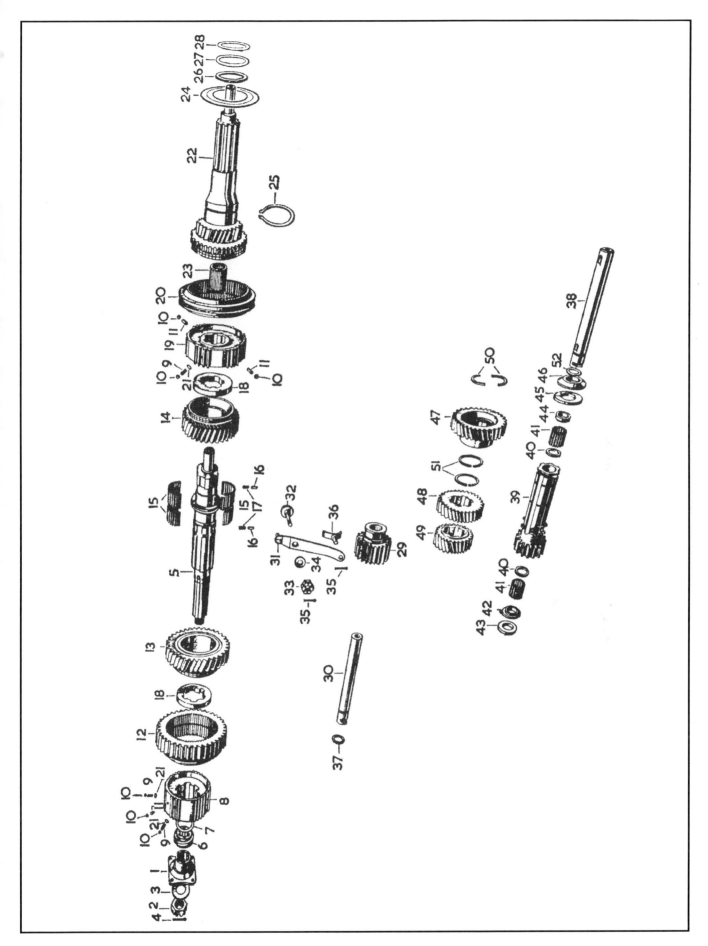

PLATE 17

PROPELLER SHAFT

Part No.	Description	Plate No.	No. per Unit	Remarks
C.15115	**PROPELLER SHAFT COMPLETE**		1	
12	**Flange Yoke** (K.2-2-239)	18– 1	2	
46	**Journal Assembly,** connecting Yokes to Propeller Shaft (K.5-L.4)	18– 2	2	
13	**Sleeve Yoke** (K.2-3-68)	18– 3	1	
26	**Dust Cap** (3-14-39)	18– 4	1	
27	**Washer** (Steel) in Dust Cap (3-15-33)	18– 5	1	
28	**Washer** (Cork) in Dust Cap (K.3-16-43)	18– 6	1	
				Fitted from Chassis No. 850001 to 850103. 875001 to 875495. 860001 to 860005. 885001 to 885025.
46	**JOURNAL ASSEMBLY, CONNECTING FLANGE YOKES TO PROPELLER SHAFT (K.5-L.4)**	18– 2	2	
8406	**Grease Nipple,** on Journals (94-GB.2204)		2	
C.19827	**Bolt,** securing Propeller Shaft to Gearbox and Final Drive Unit Flanges	18– 7	8	
C.8737/3	**Nut,** Self-Locking, on Bolts	18– 8	8	
C.3044/1	**Grease Nipple,** on Sleeve Yoke (Tec.NA.6656)	18– 9	1	
C.17694	**PROPELLER SHAFT COMPLETE (60-1336)**		1	
8404	**Flange Yoke** (2-2-329C)		2	
8405	**Journal Assembly,** connecting Yokes to Propeller Shaft (K.5.LGB.74)		2	
8407	**Sleeve Yoke** (2-3-128X)		1	
26	**Dust Cap** (3-14-39)		1	
27	**Washer** (Steel) in Dust Cap (3-15-33)		1	
28	**Washer** (Cork) in Dust Cap (K.3-16-43)		1	
				Fitted from Chassis No. 850104 to 850479. 875496 to 877044. 860006 to 860386. 885026 to 885887.
8405	**JOURNAL ASSEMBLY, CONNECTING FLANGE YOKES TO PROPELLER SHAFT (K.5-LGB.74)**		2	
8406	**Grease Nipple,** on Journals (94-GB.2204)		1	
C.19827	**Bolt,** securing Propeller Shaft to Gearbox and Final Drive Unit Flanges		8	
C.8737/3	**Nut,** Self-Locking, on Bolts		8	
8406	**Grease Nipple,** on Sleeve Yoke (94-GB.2204)		1	
C.19875	**PROPELLER SHAFT COMPLETE (61-1495)**		1	
8404	**Flange Yoke** (K.2-2-329/C)		2	
9409	**Journal Assembly,** connecting Yokes to Propeller Shaft (K.5-GB.117)		2	
9410	**Sleeve Yoke** (K.2-3-GB.3758)		1	
9411	**Gaiter,** for Sliding Joint (94-GB.4007)		1	
9412	**Ring** (Rubber) retaining Gaiter to Shaft (K.3-86-GB.139)		2	
9413	**Ring** (Steel) retaining Gaiter to Sleeve Yoke (94-GB.3951)		1	Fitted to Chassis No. 850480 and subs. 877045 and subs. 860387 and subs. 885888 and subs.
C.19827	**Bolt,** securing Propeller Shaft to Gearbox and Final Drive Unit Flanges		8	
C.8737/3	**Nut,** Self-Locking, on Bolts		8	

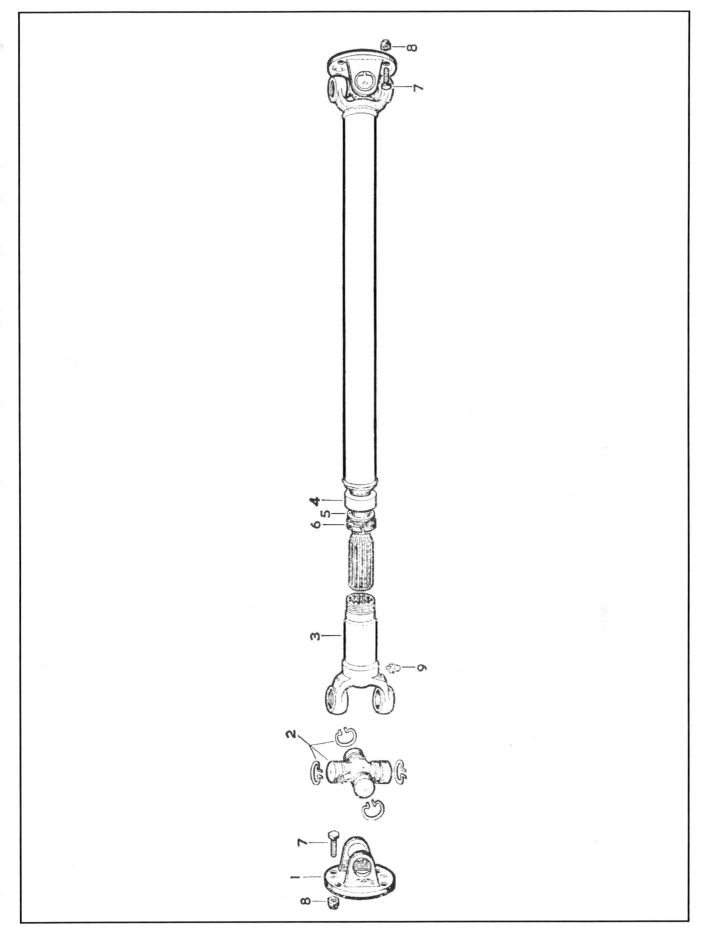

PLATE 18

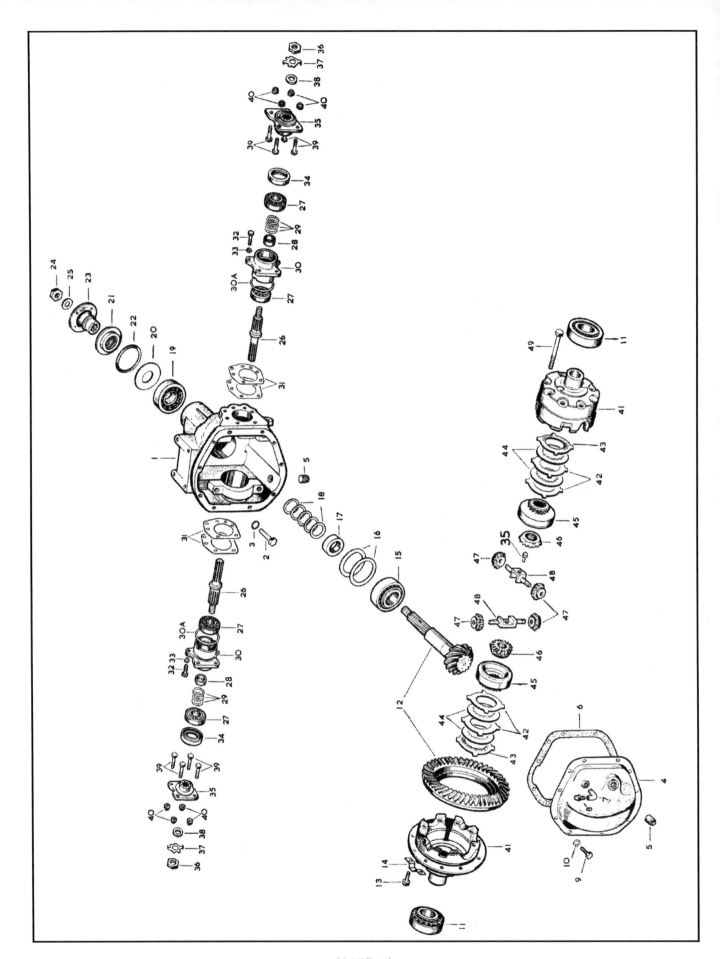

PLATE 19

Part No.	Description	Plate No.	No. per Unit	Remarks
C.18984	**FINAL DRIVE UNIT ASSEMBLY** **(4HU-001/14D) (RATIO 3.07 : 1)**		1	
8487	**Gear Carrier Sub Assembly** (4HU-061/7)	19– 1	1	
6114	**Screw,** Set, securing Differential Bearing Caps (8B-NC.36)	19– 2	4	
8489	**Lockwasher,** on Setscrews (8LW-115)	19– 3	4	
8507	**Cover,** for Carrier (4HA-010/9)	19– 4	1	
3823	**Plug,** for Filler and Drain Apertures (HA-059)	19– 5	2	
3931	**Gasket,** under Cover (4HA-026)	19– 6	1	
8509	**Elbow,** in Cover (3HA-098/4)	19– 7	1	
8508	**Breather,** at top of Elbow (3HA-098/8)	19– 8	1	
CS.131/5D	**Screw,** Set, securing Cover to Carrier (5B-NC.10)	19– 9	10	
47	**Lockwasher,** on Setscrews (5LW-95)	19–10	10	
8488	**Differential Assembly** (4HU-082/8)		1	
3845	**Roller Bearing,** on Differential Case (Timken 24780-24721) (2HA-024)	19–11	2	
8825	**Crown Wheel and Pinion** (Ratio 3.07 : 1) (4HA-105/25)	19–12	1	
6301	**Screw,** Set, securing Crown Wheel to Differential (3HA-075/6)	19–13	10	
7384	**Lock Strap,** securing Crown Wheel Setscrews (4HA-074/4)	19–14	5	
3844	**Roller Bearing,** at inner end of Pinion (Timken 31593-31520) (2HA-023)	19–15	1	
3860	**Shim,** inner, adjusting Pinion (.003″ thick) (2HA-043)	19–16	As req'd	⎱
3861	**Shim,** inner, adjusting Pinion (.005″ thick) (2HA-044)	19–16	As req'd	**USE SHIMS OF DESIRED**
3862	**Shim,** inner, adjusting Pinion (.010″ thick) (2HA-045)	19–16	As req'd	⎰ **THICKNESS.**
8029	**Distance Washer,** behind outer Pinion Shims (4HA-115)	19–17	1	
3856	**Shim,** outer, adjusting Pinion (.003″ thick) (2HA-039)	19–18	As req'd	⎱
3857	**Shim,** outer, adjusting Pinion (.005″ thick) (2HA-040)	19–18	As req'd	**USE SHIMS OF DESIRED**
3858	**Shim,** outer, adjusting Pinion (.010″ thick) (2HA-041)	19–18	As req'd	**THICKNESS.**
3859	**Shim,** outer, adjusting Pinion (.030″ thick) (2HA-042)	19–18	As req'd	⎰
3843	**Roller Bearing,** at outer end of Pinion (Timken 02872-02820) (2HA-022)	19–19	1	
3934	**Oil Slinger,** on Pinion (4HA-036)	19–20	1	
3840	**Oil Seal,** on Pinion (2HA-019)	19–21	1	
3841	**Gasket,** for Pinion Oil Seal (2HA-020)	19–22	1	
3879	**Companion Flange Assembly** (2HA-083)	19–23	1	
6126	**Nut,** securing Companion Flange to Pinion (12LN-NF.9)	19–24	1	
6128	**Washer,** under Nut (12W-24)	19–25	1	
8494	**Drive Shaft** (4HU-005/4)	19–26	2	
8495	**Roller Bearing,** on Drive Shafts (Timken 19150-1926) (4HU-025)	19–27	4	
8493	**Spacing Collar,** between Roller Bearings (4HU-018)	19–28	2	
8490	**Shim,** adjusting Bearings (.003″ thick) (4HU-116)	19–29	As req'd	⎱ **USE SHIMS OF DESIRED**
8491	**Shim,** adjusting Bearings (.005″ thick) (4HU-116/1)	19–29	As req'd	**THICKNESS.**
8492	**Shim,** adjusting Bearings (.010″ thick) (4HU-116/2)	19–29	As req'd	⎰
8499	**Housing** for Drive Shaft Bearings (4HU-014/1)	19–30	2	
8950	**'O' Ring,** on Drive Shaft Bearing Housings (4HA-079/2)	19–30A	2	
8501	**Shim,** under Bearing Housings, for Differential adjustment (.003″ thick) (4HU-050/3)	19–31	As req'd	⎱
8502	**Shim,** under Bearing Housings, for Differential adjustment (.005″ thick) (4HU-051/3)	19–31	As req'd	
8503	**Shim,** under Bearing Housings, for Differential adjustment (.010″ thick) (4HU-052/3)	19–31	As req'd	**USE SHIMS OF DESIRED THICKNESS.**
8504	**Shim,** under Bearing Housings, for Differential adjustment (.030″ thick) (4HU-053/3)	19–31	As req'd	⎰
8505	**Bolt,** securing Bearing Housings to Gear Carrier (7B-NC.24)	19–32	10	
8506	**Lockwasher,** on Bolts (7LW-13)	19–33	10	
8436	**Oil Seal,** in Bearing Housings, for Driving Flange (4HA-079/3)	19–34	2	
8500	**Flange,** on Drive Shafts (4HU-077)	19–35	2	
8496	**Nut,** securing Flange to Drive Shafts (4HU-089/1)	19–36	2	
8498	**Tab Washer,** locking Nuts (4HU-091/1)	19–37	2	
8497	**Special Washer,** under Tab Washers (16W-28)	19–38	2	
8510	**Bolt,** in Flanges, for attachment of Brake Discs and Half-Shafts (4HU-055/4)	19–39	8	
C.15349	**Nut,** Self-Locking, on Bolts (7LN-NF.75)	19–40	8	
C.17024	**Bolt,** securing Final Drive Unit to Rear Suspension Cross Member		4	
C.836	**Lockwire,** for Bolts		As req'd	

FINAL DRIVE UNIT

Part No.	Description	Plate No.	No. per Unit	Remarks
C.16618	**FINAL DRIVE UNIT ASSEMBLY** **(4HU-001/14A) (RATIO 3.54 : 1)**		1	**ALTERNATIVE RATIO.**
6305	**Crown Wheel and Pinion** (Ratio 3.54 : 1) (4HA-105/9A)		1	
	All other items are as for Final Drive Unit **C.15222.**			
C.16619	**FINAL DRIVE UNIT ASSEMBLY** **(4HU-001/14C) (RATIO 2.93 : 1)**		1	**COMPLETE FINAL DRIVE UNIT ASSEMBLY NO LONGER AVAILABLE**
6303	**Crown Wheel and Pinion** (Ratio 2.93 : 1) (4HA-105/6B)		1	
	All other items are as for Final Drive Unit **C.15222.**			
C.15522	**FINAL DRIVE UNIT ASSEMBLY** **(4HU-001/14) (RATIO 3.31 : 1)**		1	**ALTERNATIVE RATIO.**
6304	**Crown Wheel and Pinion** (Ratio 3.31 : 1) (4HA-105/8A)		1	
8488	**DIFFERENTIAL ASSEMBLY, COMPLETE** **(4HU-082/8)**		1	
7887	**Case only,** for Differential (4HA-006/9)	19–41	2 halves	
7683	**Friction Plate** (flat) (4HA-111/3)	19–42	4	
8397	**Friction Plate** (dished) (4HA-111/4)	19–43	2	
7684	**Friction Disc** (4HA-112)	19–44	4	
7682	**Ring,** for Side Gear (4HA-109/1)	19–45	2	
7681	**Side Gear** (4HA-007/1)	19–46	2	
7685	**Pinion Mate Gear** (4HA-008)	19–47	4	
7686	**Shaft,** for Pinion Mate Gears (4HA-012/1)	19–48	2 halves	
7680	**Bolt,** securing Differential Casing (6B-NC.44)	19–49	8	

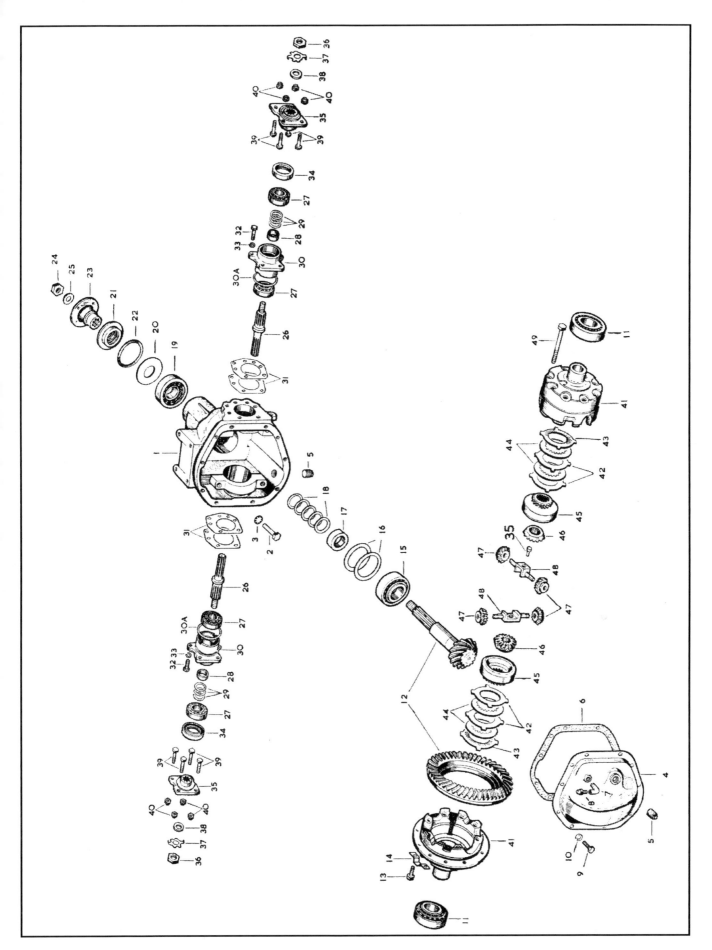

PLATE 19

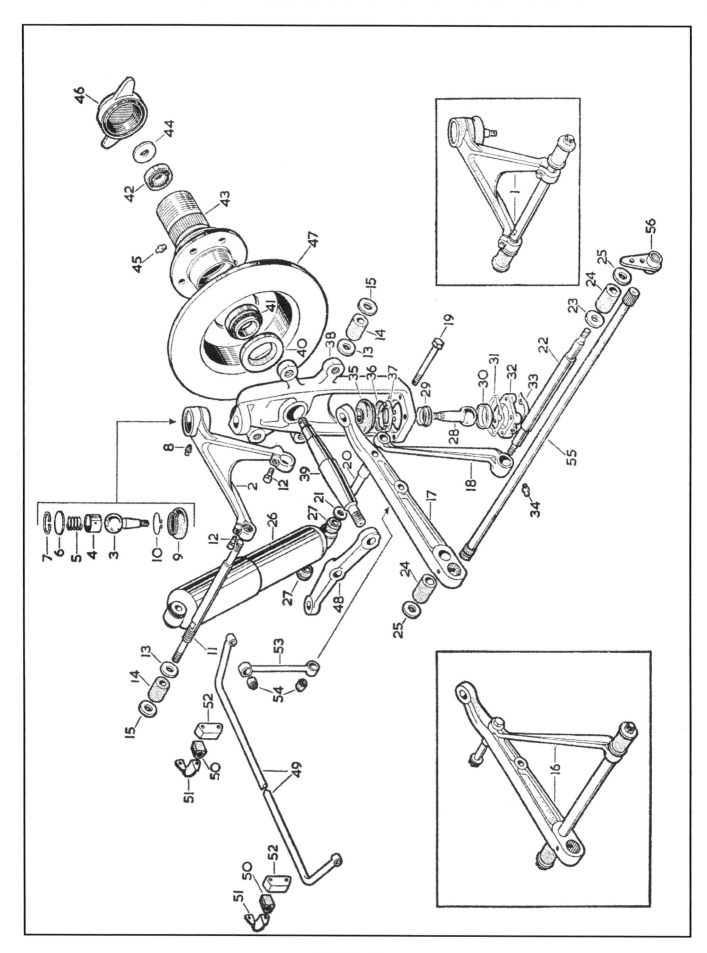

PLATE 20

Part No.	Description	Plate No.	No. per Unit	Remarks
C.15160	**FRONT SUSPENSION ASSEMBLY, R.H.**		1	Fitted from Chassis No. 850001 to 850253. 875001 to 875963. 860001 to 860022. 885001 to 885142.
C.15161	**FRONT SUSPENSION ASSEMBLY, L.H.**		1	
C.18669	**FRONT SUSPENSION ASSEMBLY, R.H.**		1	Fitted from Chassis No. 850254 to 850290. 875964 to 876129. 860023 to 860032. 885143 to 885209.
C.18670	**FRONT SUSPENSION ASSEMBLY, L.H.**		1	
C.19960	**FRONT SUSPENSION ASSEMBLY, R.H.**		1	Fitted to Chassis No. 850291 and subs. 876130 and subs. 860033 and subs. 885210 and subs.
C.19961	**FRONT SUSPENSION ASSEMBLY, L.H.**		1	
C.15361	**UPPER WISHBONE ASSEMBLY, R.H.**	20– 1	1	
C.15362	**UPPER WISHBONE ASSEMBLY, L.H.**		1	
C.15363	**Upper Wishbone,** R.H.	20– 2	1	
C.15364	**Upper Wishbone,** L.H.		1	
C.14435	**Ball Pin,** in Upper Wishbones	20– 3	2	
C.14438	**Socket,** over Ball Pins	20– 4	2	
C.19266	**Shim,** for adjustment of Upper Ball Pins (.004" thick)		As req'd	
C.635	**Spring,** over Sockets	20– 5	2	
C.15365	**Top Cover,** above Ball Pins	20– 6	2	
C.15366	**Circlip,** securing Top Cover in Wishbone Levers	20– 7	2	
C.3044/1	**Grease Nipple** in Upper Wishbones, for Ball Pin Lubrication	20– 8	2	
C.15367	**Gaiter,** on Ball Pins	20– 9	2	
C.15368	**Clip,** securing Gaiter to Upper Wishbones	20–10	2	
C.8737/5	**Nut,** Self-Locking, securing Ball Pin to Stub Axle Carriers		2	
C.791	**Washer,** Plain, under Nuts		2	
C.15369	**Fulcrum Shaft,** for Upper Wishbones	20–11	2	
C.15371	**Pinch Bolt,** clamping Wishbones on Fulcrum Shafts	20–12	4	
C.15379	**Distance Washer,** on Fulcrum Shafts	20–13	4	
C.8672	**Rubber Bush,** on Fulcrum Shafts	20–14	4	
UFN.450/L	**Slotted Nut,** securing Fulcrum Shafts in Blocks		4	
C.8676/1	**Special Washer,** under Nuts	20–15	4	
L.104/10U	**Split Pin,** retaining Slotted Nuts		4	
C.15151	**Mounting Plate,** on Front Frame Cross Member, for Upper Wishbone Fulcrum Block, front		2	
UFB.131/17R	**Bolt,** securing Mounting Plates to Cross Member		2	FOR OTHER FIXINGS PLEASE REFER TO SECTION FOR FRONT FRAME.
C.8667/2	**Nut,** Self-Locking, on Bolts		2	
C.15089	**Fulcrum Block,** front, for Upper Wishbone Shafts		2	
UFB.131/10R	**Bolt,** securing Fulcrum Block to Mounting Plates		6	
FG.105/X	**Washer,** Spring, on Bolts		6	
C.15153	**Shim,** behind Front Fulcrum Blocks, for adjustment of Camber Angle		As req'd	
C.15090	**Fulcrum Block,** rear, for Upper Wishbone Shafts		2	
UFB.131/8R	**Bolt,** securing Fulcrum Blocks to Side Members		4	
C.15113	**Washer Plate,** under head of Bolts		2	
C.8667/2	**Nut,** Self-Locking, on Bolts		4	
C.15154	**Shim,** behind Rear Fulcrum Blocks, for adjustment of Camber Angle		As req'd	

FRONT SUSPENSION

Part No.	Description	Plate No.	No. per Unit	Remarks
C.15158	**LOWER WISHBONE ASSEMBLY, R.H.**	20–16	1	
C.15159	**LOWER WISHBONE ASSEMBLY, L.H.**		1	
C.15373	**Lower Wishbone Lever,** R.H. Front	20–17	1	
C.15374	**Lower Wishbone Lever,** L.H. Front		1	
C.15375	**Lower Wishbone Lever,** rear	20–18	2	
C.15155	**Bolt,** joining front and rear Wishbone Levers and for fixing of Shock Absorbers	20–19	2	
C.9326	**Sleeve,** on Bolts	20–20	2	
FW.110/T	**Washer,** Plain, on Sleeves		2	
UFN.450/L	**Nut,** on Bolts		2	
C.11193	**Washer,** Special, under Nuts	20–21	2	
L.104/10U	**Split Pin,** retaining Nuts		2	
C.15372	**Fulcrum Shaft,** for Lower Wishbones	20–22	2	
C.15376	**Distance Washer,** on Fulcrum Shaft, between Rear Lever and Rubber Bush	20–23	2	
C.8673	**Rubber Bush,** on Fulcrum Shafts	20–24	4	
UFN.756/L	**Slotted Nut,** securing Fulcrum Shafts in Blocks		4	
C.8693/1	**Washer,** Special, under Nuts	20–25	4	
L.104/10U	**Split Pin,** retaining Nuts		4	
C.15088	**Fulcrum Block,** front, for Lower Wishbone Shafts		2	**FOR FIXINGS, PLEASE REFER TO SECTION FOR FRONT FRAME.**
C.15091	**Fulcrum Block,** rear, for Lower Wishbone Shafts		2	
UFB.131/16R	**Bolt,** securing Rear Fulcrum Blocks to Side Members		4	
C.8737/2	**Nut,** Self-Locking, on Bolts		4	
C.15071	**FRONT SHOCK ABSORBER (640-541-73)**	20–26	2	Fitted from Chassis No. 850001 to 850321. 875001 to 876394, 860001 to 860121. 885001 to 885334.
C.3273	**Bush,** in bottom "eye" of Shock Absorbers (64541640)	20–27	4	
C.20011	**FRONT SHOCK ABSORBER (NFP.64054298)**		2	Fitted to Chassis No. 850322 and subs. 876395 and subs. 860122 and subs. 885335 and subs.
C.3273	**Bush,** in bottom "eye" of Shock Absorbers (64541640)		4	
C.9380	**Bolt,** securing Shock Absorbers at top to Front Cross Member		2	
UFN.443/L	**Slotted Nut,** on Bolts		2	
C.16679	**Washer,** Plain, under Slotted Nuts		2	
L.103/10U	**Split Pin,** retaining Slotted Nuts		2	
C.15337	**BALL PIN, IN STUB AXLE CARRIER, FOR ATTACHMENT OF LOWER WISHBONES**	20–28	2	
C.15339	**Spigot,** over Ball Pins	20–29	2	
C.15904	**Railco Socket,** supporting Lower Ball Pins	20–30	2	
C.15341	**Shim** (.002" thick) between Stub Axle Carrier and Cap	20–31	As req'd	**SELECTIVE THICKNESSES. CHOOSE SHIM OF DESIRED THICKNESS.**
C.15342	**Shim** (.004" thick) between Stub Axle Carrier and Cap	20–31	As req'd	
C.17175	**Shim** (.010" thick) between Stub Axle Carrier and Cap	20–31	As req'd	
C.15338/1	**Cap,** under Lower Ball Pins	20–32	2	
C.15344	**Bolt,** securing Caps to Stub Axle Carriers		8	
C.15343	**Tab Washer,** securing Bolts	20–33	4	
C.3044/1	**Grease Nipple,** in Cap, for lubrication of Lower Ball Pins	20–34	2	

Part No.	Description	Plate No.	No. per Unit	Remarks
C.15346	**RUBBER GAITER FOR LOWER BALL PINS**	20–35	2	
C.15345	**Retainer,** for Rubber Gaiters	20–36	2	
C.17174	**Clip,** securing Rubber Gaiters to Stub Axle Carriers	20–37	2	
C.8737/6	**Nut,** Self-Locking, securing Lower Ball Pin to Stub Axle Carriers		2	
C.794/1	**Washer,** Plain, under Nuts		2	
C.15329/1	**STUB AXLE CARRIER**	20–38	2	} Fitted from Chassis No. 850001 to 850047. 875001 to 875132.
C.19224/1	**STUB AXLE CARRIER**		2	} Fitted to Chassis No. 850048 and subs.
C.16843	**Water Deflector,** on Stub Axle Carrier		2	860001 and subs. 875133 and subs. 885001 and subs.
C.19423	**STUB AXLE SHAFT**	20–39	2	
C.8667/7	**Nut,** Self-Locking, securing Stub Axle Shaft and Tie Rod Lever to Stub Axle Carriers		2	
C.15350	**OIL SEAL FOR STUB AXLE SHAFTS**	20–40	2	
C.15351	**INNER BEARING, ON STUB AXLE SHAFT, FOR HUBS (TIMKEN LM.67047-LM.67010)**	20–41	2	
C.15352	**OUTER BEARING, ON STUB AXLE SHAFT, FOR HUBS (TIMKEN LM.11949-LM.11910)**	20–42	2	

FRONT SUSPENSION

Part No.	Description	Plate No.	No. per Unit	Remarks
C.15317/1	**R.H. FRONT HUB**	20–43	1	⎫
C.15318/1	**L.H. FRONT HUB**		1	⎬ Fitted from Chassis No. 850001 to 850047. 875001 to 875132. ⎭
C.19225/1	**R.H. FRONT HUB**		1	⎫
C.19226/1	**L.H. FRONT HUB**		1	⎬ Fitted to Chassis No. 850048 and subs. 875133 and subs. 860001 and subs. 885001 and subs.
C.18842	**Water Thrower,** for Front Hubs		2	⎭
NN.756/L	**Slotted Nut,** securing Hub to Stub Axle Shafts		2	
C.3400	**"D" Washer,** under Slotted Nuts	20–44	2	
L.104/10U	**Split Pin,** retaining Slotted Nuts		2	
C.3076/1	**Grease Nipple,** in Hubs	20–45	2	
C.1102	**R.H. HUB CAP**	20–46	1	⎫
C.1103	**L.H. HUB CAP**		1	⎬ **NOT FOR USE ON CARS EXPORTED TO GERMANY.** ⎭
C.14891	**R.H. HUB CAP**		1	⎫
C.14892	**L.H. HUB CAP**		1	⎬ **REQUIRED ONLY FOR CARS EXPORTED TO GERMANY.**
C.14927	**TOOL FOR REMOVING AND FITTING HUB CAPS**		1	⎭
C.15334	**DISC FOR FRONT BRAKE CALIPERS (VBM.3748)**	20–47	2	
C.13546/1	**Bolt,** securing Discs to Hubs		10	
C.15349	**Pinnacle Nut,** on Bolts		10	

Part No.	Description	Plate No.	No. per Unit	Remarks
C.15357	**R.H. TIE ROD LEVER**	20–48	1	
C.15358	**L.H. TIE ROD LEVER**		1	
C.15378	**Bolt,** securing Tie Rod Levers to Stub Axle Carriers		2	
FG.108/X	**Washer,** Spring, on Bolts		2	
C.8667/7	**Nut,** securing Tie Rod Levers and Stub Axle Shafts to Carriers		2	
C.17653	**BRACKET, ON STUB AXLE CARRIERS, RECEIVING OUTER END OF FRONT BRAKES FLEXIBLE HOSE**		2	
C.17512	**Screw,** Set, securing Brackets to Stub Axle Carriers		2	
FG.108/X	**Washer,** Spring, on Setscrews		2	
C.16629	**ANTI-ROLL BAR**	20–49	1	
C.16633	**Rubber Bush** for Anti-Roll Bar	20–50	2	
C.15097	**Bracket,** holding Rubber Bush	20–51	2	
C.16631	**Distance Piece,** under Brackets	20–52	2	
UFB.131/18R	**Bolt,** upper, securing Brackets and Distance Pieces to Front Frame Cross Member		2	
UFB.131/31R	**Bolt,** lower, securing Brackets, Distance Pieces and lower Fulcrum Blocks to Front Frame Cross Member		2	
C.8667/2	**Nut,** Self-Locking, on Bolts		4	
C.16630	**LINK, BETWEEN ANTI-ROLL BAR AND FRONT LOWER WISHBONE LEVERS**	20–53	2	
C.10940	**Rubber Bush,** in each end of Links	20–54	4	
UFB.143/21R	**Bolt,** securing Links to Anti-Roll Bar		2	
UFB.143/22R	**Bolt,** securing Links to Front Lower Wishbone Levers		2	
C.8667/4	**Nut,** Self-Locking, on Bolts		4	
FW.107/T	**Washer,** Plain, under Nuts		4	

FRONT SUSPENSION

Part No.	Description	Plate No.	No. per Unit	Remarks
C.9331	**FRONT TORSION BAR, R.H.**	20–55	1	
C.9332	**FRONT TORSION BAR, L.H.**		1	
UFB.119/15R	**Bolt,** locating Front Torsion Bars in front Lower Wishbone Levers		2	
C.8667/17	**Nut,** Self-Locking, on Bolts		2	
C.19379	**BRACKET, RECEIVING REAR END OF FRONT TORSION BARS**	20–56	2	
C.20426	**Bolt,** securing Brackets and Reaction Plate to rear of Front Frame Side Members		4	
C.8667/3	**Nut,** Self-Locking, on Bolts		4	

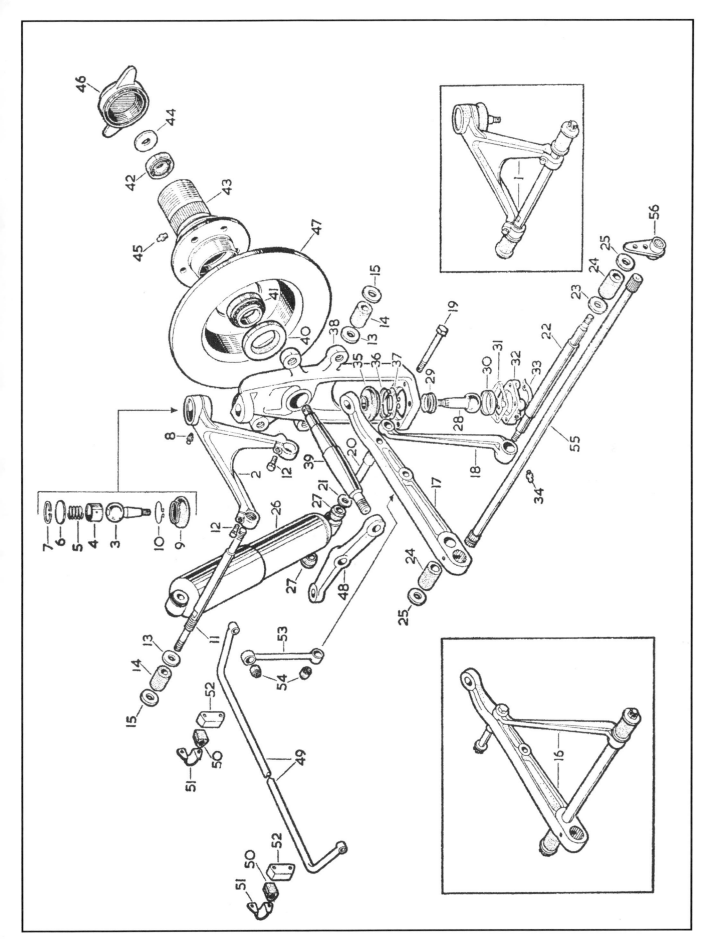

PLATE 20

REAR SUSPENSION

Part No.	Description	Plate No.	No. per Unit	Remarks
C.17014	**REAR SUSPENSION CROSS MEMBER ASSEMBLY**	21- 1	1	
C.17198	**RUBBER MOUNTING FOR ATTACH-MENT OF CROSS MEMBER TO BODY**	21- 2	4	
UFB.131/7R	**Bolt,** securing Rubber Mountings to Cross Member		8	
C.8667/2	**Nut,** Self-Locking, on Bolts and Studs		10	
C.8737/2	**Nut,** Self-Locking, on Bolts		2	
FW.105/T	**Washer,** Plain, under Nuts		2	
UFB.131/24R	**Bolt,** securing Rubber Mountings to Body		8	
C.17228	**Packing Piece,** on Bolts, at each side of Body Under-frame Members		8	
C.8737/2	**Nut,** Self-Locking, on Bolts		8	
C.16985	**MOUNTING, R.H., FOR INNER FULCRUM SHAFT**	21- 3	1	Fitted from Chassis No. 850001 to 850678. 875001 to 879131. 860001 to 861105. 885001 to 888326.
C.16986	**MOUNTING, L.H., FOR INNER FULCRUM SHAFT**		1	
C.20481	**MOUNTING FOR INNER FULCRUM SHAFTS**		2	Fitted to Chassis No. 850679 and subs. 879132 and subs. 861106 and subs. 888327 and subs.
C.17009	**Screw,** Set, long, securing Fulcrum Mountings to Final Drive Unit at rear		2	
C.17010	**Screw,** Set, short, securing Fulcrum Mountings to Final Drive Unit at front		2	
C.17722	**Shim,** .005″ thick, under Fulcrum Mountings, for Fulcrum Shaft alignment	21- 4	As req'd	
C.17723	**Shim,** .010″ thick, under Fulcrum Mountings, for Fulcrum Shaft alignment	21- 4	As req'd	
C.836	**Wire,** locking Setscrews		As req'd	
C.17023	**PLATE, BRACING LOWER FACE OF CROSS MEMBER AT CENTRE**	21- 5	1	Fitted from Chassis No. 850001 to 850678. 875001 to 879131. 860001 to 861105. 885001 to 888326.
UFS.131/5R	**Screw,** Set, securing Plate to Flanges of Cross Member		6	
UFS.131/7R	**Screw,** Set, securing Plate to Fulcrum Mountings		4	
UFB.131/23R	**Bolt,** securing Plate and clamping Fulcrum Mountings on Fulcrum Shafts		4	
C.8737/2	**Nut,** Self-Locking, on Bolts and Setscrews		14	

Part No.	Description	Plate No.	No. per Unit	Remarks
C.20651	**PLATE, BRACING LOWER FACE OF CROSS MEMBER AT CENTRE**		1	Fitted to Chassis No. 850679 and subs. 879132 and subs. 861106 and subs. 888327 and subs.
UFS.131/5R	**Screw,** Set, securing Plate to Cross Member and Fulcrum Mountings		14	
FG.105/X	**Washer,** Spring, at fixings to Fulcrum Mountings		8	
C.8737/2	**Nut,** Self-Locking, at fixings to Cross Member		6	
C.16987	**R.H. WISHBONE ASSEMBLY**	21- 6	1	Fitted from Chassis No. 850001 to 850678. 875001 to 879131. 860001 to 861105. 885001 to 888326.
C.16971	**L.H. WISHBONE ASSEMBLY**		1	
C.20255	**R.H. WISHBONE ASSEMBLY**		1	Fitted to Chassis No. 850679 and subs. 879132 and subs. 861106 and subs. 888327 and subs.
C.20256	**L.H. WISHBONE ASSEMBLY**		1	
C.17008	**FULCRUM SHAFT, FOR INNER MOUNTING OF WISHBONES**	21- 7	2	
C.17663	**Distance Tube,** on Fulcrum Shafts	21- 8	2	Fitted from Chassis No. 850001 to 850678. 875001 to 879131. 860001 to 861105. 885001 to 888326.
C.17168	**Bearing Tube,** on Fulcrum Shafts	21- 9	4	
C.17663/1	**Distance Tube,** on Fulcrum Shafts		2	Fitted to Chassis No. 850679 and subs. 879132 and subs. 861106 and subs. 888327 and subs.
C.17168/1	**Bearing Tube,** on Fulcrum Shafts		4	
C.17167	**Needle Bearing,** on Tubes, for Wishbones	21-10	8	
C.17169	**Spacing Collar,** between Bearings	21-11	4	
C.17166	**Thrust Washer,** Inner, at each end of Bearing Tubes	21-12	8	
C.17213	**Sealing Ring,** on Inner Thrust Washers	21-13	8	
C.17936	**Retainer,** for Sealing Rings	21-14	8	
C.17165	**Thrust Washer,** Outer, on Shafts	21-15	8	
C.8667/5	**Nut,** Self-Locking, on Fulcrum Shafts		4	
C.9048	**Grease Nipple,** for lubrication of Inner Fulcrum Shaft Bearings	21-16	4	Fitted from Chassis No. 850001 to 850678. 875001 to 879131. 860001 to 861105. 885001 to 888326.
C.3044/1	**Grease Nipple,** for lubrication of Inner Fulcrum Shaft Bearings		4	Fitted to Chassis No. 850679 and subs. 879132 and subs. 861106 and subs. 888327 and subs.

REAR SUSPENSION

Part No.	Description	Plate No.	No. per Unit	Remarks
C.16624	**FULCRUM SHAFT, FOR MOUNTING OF WISHBONE TO HUB CARRIER**	21–17	2	
C.16623	**Sleeve,** on Fulcrum Shafts	21–18	4	
C.16626/1	**Shim,** between Sleeves, adjusting Bearing End Float (.004″ thick)	21–19	As req'd	
C.16626/2	**Shim,** between Sleeves, adjusting Bearing End Float (.007″ thick)	21–19	As req'd	
C.16029	**Bearing** (Taper Roller) on Fulcrum Shafts (Timken 03162-03062)	21–20	4	
C.16628	**Seating Ring,** on Fulcrum Shafts, for Oil Seals	21–21	4	
C.16627	**Oil Seal,** in Hub Carriers, for Fulcrum Shafts	21–22	4	Fitted from Chassis No. 850001 to 850503. 875001 to 877182. 860001 to 860450. 885001 to 885984.
C.20178	**Oil Seal,** (Felt) in Hub Carriers, for Fulcrum Shafts		4	Fitted to Chassis No. 850504 and subs. 877183 and subs. 860451 and subs. 885985 and subs.
C.20179	**Container,** for Oil Seal		4	
C.20180	**Spacer,** between Bearing and Oil Seal Container		4	
C.20182	**Retaining Washer,** on Seating Ring, for Oil Seal		4	
C.16626	**Shim,** on Fulcrum Shafts, for centralisation of Hub Carrier in Wishbone Fork (.004″ thick)	21–23	As req'd	
C.8667/7	**Nut,** Self-Locking, securing Fulcrum Shaft in Wishbone Fork	21–24	4	
C.19063	**HUB CARRIER**	21–25	2	Fitted from Chassis No. 850001 to 850583. 875001 to 877963. 860001 to 860832. 885001 to 886685.
C.20811	**HUB CARRIER**		2	Fitted to Chassis No. 850584 and subs. 877964 and subs. 860833 and subs. 886686 and subs.
C.3044/1	**Grease Nipple,** in Carriers, for lubrication of Fulcrum Shaft Bearings	21–26	2	
C.18124	**Grease Retaining Cap,** at top of Hub Carrier	21–27	2	
C.19064	**R.H. REAR HUB**	21–28	1	Fitted from Chassis No. 850001 to 850583. 875001 to 877963. 860001 to 860832. 885001 to 886685.
C.19065	**L.H. REAR HUB**		1	
C.20889	**R.H. REAR HUB ASSEMBLY**		1	Fitted to Chassis No. 850584 and subs. 877964 and subs. 860833 and subs. 886686 and subs.
C.20813	**Water Thrower,** on Hub		1	
C.20890	**L.H. REAR HUB ASSEMBLY**		1	
C.20813	**Water Thrower,** on Hub		1	

Part No.	Description	Plate No.	No. per Unit	Remarks
C.1102	**R.H. HUB CAP**	21–29	1	
C.1103	**L.H. HUB CAP**		1	NOT FOR USE ON CARS EXPORTED TO GERMANY.
C.14891	**R.H. HUB CAP**		1	
C.14892	**L.H. HUB CAP**		1	REQUIRED ONLY FOR CARS EXPORTED TO GERMANY.
C.14927	**TOOL FOR REMOVING AND FITTING HUB CAPS**		1	
C.19068	**OIL SEAL (OUTER) FOR HUBS**	21–30	2	
C.19067	**Seating Ring,** on Hubs, for Outer Oil Seal	21–31	2	
C.19066	**OUTER BEARING (TAPER ROLLER) FOR HUBS (TIMKEN 18690-18620)**	21–32	2	
C.15230	**INNER BEARING (TAPER ROLLER) FOR HUBS (TIMKEN 18590-18520)**	21–33	2	
C.19110/A	**Spacer,** on Half-Shaft Splined Yoke, for Hub Bearing adjustment (.109″ thick)	21–34	2	
C.19110/B	**Spacer,** on Half-Shaft Splined Yoke, for Hub Bearing adjustment (.112″ thick)	21–34	2	
C.19110/C	**Spacer,** on Half-Shaft Splined Yoke, for Hub Bearing adjustment (.115″ thick)	21–34	2	
C.19110/D	**Spacer,** on Half-Shaft Splined Yoke, for Hub Bearing adjustment (.118″ thick)	21–34	2	
C.19110/E	**Spacer,** on Half-Shaft Splined Yoke, for Hub Bearing adjustment (.121″ thick)	21–34	2	
C.19110/F	**Spacer,** on Half-Shaft Splined Yoke, for Hub Bearing adjustment (.124″ thick)	21–34	2	
C.19110/G	**Spacer,** on Half-Shaft Splined Yoke, for Hub Bearing adjustment (.127″ thick)	21–34	2	
C.19110/H	**Spacer,** on Half-Shaft Splined Yoke, for Hub Bearing adjustment (.130″ thick)	21–34	2	SELECTIVE SIZES. Choose Spacer of desired thickness.
C.19110/J	**Spacer,** on Half-Shaft Splined Yoke, for Hub Bearing adjustment (.133″ thick)	21–34	2	
C.19110/K	**Spacer,** on Half-Shaft Splined Yoke, for Hub Bearing adjustment (.136″ thick)	21–34	2	
C.19110/L	**Spacer,** on Half-Shaft Splined Yoke, for Hub Bearing adjustment (.139″ thick)	21–34	2	
C.19110/M	**Spacer,** on Half-Shaft Splined Yoke, for Hub Bearing adjustment (.142″ thick)	21–34	2	
C.19110/P	**Spacer,** on Half-Shaft Splined Yoke, for Hub Bearing adjustment (.145″ thick)	21–34	2	
C.19110/Q	**Spacer,** on Half-Shaft Splined Yoke, for Hub Bearing adjustment (.148″ thick)	21–34	2	
C.19110/R	**Spacer,** on Half-Shaft Splined Yoke, for Hub Bearing adjustment (.151″ thick)	21–34	2	

REAR SUSPENSION

Part No.	Description	Plate No.	No. per Unit	Remarks
C.15231	**OIL SEAL (INNER) FOR HUBS**	21–35	2	
C.15232	**Seating Ring** for Inner Oil Seal, on Half-Shaft Splined Yoke, behind Adjustment Spacer	21–36	2	
C.15226	**HALF SHAFT ASSEMBLY**	21–37	2	
8692	**Flange Yoke** (K.3-2-GB.469)	21–38	2	
8693	**Splined Yoke** (K.3-82-GB.3711)	21–39	2	
8694	**Journal Assembly,** connecting Yokes to Half-Shafts (K.5-GB.10)	21–40	4	Fitted from Chassis No. 850001 to 850549. 850553 to 850554. 875001 to 877534. 877545 to 877549. 860001 to 860657. 885001 to 886246.
8694	**JOURNAL ASSEMBLY CONNECTING YOKES TO HALF SHAFTS (K.5-GB.10)**	21–40	4	
7153	**Gasket,** for Journals (K.3-86-119)		8	
8695	**Retainer,** for Gaskets (K.3-76-37)		8	
8696	**Circlip,** retaining Needle Bearings (K.3-7-GB.19)		8	
8406	**Grease Nipple,** on Journals (94-GB.2204)		4	
C.20398	**HALF SHAFT ASSEMBLY (05/500795)**		2	Fitted from Chassis No. 850550 to 850552. 877535 to 877544.
9406	**Flange Yoke** (05/202034)		2	
9407	**Splined Yoke** (05/221027)		2	
9408	**Journal Assembly,** connecting Yokes to Half Shafts (05/500888)		4	Also to Chassis No. 850555 and subs. 877550 and subs. 860658 and subs. 886247 and subs.
8406	**Grease Nipple,** on Journals (05/245068 or 94-GB.2204)		4	
C.16621	**Shim,** behind Flange Yokes, for adjustment of rear wheel Camber Angle	21–41	As req'd	
C.15349	**Nut,** Self-Locking, securing Flange Yoke and Brake Disc to Final Drive Unit Flanges		8	
UFN.375/L	**Slotted Nut,** securing Splined Yoke in Hubs		2	
C.21490	**Slotted Nut,** securing Splined Yoke in Hubs		2	**For use only if difficulty is experienced in fitting Split Pin.**
C.16622	**Washer,** Plain, under Slotted Nuts		2	
L.105/13U	**Split Pin,** retaining Slotted Nuts		2	
C.17011	**REAR SUSPENSION COIL SPRING**	21–42	4	Fitted from Chassis No. 850001 to 850136. 875001 to 875541. 860001 to 860007. 885001 to 885038.
C.18977	**REAR SUSPENSION COIL SPRING**		4	Fitted to Chassis No. 850137 and subs. 875542 and subs. 860008 and subs. 885039 and subs.
C.16908	**REAR SHOCK ABSORBER (64054324)**	21–43	4	Fitted from Chassis No. 850001 to 850321. 875001 to 876394. 860001 to 860121. 885001 to 885334.
8688	**Dust Shield Assembly** (64541630)		4	
8689	**Rubber Bush,** in eyes of Shock Absorber (64541636)		8	

Part No.	Description	Plate No.	No. per Unit	Remarks
C.20008	**REAR SHOCK ABSORBER** (NAP.64054299)		4	Fitted to Chassis No. 850322 and subs. 876395 and subs. 860122 and subs. 885335 and subs.
8688	Dust Shield Assembly (64541630)		4	
8689	Rubber Bush, in eyes of Shock Absorber (64541636)		8	
C.18560	Seat, for Rear Suspension Coil Spring	21—44	4	Fitted from Chassis No. 850001 to 850136. 875001 to 875541. 860001 to 860007. 885001 to 885038.
C.19820	Seat, for Rear Suspension Coil Spring (64541629)		4	Fitted to Chassis No. 850137 and subs. 875542 and subs. 860008 and subs. 885039 and subs.
8687	Retainer, for Rear Suspension Coil Springs (64540894)	21—45	8	Fitted from Chassis No. 850001 to 850136. 875001 to 875541. 860001 to 860007. 865001 to 885038.
C.19027	Packing Ring, at top of Rear Suspension Coil Springs	21—46	4	
UFB.143/16R	Bolt, securing Shock Absorbers at top to Rear Suspension Cross Member		4	
FW.107/T	Washer, Plain, on Bolts		4	
C.17012	Sleeve, on Bolts		4	
C.17013	Mounting Shaft, for lower fixing of Shock Absorbers		2	
C.3052	Washer, Plain, on Mounting Shafts		4	
C.8737/4	Nut, Self-Locking, on Bolts and Mounting Shafts		8	
C.17151	**REAR ANTI-ROLL BAR**	21—47	1	
C.16633	Rubber Bush, for Anti-Roll Bar	21—48	2	
C.3054	Bracket, holding Rubber Bushes	21—49	2	
UFS.137/7R	Screw, Set, securing Brackets to Body		4	
C.726	Washer, Shakeproof, on Setscrews		4	
C.20625	Bracket, holding Rubber Bushes		2	USE ONLY WHEN $\frac{7}{16}$" SETSCREWS ARE FITTED.
UFS.143/7R	Screw, Set, securing Brackets to Body		4	
C.727	Washer, Shakeproof, on Setscrews		4	
C.17152	**LINK, BETWEEN ANTI-ROLL BAR AND RADIUS ARMS**	21—50	2	
C.10940	Rubber Bush, in each end of Links	21—51	4	
C.18296	Bolt, Special, securing Links to Anti-Roll Bar		2	
UFB.143/15R	Bolt, securing Links to Radius Arms		2	
C.8667/4	Nut, Self-Locking, on Bolts		4	
FW.107/T	Washer, Plain, under Nuts		4	
C.17202	**BUMP STOP, ON BODY UNDERFRAME**	21—52	2	
C.8737/2	Nut, Self-Locking, securing Bump Stops		4	

REAR SUSPENSION

Part No.	Description	Plate No.	No. per Unit	Remarks
C.17207	**RADIUS ARM ASSEMBLY**	21–53	2	
C.17147	**Rubber Bush,** for front end of Radius Arms		2	
C.17146	**Rubber Bush,** for rear end of Radius Arms		2	
C.17149	**Bolt,** Special, securing Radius Arm to Wishbones		2	
C.8737/5	**Nut,** Self-Locking, on Bolts		2	
C.19031	**SAFETY STRAP ASSEMBLY, AT MOUNTING OF RADIUS ARMS TO BODY**	21–54	2	
C.19045	**Bolt,** Special, securing Radius Arms to Body		2	
C.837	**Lockwire,** for Bolts		As req'd	
UFS.131/6R	**Screw,** Set, securing Safety Straps to Body		4	
C.8667/2	**Nut,** Self-Locking, on Setscrews		4	

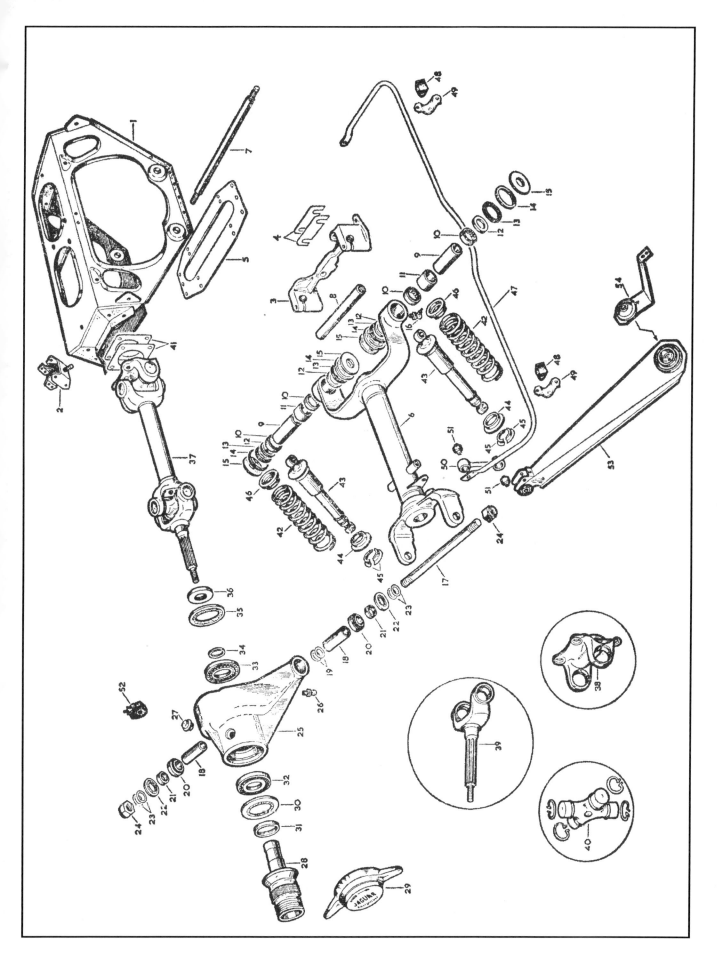

PLATE 21

ROAD WHEELS

Part No.	Description	Plate No.	No. per Unit	Remarks
C.14766	**WIRE SPOKE ROAD WHEEL (PAINTED STOVED ALUMINIUM)**		5	
7784	**Long Spoke**		120	
7790	**Short Spoke**		240	
C.5604	**Nipple**, for Spokes		360	
C.14802	**WIRE SPOKE ROAD WHEEL (CHROMIUM)**		5	**SUPPLIED TO SPECIAL ORDER ONLY.**
7796	**Long Spoke** (Chromium Plated)		120	
7801	**Short Spoke** (Chromium Plated)		240	
C.9144	**Nipple**, for Spokes		360	
C.17422	**TYRE FOR ROAD WHEELS (6.40″ × 15″ DUNLOP RS.5)**		5	
C.12567	**TUBE FOR TYRES (6.40″ × 15″)**		5	
	BALANCE WEIGHTS FOR ROAD WHEELS			
C.3985	**Balance Weight (½ Oz.)**		As req'd	
C.3986	**Balance Weight (1 Oz.)**		As req'd	
C.3987	**Balance Weight (1½ Oz.)**		As req'd	
C.3988	**Balance Weight (2 Oz.)**		As req'd	
C.3989	**Balance Weight (2½ Oz.)**		As req'd	
C.3990	**Balance Weight (3 Oz.)**		As req'd	

Part No.	Description	Plate No.	No. per Unit	Remarks
	THE UNDERMENTIONED ITEMS ARE FOR USE ONLY WHEN RACING			
C.18923	**RACING TYRE FOR FRONT ROAD WHEELS (6.00″ × 15″ DUNLOP R.5)**		2	
C.18924	**TUBE FOR FRONT RACING TYRES (6.00″ × 15″)**		2	
C.18922	**RACING REAR ROAD WHEEL (WIRE SPOKE, PAINTED STOVED ALUMINIUM)**		2	**SUPPLIED TO SPECIAL ORDER ONLY, AS ADDITIONAL ITEMS TO STANDARD EQUIPMENT.**
8822	**Front Spoke (SP.288/103)**		48	
8823	**Centre Spoke (SP.288/104)**		48	
8824	**Rear Spoke (SP.288/105)**		48	
C.9144	**Nipple,** for Spokes		144	
C.18931	**RACING TYRE FOR REAR ROAD WHEELS (6.50″ × 15″ DUNLOP R.5)**		2	
C.18932	**TUBE FOR REAR RACING TYRES (6.50″ × 15″)**		2	

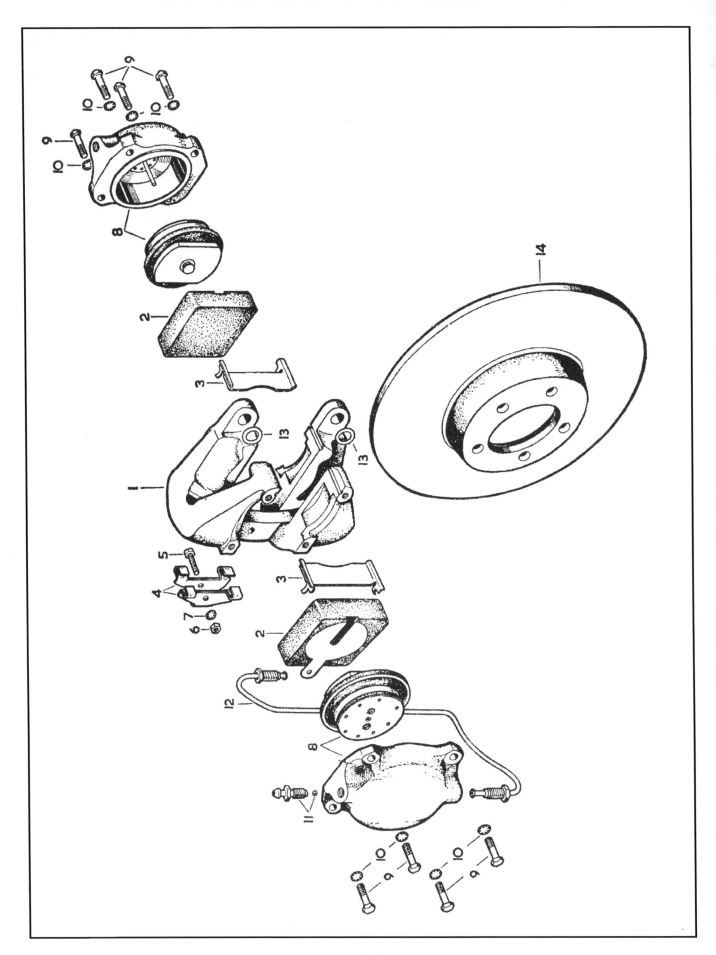

PLATE 22

Part No.	Description	Plate No.	No. per Unit	Remarks
C.18657	**R.H. FRONT CALIPER ASSEMBLY (VB.1028A/J)**		1	⎫
7715	**Front Caliper only** (VBM.1006)	22– 1	1	
8553	**Friction Pad Assembly** (VBO.5138/J)	22– 2	2	
7718	**Support Plate,** for Friction Pads (VBO.5133)	22– 3	2	
7719	**Retaining Plate,** for Friction Pads (VBO.5123)	22– 4	1	
UFB.125/7R	**Bolt,** securing Retaining Plate (VBO.6002)	22– 5	1	
UFN.125/L	**Nut,** on Bolt (VBO.6053)	22– 6	1	
C.724	**Washer,** Shakeproof, under Nut (VBO.6101)	22– 7	1	Fitted from Chassis No.
8513	**Piston and Cylinder Assembly** (VBO.5370)	22– 8	2	850001 to 850253.
7720	**Bolt,** securing Cylinders to Caliper (VBO.5100)	22– 9	8	875001 to 875963.
C.724	**Washer,** Shakeproof, on Bolts (VBO.6101)	22–10	8	860001 to 860022.
6911	**Bleed Screw and Ball Assembly** (VBO.8378)	22–11	1	885001 to 885142.
7783	**Bridge Pipe Assembly** (VBO.5203)	22–12	1	
C.18658	**L.H. FRONT CALIPER ASSEMBLY (VB.1028B/J)**		1	
7822	**Bridge Pipe Assembly** (VBO.5204)		1	
	All other items are as for R.H. Front Caliper C.18657			⎭
C.19962	**R.H. FRONT CALIPER ASSEMBLY (VB.1194A/N)**		1	⎫
8777	**Piston and Cylinder Assembly** (VBO.5505)		2	
7937	**Friction Pad Assembly** (VBO.5138/N)		2	
	All other items are as for R.H. Front Caliper C.18657.			
				Fitted to Chassis No.
				850254 and subs.
				875964 and subs.
				860023 and subs.
C.19963	**L.H. FRONT CALIPER ASSEMBLY (VB.1194B/N)**		1	885143 and subs.
8777	**Piston and Cylinder Assembly** (VBO.5505)		2	
7937	**Friction Pad Assembly** (VBO.5138/N)		2	
7822	**Bridge Pipe Assembly** (VBO.5204)		1	
	All other items are as for R.H. Front Caliper C.18657.			⎭
C.7569	**Shim,** .004" thick, for adjustment of Front Calipers	22–13	As req'd	
C.11723	**Shim,** .010" thick, for adjustment of Front Calipers	22–13	As req'd	
C.13547	**Bolt,** securing Front Calipers to Stub Axle Carriers		4	
FG.108/X	**Washer,** Spring, on Bolts		4	
C.837	**Wire,** locking Bolts		As req'd	
7727	**REPAIR KIT FOR FRONT WHEEL CYLINDERS** (VBO.8096) **(COMPRISING PISTON SEAL AND DUST SEAL)**		4	Fitted from Chassis No. 850001 to 850253. 875001 to 875963. 860001 to 860022. 885001 to 885142.

FRONT BRAKES

Part No.	Description	Plate No.	No. per Unit	Remarks
8820	**REPAIR KIT FOR FRONT WHEEL CYLINDERS (VBO.8210)** (COMPRISING PISTON SEAL AND DUST SEAL)		4	Fitted to Chassis No. 850254 and subs. 875964 and subs. 860023 and subs. 885143 and subs.
9251	**REPAIR KIT FOR CALIPER PADS (VBO.8328/N)**		1	
7840	**PISTON RETRACTION TOOL (AO.103741)**		1	FOR USE WHEN RENEWING FRICTION PADS.
C.15334	**DISC FOR FRONT CALIPERS (VBM.3748)**	22–14	2	
C.13546/1	**Bolt,** securing Disc to Hubs		10	
C.15349	**Nut,** Self-Locking, on Bolts		10	
C.15317/1	**R.H. FRONT HUB**		1	
C.15318/1	**L.H. FRONT HUB**		1	
C.3076/1	**Grease Nipple,** for Hubs		2	

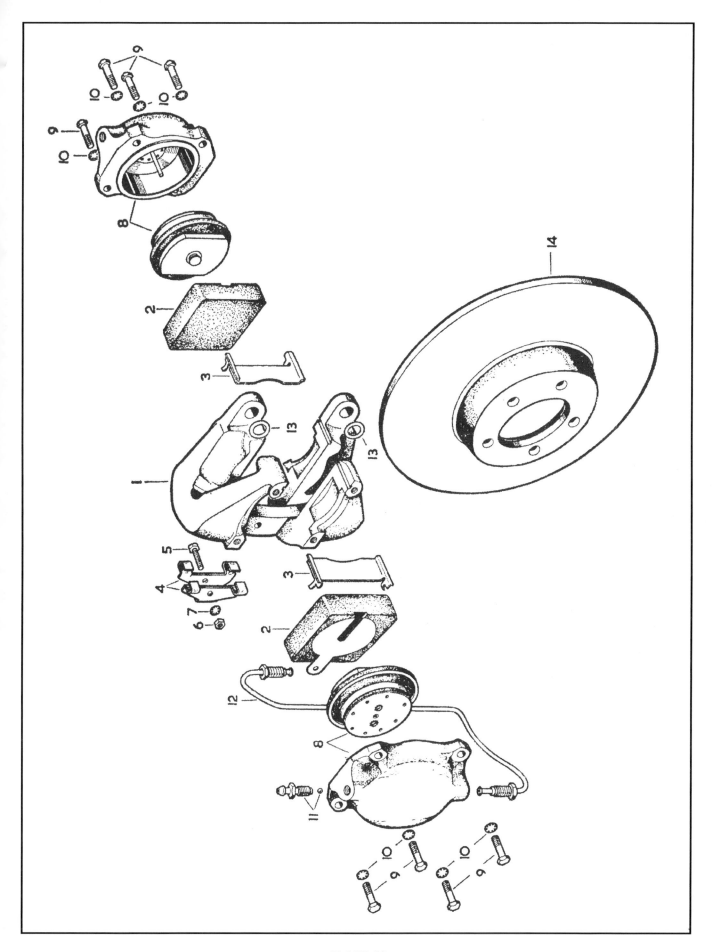

PLATE 22

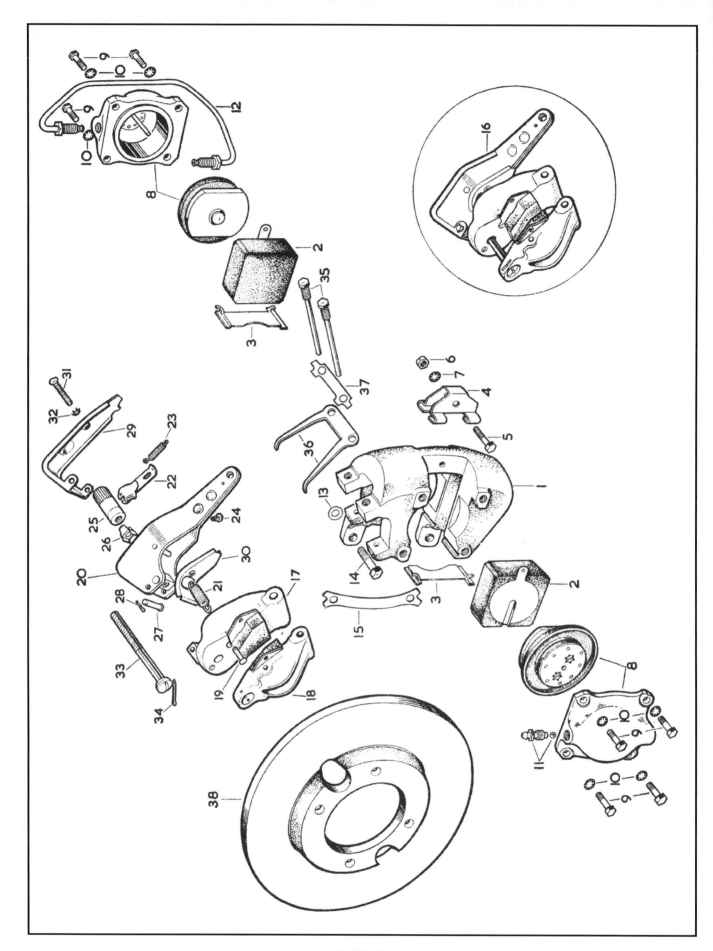

PLATE 23

108

Part No.	Description	Plate No.	No. per Unit	Remarks
C.17448	**R.H. REAR CALIPER ASSEMBLY (VB.1134A/J)**		1	
8010	**R.H. Rear Caliper only** (VBM.1081)	23- 1	1	
8553	**Friction Pad Assembly** (VBO.5138/J)	23- 2	2	
7718	**Support Plate,** for Friction Pads (VBO.5133)	23- 3	2	
7719	**Retaining Plate,** for Friction Pads (VBO.5123)	23- 4	1	
UFB.125/7R	**Bolt,** securing Retaining Plate (VBO.6002)	23- 5	1	
UFN.125/L	**Nut,** on Bolt (VBO.6053)	23- 6	1	
C.724	**Washer,** Shakeproof, under Nut (VBO.6101)	23- 7	1	
8514	**Piston and Cylinder Assembly** (VBO.5375)	23- 8	2	Fitted from Chassis No.
7720	**Bolt,** securing Cylinders to Caliper (VBO.5100)	23- 9	8	850001 to 850253.
C.724	**Washer,** Shakeproof, on Bolts (VBO.6101)	23-10	8	875001 to 875963.
6911	**Bleed Screw and Ball Assembly** (VBO.8378)	23-11	1	860001 to 860022.
7826	**Bridge Pipe Assembly** (VBO.3588)	23-12	1	885001 to 885142.
C.17449	**L.H. REAR CALIPER ASSEMBLY (VB.1134B/J)**		1	
8009	**L.H. Rear Caliper only** (VBM.1080)		1	
7827	**Bridge Pipe Assembly** (VBO.3589)		1	
	All other items are as for R.H. Rear Caliper C.17448			
C.20006	**R.H. REAR CALIPER ASSEMBLY (VB.1166A/N)**		1	
8778	**Piston and Cylinder Assembly** (VBO.5506)		2	
7937	**Friction Pad Assembly** (VBO.5138/N)		2	
	All other items are as for R.H. Rear Caliper C.17448.			Fitted to Chassis No.
				850254 and subs.
				875964 and subs.
				860023 and subs.
C.20007	**L.H. REAR CALIPER ASSEMBLY (VB.1166B/N)**		1	885143 and subs.
8009	**L.H. Rear Caliper only** (VBM.1080)		1	
8778	**Piston and Cylinder Assembly** (VBO.5506)		2	
7937	**Friction Pad Assembly** (VBO.5138/N)		2	
7827	**Bridge Pipe Assembly** (VBO.3589)		1	
	All other items are as for R.H. Rear Caliper C.17448.			
C.13198	**Shim,** .005″ thick, for adjustment of Rear Calipers (VBO.1333)	23-13	As req'd	
C.13199	**Shim,** .020″ thick, for adjustment of Rear Calipers (VBO.1334)	23-13	As req'd	
C.19759	**Screw,** Set, securing Rear Calipers to Final Drive Unit Housing	23-14	4	Fitted from Chassis No.
C.18491	**Tab Washer,** locking Setscrews	23-15	2	850001 to 850577. 875001 to 877735. 860001 to 860740. 885001 to 886455.
C.20624	**Screw,** Set, securing Rear Calipers to Final Drive Unit Housing		4	Fitted to Chassis No. 850578 and subs.
FG.107/X	**Washer,** Spring, on Setscrews		4	877736 and subs. 860741 and subs.
C.21126	**Locking Wire,** Stainless, for Setscrews		4	886456 and subs. May be used to replace C.19759 & C.18491.

REAR BRAKES

Part No.	Description	Plate No.	No. per Unit	Remarks
8665	**REPAIR KIT FOR REAR WHEEL CYLINDER (VBO.8097)** **(COMPRISING PISTON SEAL AND DUST SEAL)**		4	Fitted from Chassis No. 850001 to 850253. 875001 to 875963. 860001 to 860022. 885001 to 885142.
8972	**REPAIR KIT FOR REAR WHEEL CYLINDERS (VBO.8211)** **(COMPRISING PISTON SEAL AND DUST SEAL)**		4	Fitted to Chassis No. 850254 and subs. 875964 and subs. 860023 and subs. 885143 and subs.
9251	**REPAIR KIT FOR CALIPER PADS (VBO.8328/N)**		1	
7840	**PISTON RETRACTION TOOL (AO.103741)**		1	**FOR USE WHEN RENEWING FRICTION PADS.**
C.17450	**HANDBRAKE MECHANISM ASSEMBLY R.H. (VBM.4148/A)**		1	
8515	**R.H. Inner Pad Carrier Assembly (VBM.4173/A)**		1	
8516	**R.H. Outer Pad Carrier Assembly (VBO.7138/A)**		1	
8024	**Operating Lever Assembly (VBO.4176)**		1	
8517	**Bolt,** securing Pad Carriers to Operating Lever (VBO.4819)		1	
C.8667/2	**Nut,** Self-Locking, on Bolt (VBO.6056)		1	
6923	**Pivot Seat,** for Operating Lever (VBO.2350)		1	
8015	**Clevis Pin,** securing Operating Lever to Pivot Seat (VBO.4182)		1	
8519	**Split Pin,** retaining Clevis Pin (VBO.6154)		1	Fitted from Chassis No. 850001 to 850089. 875001 to 875331. 860001 to 860003. 885001 to 885014.
C.17451	**HANDBRAKE MECHANISM ASSEMBLY L.H. (VBM.4148/B)**		1	
8520	**L.H. Inner Pad Carrier Assembly (VBM.4173/B)**		1	
8521	**L.H. Outer Pad Carrier Assembly (VBO.7138/B)**		1	
	All other items are as for R.H. Handbrake Mechanism C.17450			
8016	**Bolt,** securing Handbrake Mechanism to Rear Calipers (VBO.4190)		4	
8017	**Retraction Plate,** on Bolts (VBO.3764/1)		2	
8014	**Tab Washer,** locking Bolts (VBO.4226)		2	

Part No.	Description	Plate No.	No. per Unit	Remarks
C.19904	**HANDBRAKE MECHANISM ASSEMBLY R.H. (VBM.4220/A)**		1	
8934	**R.H. Inner Pad Carrier Assembly** (VBM.4694/A)		1	
8936	**R.H. Outer Pad Carrier Assembly** (VBO.8160/A)		1	
8938	**Anchor Pin,** in Inner Pad Carrier, retaining Return Spring (VBO.8157)		1	
8943	**Operating Lever Assembly** (VBO.7856)		1	
8940	**Return Spring,** between Operating Lever and Anchor Pin (VBO.8190)		1	Fitted from Chassis No.
8836	**Pawl Assembly** (VBO.7995)		1	850090 to 850550.
8837	**Tension Spring,** for Pawl (VBO.7367)		1	850553 to 850554.
8838	**Anchor Pin.** retaining Tension Spring (VBO.7385)		1	875332 to 877534.
8980	**Adjusting Nut** (VBO.7667)		1	877540 to 877566.
8840	**Friction Spring,** on Adjusting Nut (VBO.7588)		1	860004 to 860663.
8941	**Hinge Pin,** securing Operating Lever (VBO.8198)		1	885015 to 886262.
L.102/3U	**Split Pin,** retaining Hinge Pin		1	
8939	**Protection Cover Assembly,** at rear of Operating Lever (VBO.8159)		1	
8942	**Protection Cover,** at front of Operating Lever (VBO.7950)		1	
8844	**Bolt,** securing Protection Covers (VBO.8090)		1	
8845	**Bolt,** securing Pad Carriers to Operating Lever (VBO.8024)		1	
L.102.5/8U	**Split Pin,** retaining Bolt		1	
C.19905	**HANDBRAKE MECHANISM ASSEMBLY L.H. (VBM.4220/B)**		1	Fitted from Chassis No. 850090 to 850550.
8935	**L.H. Inner Pad Carrier Assembly** (VBM.4694/B)		1	850553 to 850554. 875332 to 877534.
8937	**L.H. Outer Pad Carrier Assembly** (VBO.8160/B)		1	877540 to 877566. 860004 to 860663.
	All other items are as for R.H. Handbrake Mechanism C.19904.			885015 to 886262.
C.19830	**HANDBRAKE MECHANISM ASSEMBLY R.H. (VBM.4234/A)**	23–16	1	
9326	**R.H. Inner Pad Carrier Assembly** (VBM.4647/A)	23–17	1	
9328	**R.H. Outer Pad Carrier Assembly** (VBO.8235/A)	23–18	1	
8938	**Anchor Pin,** in Inner Pad Carrier, retaining Return Spring (VBO.8157)	23–19	1	
9330	**Operating Lever Assembly** (VBO.8379)	23–20	1	
8940	**Return Spring,** between Operating Lever and Anchor Pin (VBO.8190)	23–21	1	
8836	**Pawl Assembly** (VBO.7995)	23–22	1	Fitted from Chassis No.
8837	**Tension Spring,** for Pawl (VBO.7367)	23–23	1	850551 to 850552.
8838	**Anchor Pin,** retaining Tension Spring (VBO.7385)	23–24	1	850555 and subs.
8980	**Adjusting Nut** (VBO.7667)	23–25	1	877535 to 877539.
8840	**Friction Spring,** on Adjusting Nut (VBO.7588)	23–26	1	877567 and subs.
8841	**Hinge Pin,** securing Operating Lever (VBO.7289)	23–27	1	860664 and subs.
L.102/3U	**Split Pin,** retaining Hinge Pin	23–28	1	886263 and subs.
9334	**Protection Cover Assembly,** at rear of Operating Lever (VBO.8467)	23–29	1	
9335	**Protection Cover,** at front of Operating Lever (VBO.8215)	23–30	1	
9336	**Bolt,** securing Protection Covers (VBO.6015/F)	23–31	1	
BD.2906/3	**Washer,** Countersunk, Shakeproof, on Bolt (VBO.6100/P)	23–32	1	
9332	**Bolt,** securing Pad Carriers to Operating Lever (VBO.8217)	23–33	1	
L.102.5/8U	**Split Pin,** retaining Bolts	23–34	1	

REAR BRAKES

Part No.	Description	Plate No.	No. per Unit	Remarks
C.19833	**HANDBRAKE MECHANISM ASSEMBLY L.H. (VBM.4230/B)**		1	Fitted from Chassis No. 850551 to 850552. 850555 and subs. 877535 to 877539. 877567 and subs. 860664 and subs. 886263 and subs.
9327	**L.H. Inner Pad Carrier Assembly (VBM.4647/B)**		1	
9329	**L.H. Outer Pad Carrier Assembly (VBO.8235/B)**		1	
	All other items are as for R.H. Handbrake Mechanism C.19830.			
8016	**Bolt,** securing Handbrake Mechanism to Rear Calipers (VBO.4190)	23–35	4	
9333	**Retraction Plate,** on Bolts (VBO.4646/1)	23–36	2	
8014	**Tab Washer,** locking Bolts (VBO.4226)	23–37	2	
8522	**REPAIR KIT FOR HANDBRAKE MECHANISM (VBO.8073)** (COMPRISING FRICTION PADS, FIXING BOLTS, NUTS AND WASHERS)		1	Fitted from Chassis No. 850001 to 850550. 850553 to 850554. 875001 to 877534. 877540 to 877566. 860001 to 860663. 885001 to 886262.
9245	**REPAIR KIT FOR HANDBRAKE MECHANISM (VBO.8737/R)** (COMPRISING FRICTION PADS, FIXING BOLTS, NUTS AND WASHERS)		1	Fitted from Chassis No. 850551 to 850552. 850555 and subs. 877535 to 877539. 877567 and subs. 860664 and subs. 886263 and subs.
C.15223	**DISC FOR REAR CALIPERS (VBM.3981)**	23–38	2	

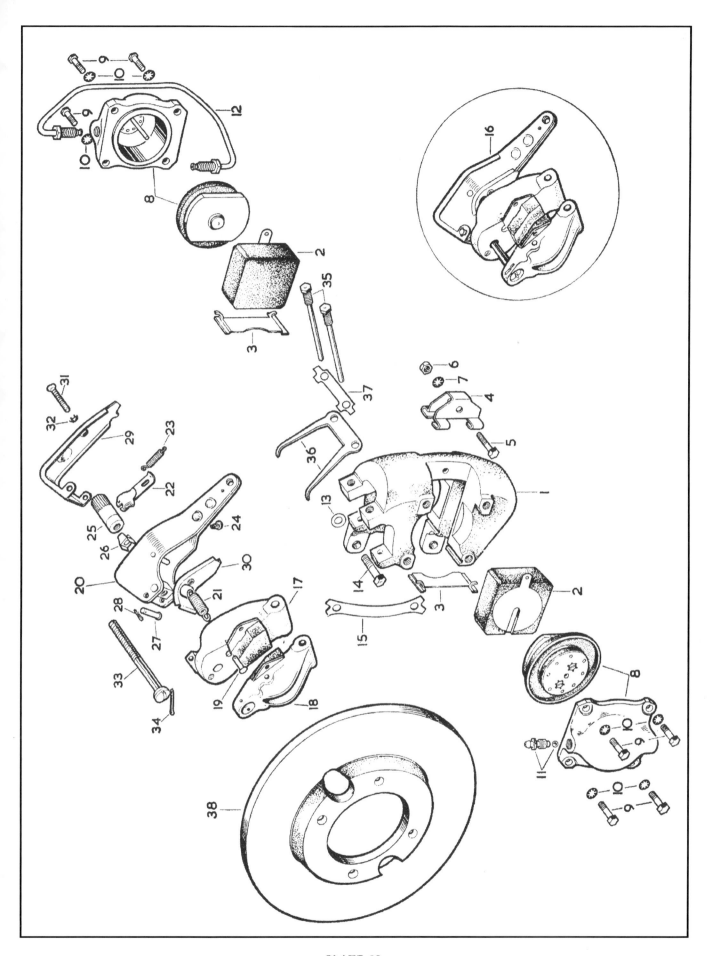

PLATE 23

113

BRAKE SERVO UNIT

Part No.	Description	Plate No.	No. per Unit	Remarks
C.17266	**BRAKE SERVO UNIT ASSEMBLY** **(VB.10000)**		1	
8723	**Valve Housing** (VB.10001)	24– 1	1	
8724	**Nipple,** for Vacuum test (VBO.10065)	24– 2	1	
8725	**Adaptor,** for testing take-off (VBO.10066)	24– 3	1	
8726	**Screwed Plug,** in Adaptor (VBO.10067)	24– 4	1	
8727	**Gasket,** under Screwed Plug and Adaptor (VBO.10068)	24– 5	2	
8728	**Air Valve Assembly** (VBO.10001)	24– 6	1	
8729	**Vacuum Valve Assembly** (VBM.10002)	24– 7	1	
8730	**Return Spring,** for Vacuum Valve (VBO.10006)	24– 8	1	
8731	**Balancing Washer,** inside Diaphragm (VBO.10007)	24– 9	1	
8732	**Valve Balancing Diaphragm** (VBM.10003)	24–10	1	
8733	**Retainer,** for Diaphragm (VBO.10008)	24–11	1	
8734	**Control Spring,** for Air Valve (VBO.10009)	24–12	1	
8735	**Retainer and Sleeve Assembly** (VBM.10004)	24–13	1	
8736	**Bellows** (VBM.10008)	24–14	1	
8737	**Support Ring,** inside Bellows (VBO.10025)	24–15	3	
8738	**Bolt,** securing Retainer and Sleeve to Valve Housing (VBO.10011)	24–16	3	
8739	**Main Return Spring** (VBO.10012)	24–17	1	
8740	**Mounting Hub Assembly** (VBM.10010)	24–18	1	
8741	**Seal,** for Hub (VBO.10014)	24–19	1	
8742	**Guide Sleeve,** behind Seal (VBM.10012)	24–20	1	
8743	**Rubber Buffer,** between Mounting Hub and Stop Washer (VBO.10015)	24–21	1	
8744	**Stop Washer,** for Mounting Hub (VBO.10016)	24–22	1	
8745	**Circlip,** retaining Hub to Sleeve (VBO.10017)	24–23	1	
8746	**Air Filter,** inside Sleeve (VBO.10018)	24–24	1	
8747	**Baffle,** for Air Filter (VBO.10019)	24–25	1	
8748	**Mounting Bracket Assembly** (VBO.10027)	24–26	1	
UFN.225/L	**Nut,** securing Mounting Bracket to Hub (VBO.10021)	24–27	3	
C.724	**Washer,** Shakeproof, under Nuts (VBO.10020)	24–28	3	
C.17267	**Nylon Bush,** for Valve Housing (VBM.10000)	24–29	1	
C.17268	**Eccentric Bush,** for Valve Housing (VBM.10036)	24–30	1	
C.17269	**Spring,** for Valve Housing (VBM.10037)	24–31	1	

Part No.	Description	Plate No.	No. per Unit	Remarks
8749	**REPAIR KIT FOR BRAKE SERVO UNIT**		1	

comprising:—

C.17239	Rubber Buffer	1 off
C.17267	Bush	1 off
C.17262	Bush	10 off
8743	Rubber Buffer	1 off
8728	Air Valve Assembly	1 off
8729	Vacuum Valve Assembly	1 off
8732	Valve Balancing Diaphragm	1 off
8741	Seal	1 off
8745	Circlip	1 off
	Tube, Silicon Grease	

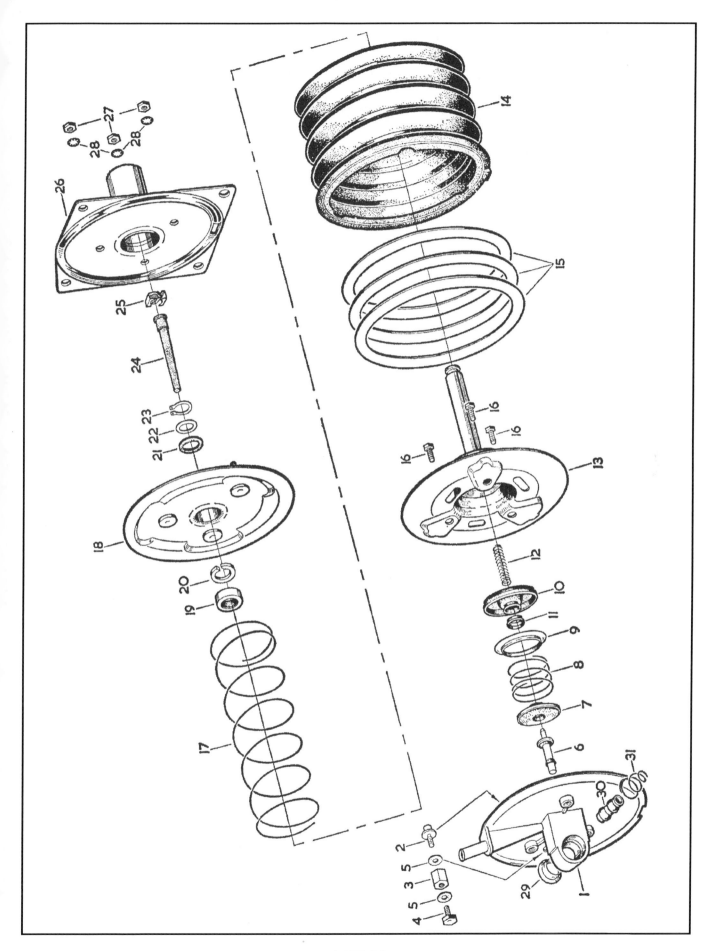

PLATE 24

RESERVAC TANK FOR BRAKE SERVO

Part No.	Description	Plate No.	No. per Unit	Remarks
C.17488	**RESERVAC TANK ASSEMBLY**	25– 1	1	
UFS.125/4R	**Screw,** Set, securing Reservac Tank to Body		4	
FG.104/X	**Washer,** Spring, on Setscrews		4	
C.14693	**CHECK VALVE ASSEMBLY ON RESERVAC TANK**	25– 2	1	
C.17493	**VACUUM HOSE FROM RESERVAC TANK TO SERVO**	25– 3	1	**R.H. DRIVE CARS ONLY.**
C.18459	**VACUUM HOSE FROM RESERVAC TANK TO SERVO**		1	**L.H. DRIVE CARS ONLY.**
C.15886/5	**Clip,** securing Hose to Tank and Servo	25– 4	2	
C.1040/4	**Clip,** securing Hose to Dash and Master Cylinder Bracket	25– 5	See Remarks	1 off required for R.H. Drive Cars 3 off required for L.H. Drive Cars
C.17494	**VACUUM HOSE FROM CHECK VALVE TO AIR BALANCE PIPE ON ENGINE**	25– 6	1	
C.15886/5	**Clip,** securing Hose	25– 7	2	
C.14746	**ADAPTOR ASSEMBLY, AT REAR OF AIR BALANCE PIPE, FOR CONNECTION OF VACUUM HOSE**	25– 8	1	
C.14089	**Gasket,** under Adaptor	25– 9	1	
UFN.125/L	**Nut,** securing Adaptor		2	
FG.104/X	**Washer,** Spring, under Nuts		2	

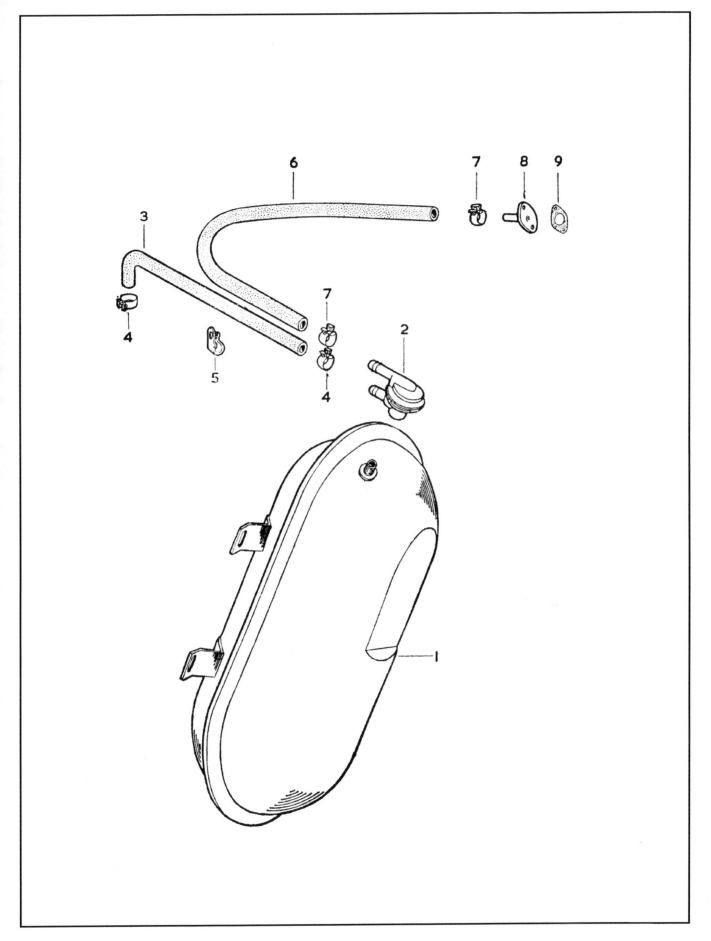

PLATE 25

BRAKE CONTROLS

Part No.	Description	Plate No.	No. per Unit	Remarks
C.17254	**BRAKE PEDAL**	26– 1	1	**R.H. DRIVE CARS ONLY.**
C.17592	**BRAKE PEDAL**		1	**L.H. DRIVE CARS ONLY.**
C.14366	**Return Spring,** for Brake Pedal		1	
C.15245	**STEEL PAD ON BRAKE PEDAL**		1	Fitted from Chassis No. 850001 to 850474. 875001 to 876998. 860001 to 860374 except 860365. 885001 to 885870.
C.20221	**STEEL PAD ON BRAKE PEDAL**	26– 2	1	Fitted to Chassis No. 850475 and subs. 876999 and subs. 860375 and subs. also 860365. 885871 and subs.
C.8667/2	**Nut,** Self-Locking, securing Pad to Pedal		1	
C.9934	**RUBBER PAD ON BRAKE PEDAL**	26– 3	1	
C.17253	**HOUSING FOR BRAKE PEDAL**		1	
C.12473	**Stud,** for mounting of Brake Master Cylinder and Servo Brackets to Housing		9	
C.18203	**Stud,** for fixing of Housing to Scuttle and for mounting of Clutch Master Cylinder		6	Fitted from Chassis No. 850001 to 850232. 875001 to 875858. 860001 to 860020. 885001 to 885104.
C.17260	**Bush, in** Housing, for Brake Pedal Shaft and Clutch Pedal		1	
UCS.125/3R	**Screw,** Set, retaining Bush		1	
C.17498	**Bearing** (Torrington B.128), in Housing, for Brake Pedal Shaft		1	
C.18262	**Gasket,** between Housing and Scuttle		1	
C.8667/2	**Nut,** Self-Locking, securing Housing to Scuttle		5	
FW.105/T	**Washer,** Plain, under Nuts		5	

Part No.	Description	Plate No.	No. per Unit	Remarks
C.19666	**HOUSING FOR BRAKE PEDAL**	26– 4	1	
C.12473	**Stud,** for mounting of Brake Master Cylinder and Servo Brackets to Housing		9	
C.18203	**Stud,** for fixing of Housing to Scuttle and for mounting of Clutch Master Cylinder		6	
C.19613	**Flanged Bearing Tube,** at side of Pedal Housing	26– 5	1	Fitted to Chassis No.
UCS.125/4R	**Screw,** Set, securing Bearing Tube		2	850233 and subs.
C.724	**Washer,** Shakeproof, on Setscrews		2	875859 and subs.
C.19623	**Bush,** in Bearing Tube, for Brake Pedal Shaft	26– 6	1	860021 and subs.
C.17498	**Bearing** (Torrington B.128), in Housing, for Brake Pedal Shaft	26– 7	1	885105 and subs.
C.18262	**Gasket,** between Housing and Scuttle	26– 8	1	
C.8667/2	**Nut,** Self-Locking, securing Housing to Scuttle		5	
FW.105/T	**Washer,** Plain, under Nuts		5	
C.17256	**SHAFT AND PIN ASSEMBLY, FOR MOUNTING OF BRAKE PEDAL**	26– 9	1	
UFS.131/8R	**Screw,** Set, clamping Pedal on Shaft		1	
C.17485	**Circlip,** retaining Shaft	26–10	1	
C.17481	**Washer,** behind Circlip		1	Fitted from Chassis No.
				850001 to 850232.
				875001 to 875858.
				860001 to 860020.
				885001 to 885104.
C.21755	**Washer** (Tufnol) between Brake and Clutch Pedals		1	
C.17261	**CONNECTING LEVER, BETWEEN PEDAL SHAFT AND END PLATE OF SERVO BELLOWS**		1	Fitted from Chassis No. 850001 to 850474. 875001 to 876998. 860001 to 860374. 885001 to 885870. Except 860365.
C.20320	**CONNECTING LEVER, BETWEEN PEDAL SHAFT AND END PLATE OF SERVO BELLOWS**	26–11	1	Fitted from Chassis No. 850475 to 850649. 876999 to 878963. 860375 to 861079. 885871 to 888168. Also to 860365.
C.21609	**CONNECTING LEVER, BETWEEN PEDAL SHAFT AND END PLATE OF SERVO BELLOWS**		1	Fitted to Chassis No. 850650 and subs. 878964 and subs. 861080 and subs. 888169 and subs.
C.17262	**Nylon Bush,** for Lever, on lower pin of Pedal Shaft	26–12	2	
C.17239	**Rubber Buffer,** for Lever, on upper pin of Pedal Shaft	26–13	1	
FW.204/T	**Washer,** Plain, at top of Rubber Buffer	26–14	1	
C.17240	**Spacing Collar,** at top of Washer	26–15	1	
C.17241	**Belleville Washer,** between Spacing Collar and Servo Operating Arm	26–16	1	

BRAKE CONTROLS

Part No.	Description	Plate No.	No. per Unit	Remarks
C.17242	**ARM, OPERATING BRAKE SERVO**	26–17	1	
C.17243	**Eccentric Barrel Nut,** for fine adjustment of Operating Arm and retaining Operating Arm and Connecting Lever		1	Fitted from Chassis No. 850001 to 850474. 875001 to 876998. 860001 to 860374. 885001 to 885870. Except 860365.
C.20787	**Eccentric Barrel Nut,** for fine adjustment of Operating Arm and retaining Operating Arm and Connecting Lever	26–18	1	Fitted to Chassis No. 850475 and subs. 876999 and subs. 860375 and subs. 885871 and subs. Also to 860365.
UFN.425/L	**Slotted Nut,** locking Eccentric Nut to upper pin of Pedal Shaft	26–19	1	
L.102/6U	**Split Pin,** retaining Nut	26–20	1	
C.8667/2	**Nut,** Self Locking, retaining Operating Arm and Connecting Lever on lower pin of Pedal Shaft		1	
FW.205/T	**Washer,** Plain, at each side of Operating Arm		2	
C.17238	**SERRATED PIN, IN UPPER END OF CONNECTING LEVER**	26–21	1	
C.17267	**Nylon Bush,** on Pin (VBM.10000)	26–22	1	
C.17268	**Steel Bush,** for "eye" on Servo Bellows End Plate (VBM.10036)	26–23	1	
C.17269	**Conical Spring,** above Steel Bush (VBM.10037)	26–24	1	
C.8667/2	**Nut,** retaining Servo Bellows End Plate on Pin		1	
C.1904	**Washer,** Plain, under Nut		1	
C.17264	**FORK END BETWEEN CONNECTING LEVER AND BALANCE LINK**	26–25	1	
C.17265	**Joint Pin,** securing Fork End to Connecting Lever	26–26	1	
C.17262	**Nylon Bush,** on Joint Pin	26–27	2	
C.17486	**Grub Screw** (Allen Head) retaining Joint Pin in Connecting Lever	26–28	1	Fitted from Chassis No. 850001 to 850649. 875001 to 878963. 860001 to 861079. 885001 to 888168.
C.20724/12	**Roll Pin,** retaining Joint Pin in Connecting Lever		1	Fitted to Chassis No. 850650 and subs. 878964 and subs. 861080 and subs. 888169 and subs.
C.17244	**BALANCE LINK ASSEMBLY FOR OPERATION OF MASTER CYLINDERS**		1	Fitted from Chassis No. 850001 to 850376. 875001 to 876638. 860001 to 860192. 885001 to 885571. **USE C.20341 FOR ALL REPLACEMENTS.**

Part No.	Description	Plate No.	No. per Unit	Remarks
C.20341	**BALANCE LINK ASSEMBLY FOR OPERATION OF MASTER CYLINDERS**	26–29	1	Fitted to Chassis No. 850377 and subs. 876639 and subs. 860193 and subs. 885572 and subs.
UFB.131/12R	**Bolt,** securing Fork End and Balance Link to Pivot Bracket		1	
C.17249	**Spacing Tube,** on Bolt	26–30	1	
C.17262	**Nylon Bush,** on Spacing Tube	26–31	4	
C.8667/2	**Nut,** Self-Locking, on Bolt		1	
C.17246	**PIVOT BRACKET ASSEMBLY FOR BALANCE LINK**	26–32	1	
UFB.131/28R	**Bolt,** mounting Pivot Bracket to Brake Master Cylinder Bracket		1	
C.17236	**Sleeve,** on Bolt	26–33	1	
C.17262	**Nylon Bush,** at each end of Sleeve	26–34	2	
C.8667/2	**Nut,** Self-Locking, on Bolt		1	
C.18195	**BRACKET ASSEMBLY FOR MOUNTING OF BRAKE MASTER CYLINDERS**	26–35	1	
UFN.131/L	**Nut,** securing Bracket to Pedal Housing		4	
C.725	**Washer,** Shakeproof, under Nuts		4	
UCS.131/4R	**Screw,** Set, securing Bracket to Pedal Housing		1	
C.8667/2	**Nut,** Self-Locking, securing Bracket to Scuttle		2	
C.17235	**BRAKE MASTER CYLINDER ASSEMBLY (UPPER) OPERATING REAR BRAKES (VBM.4039)**		1	Fitted from Chassis No. 850001 to 850254. 875001 to 876014. 860001 to 860026. 885001 to 885155.
C.19968	**BRAKE MASTER CYLINDER ASSEMBLY (UPPER) OPERATING REAR BRAKES (VBM.4706)**	26–36	1	Fitted to Chassis No. 850255 and subs. 876015 and subs. 860027 and subs. 885156 and subs.
	For individual items, please refer to section for "Hydraulic Brake Pipes"			
C.17482	**Fork End,** for connection of Master Cylinder to Balance Link	26–37	1	
UFN.231/L	**Nut,** securing Fork End to Push Rod		1	
J.105/12S	**Clevis Pin,** securing Balance Link to Upper Master Cylinder		1	
L.102·5/6U	**Split Pin,** retaining Clevis Pin		1	
FW.105/T	**Washer,** Plain, behind Split Pin		1	

BRAKE CONTROLS

Part No.	Description	Plate No.	No. per Unit	Remarks
C.17234	**BRAKE MASTER CYLINDER ASSEMBLY (LOWER) OPERATING FRONT BRAKES (VBM.4038)**		1	Fitted from Chassis No. 850001 to 850254. 875001 to 876014. 860001 to 860026. 885001 to 885155.
C.19967	**BRAKE MASTER CYLINDER ASSEMBLY (LOWER) OPERATING FRONT BRAKES (VBM.4705)**	26–38	1	Fitted to Chassis No. 850255 and subs. 876015 and subs. 860027 and subs. 885156 and subs.
	For individual items, please refer to section for "Hydraulic Brake Pipes"			
J.105/10S	**Clevis Pin,** securing Balance Link to Master Cylinder	26–39	1	
L.102·5/6U	**Split Pin,** retaining Clevis Pin		1	
FW.105/T	**Washer,** Plain, behind Split Pin		1	
UFS.131/8R	**Screw,** Set, securing Master Cylinders to Bracket		4	
C.8667/2	**Nut,** Self-Locking, on Setscrews		4	
C.18172	**BRACKET ASSEMBLY FOR MOUNTING OF BRAKE SERVO**	26–40	1	
UFN.131/L	**Nut,** securing Bracket to Pedal Housing		4	
C.725	**Washer,** Shakeproof, under Nuts		4	
C.17266	**BRAKE VACUUM SERVO ASSEMBLY (VB.10000)**	26–41	1	
C.8667/2	**Nut,** Self-Locking, retaining Servo Bellows on Connecting Lever Pin		1	
C.1904	**Special Washer,** behind Self-Locking Nut		1	
C.8667/2	**Nut,** Self-Locking, securing Brake Servo to Mounting Bracket		4	
FW.105/T	**Washer,** Plain, under Nuts		4	
C.18266	**RUBBER SEAL, BETWEEN SERVO BRACKET AND DASH**	26–42	1	

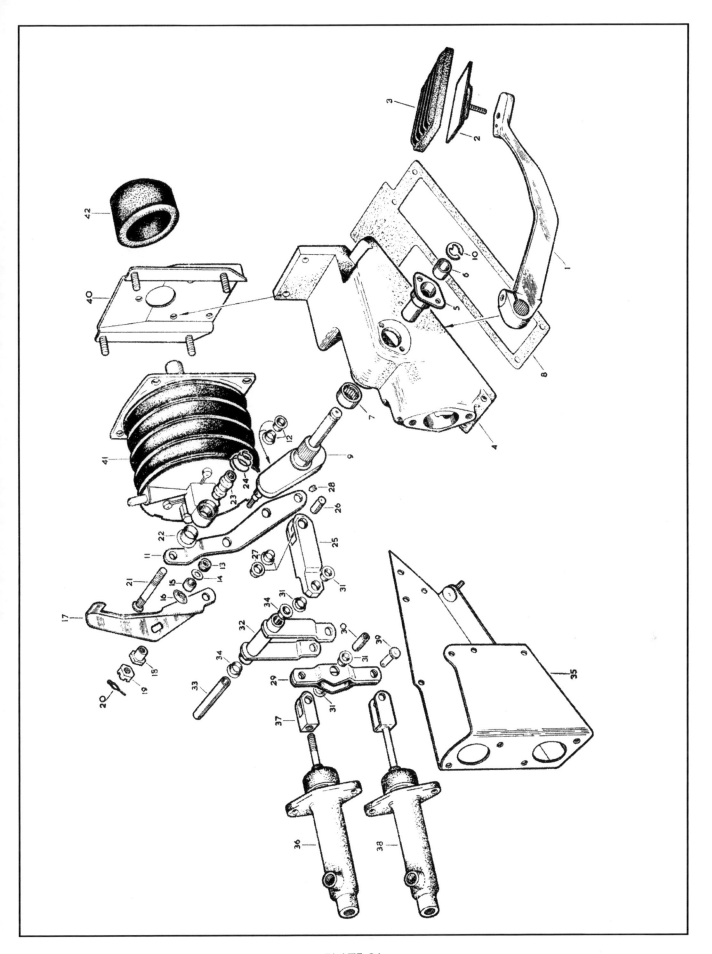

PLATE 26

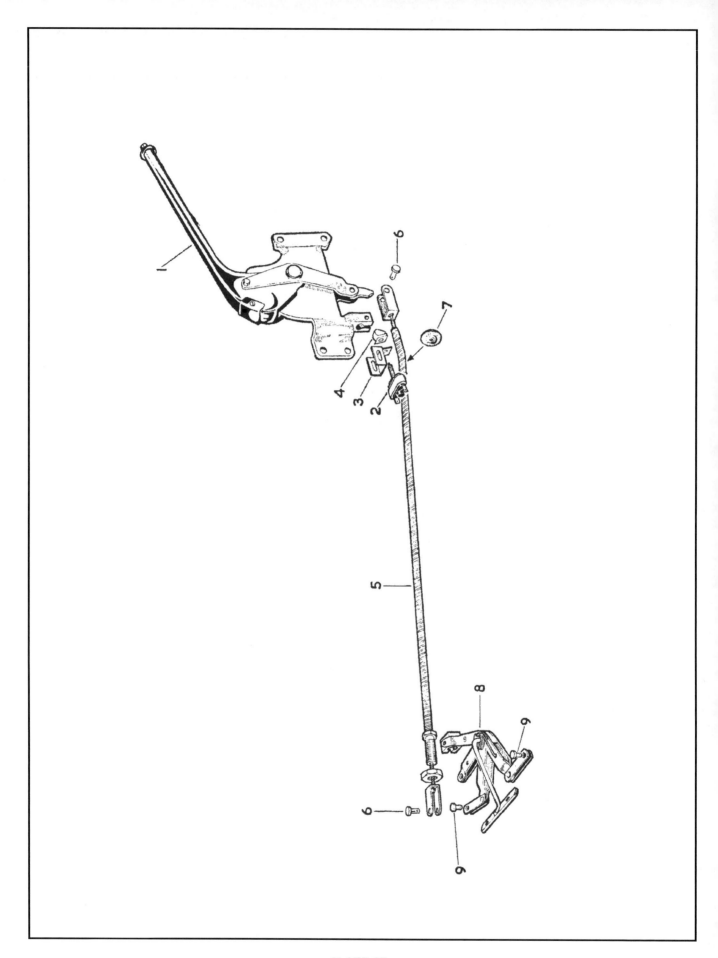

PLATE 27

124

Part No.	Description	Plate No.	No. per Unit	Remarks
C.16823	**HANDBRAKE LEVER ASSEMBLY**	27- 1	1	
C.17736	**Chrome Thumb Button**, in end of Lever		1	
C.17737	**Spring**, under Button		1	
C.17735	**Push Rod Assembly**, operating Pawl		1	
J.103/5.5S	**Clevis Pin**, securing Push rod to Pawl		1	
L.102/4U	**Split Pin**, retaining Clevis Pin		1	
C.17738	**Pawl**		1	
C.17162	**Cover Plate**, sealing Pawl Access Hole		1	
BD.711/6	**Screw**, Self-Tapping, securing Cover Plate		2	
C.17741	**Bolt** (Chromed Head) pivoting Pawl		1	
C.17740	**Spacing Tube**, on Bolt		1	
C.17739	**Spacing Collar**, on Tube		2	
C.8737/2	**Nut**, Self-locking, on Bolt		1	
C.17742	**Lever Assembly**, for operation of Handbrake Cable		1	
C.17750	**Pivot Pin**, for Lever		1	} SUPERSEDED BY C.21123, C.21125, C.21124 AND L.104/12U.
C.17751	**Circlip**, retaining Pivot Pin		1	
C.21123	**Pivot Pin**, for Lever		1	
C.21125	**Nut**, retaining Pivot Pin		1	} SUPERSEDES C.17751 AND C.17750.
C.21124	**Washer**, under Nut		1	
L.104/12U	**Split Pin**, securing Nut		1	
C.17746	**Mounting Plate Assembly**, for Handbrake		1	
UFS.531/6R	**Screw**, Set, securing Handbrake Assembly to Propeller Shaft Tunnel		4	
C.17879	**Tapped Plate**, at rear fixing		1	
C.16660	**SWITCH FOR OPERATION OF HAND-BRAKE WARNING LIGHT** (31893-12.SA)	27- 2	1	
C.18737	**Bracket**, mounting Switch to Handbrake	27- 3	1	
UFS.119/8R	**Screw**, Set, securing Bracket to Cable Abutment Block		1	
C.8667/17	**Nut**, on Setscrew		1	
AW.102/T	**Washer**, Plain, on Setscrew		2	
C.18738	**Spring Striker**, operating Warning Light Switch	27- 4	1	
C.17415	**HANDBRAKE CABLE ASSEMBLY**		1	Fitted from Chassis No. 850001 to 850554. 875001 to 877566. 860001 to 860663. 885001 to 886262.
C.20401	**HANDBRAKE CABLE ASSEMBLY**	27- 5	1	Fitted to Chassis No. 850555 and subs. 877567 and subs. 860664 and subs. 886263 and subs.
J.105/10S	**Clevis Pin**, securing Handbrake Cable to Lever and Compensator	27- 6	2	
L.103/7U	**Split Pin**, retaining Clevis Pins		2	
FW.105/T	**Washer**, Plain, behind Split Pins		2	
C.17432	**Grommet**, in Propeller Shaft Tunnel, for Cable	27- 7	1	

HANDBRAKE CONTROL

Part No.	Description	Plate No.	No. per Unit	Remarks
C.18374	**HANDBRAKE COMPENSATOR ASSEMBLY, COMPLETE**		1	
C.18375	**Outer Lever Assembly,** complete with Link and Abutment Block		1	Fitted from Chassis No.
C.18383	**Inner Lever Assembly,** complete with Link		1	850001 to 850554.
C.18387	**Return Spring,** for Compensator Levers		1	875001 to 877566.
C.18389	**Pivot Bracket Assembly,** for mounting of Compensator		1	860001 to 860663.
L.103/7U	**Split Pin,** retaining Levers and Spring on Pivot Bracket		1	885001 to 886262.
FW.106/T	**Washer,** Plain, behind Split Pin		1	
C.18414	**Corrugated Washer,** behind Plain Washer		1	
C.20402	**HANDBRAKE COMPENSATOR ASSEMBLY, COMPLETE**	27- 8	1	
C.20403	**Outer Lever Assembly,** complete with Link and Abutment Block		1	Fitted to Chassis No.
C.20404	**Inner Lever Assembly,** complete with Link		1	850555 and subs.
C.18387	**Return Spring,** for Compensator Levers		1	877567 and subs.
C.20406	**Pivot Bracket Assembly,** for mounting of Compensator Levers		1	860664 and subs.
L.103/7U	**Split Pin,** retaining Levers and Spring on Pivot Bracket		1	886263 and subs.
FW.106/T	**Washer,** Plain, behind Split Pin		1	
C.18414	**Corrugated Washer,** behind Plain Washer		1	
UFS.131/5R	**Screw,** Set, securing Pivot Bracket to Rear Suspension Cross Member		2	
FG.105/X	**Washer,** Spring, on Setscrews		2	
J.105/10S	**Clevis Pin,** securing Compensator Links to Operating Lever on Handbrake Calipers	27- 9	2	
L.103/7U	**Split Pin,** retaining Clevis Pins		2	
FW.105/T	**Washer,** Plain, behind Split Pins		2	
C.14366	**ANCHOR SPRING, BETWEEN HANDBRAKE CABLE AND REAR BRAKE HOSE BRACKET ON BODY**		1	
C.1040/1	**Clip,** for fixing of Spring to Handbrake Cable		1	
UFS.119/3R	**Screw,** Set, through Clip		1	
AW.102/T	**Washer,** Plain, on Setscrew		1	
UFN.119/L	**Nut,** on Setscrew		1	
C.723/A	**Washer,** Shakeproof, under Nut		1	

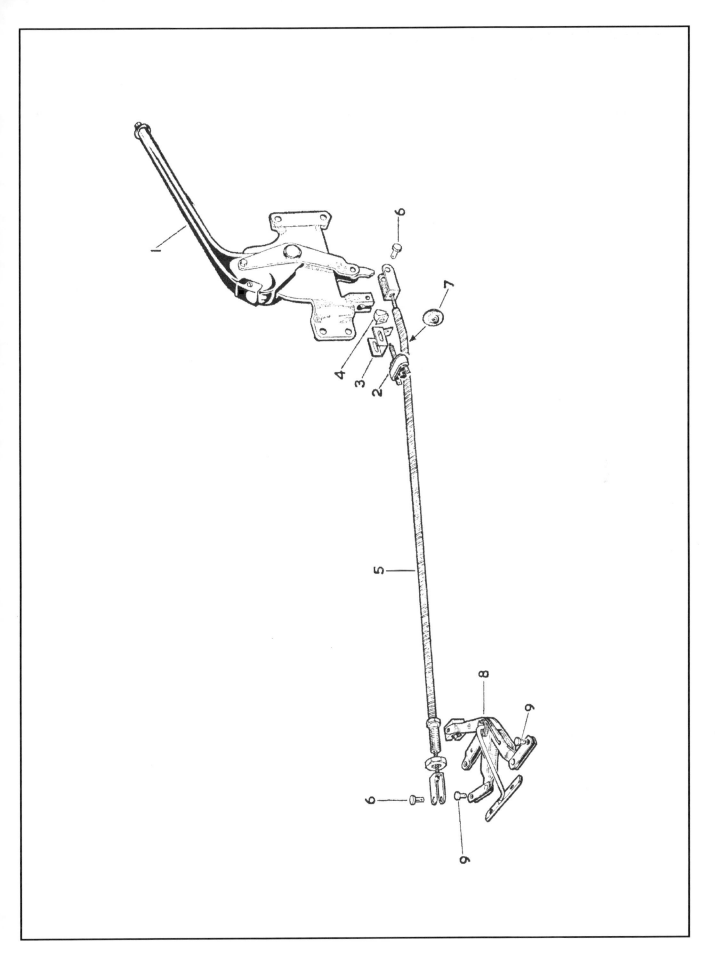

PLATE 27

HYDRAULIC BRAKE PIPES
(R.H. DRIVE CARS ONLY)

Part No.	Description	Plate No.	No. per Unit	Remarks
C.18617	RESERVOIR ASSEMBLY FOR BRAKE FLUID (COMPLETE WITH FILLER CAP AND LEVEL INDICATOR)	28– 1	2	Fitted from Chassis No. 850001 to 850555. 860001 to 860677.
C.18197	Filler Cap and Level Indicator	28–1A	2	
C.21896	RESERVOIR ASSEMBLY FOR BRAKE FLUID (COMPLETE WITH FILLER CAP AND LEVEL INDICATOR)		2	Fitted to Chassis No. 850556 and subs. 860678 and subs.
C.21889	Filler Cap and Level Indicator		2	
C.21890	Protective Cap over Indicator Plunger		2	
C.17476	BRACKET ASSEMBLY FOR MOUNTING OF FLUID RESERVOIRS	28– 2	1	Fitted from Chassis No. 850001 to 850555. 860001 to 860677.
UFS.125/4R	Screw, Set, clamping Reservoir Clips		3	
C.8667/1	Nut, Self-Locking, on Setscrews		3	
UFS.131/4R	Screw, Set, securing Bracket to Dash		2	
C.725	Washer, Shakeproof, on Setscrews		2	
C.20232	BRACKET FOR MOUNTING OF FLUID RESERVOIRS		1	
UFS.131/4R	Screw, Set, securing Brackets to Dash		2	
C.725	Washer, Shakeproof, on Setscrews		2	
				Fitted to Chassis No. 850556 and subs. 860678 and subs.
C.19497	CLAMP, SECURING RESERVOIRS TO BRACKET		2	
C.20235	Stud, securing Clamp		2	
C.8737/1	Nut, Self-Locking, on Studs		4	
C.6854	LOW PRESSURE HOSE FROM RESERVOIR TO PIPE	28– 3	2	
C.15886/5	Clip, securing Hose to Reservoirs	28– 4	2	
C.15886/4	Clip, securing Hose to Hydraulic Pipes	28– 5	2	

Part No.	Description	Plate No.	No. per Unit	Remarks
C.17385	**HYDRAULIC PIPE ASSEMBLY FROM HOSE TO FRONT BRAKES MASTER CYLINDER (LOWER) (VBO.7598)**	28– 6	1	
C.17387	**HYDRAULIC PIPE ASSEMBLY FROM HOSE TO REAR BRAKES MASTER CYLINDER (UPPER) (VBO.7597)**	28– 7	1	
C.17234	**BRAKE MASTER CYLINDER ASSEMBLY (LOWER) OPERATING FRONT BRAKES (VBM.4038)**	28– 8	1	
8528	Body only (VBM.4126)	28– 9	1	
8296	Seal, on Valve (VBO.4842)	28–10	1	
7676	Valve (VBO.3539)	28–11	1	
6943	Spring, on Valve (VBO.1410)	28–12	1	
8531	Spring Support, at front of Cylinder Body (VBM.4423)	28–13	1	Fitted from Chassis No. 850001 to 850254. 860001 to 860026.
8532	Main Spring (VBO.7008)	28–14	1	
8530	Spring Support at rear of Cylinder Body (VBO.7010)	28–15	1	
8533	Cup Seal, on Piston (VBO.8205)	28–16	1	
8529	Piston (VBO.7007)	28–17	1	
8536	Static Seal, on Piston (VBO.4998)	28–18	1	
8537	Push Rod Assembly (VBO.7173)	28–19	1	
8535	Circlip, retaining Push Rod in Cylinder Body (VBO.7024)	28–20	1	
8534	Dust Excluder, over end of Cylinder Body (VBO.7022)	28–21	1	
C.19967	**BRAKE MASTER CYLINDER ASSEMBLY (LOWER) OPERATING FRONT BRAKES (VBM.4705)**		1	Fitted to Chassis No. 850255 and subs. 860027 and subs.
8981	Spring Support, at rear of Cylinder Body (VBO.8599)		1	
8983	Piston (VBO.8612)		1	**C.19967 MAY BE USED TO REPLACE C.17234.**
	All other items are as for Master Cylinder C.17234.			
C.17235	**BRAKE MASTER CYLINDER ASSEMBLY (UPPER) OPERATING REAR BRAKES (VBM.4039)**	28–22	1	Fitted from Chassis No. 850001 to 850254. 860001 to 860026.
8539	Valve (VBO.7106)		1	
8538	Piston (VBO.7105)		1	
8540	Push Rod (VBO.7515)		1	
8541	Washer, on Push Rod (VBO.7023/1)		1	
8542	Locknut, on Push Rod (VBO.6054)		1	
	All other items are as for Master Cylinder C.17234.			

HYDRAULIC BRAKE PIPES
(R.H. DRIVE CARS ONLY)

Part No.	Description	Plate No.	No. per Unit	Remarks
C.19968	**BRAKE MASTER CYLINDER ASSEMBLY (UPPER) OPERATING REAR BRAKES (VBM.4706)**		1	
8981	**Spring Support,** at rear end of Cylinder Body (VBO.8599)		1	Fitted to Chassis No. 850255 and subs.
8539	**Valve** (VBO.7106)		1	860027 and subs.
8982	**Piston** (VBO.8600)		1	
8540	**Push Rod** (VBO.7515)		1	**C.19968 MAY BE USED TO REPLACE C.17235.**
8541	**Washer,** on Push Rod (VBO.7023/1)		1	
8542	**Locknut,** on Push Rod (VBO.6054)		1	
	All other items are as for Master Cylinder C.17234.			
8666	**REPAIR KIT FOR SERVICING OF BRAKE MASTER CYLINDERS (VBO.8062)** **(COMPRISING CUP SEAL, STATIC SEAL, VALVE SEAL, DUST EXCLUDER AND TUBE OF RUBBER GREASE)**		2	
UFS.131/8R	**Screw,** Set, securing Master Cylinders to Bracket on Pedal Housing		4	
C.8667/2	**Nut,** Self-Locking, on Setscrews		4	
C.17389	**HYDRAULIC PIPE ASSEMBLY FROM FRONT BRAKES MASTER CYLINDER TO 4-WAY UNION (VBO.7449)**	28–23	1	
C.17464	**4-WAY UNION (VBO.7301)**	28–24	1	
UFB.131/24R	**Bolt,** securing 4-Way Union to Cross Member		1	
C.8667/2	**Nut,** Self-Locking, on Bolt		1	
C.17391	**HYDRAULIC PIPE ASSEMBLY FROM 4-WAY UNION TO R.H. FRONT FLEXIBLE HOSE (VBO.7370)**	28–25	1	

Part No.	Description	Plate No.	No. per Unit	Remarks
C.17392	**HYDRAULIC PIPE ASSEMBLY FROM 4-WAY UNION TO L.H. FRONT FLEXIBLE HOSE (VBO.7372)**	28–26	1	
C.13182	**FRONT FLEXIBLE HOSE (WDO.22680/16½)**	28–27	2	
UFN.237/L	**Locknut,** securing ends of Flexible Hoses to Brackets on Front Frame and Stub Axle Carriers		4	
C.741	**Washer,** Shakeproof, under Locknuts		4	
C.17393	**HYDRAULIC PIPE ASSEMBLY FROM FRONT FLEXIBLE HOSE TO BRAKE CALIPER (VBO.7371)**	28–28	2	
C.17395	**HYDRAULIC PIPE ASSEMBLY FROM REAR BRAKES MASTER CYLINDER TO PIPE CONNECTOR (VBO.7450)**	28–29	1	
C.13187	**PIPE CONNECTOR (VBO.1766)**	28–30	1	
C.17459	**HYDRAULIC PIPE ASSEMBLY FROM PIPE CONNECTOR TO REAR FLEXIBLE HOSE (VBO.7373)**	28–31	1	
C.13188	**REAR FLEXIBLE HOSE (WDO.22681/13¾)**	28–32	1	
UFN.237/L	**Locknut,** securing Rear Flexible Hose to Bracket on Body		1	
C.741	**Washer,** Shakeproof, under Locknut		1	
C.11239	**Copper Gasket,** at connection of Hose to 3-Way Union (KL.44516)		1	

HYDRAULIC BRAKE PIPES
(R.H. DRIVE CARS ONLY)

Part No.	Description	Plate No.	No. per Unit	Remarks
C.18834	**3-WAY UNION (VBO.1227)**	28–33	1	
UFS.131/5R	**Screw,** Set, securing 3-Way Union to edge of Rear Suspension Cross Member		1	
UFN.131/L	**Nut,** on Setscrew		1	
C.740	**Washer,** Shakeproof, under Nut		1	
C.17397	**HYDRAULIC PIPE ASSEMBLY FROM 3-WAY UNION TO R.H. REAR CALIPER (VBO.7374)**	28–34	1	
C.17398	**HYDRAULIC PIPE ASSEMBLY FROM 3-WAY UNION TO L.H. REAR CALIPER (VBO.7375)**	28–35	1	
C.3727	**CLIP, SECURING HYDRAULIC PIPES**	28–36	2	
C.10268	**CLIP, SECURING HYDRAULIC PIPES**	28–37	4	

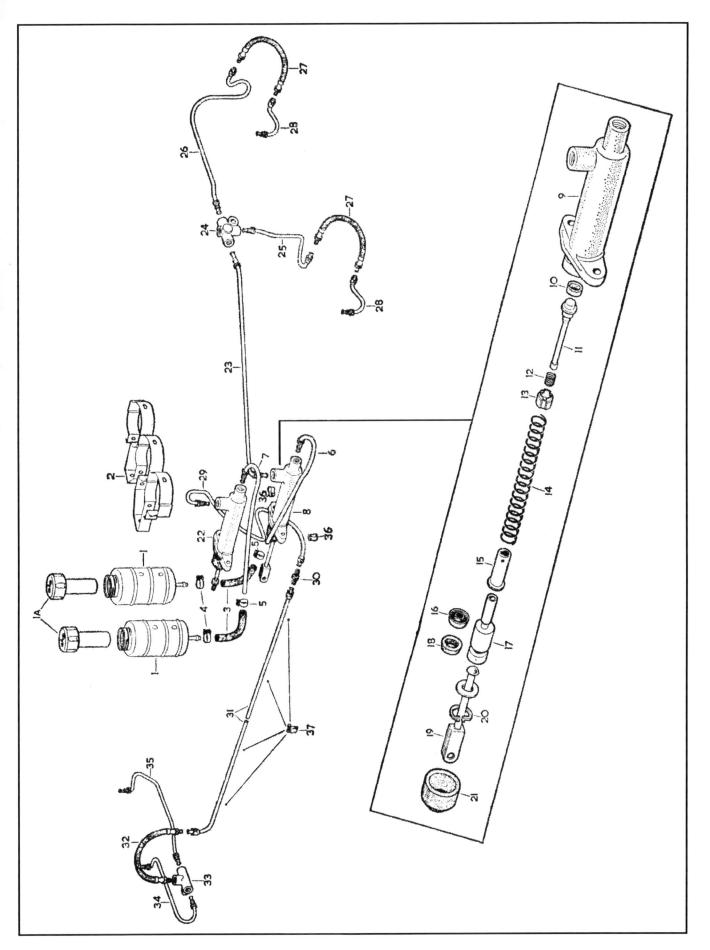

PLATE 28

HYDRAULIC BRAKE PIPES
(L.H. DRIVE CARS ONLY)

Part No.	Description	Plate No.	No. per Unit	Remarks
C.18617	RESERVOIR ASSEMBLY FOR BRAKE FLUID (COMPLETE WITH FILLER CAP AND LEVEL INDICATOR)	29- 1	2	Fitted from Chassis No. 875001 to 877556. 885001 to 886282.
C.18197	Filler Cap and Level Indicator	29–1A	2	
C.21896	RESERVOIR ASSEMBLY FOR BRAKE FLUID (COMPLETE WITH FILLER CAP AND LEVEL INDICATOR)		2	Fitted to Chassis No. 877557 and subs. 886283 and subs.
C.21889	Filler Cap and Level Indicator		2	
C.21890	Protective Cap over Indicator Plunger		2	
C.18693	BRACKET ASSEMBLY FOR MOUNTING OF FLUID RESERVOIRS	29- 2	1	Fitted from Chassis No. 875001 to 877556. 885001 to 886282.
UFS.125/4R	Screw, Set, clamping Reservoir Clips		3	
C.8667/1	Nut, Self-Locking, on Setscrews		3	
C.20234	BRACKET FOR MOUNTING OF FLUID RESERVOIRS		1	Fitted to Chassis No. 877557 and subs. 886283 and subs.
C.19497	CLAMP, SECURING RESERVOIRS TO BRACKET		2	
C.20235	Stud, securing Clamp		2	
C.8737/1	Nut, Self-Locking, on Studs		4	
C.17812	BRACKET ASSEMBLY, FOR FIXING OF RESERVOIR BRACKET TO L.H. SIDE MEMBER	29- 3	2	
C.17811	Clamping Piece, for Brackets	29- 4	2	
UFS.125/9R	Screw, Set, through Clamps		2	
UFN.125/L	Nut, on Setscrews		2	
C.724	Washer, Shakeproof, under Nuts		2	
C.18695	SHIELD ASSEMBLY, PROTECTING RESERVOIRS FROM EXHAUST HEAT	29- 5	1	
UFS.131/7R	Screw, Set, securing Shield and Reservoir Bracket to Fixing Bracket		4	
C.18698	Spacer, on Setscrews		4	
FW.105/T	Washer, Plain, on Setscrews		8	Fitted from Chassis No. 875001 to 877556. 885001 to 886282.
UFN.131/L	Nut, on Setscrews		4	
C.725	Washer, Shakeproof, under Nut		4	
FW.105/T	Washer, Plain, on Setscrews		6	Fitted to Chassis No. 877557 and subs. 886283 and subs.
UFN.131/L	Nut, on Setscrews		2	
C.725	Washer, Shakeproof, on Setscrews		4	
C.21255	Nut Retainer Clip		2	

Part No.	Description	Plate No.	No. per Unit	Remarks
C.18717	**LOW PRESSURE HOSE FROM RESERVOIR TO PIPE**	29– 6	2	
C.15886/5	**Clip,** securing Hose to Reservoirs	29– 7	2	
C.15886/4	**Clip,** securing Hose to Hydraulic Pipes	29– 8	2	
C.18715	**HYDRAULIC PIPE ASSEMBLY FROM HOSE TO FRONT BRAKES MASTER CYLINDER (LOWER)**	29– 9	1	
C.18714	**HYDRAULIC PIPE ASSEMBLY FROM HOSE TO REAR BRAKES MASTER CYLINDER (UPPER)**	29–10	1	
C.17234	**BRAKE MASTER CYLINDER ASSEMBLY (LOWER) OPERATING FRONT BRAKES (VBM.4038)**	29–11	1	
8528	**Body only** (VBM.4126)	29–12	1	
8296	**Seal,** on Valve (VBO.4842)	29–13	1	
7676	**Valve** (VBO.3539)	29–14	1	
6943	**Spring,** on Valve (VBO.1410)	29–15	1	
8531	**Spring Support,** at forward end of Cylinder Body (VBM.4423)	29–16	1	Fitted from Chassis No. 875001 to 876014. 885001 to 885155.
8532	**Main Spring** (VBO.7008)	29–17	1	
8530	**Spring Support,** at rear end of Cylinder Body (VBO.7010)	29–18	1	
8533	**Cup Seal,** on Piston (VBO.8205)	29–19	1	
8529	**Piston** (VBO.7007)	29–20	1	
8536	**Static Seal,** on Piston (VBO.4998)	29–21	1	
8537	**Push Rod Assembly** (VBO.7173)	29–22	1	
8535	**Circlip,** retaining Push Rod in Cylinder Body (VBO.7024)	29–23	1	
8534	**Dust Excluder,** over end of Cylinder Body (VBO.7022)	29–24	1	
C.19967	**BRAKE MASTER CYLINDER ASSEMBLY (LOWER) OPERATING FRONT BRAKES (VBM.4705)**		1	Fitted to Chassis No. 876015 and subs. 885156 and subs.
8981	**Spring Support,** at rear end of Cylinder Body (VBO.8599)		1	**C.19967 MAY BE USED TO REPLACE C.17234.**
8983	**Piston** (VBO.8612)		1	
	All other items are as for Master Cylinder C.17234.			
C.17235	**BRAKE MASTER CYLINDER ASSEMBLY (UPPER) OPERATING REAR BRAKES (VBM.4039)**	29–25	1	
8539	**Valve** (VBO.7106)		1	Fitted from Chassis No. 875001 to 876014. 885001 to 885155.
8538	**Piston** (VBO.7105)		1	
8540	**Push Rod** (VBO.7515)		1	
8541	**Washer,** on Push Rod (VBO.7023/1)		1	
8542	**Locknut,** on Push Rod (VBO.6054)		1	
	All other items are as for Master Cylinder C.17234			

HYDRAULIC BRAKE PIPES
(L.H. DRIVE CARS ONLY)

Part No.	Description	Plate No.	No. per Unit	Remarks
C.19968	**BRAKE MASTER CYLINDER ASSEMBLY (UPPER) OPERATING REAR BRAKES (VBM.4706)**		1	Fitted to Chassis No. 876015 and subs. 885156 and subs.
8981	**Spring Support,** at rear end of Cylinder Body (VBO.8599)		1	
8539	**Valve** (VBO.7106)		1	**C.19968 MAY BE USED TO REPLACE C.17235.**
8982	**Piston** (VBO.8600)		1	
8540	**Push Rod** (VBO.7515)		1	
8541	**Washer,** on Push Rod (VBO.7023/1)		1	
8542	**Locknut,** on Push Rod (VBO.6054)		1	
	All other items are as for Master Cylinder C.17234.			
8666	**REPAIR KIT FOR SERVICING OF BRAKE MASTER CYLINDERS (VBO.8062) (COMPRISING CUP SEAL, STATIC SEAL, VALVE SEAL, DUST EXCLUDER AND TUBE OF RUBBER GREASE**		2	
UFS.131/8R	**Screw,** Set, securing Master Cylinders to Bracket on Pedal Housing		4	
C.8667/2	**Nut,** Self-Locking, on Setscrews		4	
C.17390	**HYDRAULIC PIPE ASSEMBLY FROM FRONT BRAKES MASTER CYLINDER TO 4-WAY UNION (VBO. 7449)**	29–26	1	
C.17464	**4-WAY UNION (VBO.7301)**	29–27	1	
UFB.131/24R	**Bolt,** securing 4-Way Union to Front Frame Cross Member		1	
C.8667/2	**Nut,** Self-Locking, on Bolt		1	
C.17465	**HYDRAULIC PIPE ASSEMBLY FROM 4-WAY UNION TO R.H. FRONT FLEXIBLE HOSE (VBO.7651)**	29–28	1	
C.17466	**HYDRAULIC PIPE ASSEMBLY FROM 4-WAY UNION TO L.H. FRONT FLEXIBLE HOSE (VBO.7650)**	29–29	1	

Part No.	Description	Plate No.	No. per Unit	Remarks
C.13182	**FRONT FLEXIBLE HOSE (WDO.22680/16½)**	29–30	2	
UFN.237/L	Locknut, securing ends of Flexible Hoses to Brackets on Front Frame and Stub Axle Carriers		4	
C.741	Washer, Shakeproof, under Locknuts		4	
C.17393	**HYDRAULIC PIPE ASSEMBLY FROM FRONT FLEXIBLE HOSES TO BRAKE CALIPER (VBO.7371)**	29–31	2	
C.17396	**HYDRAULIC PIPE ASSEMBLY FROM REAR BRAKES MASTER CYLINDER TO PIPE CONNECTOR (VBO.7643)**	29–32	1	
C.13187	**PIPE CONNECTOR (VBO.1766)**	29–33	1	
C.17459	**HYDRAULIC PIPE ASSEMBLY FROM PIPE CONNECTOR TO REAR FLEXIBLE HOSE (VBO.7373)**	29–34	1	
C.13188	**REAR FLEXIBLE HOSE (WDO.22681/13¾)**	29–35	1	
UFN.237/L	Locknut, securing Rear Flexible Hose to Bracket on Body		1	
C.741	Washer, Shakeproof, under Locknut		1	
C.11239	Copper Gasket, at connection of Hose to 3-Way Union (KL.44516)		1	

HYDRAULIC BRAKE PIPES

(L.H. DRIVE CARS ONLY)

Part No.	Description	Plate No.	No. per Unit	Remarks
C.18834	**3-WAY UNION (VBO.1227)**	29–36	1	
UFS.131/5R	**Screw,** Set, securing 3-Way Union to edge of Rear Suspension Cross Member		1	
UFN.131/L	**Nut,** on Setscrew		1	
C.740	**Washer,** Shakeproof, under Nut		1	
C.17824	**HYDRAULIC PIPE ASSEMBLY FROM 3-WAY UNION TO R.H. REAR CALIPER (VBO.7653)**	29–37	1	
C.17825	**HYDRAULIC PIPE ASSEMBLY FROM 3-WAY UNION TO L.H. REAR CALIPER (VBO.7654)**	29–38	1	
C.5023	**CLIP, SECURING HYDRAULIC PIPES**	29–39	4	
C.18461	**EDGE CLIP, SECURING HYDRAULIC PIPES**	29–40	2	

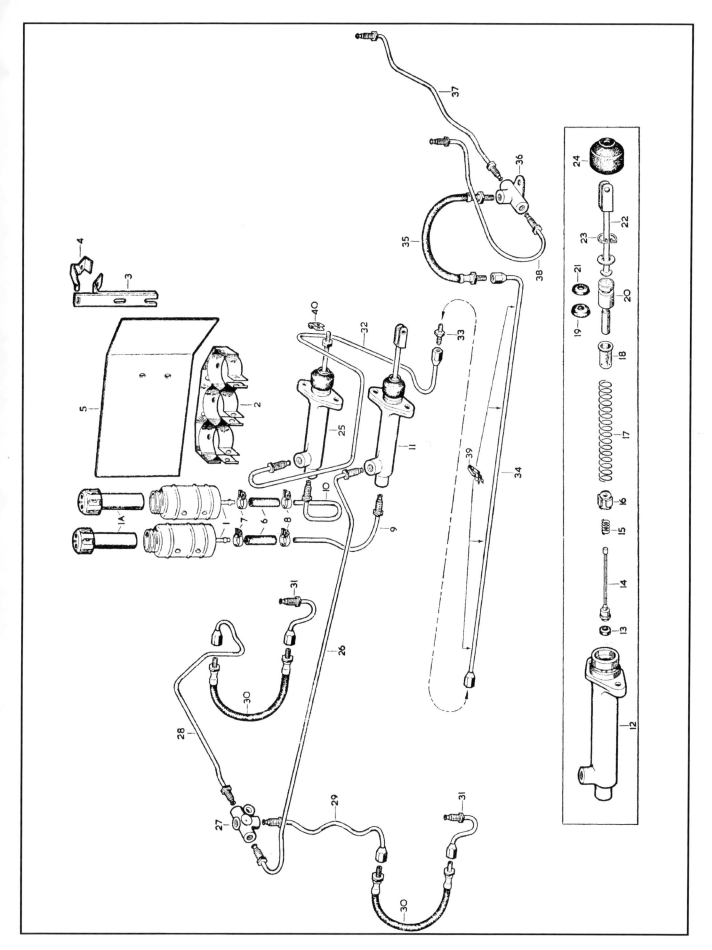

PLATE 29

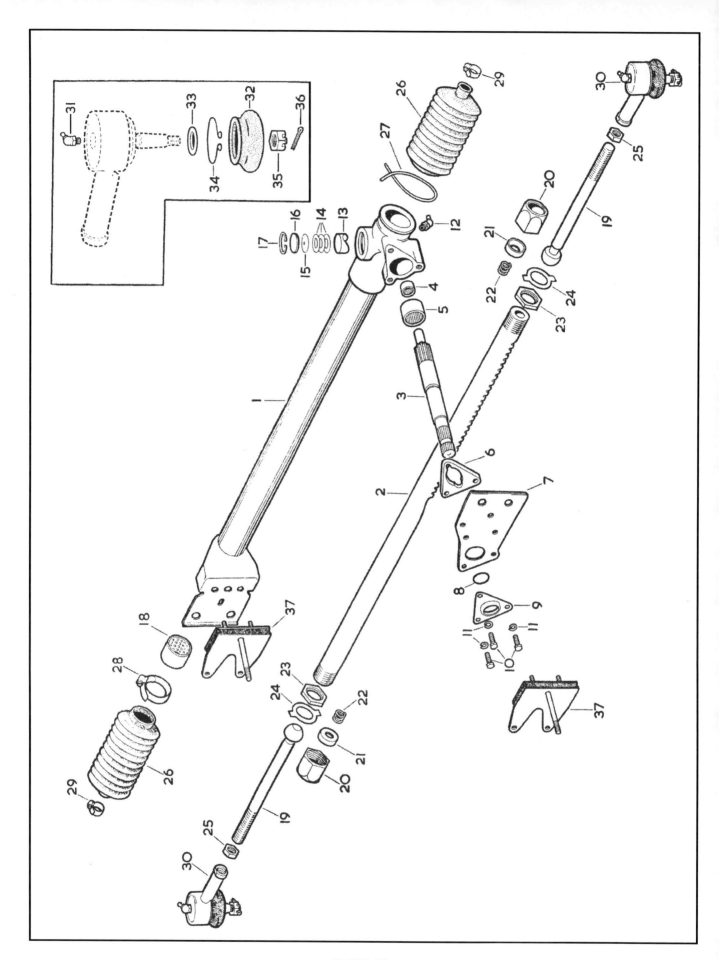

PLATE 30

Part No.	Description	Plate No.	No. per Unit	Remarks
C.15380	**RACK & PINION ASSEMBLY, COMPLETE**		1	**R.H. DRIVE CARS ONLY.**
C.15381	**RACK & PINION ASSEMBLY, COMPLETE**		1	**L.H. DRIVE CARS ONLY.**
C.15191	**Housing Assembly,** for Rack and Pinion	30– 1	1	**R.H. DRIVE CARS ONLY.**
C.15192	**Housing Assembly,** for Rack and Pinion		1	**L.H. DRIVE CARS ONLY.**
C.15093	**Rack only**	30– 2	1	
C.15094	**Pinion only**	30– 3	1	
C.15203	**Bearing** (Torrington M.8121) supporting lower end of Pinion	30– 4	1	
C.15204	**Bearing** (Torrington B.1516) supporting upper end of Pinion	30– 5	1	
C.15205	**Thrust Plate,** retaining Pinion	30– 6	1	
C.15206	**Attachment Bracket,** for fixing of Rack and Pinion to Mounting	30– 7	1	**R.H. DRIVE CARS ONLY.**
C.15207	**Attachment Bracket,** for fixing of Rack and Pinion to Mounting		1	**L.H. DRIVE CARS ONLY.**
C.15208	**'O' Ring,** at upper end of Pinion	30– 8	1	
C.15209	**Retainer,** for 'O' Ring	30– 9	1	
UFS.131/7R	**Screw,** Set, securing Thrust Plate, Attachment Bracket and 'O' Ring Retainer to Rack and Pinion Housing	30–10	2	Fitted from Chassis No. 850001 to 850499. 875001 to 877275. 860001 to 860425. 885001 to 886045.
FG.105/X	**Washer,** Spring, on Setscrews	30–11	2	
C.18965	**Screw** (Allen Head) securing Thrust Plate, Attachment Bracket and 'O' Ring Retainer to Rack and Pinion Housing		1	Fitted from Chassis No. 850001 to 850558. 875001 to 877578. 860001 to 860691. 885001 to 886305.
C.725	**Washer,** Shakeproof, on Allen Head Screw		1	
C.20107	**Stud,** in Pinion Housing, securing Thrust Plate, Attachment Bracket and 'O' Ring Retainer to Rack and Pinion Housing		2	Fitted from Chassis No. 850500 to 850558. 877276 to 877578. 860426 to 860691. 886046 to 886305.
C.8737/2	**Nut,** Self-Locking, on Studs		2	3 off each fitted to Chassis No. 850559 and subs. 877579 and subs. 860692 and subs. 886306 and subs.
C.3363/1	**Grease Nipple,** on Rack and Pinion Housing	30–12	1	
C.15197	**Plunger,** at top of Housing, applying Friction to Rack	30–13	1	Fitted from Chassis No. 850001 to 850403. 875001 to 876846. 860001 to 860231. 875001 to 885735.
C.20145	**Plunger,** at top of Housing, applying Friction to Rack		1	Fitted to Chassis No. 850404 and subs. 876847 and subs. 860232 and subs. 885736 and subs.
C.15199	**Shim** (.004" thick) at top of Plunger	30–14	As req'd	
C.15198	**Shim** (.010" thick) at top of Plunger	30–14	As req'd	
C.15200	**Plate Spring,** under Cover	30–15	1	Fitted from Chassis No. 850001 to 850403. 875001 to 876846. 860001 to 860231. 885001 to 885735.
C.15201	**Cover,** retaining Plunger Shims and Plate Spring	30–16	1	
C.20146	**Plate Spring,** under Cover		1	Fitted to Chassis No. 850404 and subs. 876847 and subs. 860232 and subs. 885736 and subs.
C.20147	**Cover,** retaining Plunger Shims and Plate Spring		1	
C 15202	**Circlip,** securing Cover	30–17	1	
C.15210	**Bush,** in Tube, for Rack	30–18	1	
C.15418	**Ball Pin and Tie Rod,** at ends of Rack	30–19	2	
C.10026	**Housing,** for Ball Pins	30–20	2	
C.7599	**Socket,** under Ball Pins	30–21	2	
C.8472	**Spring,** behind Sockets	30–22	2	
C.15407	**Nut,** locking Ball Pin Housings to Rack	30–23	2	
C.15408	**Tab Washer,** locking Nuts	30–24	2	
C.15409	**Nut,** locking Tie Rod Ends to Tie Rods	30–25	2	
C.6623	**Bellows,** at each end of Rack and Pinion Housing	30–26	2	
C.15211	**Tie Wire,** securing Bellows at pinion end of Housing	30–27	1	
C.2905/4	**Clip,** securing Bellows to Rack Tube	30–28	1	**FITTED AT L.H. SIDE ON R.H. DRIVE CARS AND R.H. SIDE ON L.H. DRIVE CARS.**
C.2905/2	**Clip,** securing Bellows to Ball Pins	30–29	2	
C.15410	**End Assembly,** for Tie Rods	30–30	2	

STEERING UNIT

Part No.	Description	Plate No.	No. per Unit	Remarks
C.15410	**END ASSEMBLY FOR TIE RODS**	30–30	2	
C.3363/1	**Grease Nipple,** for lubrication of Ball Joint in Tie Rod Ends	30–31	2	
C.15414	**Gaiter,** protecting Ball Joints	30–32	2	
C.15416	**Retainer,** inside Gaiters	30–33	2	
C.15415	**Clip,** securing Gaiter to Tie Rod Ends	30–34	2	
UFN.450/L	**Slotted Nut,** securing Tie Rod Ends to Tie Rod Levers	30–35	2	
L.104/10U	**Split Pin,** retaining Slotted Nuts	30–36	2	
C.15092	**RUBBER MOUNTING FOR RACK AND PINION ASSEMBLY**	30–37	2	Fitted from Chassis No. 850001 to 850558. 875001 to 877578. 860001 to 860691. 885001 to 886305.
C.20087	**RUBBER MOUNTING FOR RACK AND PINION ASSEMBLY**		2	Fitted to Chassis No. 850559 and subs. 877579 and subs. 860692 and subs. 886306 and subs.
UFS.131/6R	**Screw,** Set, securing Rack and Pinion Assembly to Rubber Mountings		2	
UFS.131/24R	**Screw,** Set, securing Rubber Mounting to Front Frame Cross Member		1	FITTED AT R.H. SIDE ON R.H. DRIVE CARS AND L.H. SIDE ON L.H. DRIVE CARS.
UFB.131/13R	**Bolt,** securing Rubber Mounting to Front Frame Cross Member		1	
C.18901	**Distance Tube,** on Bolt and Setscrew		2	
C.15183	**Washer,** Special, on Bolt and Setscrew		2	
UFS.131/24R	**Screw,** Set, securing Rubber Mounting to Front Frame Cross Member		1	FITTED AT R.H. SIDE ON L.H. DRIVE CARS AND L.H. SIDE ON R.H. DRIVE CARS.
UFS.131/12R	**Screw,** Set, securing Rubber Mounting to Front Frame Cross Member		1	
UFN.131/L	**Nut,** locking Setscrews		2	
C.725	**Washer,** Shakeproof, under Nuts		2	
C.15183	**Washer,** Special, under head of Setscrews		2	
C.8667/2	**Nut,** Self-Locking, on Bolts and Setscrews and on Studs of Rubber Mountings		12	

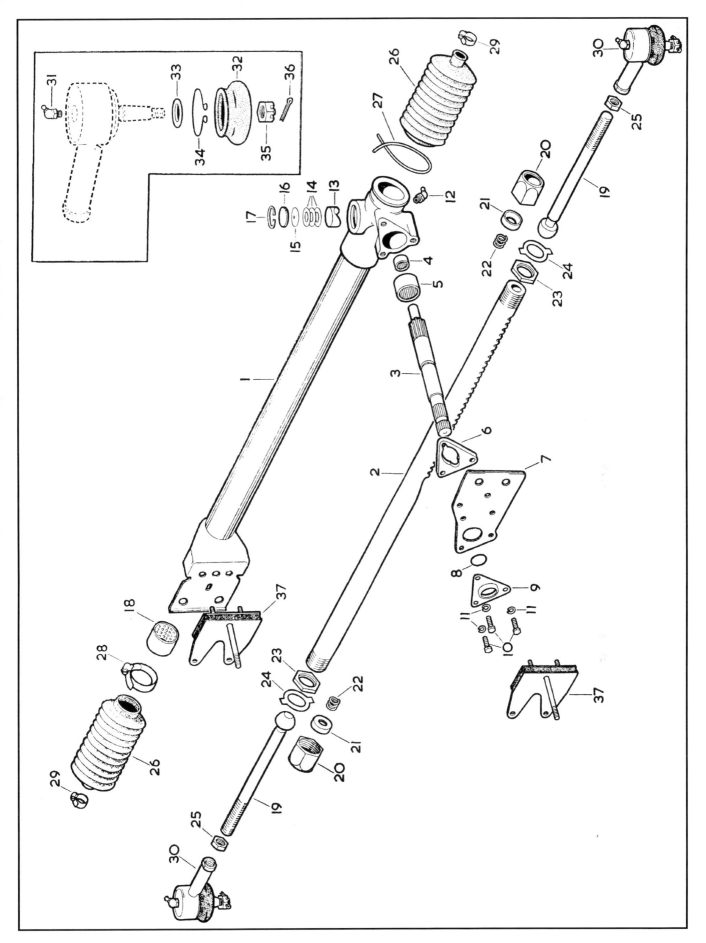

PLATE 30

143

STEERING COLUMN

Part No.	Description	Plate No.	No. per Unit	Remarks
C.17759	**UPPER STEERING COLUMN ASSEMBLY**		1	
C.17648	**Outer Tube Assembly**	31– 1	1	
C.15179	**Inner Column**, Female	31– 2	1	
C.19131	**Felt Bearing**, upper	31– 3	1	Fitted from Chassis No.
C.13855	**Felt Bearing**, lower	31– 4	1	850001 to 850587.
C.10790	**Washer**, retaining Felt Bearings	31– 5	4	875001 to 878036.
C.10788	**Spring Clip**, retaining Washers	31– 6	2	860001 to 860862.
C.15619	**Inner Column**, Male	31– 7	1	885001 to 886753.
C.16676	**Stop Button**, for Male Inner Column	31– 8	1	
C.15419	**Locknut**, clamping Male Inner Column on Telescopic Device	31– 9	1	**SEE EXPORT GERMANY C.20157.**
8671	**Split Collet**, inside Locknut (complete with Circlip C.18235)	31–10	1	
C.18235	**Circlip**, for Split Collet	31–11	1	
C.20157	**UPPER STEERING COLUMN ASSEMBLY**		1	
C.20158	**Outer Tube Assembly**		1	
C.20160	**Inner Column**, Female		1	
C.20090	**Bearing**, Upper (Vulkollan)		1	**EXPORT GERMANY.**
C.20091	**Bearing**, Lower (Vulkollan)		1	
C.15619	**Inner Column**, Male		1	Fitted from Chassis No.
C.16676	**Stop Button**, for Male Inner Column		1	876665 to 878036.
C.15419	**Locknut**, clamping Male Inner Column on Telescopic Device		1	885567 to 886753.
8671	**Split Collet**, inside Locknut (complete with Circlip C.18235)		1	
C.18235	**Circlip**, for Split Collet		1	
C.20239	**Lock and Ignition Switch Assembly** (Neiman)		1	
C.20557	**UPPER STEERING COLUMN ASSEMBLY**		1	
C.20558	**Outer Tube Assembly**		1	
C.20160	**Inner Column**, Female		1	
C.20090	**Bearing**, Upper (Vulkollan)		1	
C.20091	**Bearing**, Lower (Vulkollan)		1	Fitted to Chassis No.
C.15619	**Inner Column**, Male		1	850588 and subs.
C.16676	**Stop Button**, for Male Inner Column		1	878037 and subs.
C.15419	**Locknut**, clamping Male Inner Column on Telescopic Device		1	860863 and subs.
8671	**Split Collet**, inside Locknut (complete with Circlip C.18235)		1	886754 and subs.
C.18235	**Circlip**, for Split Collet		1	
C.20171	**Lock and Ignition Switch Assembly** (Waso Werkin)		1	
C.16884	**HORN SLIP RING ASSEMBLY** (38274/A)		1	
C.16876	**Contact Pin Assembly** (54300581)	31–12	1	
C.16879	**Insulating Bush**, upper, for Contact Pin (54300814)	31–13	1	
C.16880	**Spring**, under Insulating Bush (324866)	31–14	1	
C.16881	**Washer**, under Spring (143276)	31–15	1	
C.16882	**Insulating Bush**, lower, for Contact Pin (54300582)	31–16	1	
C.16886	**Contact Nipple**, between Pin and Slip Ring (54300584)	31–17	1	
C.16887	**Spring**, for Nipple (54300585)	31–18	1	
8400	**Rotor Assembly** (comprising top and bottom Rotors) (54300829)	31–19	1	
C.10317	**Slip Ring only** (348276)	31–20	1	
C.17685	**Sleeve**, insulating lower end of Contact Pin from Female Inner Column	31–21	1	

Part No.	Description	Plate No.	No. per Unit	Remarks
C.8157	**CONTACT ASSEMBLY FOR HORN SLIP RING (348262/A)**		1	
C.8158	**Contact Holder** (348269)	31–22	2	
C.8159	**Contact** (348268)	31–23	1	
C.8161	**Bolt,** securing Contact to Holders (139444)	31–24	1	
C.8160	**Nut,** on Bolts (348270)	31–25	1	
C.10650	**Sleeve,** insulating Contacts (348272)	31–26	1	
C.13024	**Insulating Strip** (Fibre) protecting Contact from above (348486)	31–27	1	
C.12194	**Eyelet,** for Cable connection to Earth Contact (188818)		1	
C.11746	**EARTH CONTACT FOR OPERATION OF HORN (348313)**	31–28	1	
UCS.313/3H	**Screw,** Set, securing Contacts to Bracket on Outer Tube		1	
UCN.113/L	**Nut,** on Setscrew		1	
C.721	**Washer,** Shakeproof, under Nut		1	
C.16069	**DIRECTION INDICATOR CONTROL ASSEMBLY (34361-37.SA)**	31–29	1	
C.16451	**STRIKER FOR RETURN OF DIRECTION INDICATOR TO NEUTRAL POSITION (54332927)**	31–30	1	
C.14007/1	**Screw,** Set, securing Striker		2	
C.723/A	**Washer,** Shakeproof, on Setscrews		2	
C.3377	**Washer,** Plain, under Shakeproof Washers		2	
C.15168	**STEERING WHEEL ASSEMBLY (16″)**	31–31	1	**SUPERSEDED BY C.20267.**
C.20267	**STEERING WHEEL ASSEMBLY (16″)**		1	**SUPERSEDES C.15168.**
C.18304	**Grub Screw,** in Hub of Steering Wheel	31–32	3	
C.7878	**Split Cone,** on Male Inner Column, for seating of Steering Wheel	31–33	2 halves	
C.7879	**Nut,** securing Steering Wheel to Male Inner Column	31–34	1	
C.15885	**Washer,** Plain, under Nut	31–35	1	
C.11820/7	**Palnut,** locking Nut	31–36	1	
C.17684	**BRACKET, UPPER, MOUNTING UPPER STEERING COLUMN TO DASH**	31–37	1	
UFS.131/4R	**Screw,** Set, securing Bracket to Dash		4	
FG.105/X	**Washer,** Spring, on Setscrews		4	
UFB.125/18R	**Bolt,** securing Upper Steering Column in Bracket and for locking of Steering Wheel Rake adjustment		1	
C.17815	**Spacing Tube,** on Bolt		1	
C.8667/1	**Nut,** Self-Locking, on Bolt		1	
BD.541/20	**Washer,** Plain, under Nut		1	

STEERING COLUMN

Part No.	Description	Plate No.	No. per Unit	Remarks
C.15181	**BRACKET, LOWER, MOUNTING UPPER STEERING COLUMN TO DASH**	31–38	1	
UFS.131/6R	**Screw,** Set, securing Bracket to Dash		4	
FG.105/X	**Washer,** Spring, on Setscrews		4	
UFB.131/12R	**Bolt,** through Bracket, pivoting Upper Steering Column for Rake Adjustment		2	
C.15183	**Plain Washer,** under head of Bolts		2	
C.15182	**Rubber Bush,** on Bolts		2	
C.8667/2	**Nut,** Self-Locking, on Bolts		2	
C.15163	**LOWER STEERING COLUMN ASSEMBLY**	31–39	1	Fitted from Chassis No. 850001 to 850547. 875001 to 877487. 860001 to 860646. 885001 to 886213.
C.17437	Universal Joint Assembly, at lower end of Steering Column		1	**C.17437 NOT SUPPLIED**
C.20487	**LOWER STEERING COLUMN ASSEMBLY (O1/500973)**		1	Fitted to Chassis No. 850548 and subs. 877488 and subs. 860647 and subs. 886214 and subs.
C.17437	Universal Joint Assembly, at lower end of Steering Column		1	**C.17437 NOT SUPPLIED**
C.17469	**Screw,** Allen Head, securing lower Universal Joint to Pinion Shaft		1	
FG.104/X	**Washer,** Spring, on Screw		1	
UFB.131/14R	**Bolt,** securing upper Universal Joint to lower and upper Steering Columns		2	
UFN.131/L	**Nut,** on Bolts		2	
FG.105/X	**Washer,** Spring, under Nuts		2	
C.17437	**UNIVERSAL JOINT ASSEMBLY AT LOWER END OF LOWER STEERING COLUMN (SK.3377/B)**		1	**ASSEMBLY NOT SUPPLIED. USE INDIVIDUAL ITEMS.**
8699	**End Yoke,** for Universal Joint (KO.5-4-GB.1373)	31–40	1	
5426	**Journal Assembly** for Universal Joint (KO.5-GB.1)	31–41	1	
C.15180	**UNIVERSAL JOINT ASSEMBLY AT UPPER END OF LOWER STEERING COLUMN (SK.2938/F)**	31–42	1	
8700	**End Yoke,** for Universal Joint (KO. 5-4-GB.1151)	31–43	2	
5426	**Journal Assembly,** connecting Yokes (KO. 5-GB.1)	31–44	1	

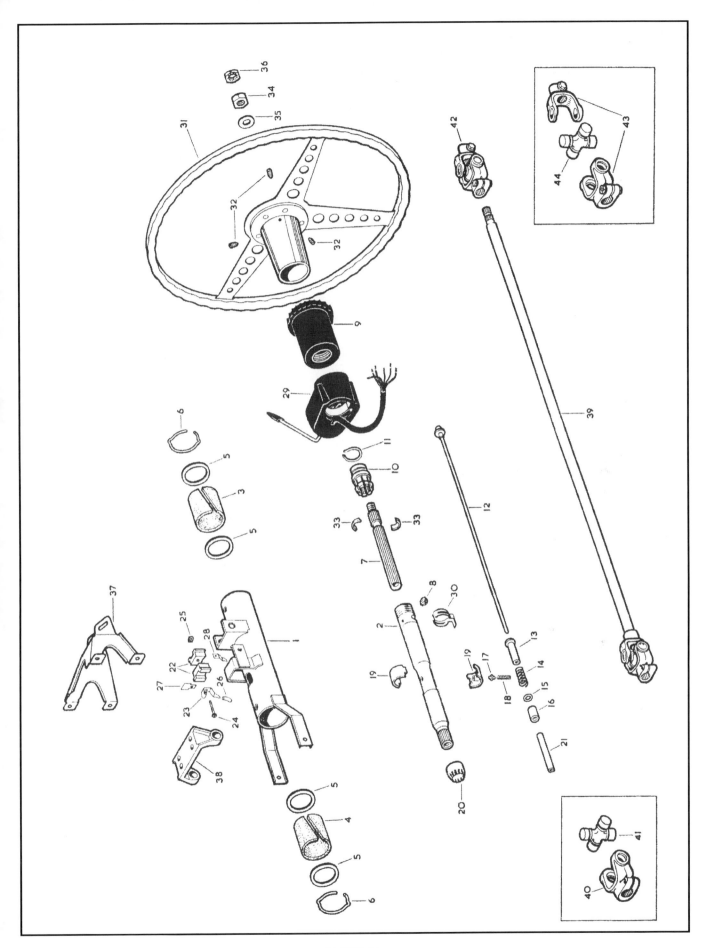

PLATE 31

COOLING SYSTEM

Part No.	Description	Plate No.	No. per Unit	Remarks
C.16770	**RADIATOR BLOCK ASSEMBLY**	32– 1	1	
C.8975	**Rubber Mounting Pad,** for Radiator Block	32– 2	4	
C.18283	**Distance Collar,** through Pads	32– 3	2	
C.8737/3	**Nut,** securing Radiator Block to Front Sub-Frame		2	
BD.541/2	**Washer,** Plain, under Nuts		2	
C.16764	**Tie Bar,** R.H., between Radiator Block and Header Tank Support Bracket	32– 4	1	
C.16765	**Tie Bar,** L.H., between Radiator Block and Header Tank Support Bracket	32– 5	1	
C.16766	**Distance Piece,** under forward end of Tie Bars	32– 6	2	
C.8737/2	**Nut,** Self-Locking, securing Tie Bars to Radiator Block		2	
C.2354	**DRAIN TAP FOR RADIATOR BLOCK**	32– 7	1	
C.316	**Fibre Washer,** on Drain Tap	32– 8	As req'd	
C.16998	**RADIATOR HEADER TANK ASSEMBLY**	32– 9	1	Fitted from Chassis No. 850001 to 850656.
C.18460	**Filler Cap** (4 lbs. pressure)	32–10	1	875001 to 879043. 860001 to 861090. 885001 to 888240.
C.21512	**RADIATOR HEADER TANK ASSEMBLY**		1	Fitted to Chassis No. 850657 and subs.
C.18485	**Filler Cap** (9 lbs. pressure)		1	879044 and subs. 861091 and subs.
BD.4052/1	**Rubber Overflow Pipe,** for Header Tank	32–11	1	888241 and subs.
C.16768	**BRACKET ASSEMBLY SUPPORTING HEADER TANK**	32–12	1	
C.8975	**Rubber Mounting Pad,** for Support Bracket	32–13	4	
C.8976	**Distance Collar,** through Pads	32–14	2	
UFB.137/10R	**Bolt,** securing Support Bracket to Cross Member		2	
BD.541/2	**Washer,** Plain, on Bolts		2	
UFS.131/5R	**Screw,** Set, securing Header Tank to Support Bracket and securing Radiator Tie Bars		2	
UFS.131/6R	**Screw,** Set, securing Header Tank to Support Bracket and securing Radiator Tie Bars		1	
C.8667/2	**Nut,** Self-locking, on Setscrews		3	

Part No.	Description	Plate No.	No. per Unit	Remarks
C.18559	**THERMOSTAT, IN HEADER TANK, CONTROLLING ELECTRIC COOLING FAN**	32–15	1	
C.2475	**Gasket,** under Thermostat	32–16	1	
UFS.419/4H	**Screw,** Set, securing Thermostat		3	
AW102/E	**Washer,** on Setscrews		3	
C.16687	**COOLING FAN ASSEMBLY**	32–17	1	
C.8667/1	**Nut,** Self-Locking, securing Fan to Motor		1	
FW.104/T	**Washer,** Plain, under Nut		1	
C.16452	**ELECTRIC MOTOR, DRIVING FAN (LUCAS 78378/B)**	32–18	1	
C.18110	**Grommet,** in Mounting Bracket	32–19	4	
C.18123	**Washer,** under Grommets	32–20	4	
C.8667/17	**Nut,** Self-Locking, securing Electric Motor to Mounting Bracket on Cross Member		4	
C.18111	**Washer,** Plain, under Nuts		4	
C.18109	**COWL, SURROUNDING COOLING FAN**	32–21	1	
C.18107/1	**Sealing Strip** (Polyurethane) at top and bottom of Cowl	32–22	2	
C.18106	**Sealing Strip** (Polyurethane) at L.H. Side of Cowl	32–23	1	
C.18108	**Sealing Strip** (Polyurethane) at R.H. Side of Cowl	32–24	1	
UFB.125/8R	**Bolt,** securing Cowl to Radiator Tie Bars		2	
C.15712	**Distance Piece,** between Cowl and Tie Bars		2	
C.8667/1	**Nut,** Self-Locking, on Bolts		2	
FW.104/T	**Washer,** Plain, under Nuts		2	
C.18105	**Bracket,** under Radiator Block, for mounting of Cowl and Duct Shield		2	
UFS.125/6R	**Screw,** Set, securing Cowl to Bracket		2	
BD.541/9	**Distance Washer,** on Setscrews		2	
C.8667/1	**Nut,** Self-Locking, on Setscrews		2	
FW.104/T	**Washer,** Plain, under Nuts		2	
C.18282	**DUCT SHIELD, BETWEEN LOWER EDGE OF RADIATOR AND SUB-FRAME CROSS TUBE**	32–25	1	
C.1040/20	**Clip,** for fixing of Duct Shield to Sub-Frame		3	
UFS.125/4R	**Screw,** Set, securing Duct Shield		5	
C.8737/1	**Nut,** Self-Locking, on Setscrews		5	
FW.104/T	**Washer,** Plain, at Clip fixing		3	

COOLING SYSTEM

Part No.	Description	Plate No.	No. per Unit	Remarks
C.16767	**ELBOW HOSE, CONNECTING RADIATOR TO HEADER TANK**	32–26	1	
C.2905/4	**Clip,** securing Hose	32–27	2	
C.12424	**HOSE, CONNECTING HEADER TANK TO OUTLET ELBOW ON ENGINE**	32–28	1	**MUST NOT BE USED IF 9 LBS. PRESSURE CAP IS FITTED TO HEADER TANK.**
C.21489	**HOSE, CONNECTING HEADER TANK TO OUTLET ELBOW ON ENGINE**		1	Fitted to Chassis No. 850657 and subs. 879044 and subs. 861091 and subs. 888241 and subs.
C.2905/4	**Clip,** securing Hose	32–29	2	
C.7548	**BY-PASS HOSE**	32–30	1	
C.2905/4	**Clip,** securing By-Pass Hose	32–31	2	
C.12630	**ELBOW HOSE, CONNECTING WATER PUMP TO PIPE**	32–32	1	
C.2905/5	**Clip,** securing Hose to Pipe	32–33	1	
C.2905/4	**Clip,** securing Hose to Water Pump		1	
C.16999	**PIPE, CONNECTING HOSES**	32–34	1	
C.15099	**HOSE, CONNECTING PIPE TO BOTTOM OF RADIATOR**	32–35	1	
C.2905/5	**Clip,** securing Hose to Pipe	32–36	1	
C.2905/4	**Clip,** securing Hose to Radiator	32–37	1	

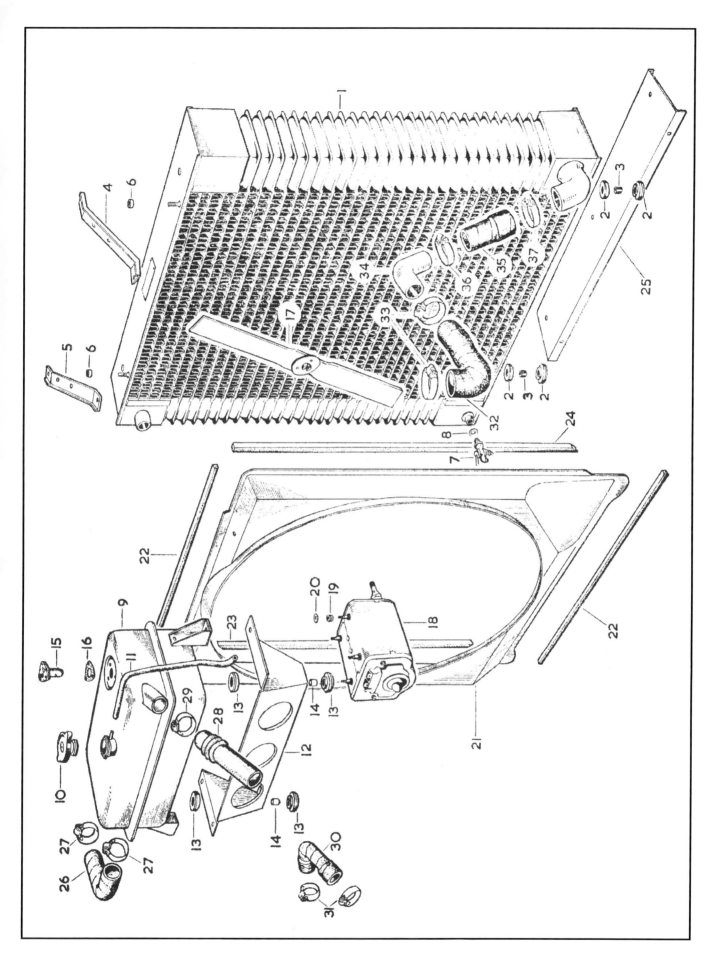

PLATE 32

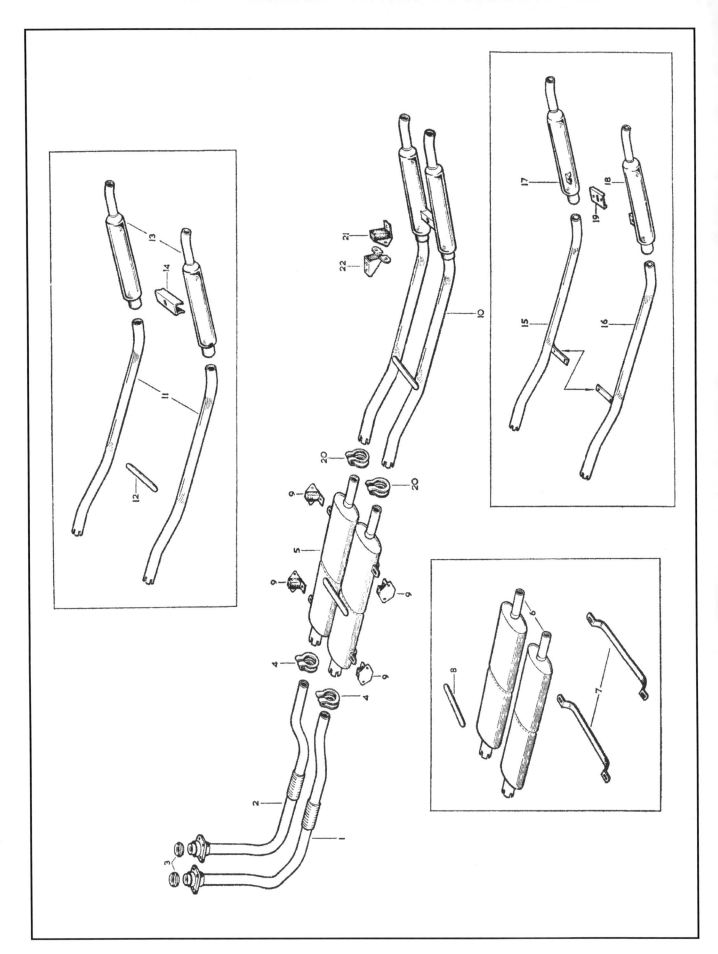

PLATE 33

Part No.	Description	Plate No.	No. per Unit	Remarks
C.18426	**FRONT DOWN PIPE ASSEMBLY, FROM MANIFOLD TO SILENCER**	33– 1	1	
C.1759	**Flexible Pipe,** on Down Pipe (12″ long)		1	
C.18401	**Flange**		1	
C.18427	**REAR DOWN PIPE ASSEMBLY, FROM MANIFOLD TO SILENCER**	33– 2	1	
C.1759	**Flexible Pipe,** on Down Pipe (12″ long)		1	
C.18401	**Flange**		1	
C.18405/1	**Gasket,** between Down Pipe and Exhaust Manifold	33– 3	2	
C.17916	**Nut,** securing Down Pipe to Exhaust Manifold		8	
FG.106/X	**Washer,** Spring, under Nuts		8	
C.13063	**CLIP, SECURING DOWN PIPES TO SILENCERS**	33– 4	2	
UFB.131/22R	**Bolt,** through Clips		2	
UFN.131/L	**Nut,** on Bolts		2	
FW.105/T	**Washer,** Plain, under Nuts		2	
C.17123	**TWIN SILENCERS ASSEMBLY**	33– 5	1	
C.17124	**Silencer only**	33– 6	2	
C.17127	**Mounting Strap,** for Silencers	33– 7	2	
C.18986	**Stiffener,** for Silencers	33– 8	1	
1363	**RUBBER MOUNTING FOR SUS-PENSION OF SILENCERS TO BODY**	33– 9	4	
UFN.131/L	**Nut,** securing Rubber Mountings to Body		4	
C.725	**Washer,** Shakeproof, under Nuts		4	
UFS.131/7R	**Screw,** Set, securing Silencers to Rubber Mountings		4	
C.12027	**Spacer,** between Silencers and Rubber Mountings		4	
C.8667/2	**Nut,** Self-Locking, on Setscrews		4	
FW.105/T	**Washer,** Plain, under Nuts		4	
C.18432	**EXHAUST TAIL PIPE ASSEMBLY**	33–10	1	Fitted from Chassis No. 850001 to 850178.
C.18433	**Tail Pipe only**	33–11	2	875001 to 875607.
C.17131	**Strap,** linking Tail Pipes at front	33–12	1	860001 to 860011.
C.18434	**Muffler Box Assembly**	33–13	2	885001 to 885058.
C.18436	**Mounting Bracket,** between Muffler Boxes	33–14	1	

EXHAUST SYSTEM

Part No.	Description	Plate No.	No. per Unit	Remarks
C.18660	**EXHAUST TAIL PIPE ASSEMBLY, R.H.**	33–15	1	⎫
				⎪
				Fitted to Chassis No.
				850179 and subs.
				875608 and subs.
C.18661	**EXHAUST TAIL PIPE ASSEMBLY, L.H.**	33–16	1	860012 and subs.
UFS.125/5R	**Setscrew,** securing Tail Pipe to Tail Pipe		2	885059 and subs.
C.8667/1	**Nut,** Self-Locking, on Setscrews		2	⎭
C.18655	**MUFFLER ASSEMBLY, R.H.**	33–17	1	⎫
				⎪
				Fitted to Chassis No.
				850179 and subs.
				875608 and subs.
C.18656	**MUFFLER ASSEMBLY, L.H.**	33–18	1	860012 and subs.
				885059 and subs.
C.18975	**Tie Plate,** between Mufflers	33–19	2	
UFS.125/5R	**Setscrew,** securing Tie Plate to Mufflers		2	
C.8667/1	**Nut,** Self-Locking, on Setscrews		1	⎭
C.18196	**CLIP, SECURING TAIL PIPES TO SILENCERS**	33–20	2	
UFB.131/22R	**Bolt,** through Clips		2	
UFN.131/L	**Nut,** on Bolts		2	
FW.105/T	**Washer,** Plain, under Nuts		2	
1363	**RUBBER MOUNTING FOR SUSPENSION OF TAIL PIPES TO BODY**	33–21	1	
UFS.131/6R	**Screw,** Set, securing Mounting to Tail Pipes		1	
UFN.131/L	**Nut,** on Setscrews		1	
C.725	**Washer,** Shakeproof, under Nut		1	
C.17462	**BRACKET FOR FIXING OF RUBBER MOUNTING TO BODY**	33–22	1	
C.8667/2	**Nut,** Self-Locking, securing Bracket to Boot Floor		2	
UFS.131/5R	**Screw,** Set, securing Rubber Mounting to Bracket		2	
UFN.131/L	**Nut,** on Setscrews		2	
C.725	**Washer,** Shakeproof, under Nuts		2	
C.19018	**Hooked Safety Bracket,** on Setscrews		1	

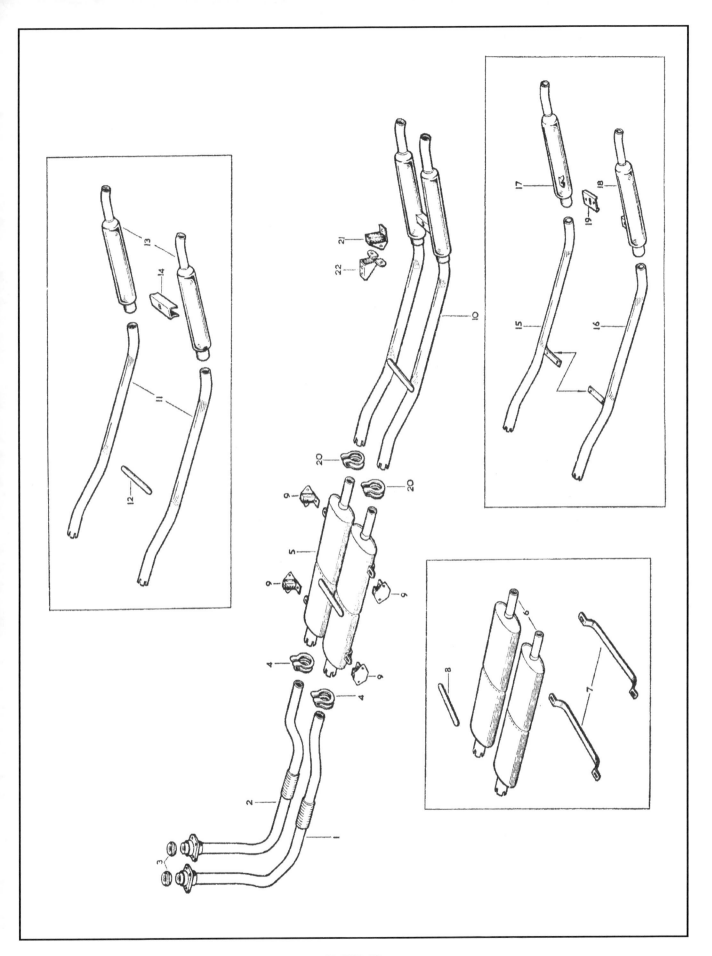

PLATE 33

FUEL SYSTEM

Part No.	Description	Plate No.	No. per Unit	Remarks
C.15076	**PETROL TANK ASSEMBLY**		1	⎫ Fitted from Chassis No.
C.19107	**Sump Assembly,** at bottom of Petrol Tank		1	⎪ 850001 to 850091.
C.1617	**Washer,** on Sump		1	⎬ 875001 to 875385.
C.19117	**Petrol Filter and Drain Plug Assembly,** at bottom of Sump		1	⎪ 860001 to 860004. 885001 to 885020.
C.19108	**'O' Ring,** for top of Petrol Filter		1	
C.1617	**Washer,** on Petrol Filter		1	⎭
C.19801	**PETROL TANK ASSEMBLY**	34– 1	1	⎫ Fitted to Chassis No. 850092 and subs.
C.19302	**Sump Assembly,** at bottom of Petrol Tank	34– 2	1	⎬ 875386 and subs.
C.1617	**Washer,** on Sump	34– 3	1	⎪ 860005 and subs.
C.19298	**Screwed Ring,** for Sump	34– 4	1	⎭ 885021 and subs.
C.15150	**Ventilation Hose,** from Tank to Petrol Filler Box	34– 5	1	
C.2905/1	**Clip,** securing Hose	34– 6	2	
C.18906	**Rubber Pad,** under Petrol Tank		1	
C.9024	**FILLER CAP FOR PETROL TANK**	34– 7	1	
C.18936	**HOSE, CONNECTING TANK TO PETROL FILLER BOX**	34– 8	1	
C.2905/7	**Clip,** securing Hose	34– 9	2	
C.16077	**PETROL TANK ELEMENT UNIT (TF.1104/051)**		1	**For Spares Replacements use C.20429.**
C.20429	**PETROL TANK ELEMENT UNIT (TF.1104/049)**	34–10	1	
C.937	**Gasket,** under Element Unit	34–11	1	
UFS.313/3H	**Screw,** Set, securing Element Unit		6	
C.2296/9	**Copper Washer,** on Setscrews		12	
C.17468	**PETROL PUMP ASSEMBLY (LUCAS 78388/A-2.FP)**		1	⎫ Fitted from Chassis No. 850001 to 850091.
C.17570	**Outlet Union,** for Petrol Pump (771390)		1	⎪ 875001 to 875385.
8811	**Washer** (Fibre) on Outlet Union (54140054)		1	⎬ 860001 to 860004.
UFB.125/8R	**Bolt,** securing Petrol Pump to Mounting Bracket		2	⎪ 885001 to 885020.
C.8667/1	**Nut,** Self-Locking, on Bolts		2	
FW.104/T	**Washer,** Plain, under Nuts		2	⎭
C.19919	**PETROL PUMP ASSEMBLY (78387/D-2.FP)**	34–12	1	⎫ Fitted to Chassis No. 850092 and subs.
C.18952	**Special Washer,** for Pump Mounting	34–13	2	⎬ 875386 and subs.
C.18953	**Special Washer,** for Pump Mounting	34–14	2	⎪ 860005 and subs.
8667/1	**Self-Locking Nut,** securing Pump		2	⎭ 885021 and subs.
C.19271	**FILTER ASSEMBLY FOR FEED PIPE ON PETROL PUMP**	34–15	1	⎫ Fitted to Chassis No. 850092 and subs.
C.11576	**Union Nut,** securing Filter to Feed Pipe	34–16	1	⎬ 875386 and subs. 860005 and subs.
C.11575	**Olive,** on Feed Pipe, for Union Nut	34–17	1	⎭ 885021 and subs.
C.17499	**BRACKET ASSEMBLY, FOR MOUNTING OF PETROL PUMP**		1	Fitted from Chassis No. 850001 to 850091. 875001 to 875385. 860001 to 860004. 885001 to 885020.

Part No.	Description	Plate No.	No. per Unit	Remarks
C.18907	**PLATE ASSEMBLY, FOR MOUNTING OF PETROL PUMP**	34–18	1	Fitted to Chassis No. 850092 and subs. 875386 and subs. 860005 and subs. 885021 and subs.
C.17504	**Gasket,** under Bracket (or Plate)	34–19	1	
UFS.119/4R	**Screw,** Set, securing Bracket to Petrol Tank		8	
AW.102/E	**Copper Washer,** on Setscrews		8	
C.19262	**PETROL PIPE ASSEMBLY BETWEEN FILTER AND PUMP**		1	Fitted from Chassis No. 850001 to 850091. 875001 to 875385. 860001 to 860004. 885001 to 885020.
8812	**Banjo Bolt,** securing Petrol Pipe to inlet side of Pump (54710343)		1	
8813	**Washer,** at each side of Banjo (54148514)		2	
C.19264	**PETROL PIPE ASSEMBLY BETWEEN FILTER AND PUMP**	34–20	1	Fitted to Chassis No. 850092 and subs. 875386 and subs. 860005 and subs. 885021 and subs.
C.19259	**Banjo Bolt,** securing Petrol Pipe to inlet side of Pump	34–21	1	
C.11489	**Washer,** at each side of Banjo	34–22	2	

NOTE:—WHEN SERVICING THE PETROL PUMP, THE BATTERY SHOULD BE DISCONNECTED AS A PRECAUTION AGAINST FIRE.

Part No.	Description	Plate No.	No. per Unit	Remarks
BD.16008	**BRACKET ASSEMBLY, FOR FORWARD MOUNTING OF PETROL TANK**	34–23	1	
UFN.131/L	**Nut,** securing Bracket to Boot Floor		4	
C.725	**Washer,** Shakeproof, under Nuts		4	
C.19846	**Rubber Pad,** at Petrol Tank Mountings	34–24	6	
C.6390	**Distance Tube,** through Rubber Pads	34–25	3	
C.11920	**Bolt,** securing Petrol Tank		3	
FG.106/X	**Washer,** Spring, on Bolts		3	
C.410	**Washer,** Special, under Spring Washers		3	
C.19095	**PETROL PIPE BETWEEN OUTLET UNION ON PUMP AND CONNECTOR ON PUMP MOUNTING BRACKET**		1	Fitted from Chassis No. 850001 to 850091. 875001 to 875385. 860001 to 860004. 885001 to 885020.
C.16267	**Nipple,** for connection of Pipe to Union on Mounting Bracket		1	
C.16266	**Nut,** securing Nipple to Union		1	
C.20834	**PETROL PIPE ASSEMBLY FROM PUMP TO CONNECTOR ON PUMP MOUNTING PLATE**	34–26	1	Fitted to Chassis No. 850092 and subs. 875386 and subs. 860005 and subs. 885021 and subs.
C.11488	**Bolt,** securing Banjo	34–28	1	
C.11489	**Fibre Washer,** on Banjo Bolt	34–29	2	
C.17506	**PETROL PIPE ASSEMBLY BETWEEN PUMP MOUNTING BRACKET AND BULKHEAD CONNECTOR**	34–27	1	
C.11488	**Banjo Bolt,** securing Pipe to Pump Bracket and Connector	34–28	2	
C.11489	**Fibre Washer,** at each side of Banjos	34–29	4	

FUEL SYSTEM

Part No.	Description	Plate No.	No. per Unit	Remarks
C.17630	**BULKHEAD CONNECTOR AT R.H. FRONT CORNER OF BOOT FLOOR**	34–30	1	
C.18254	**Mounting Plate,** for Bulkhead Connector	34–31	1	
C.10267	**Nut,** securing Connector to Mounting Plate	34–32	1	
C.3729	**Brass Washer,** under Nut	34–33	1	
UFS.125/4R	**Screw,** Set, securing Mounting Plate to Boot Floor		2	
C.724	**Washer,** Shakeproof, on Setscrews		2	
C.17222	**PETROL PIPE ASSEMBLY BETWEEN CONNECTOR AND PETROL FILTER**	34–34	1	
C.3727	**Clip,** securing Petrol Pipe to Wheel Arch	34–35	2	
C.10268	**Clip,** securing Petrol Pipe to Underframe	34–36	4	
C.1040/9	**Clip,** securing Petrol Pipe to Underframe	34–37	1	
C.1040/12	**Clip,** securing Petrol Pipe at Reservac Tank Mounting	34–38	1	
C.13681	**PETROL FILTER ASSEMBLY (AC.7950001)**	34–39	1	
7297	**Filter Casting**	34–40	1	
7298	**Sealing Washer,** between Filter Casting and Glass Bowl	34–41	1	
7299	**Filter Gauze**	34–42	1	
7300	**Glass Bowl**	34–43	1	
7301	**Retaining Strap Assembly**	34–44	1	
C.13705	**Banjo Bolt,** securing Petrol Pipes to Filter	34–45	2	
C.784	**Fibre Washer,** at each side of Banjos	34–46	4	
C.17354	**BRACKET ON FRONT FRAME FIXING BOLT, FOR MOUNTING OF PETROL FILTER**		1	Fitted from Chassis No. 850001 to 850091. 875001 to 875385. 860001 to 860004. 885001 to 885020.
C.18964	**BRACKET ON FRONT FRAME FIXING BOLT, FOR MOUNTING OF PETROL FILTER**	34–47	1	Fitted to Chassis No. 850092 and subs. 875386 and subs. 860005 and subs. 885021 and subs.
UFS.131/6R	**Screw,** Set, securing Filter to Bracket		2	
UFN.131/L	**Nut,** on Setscrews		2	
FG.105/X	**Washer,** Spring, under Nuts		2	
C.17335	**PETROL PIPE ASSEMBLY FROM FILTER TO CARBURETTER FEED PIPE**	34–48	1	
C.11576	**Union Nut,** securing Feed Pipe to Pipe from Filter		1	
C.11575	**Olive,** on Carburetter Feed Pipe		1	
C.15823	**FEED PIPE ASSEMBLY, LINKING CARBURETTERS**	34–49	1	
C.11488	**Banjo Bolt,** securing Feed Pipe to Float Chambers	34–50	3	
C.11489	**Fibre Washer,** at each side of Banjos	34–51	6	

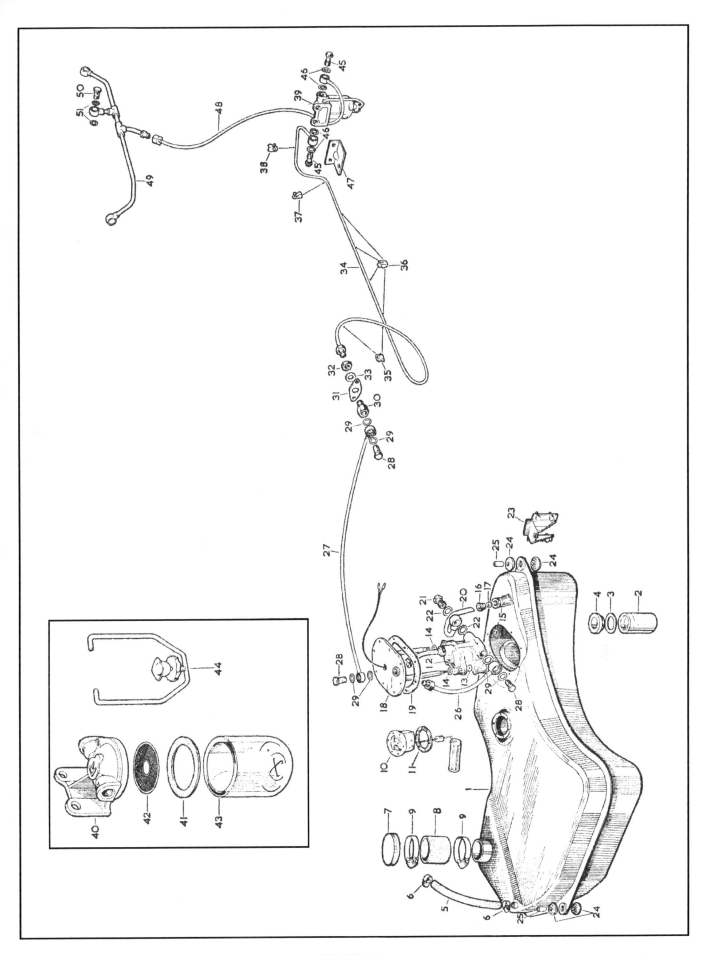

PLATE 34

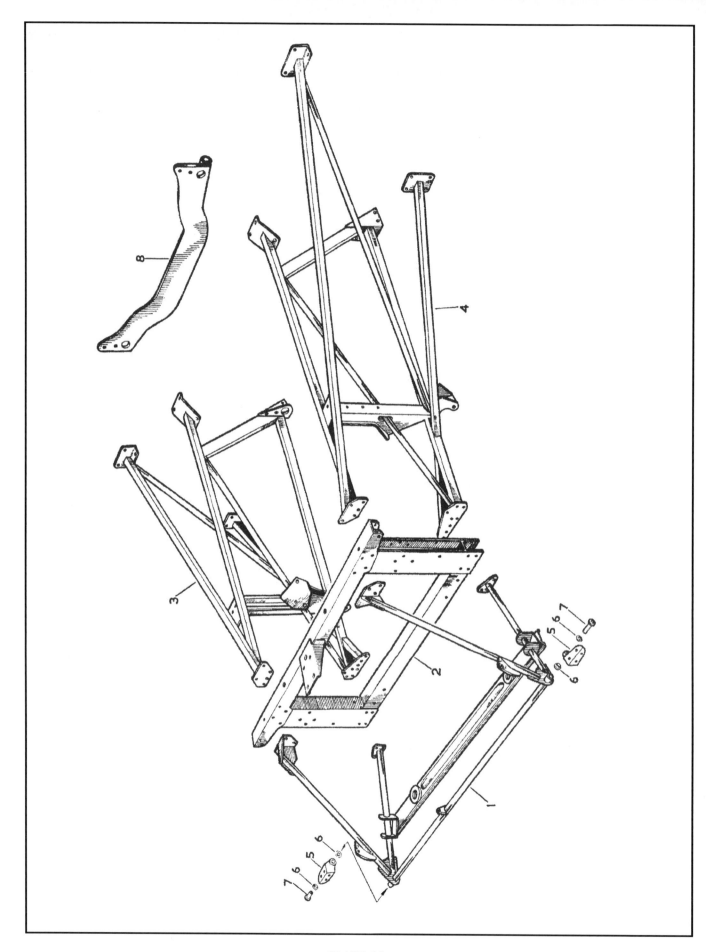

PLATE 35

Part No.	Description	Plate No.	No. per Unit	Remarks
C.20352	**FRONT SUB-FRAME ASSEMBLY**	35– 1	1	
C.15014	**FRONT CROSS MEMBER ASSEMBLY**	35– 2	1	
C.15029	**R.H. SIDE MEMBER ASSEMBLY**	35– 3	1	
C.15030	**L.H. SIDE MEMBER ASSEMBLY**	35– 4	1	
UFB.131/25R	**Bolt,** securing Side Members and Front Sub-Frame to Cross Member at top and fixing Hydraulic Brakes 4-Way Union		1	**FITTED AT R.H. SIDE ON R.H. DRIVE CARS AND L.H. SIDE ON L.H. DRIVE CARS.**
UFB.131/20R	**Bolt,** securing upper front Fulcrum Mounting Plates, Side Members and Front Sub-Frame to Cross Member at top		7	
UFB.131/31R	**Bolt,** securing lower front Fulcrum Blocks, Side Members, Front Sub-Frame and Anti-Roll Bar Brackets to Cross Member at bottom		2	
UFB.131/19R	**Bolt,** securing lower front Fulcrum Blocks, Side Members and Front Sub-Frame to Cross Member at bottom		6	
UFB.131/18R	**Bolt,** securing Side Members and Front Sub-Frame to Cross Member at bottom		4	
C.15045	**Packing Plate,** between attachment flange of Side Members and lower rail of Cross Member		2	
C.17510	**Bracket,** on Cross Member side channels, for Front Brake Hoses		2	
UFS.131/6R	**Screw,** Set, securing Brackets to Cross Member		2	
C.8667/2	**Nut,** Self-Locking, on Bolts and Setscrews		22	
UFS.131/7R	**Screw,** Set, securing Side Members to Dash		24	
C.8667/2	**Nut,** Self-Locking, on Setscrews		12	
FW.105/T	**Washer,** Plain, under Nuts		12	
UFB.137/18R	**Bolt,** securing Side Members to Body Underframe Channels		2	
C.8667/3	**Nut,** Self-Locking, on Bolts		2	
FW.106/T	**Washer,** Plain, under Nuts		2	

FRONT FRAME

Part No.	Description	Plate No.	No. per Unit	Remarks
C.19326	**BONNET HINGE**	35– 5	2	
C.16804	**Nylon Bush,** for Bonnet Hinges	35– 6	4	
C.19330	**Bearing** (Steel) for Bonnet Hinges	35– 7	2	
UFB.137/18R	**Bolt,** securing Bonnet Hinges to Front Sub Frame		2	
FG.106/X	**Washer,** Spring, on Bolts		2	
C.19179	**REACTION PLATE, BETWEEN SIDE MEMBERS AT REAR, STIFFENING TORSION BAR ANCHOR BRACKET MOUNTINGS**	35– 8	1	
C.18730	**Bolt,** securing Reaction Plate and Torsion Bar Anchor Brackets to Side Members		4	
C.8667/3	**Nut,** Self-Locking, on Bolts		4	
C.8060	**Bolt,** securing Reaction Plate to Body Underframe Channels through Side Members		2	
C.8667/5	**Nut,** Self-Locking, on Bolts		2	

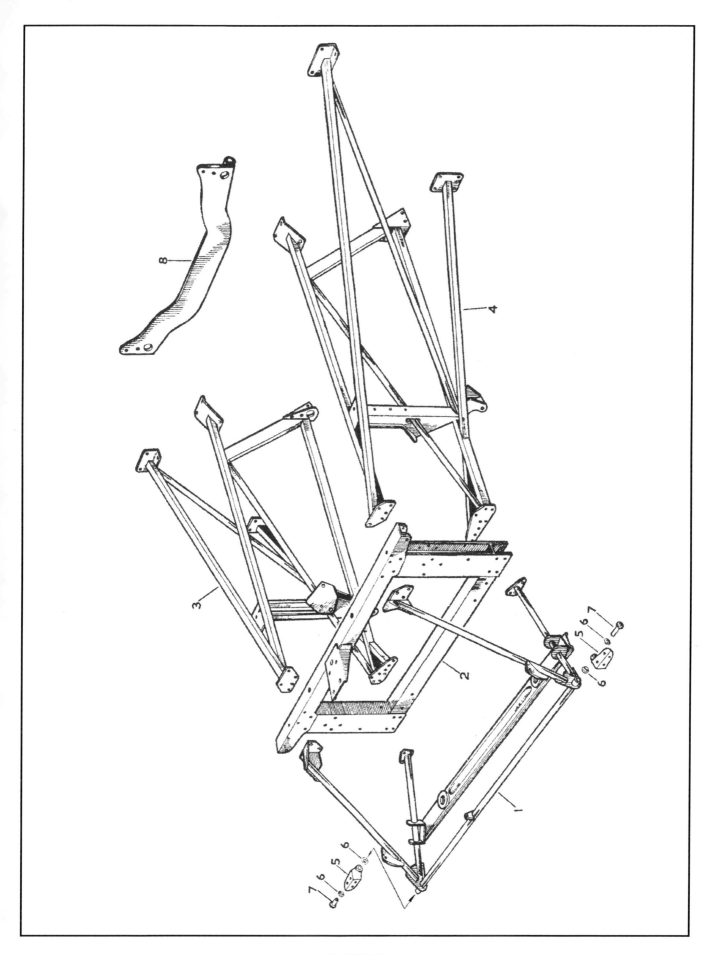

PLATE 35

BODY SHELL
FOR OPEN CARS ONLY

Part No.	Description	Plate No.	No. per Unit	Remarks
BD.22825	**BODY SHELL ASSEMBLY, COMPLETE**		1	
BD.22823	**Underframe Assembly**		1	
BD.19929	**Bonnet and Front Wings Assembly**		1	
C.20352	**Front Sub-Frame Assembly**		1	FOR FIXINGS TO MAIN BODY PORTION, PLEASE REFER TO SECTION FOR FRONT FRAME.
C.15014	**Front Cross Member Assembly**		1	
C.15029	**R.H. Side Member Assembly**		1	
C.15030	**L.H. Side Member Assembly**		1	
C.19326	**Hinge,** for Bonnet		2	
BD.15168	**Door Shell Assembly,** R.H.		1	
BD.15169	**Door Shell Assembly,** L.H.		1	
BD.15495	**Hinge Assembly,** for R.H. Door		1	
BD.15496	**Hinge Assembly,** for L.H. Door		1	
BD.14768	**Scuttle Top Panel**		1	
BD.16547	**R.H. Windscreen Pillar Assembly**		1	
BD.16548	**L.H. Windscreen Pillar Assembly**		1	
BD.15217	**Filler Panel,** between R.H. Screen Pillar and Scuttle Top Panel		1	
BD.15218	**Filler Panel,** between L.H. Screen Pillar and Scuttle Top Panel		1	
BD.15467	**Closing Panel,** under R.H. Screen Pillar		1	
BD.15468	**Closing Panel,** under L.H. Screen Pillar		1	
BD.17069	**Corner Panel,** Dash to Scuttle Top, R.H.		1	
BD.17070	**Corner Panel,** Dash to Scuttle Top, L.H.		1	
BD.15180	**Exterior Panel Assembly,** R.H. Dash side		1	
BD.15181	**Exterior Panel Assembly,** L.H. Dash side		1	
BD.15133	**R.H. Sill Outer Panel**		1	
BD.15134	**L.H. Sill Outer Panel**		1	
BD.15184	**End Plate,** at front of R.H. Sill		1	
BD.15187	**Bracket Assembly,** at front of R.H. Sill, mounting Air Cleaner		1	
BD.15185	**End Plate Assembly,** at front of L.H. Sill		1	
BD.15186	**Bracket Assembly,** at front of L.H. Sill, mounting Battery Tray		1	
BD.19586	**Bracket Assembly,** for Jack Location		1	
BD.15188	**Panel Assembly,** lower rear		1	
BD.15190	**Tonneau Panel and Rear Wings Assembly**		1	
BD.18872	**Top Quarter Panel Assembly, R.H.**		1	
BD.18873	**Top Quarter Panel Assembly, L.H.**		1	
BD.15934	**Lid Assembly,** for Petrol Filler Box		1	
BD 18945	**Filler Panel,** seating R.H. Stop/Tail Lamp		1	
BD.18946	**Filler Panel,** seating L.H. Stop/Tail Lamp		1	
BD.18952	**Fixing Bracket,** inner, for R.H. Stop/Tail Lamp		1	
BD.19532	**Fixing Bracket,** outer, for R.H. Stop/Tail Lamp		1	
BD.18953	**Fixing Bracket,** inner, for L.H. Stop/Tail Lamp		1	
BD.19533	**Fixing Bracket,** outer, for L.H. Stop/Tail Lamp		1	
BD.15172	**Boot Lid Shell Assembly**		1	
BD.19211	**R.H. Hinge Assembly,** for Boot Lid		1	
BD.19212	**L.H. Hinge Assembly,** for Boot Lid		1	

Part No.	Description	Plate No.	No. per Unit	Remarks
BD.15170	**BODY UNDERFRAME ASSEMBLY**		1	Fitted from Chassis No. 850001 to 850526. 875001 to 877355.
BD.15171	**Floor Assembly**		1	Fitted from Chassis No. 850001 to 850357. 875001 to 876381.
BD.23141	**Floor Assembly**		1	Fitted from Chassis No. 850358 to 850526. 876382 to 877353.
BD.15196	**Rear End Assembly**		1	
BD.22823	**BODY UNDERFRAME ASSEMBLY**		1	Fitted to Chassis No. 850527 and subs. 877356 and subs.
BD.22819	**Floor Assembly**	36– 1	1	
BD.23101	**Rear End Assembly**		1	
BD.15171	**FLOOR ASSEMBLY**		1	Fitted from Chassis No. 850001 to 850357. 875001 to 876381.
BD.19238	**Bracket Assembly,** for Exhaust Silencer Mounting		4	
BD.23141	**FLOOR ASSEMBLY (COMPLETE WITH HEEL WELLS)**		1	Fitted from Chassis No. 850358 to 850526. 876382 to 877355.
BD.15131/2	**Heel Well** only		2	
BD.19238	**Bracket Assembly,** for Exhaust Silencer Mounting		4	
BD.22819	**FLOOR ASSEMBLY (COMPLETE WITH HEEL WELLS)**	36– 1	1	Fitted to Chassis No. 850527 and subs. 977356 and subs.
BD.15131/2	**Heel Well** only		2	
BD.19238	**Bracket Assembly,** for Exhaust Silencer Mounting		4	
BD.15588/1	**Plastic Plug,** in Floor ($\frac{3}{8}$" dia.)		26	
BD.15588/2	**Plastic Plug,** in Floor ($\frac{1}{2}$" dia.)		2	**R.H. DRIVE CARS ONLY.**
BD.15588/4	**Plastic Plug,** in Floor ($\frac{3}{4}$" dia.)		2	
BD.15588/5	**Plastic Plug,** in Floor ($\frac{7}{8}$" dia.)		10	
BD.19902	**Plastic Plug,** in Floor		1	
BD.22756	**Plastic Plug,** in Floor (Safety Harness)		4	

BODY UNDERFRAME AND PANELS
FOR OPEN CARS ONLY

Part No.	Description	Plate No.	No. per Unit	Remarks
BD.15196	**REAR END ASSEMBLY**		1	
BD.16650	**Tunnel Assembly**	36– 2	1	
BD.15223	**Shut Pillar Assembly,** R.H.	36– 3	1	
BD.15224	**Shut Pillar Assembly,** L.H.	36– 4	1	
BD.18839	**Support Panel,** for R.H. Rear Quarter	36– 5	1	
BD.18840	**Support Panel,** for L.H. Rear Quarter	36– 6	1	
BD.18831	**Mounting Panel,** R.H., for Hoodsticks		1	
BD.18832	**Mounting Panel,** L.H., for Hoodsticks		1	
BD.15232	**Wheel Arch Panel Assembly,** R.H. Forward	36– 7	1	
BD.15233	**Wheel Arch Panel Assembly,** L.H. Forward	36– 8	1	
BD.15225	**Wheel Arch Panel Assembly,** R.H. Rear	36– 9	1	
BD.15226	**Wheel Arch Panel Assembly,** L.H. Rear	36–10	1	
BD.15230	**Valance Assembly,** behind R.H. Wheel Arch	36–11	1	
BD.15231	**Valance Assembly,** behind L.H. Wheel Arch	36–12	1	
BD.22693	**Floor Panel Assembly,** Rear	36–13	1	
BD.20162	**Cross Member Assembly,** for Rear Floor	36–14	1	
BD.17445	**Stiffening Bracket,** at sides of Rear Cross Member	36–15	2	Fitted from Chassis No. 850001 to 850526. 875001 to 877355.
BD.19077	**Bracket Assembly,** R.H., for mounting of Rear Suspension Cross Member		1	
BD.19078	**Bracket Assembly,** L.H., for mounting of Rear Suspension Cross Member		1	
BD.17442	**Top Panel Assembly,** above Rear Floor	36–16	1	
BD.19681	**Rear Bulkhead Panel Assembly**	36–17	1	
BD.15228	**Panel Assembly,** for front of Spare Wheel Compartment	36–18	1	
BD.15238	**Reinforcement Angle,** between Spare Wheel Compartment Panel and Top Panel		1	
BD.18963	**Shield,** for Interior Light	36–19	1	
BD.16212	**Panel Assembly,** reinforcing Tonneau	36–20	1	
BD.18949	**Bracket Assembly,** mounting R.H. Hinge for Boot Lid		1	
BD.18950	**Bracket Assembly,** mounting L.H. Hinge for Boot Lid		1	
BD.20504	**Extension,** between R.H. Hinge Bracket and Rear Bulkhead Panel		1	
BD.20505	**Extension,** between L.H. Hinge Bracket and Rear Bulkhead Panel		1	
BD.23101	**REAR END ASSEMBLY**		1	
BD.22808	**Floor Panel Assembly,** rear		1	Fitted to Chassis No. 850527 and subs. 877356 and subs.
BD.22816	**Stiffening Bracket,** at R.H. side of Rear Cross Member		1	
BD.22817	**Stiffening Bracket,** at L.H. side of Rear Cross Member		1	
	All other items are as for Rear End Assembly BD.15196.			
BD.19221	**Extension,** on R.H. Shut Pillar, for Door Seal Retainer		1	
BD.19222	**Extension,** on L.H. Shut Pillar, for Door Seal Retainer		1	
BD.19132	**Bracket Assembly,** for mounting of Rear Suspension Bump Stop Rubbers		2	
BD.15137	**Panel Assembly,** at R.H. side of Gearbox	36–21	1	
BD.15138	**Panel Assembly,** at L.H. side of Gearbox	36–22	1	
BD.15198	**Reinforcement Panel,** for R.H. Shut Pillar	36–23	1	
BD.15994	**Closing Panel,** for R.H. Shut Pillar	36–24	1	
BD.15199	**Reinforcement Panel,** for L.H. Shut Pillar	36–25	1	
BD.15995	**Closing Panel,** for L.H. Shut Pillar	36–26	1	
BD.17456	**Support Panel,** for Shut Pillars		2	
BD.18368	**Reinforcement Panel,** lower rear, for Propeller Shaft Tunnel		1	
BD.15982	**Reinforcement Panel,** at rear of R.H. Sill	36–27	1	
BD.15983	**Reinforcement Panel,** at rear of L.H. Sill	36–28	1	
BD.16488	**Reinforcement Panel,** at front of Sills	36–29	2	
BD.15202	**Closing Panel,** for front of R.H. Sill	36–30	1	
BD.15203	**Closing Panel,** for front of L.H. Sill	36–31	1	
BD.14918	**Reinforcement Panel,** for R.H. Dash side		1	
BD.14919	**Reinforcement Panel,** for L.H. Dash side	36–32	1	
BD.16942	**Closing Panel Assembly,** R.H. lower Dash front		1	
BD.16943	**Closing Panel,** L.H. lower Dash front		1	

Part No.	Description	Plate No.	No. per Unit	Remarks
BD.15180	**EXTERIOR PANEL ASSEMBLY, R.H. DASH SIDE**	36–33	1	
BD.15181	**EXTERIOR PANEL ASSEMBLY, L.H. DASH SIDE**	36–34	1	
BD.15133	**R.H. SILL OUTER PANEL**	36–35	1	
BD.15184	**End Plate,** at front of R.H. Sill		1	
BD.15187	**Bracket Assembly,** at side of R.H. Sill for Mounting Air Cleaner		1	
BD.15134	**L.H. SILL OUTER PANEL**	36–36	1	
BD.15185	**End Plate Assembly,** at front of L.H. Sill		1	
BD.15186	**Bracket Assembly,** at side of L.H. Sill for Mounting Battery Tray		1	
BD.19586	**BRACKET, UNDER SILLS, FOR JACK LOCATION**		2	
BD.15168	**DOOR SHELL ASSEMBLY, R.H.**		1	
BD.15178	**Outer Panel Assembly,** for R.H. Door		1	
BD.15453	**Inner Panel Assembly,** for R.H. Door		1	
BD.21030	**Drain Tray,** at top of R.H. Door		1	
BD.11712/2	**Pop Rivet,** securing Drain Tray		2	
BD.20878	**Shroud,** for Drain Holes at bottom of Door		2	
BD.1814/1	**Pop Rivet,** securing Shroud		6	
BD.21180	**Drain Tube,** Rubber, for Trays		1	
BD.20978	**Shroud,** for Drain Holes at front of Door		1	
BD.20979	**Shroud,** for Drain Holes at rear of Door		1	
BD.1814/2	**Pop Rivet,** securing Shrouds at front and rear of Door		7	Fitted from Chassis No. 850001 to 850506. 875001 to 877201.
BD.15169	**DOOR SHELL ASSEMBLY, L.H.**		1	
BD.15179	**Outer Panel Assembly,** for L.H. Door		1	
BD.15454	**Inner Panel Assembly,** for L.H. Door		1	
BD.21031	**Drain Tray,** at top of L.H. Door		1	

All other items are as for Door Shell Assembly BD.15168.

BODY UNDERFRAME AND PANELS
FOR OPEN CARS ONLY

Part No.	Description	Plate No.	No. per Unit	Remarks
BD.21317	**DOOR SHELL ASSEMBLY, R.H.**	36–37	1	
BD.21319	**Outer Panel Assembly,** for R.H. Door		1	
BD.15453	**Inner Panel Assembly,** for R.H. Door		1	
BD.21030	**Drain Tray,** at top of R.H. Door		1	
	All other items are as for Door Shell Assembly BD.15168.			
				Fitted to Chassis No. 850507 and subs. 877202 and subs.
BD.21318	**DOOR SHELL ASSEMBLY, L.H.**	36–38	1	
BD.21320	**Outer Panel Assembly,** for L.H. Door		1	
BD.15454	**Inner Panel Assembly,** for L.H. Door		1	
BD.21031	**Drain Tray,** at top of L.H. Door		1	
	All other items are as for Door Shell Assembly BD.15168.			
BD.15495	**HINGE ASSEMBLY FOR R.H. DOOR**	36–39	1	
BD.15496	**HINGE ASSEMBLY FOR L.H. DOOR**	36–40	1	
C.16168	**Grease Nipple,** for Door Hinges (Tec.YH.109)		2	
BD.22662	**CHECK ARM ASSEMBLY FOR DOORS**	36–41	2	
BD.22661	**Brass Cam,** for Check Arms		2	
UCS.519/4H	**Screw,** Set, Csk. Hd., securing Cam to Check Arms		4	**Self-Tapping Screw BD.17503/1 may be required for some cars.**
UFS.425/5H	**Screw,** Set, securing Check Arm to Door Hinges		4	
C.724	**Washer,** Shakeproof, on Setscrews		4	
BD.17034/5	**Screw,** Set, securing Hinge to Doors		8	
BD.711/20	**Screw,** Self-Tapping, securing Hinge to Doors		4	
BD.13565/3	**Screw,** Set, securing Hinges to Body		8	
FG.105/X	**Washer,** Spring, on Setscrews		8	
BD.15191	**REAR WING ASSEMBLY, R.H.**	36–42	1	
BD.15192	**REAR WING ASSEMBLY, L.H.**	36–43	1	

BODY UNDERFRAME AND PANELS
FOR OPEN CARS ONLY

Part No.	Description	Plate No.	No. per Unit	Remarks
BD.15933	**PETROL FILLER BOX ASSEMBLY, IN L.H. WING**	36–44	1	
BD.15189	**TONNEAU TOP PANEL**	36–45	1	
BD.18801	**SUPPORT PANEL ASSEMBLY, UNDER FRONT OF TONNEAU TOP PANEL**	36–46	1	
BD.15219	**TONNEAU REAR PANEL ASSEMBLY**	36–47	1	
BD.18872	**TOP QUARTER PANEL ASSEMBLY, R.H.**	36–48	1	
BD.18873	**TOP QUARTER PANEL ASSEMBLY, L.H.**	36–49	1	
BD.15172	**BOOT LID SHELL ASSEMBLY**	36–50	1	
BD.20622	**R.H. HINGE ASSEMBLY FOR BOOT LID**	36–51	1	
BD.19204	**Leaf Spring,** on Hinge		5	
UFS.119/4R	**Screw,** Set, securing Springs to Bracket		1	
UFN.119/L	**Nut,** on Setscrew		1	
C.723/A	**Washer,** Shakeproof, under Nut		1	
AW.102/T	**Washer,** Plain, on Setscrew		2	
BD.20628	**Anchor Pin,** for Spring		1	
BD.19202	**Distance Tube,** on Anchor Pin		1	
BD.19203	**Distance Collar,** below Tube		1	

BODY UNDERFRAME AND PANELS
FOR OPEN CARS ONLY

Part No.	Description	Plate No.	No. per Unit	Remarks
BD.20623	**L.H. HINGE ASSEMBLY FOR BOOT LID**	36–52	1	
BD.19204	**Leaf Spring,** on Hinge		5	
UFS.119/4R	**Screw,** Set, securing Springs to Bracket		1	
UFN.119/L	**Nut,** on Setscrew		1	
C.723/A	**Washer,** Shakeproof, under Nut		1	
AW.102/T	**Washer,** Plain, on Setscrew		2	
BD.20628	**Anchor Pin,** for Spring		1	
BD.19202	**Distance Tube,** on Anchor Pin		1	
BD.19203	**Distance Collar,** below Tube		1	
BD.8291/2	**Screw,** Set, securing Hinges to Boot Lid		4	
C.724	**Washer,** Shakeproof, on Setscrews		4	
FW.104/T	**Washer,** Plain, under Shakeproof Washers		4	
BD.13565/2	**Screw,** Set (¾″ long) securing Hinges to Body		4	
C.725	**Washer,** Shakeproof, on Setscrews		4	
FW.105/T	**Washer,** Plain, under Shakeproof Washers		4	
BD.6265/1	**Shim** (.036″ thick) for Hinges		As req'd	
BD.6265/2	**Shim** (.064″ thick) for Hinges		As req'd	
UFN.125/L	**Nut,** securing Hinges to Body		4	
C.724	**Washer,** Shakeproof, under Nuts		4	
FW.104/T	**Washer,** Plain, under Shakeproof Washers		4	
BD.15934	**LID ASSEMBLY FOR PETROL FILLER BOX**	36–53	1	
BD.15932	**HINGE ASSEMBLY FOR PETROL FILLER LID**	36–54	1	
BD.8291/1	**Screw,** Set, securing Hinge to Lid and to Body		4	
C.724	**Washer,** Shakeproof, on Setscrews		4	
FW.104/T	**Washer,** Plain, under Shakeproof Washers		4	
BD.15930	**SPRING, BETWEEN LID AND HINGE**	36–55	1	
BD.15188	**PANEL ASSEMBLY, LOWER REAR**	36–56	1	
BD.18837	**Lower Panel,** R.H. Outer		1	
BD.18838	**Lower Panel,** L.H. Outer	36–57	1	
BD.16207	**PANEL ASSEMBLY, FOR REAR NUMBER PLATE**		1	
BD.18945	**FILLER PANEL, SEATING R.H. STOP/ TAIL LAMP**	36–58	1	
BD.18952	**Fixing Bracket,** inner, for R.H. Stop/Tail Lamp		1	
BD.18955	**Fixing Bracket,** outer, for R.H. Stop/Tail Lamp		1	

Part No.	Description	Plate No.	No. per Unit	Remarks
BD.18946	**FILLER PANEL, SEATING L.H. STOP/ TAIL LAMP**	36–59	1	
BD.18953	**Fixing Bracket,** inner, for L.H. Stop/Tail Lamp		1	
BD.18956	**Fixing Bracket,** outer, for L.H. Stop/Tail Lamp		1	
BD.16550	**BONNET AND FRONT WINGS ASSEMBLY**		1	Fitted from Chassis No. 850001 to 850091. 875001 to 875385.
BD.15174	**Centre Panel Assembly,** for Bonnet	37– 1	1	
BD.15175	**Front Under Panel Assembly**	37– 2	1	
BD.16557	**Air Duct Lower Panel Assembly**	37– 3	1	
BD.16839/2	**Screw,** Self-Tapping, securing Air Duct Panel to Valances		6	
UCS.125/5R	**Screw,** Set, securing Front Under Panel to Valances, Centre Panel and Wings		14	
UCN.125/L	**Nut,** on Setscrews		14	
FG.104/X	**Washer,** Spring, on Setscrews and Self-Tapping Screws		20	
BD.542/3	**Washer,** Special, on Setscrews and Self-Tapping Screws		34	
BD.15176	**Front Wing Assembly,** R.H.	37– 4	1	
BD.15177	**Front Wing Assembly,** L.H.	37– 5	1	
UCS.125/5R	**Screw,** Set, securing Wings to Centre Panel		18	
UCN.125/L	**Nut,** on Setscrews		18	
FG.104/X	**Washer,** Spring, under Nuts		18	
BD.542/3	**Washer,** Special, on Setscrews		36	
BD.19021	**R.H. Valance and Air Duct Assembly**	37– 6	1	
BD.19022	**L.H. Valance and Air Duct Assembly**	37– 7	1	
BD.16839/2	**Screw,** Self-Tapping, securing Valance and Duct Assemblies to Centre and Front Under Panels		23	
FG.104/X	**Washer,** Spring, on Self-Tapping Screws		23	
BD.542/3	**Washer,** Special, under Spring Washers		23	
BD.16422	**R.H. Front Diaphragm Assembly,** mounting Headlamp	37– 8	1	
BD.16423	**L.H. Front Diaphragm Assembly,** mounting Headlamp	37– 9	1	
UCS.125/5R	**Screw,** Set, securing Diaphragms to Wings		8	
UCN.125/L	**Nut,** on Setscrews		8	
BD.16839/2	**Screw,** Self-Tapping, securing Diaphragms to Valances, Wings and Front Under Panel		26	
FG.104/X	**Washer,** Spring, on Setscrews and Self-Tapping Screws		34	
BD.542/3	**Washer,** Special, on Setscrews and Self-Tapping Screws		42	
BD.22749	**Sealing Panel,** for R.H. Headlamp Diaphragm		1	
BD.22750	**Sealing Panel,** for L.H. Headlamp Diaphragm		1	
BD.22749/1	**Felt,** on Sealing Panel		4	
BD.1328/2	**Rivet,** securing Felt to Panel		8	
UFS.419/3H	**Screw,** Set, securing Sealing Panel		2	
UFN.119/L	**Nut,** on Setscrews		2	
C.723/A	**Washer,** Shakeproof, on Setscrews		2	
AW.102/T	**Washer,** Plain, under Shakeproof Washers		2	
BD.16381	**R.H. Diaphragm Assembly,** at rear of Bonnet	37–10	1	
BD.16382	**L.H. Diaphragm Assembly,** at rear of Bonnet	37–11	1	
UCS.125/5R	**Screw,** Set, securing Rear Diaphragms to Wings, Valances and Centre Panel		18	
UCN.125/L	**Nut,** on Setscrews		18	
BD.16839/2	**Screw,** Self-Tapping, securing Rear Diaphragms to Centre Panel		7	
FG.104/X	**Washer,** Spring, on Setscrews and Self-Tapping Screws		25	
BD.542/3	**Washer,** Special, on Setscrews and Self-Tapping Screws		43	
BD.18767	**Reinforcing Angle,** between Wings and Centre Panel at rear		2	
UFS.125/4R	**Screw,** Set, securing Reinforcing Angles		8	
FG.104/X	**Washer,** Spring, on Setscrews		8	
FW.104/T	**Washer,** Plain, under Spring Washers		8	

BODY UNDERFRAME AND PANELS
FOR OPEN CARS ONLY

Part No.	Description	Plate No.	No. per Unit	Remarks
BD.19929	**BONNET AND FRONT WINGS ASSEMBLY**		1	
BD.19930	Front Wing Assembly, R.H.		1	Fitted to Chassis No. 850092 and subs. 875386 and subs.
BD.19931	Front Wing Assembly, L.H.		1	
	All other items are as for Bonnet and Front Wings Assembly BD.16550.			
C.16803	**BONNET HINGE**	37–12	2	
C.16804	**Nylon Bush,** in Hinges	37–13	4	Fitted from Chassis No. 850001 to 850238. 875001 to 876457.
C.8667/5	**Nut,** Self-Locking, retaining Hinges on Sub Frame Cross Bar		2	
C.8676	**Washer,** Plain, under Self-Locking Nuts		2	
C.19326	**BONNET HINGE**		2	
C.16804	**Nylon Bush,** in Bonnet Hinges		4	Fitted to Chassis No. 850239 and subs. 876458 and subs.
C.19330	**Bearing** (Steel), for Bonnet Hinges		2	
UFB.137/18R	**Bolt,** retaining Bonnet Hinges to Front Sub Frame		2	
FG.106/X	**Washer,** Spring, on Bolts		2	
BD.13565/6	**Screw,** Set, securing Hinges to Bonnet		4	
BD.13565/8	**Screw,** Set, securing Hinges to Bonnet		4	
C.725	**Washer,** Shakeproof, on Setscrews		8	
C.985	**Washer,** Plain, under Shakeproof Washers		8	
BD.18951	**Shim** (.064″ thick) for Bonnet Hinges		As req'd	
BD.18951/1	**Shim** (.036″ thick) for Bonnet Hinges		As req'd	
BD.20950/1	**Special Shim** (Slotted) (.036″ thick) for Bonnet Hinges		As req'd	
BD.20950/2	**Special Shim** (Slotted) (.128″ thick) for Bonnet Hinges		As req'd	
BD.20957	**SCUTTLE TOP PANEL ASSEMBLY**	37–14	1	
BD.16547	**R.H. WINDSCREEN PILLAR ASSEMBLY**	37–15	1	
BD.16548	**L.H. WINDSCREEN PILLAR ASSEMBLY**	37–16	1	
BD.15217	**Filler Panel,** between R.H. Windscreen Pillar and Scuttle Top Panel	37–17	1	
BD.15218	**Filler Panel,** between L.H. Windscreen Pillar and Scuttle Top Panel	37–18	1	

Part No.	Description	Plate No.	No. per Unit	Remarks
BD.17069	**CORNER PANEL, DASH TO SCUTTLE TOP PANEL, R.H.**	37–19	1	
BD.17070	**CORNER PANEL, DASH TO SCUTTLE TOP PANEL, L.H.**	37–20	1	
BD.15467	**CLOSING PANEL, UNDER R.H. WINDSCREEN PILLAR**	37–21	1	
BD.15468	**CLOSING PANEL, UNDER L.H. WINDSCREEN PILLAR**	37–22	1	
BD.18710	**FRAME ASSEMBLY MOUNTING STONEGUARD**	37–23	1	

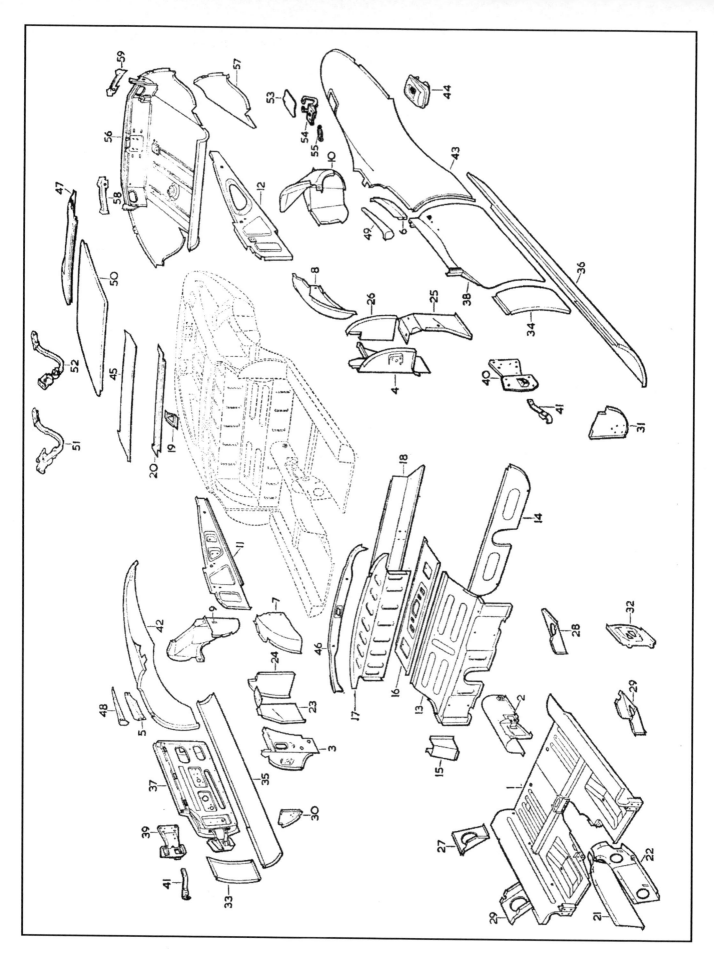

PLATE 36

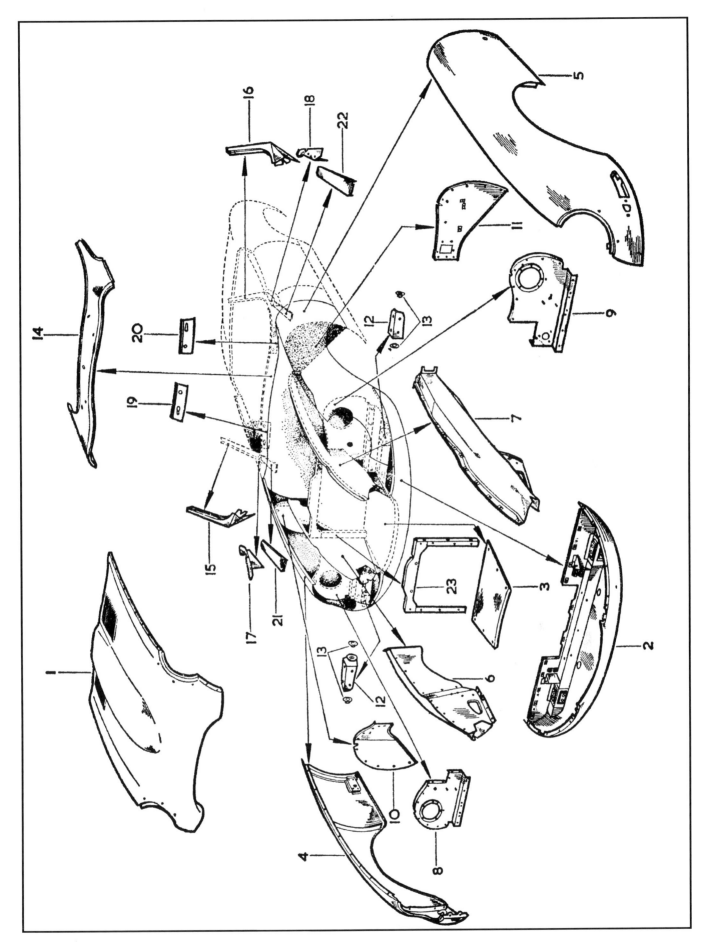

PLATE 37

175

BODY FITTINGS
FOR OPEN CARS ONLY

Part No.	Description	Plate No.	No. per Unit	Remarks
BD.19145	**R.H. FRONT BUMPER ASSEMBLY**		1	
BD.19146	**L.H. FRONT BUMPER ASSEMBLY**		1	
BD.15533	**Bar Assembly only,** for R.H. Front Bumper	38– 1	1	
BD.15532	**Bar Assembly only,** for L.H. Front Bumper	38– 2	1	
BD.19111	**Over Rider Assembly,** on R.H. Front Bumper	38– 3	1	
BD.19112	**Over Rider Assembly,** on L.H. Front Bumper	38– 4	1	
BD.19149	**Beading,** between Over Rider and Front Bumpers	38– 5	4	
UFN.137/L	**Nut,** securing Over Rider to Front Bumpers		2	
FG.106/X	**Washer,** Spring, under Nuts		2	
FW.106/T	**Washer,** Plain, under Spring Washers		2	
BD.19113	**Extension Assembly,** for fixing of Motif Bar	38– 6	2	
UFS.125/6R	**Screw,** Set, securing Extension Bracket to Over Riders		4	
C.724	**Washer,** Shakeproof, on Setscrews		4	
FW.104/T	**Washer,** Plain, under Shakeproof Washers		4	
BD.19119	**Distance Piece,** on Setscrews		4	
UFS.137/10R	**Screw,** Set, securing Front Bumpers to Bonnet		4	
FG.106/X	**Washer,** Spring, on Setscrews		4	
C.410	**Washer,** Plain, under Spring Washers		4	
BD.20893	**Spacer,** on Setscrews, at side fixings		2	
BD.20663	**Spacer,** on Setscrews, at front fixings		2	
BD.18947/2	**Rubber Seal,** between Front Bumpers and Bonnet	38– 7	2	
BD.10313	**Clip,** securing Seal	38– 8	2	
BD.17700	**MOTIF BAR IN AIR INTAKE APERTURE**	38– 9	1	
C.16336	**MOTIF**	38–10	1	
BD.19033	**Backing Piece,** behind Motif	38–11	1	
BD.19034	**Spring Clip,** retaining Motif	38–12	1	
BD.11501	**Screw,** Self-Tapping, securing Spring Clip	38–13	2	
UFS.125/5R	**Screw,** Set, securing Motif Bar		2	
FG.104/X	**Washer,** Spring, on Setscrews		2	
BD.19147	**R.H. REAR BUMPER ASSEMBLY**		1	
BD.19148	**L.H. REAR BUMPER ASSEMBLY**		1	
BD.15887	**Bar Assembly only,** for R.H. Rear Bumper	38–14	1	
BD.15888	**Bar Assembly only,** for L.H. Rear Bumper	38–15	1	
BD.19135	**Over Rider Assembly,** for R.H. Rear Bumper	38–16	1	
BD.19136	**Over Rider Assembly,** for L.H. Rear Bumper	38–17	1	
UFN.137/L	**Nut,** securing Over Rider to Rear Bumpers		2	
FG.106/X	**Washer,** Spring, under Nuts		2	
FW.106/T	**Washer,** Plain, under Spring Washers		2	
BD.19149	**Beading,** between Over Rider and Rear Bumpers	38–18	4	
UFS.131/6R	**Screw,** Set, securing Rear Bumpers to Body		2	
FG.105/X	**Washer,** Spring, on Setscrews		2	
FW.105/T	**Washer,** Plain, under Spring Washers		2	
UFS.137/10R	**Screw,** Set, securing Rear Bumpers to Body		2	
UFN.137/L	**Nut,** securing Rear Bumpers to Body		2	
FG.106/X	**Washer,** Spring, on Setscrews and under Nuts		4	
FW.106/T	**Washer,** Plain, under Spring Washers		4	
BD.20893	**Nylon Spacer,** at Rear Bumper mountings		4	
BD.18947/1	**Rubber Seal,** between Rear Bumpers and Body	38–19	2	

Part No.	Description	Plate No.	No. per Unit	Remarks
BD.16789	**CHROME FINISHER ASSEMBLY AROUND R.H. HEADLAMP APERTURE**	38–20	1	
BD.16790	**CHROME FINISHER ASSEMBLY AROUND L.H. HEADLAMP APERTURE**	38–21	1	
BD.16786	**GLASS IN R.H. HEADLAMP APERTURE**	38–22	1	
BD.16787	**GLASS IN L.H. HEADLAMP APERTURE**	38–23	1	
BD.16788	**RUBBER SEAL AROUND HEADLAMP GLASSES**	38–24	2	
BD.19013/2	**Screw,** Self-Tapping, securing Finishers and Headlamp Glasses to Bonnet		12	**FOR USE ONLY WITH SPIRE NUT FIXING.**
BD.8633/5	**Spire Nut,** on Self-Tapping Screws		12	
BD.22780/4	**Screw,** Set, securing Finishers and Headlamp Glasses to Bonnet		12	**FOR USE ONLY WITH TAPPED PLATE FIXING.**
BD.17651	**FINISHING PANEL ASSEMBLY IN R.H. HEADLAMP RECESS**	38–25	1	
BD.17652	**FINISHING PANEL ASSEMBLY IN L.H. HEADLAMP RECESS**	38–26	1	
BD.20543/1	**Rubber Seal,** for Panels	38–27	2	
UFS.119/6R	**Screw,** Set, securing Panels to Headlamp Diaphragms		2	
UFS.119/8R	**Screw,** Set, securing Panels to Headlamp Diaphragms		4	
AG.102/X	**Washer,** Spring, on Setscrews		6	
AW.102/T	**Washer,** Plain, under Spring Washers		6	
UFN.119/L	**Nut,** on Setscrews		6	
C.1094	**Distance Piece,** for Panels		As req'd	

BODY FITTINGS
FOR OPEN CARS ONLY

Part No.	Description	Plate No.	No. per Unit	Remarks
BD.19029/2	**CHROME BEADING, FORWARD OF HEADLAMP APERTURES**	38–28	2	
BD.19029/1	**CHROME BEADING, AT REAR OF HEADLAMP APERTURES**	38–29	2	
BD.19030	**Brass Clip**, securing Chrome Beads	38–30	22	
BD.20934	**PIVOTED CARRIER BRACKET ASSEMBLY FOR FRONT NUMBER PLATE**		1	
UFN.125/L	**Nut**, securing Carrier Bracket to Bonnet Front Under Panel		2	
C.724	**Washer**, Shakeproof, under Nuts		2	
BD.20939	**Packing Block** (Aluminium) at Carrier Bracket fixings		2	TO BE FITTED ONLY AS REQUIRED.
BD.20936	**CONTROL ROD, OPERATING CARRIER BRACKET PIVOT WHEN BONNET IS MOVED**		1	
C.13806	**Clip**, securing Control Rod to Carrier Bracket		1	
C.4548	**GROMMET, IN BONNET FRONT UNDER PANEL, FOR CONTROL ROD**		1	
BD.20937	**FORK END FOR CONNECTION OF CONTROL ROD TO BRACKET ON FRONT SUB-FRAME**		1	TO BE FITTED ONLY AS REQUIRED.
UFN.125/L	**Nut**, locking Fork End to Control Rod		1	
J.103/10S	**Clevis Pin**, securing Fork End to Bracket on Front Sub-Frame		1	
L.102/4U	**Split Pin**, retaining Clevis Pin		1	
AW.102/T	**Washer**, Plain, behind Split Pin		1	

Part No.	Description	Plate No.	No. per Unit	Remarks
BD.20989	**RUBBER PLUG SEALING REDUNDANT APERTURE IN BONNET FRONT UNDER PANEL**		1	NOT REQUIRED WHEN FRONT NUMBER PLATE CARRIER IS FITTED.
BD.20093	**STONE GUARD ASSEMBLY AT REAR OF BONNET AIR INTAKE APERTURE**	38–31	1	
BD.20150/3	**Screw,** Set, securing Stone Guard to Bonnet		8	
C.723/A	**Washer,** Shakeproof, on Setscrews		8	
BD.541/34	**Special Washer,** under Shakeproof Washers at side fixings		6	
AW.102/T	**Washer,** Plain, under Shakeproof Washers at top fixings		2	
BD.20579	**Bracket,** for lower fixing of Stone Guard		2	
UFS.125/4R	**Screw,** Set, securing Brackets and Stone Guard		4	
UFN.125/L	**Nut,** on Setscrews		4	
C.724	**Washer,** Shakeproof, under Nuts		4	
FW.104/T	**Washer,** Plain, under Shakeproof Washers		4	
BD.18710	**FRAME ASSEMBLY FOR FIXING OF STONE GUARD**	38–32	1	
BD.19031	**Felt Strip** at top of Frame ($\frac{1}{4}'' \times \frac{5}{8}'' \times 23''$)		1	
BD.16839/2	**Screw,** Self-Tapping, securing Frame to Bonnet		6	
BD.542/3	**Special Washer,** on Self-Tapping Screws		6	
BD.20014	**BONNET BALANCE LINK ASSEMBLY, R.H.**	38–33	1	
BD.20015	**BONNET BALANCE LINK ASSEMBLY, L.H.**	38–34	1	
BD.19972	**Spring,** on Bonnet Balance Links		4	
BD.20013/4	**Brass Washer,** at each side of spring "eyes"		16	
L.102/6U	**Split Pin,** retaining Springs		8	
BD.8291/2	**Screw,** Set, securing Balance Links to Bonnet		8	
C.724	**Washer,** Shakeproof, on Setscrews		8	
BD.541/20	**Special Washer,** under Shakeproof Washers		8	
BD.19736	**Bolt** (Shouldered) securing Balance Links to Front Frame		2	
BD.20013/1	**Brass Washer,** on Bolts		2	
BD.20013/2	**Brass Washer,** on Bolts		2	
C.8667/1	**Nut,** Self-Locking, on Bolts		2	

BODY FITTINGS
FOR OPEN CARS ONLY

Part No.	Description	Plate No.	No. per Unit	Remarks
BD.19178	**GRILLE AT REAR OF BONNET**	38–35	1	
BD.17290	**Thread Cutting Fix**, securing Grille to Bonnet		2	
UFS.419/4H	**Screw**, Set, securing Grille to Bonnet		2	
C.723/A	**Washer**, Shakeproof, on Setscrews		2	
BD.20315	**BONNET SAFETY CATCH ASSEMBLY**	38–36	1	
BD.20318	**Spring**, on Safety Catch		1	
J.103/15S	**Clevis Pin**, through Safety Catch		1	
L.102/4U	**Split Pin**, retaining Clevis Pin		1	
BD.541/28	**Washer**, Special, behind Split Pin		1	
BD.20319	**Tapped Plate**, for fixing of Safety Catch		1	
UFS.419/3H	**Screw**, Set, securing Safety Catch to Bonnet		4	
C.723/A	**Washer**, Shakeproof, on Setscrews		4	
BD.20320	**BRACKET RECEIVING SAFETY CATCH**	38–37	1	
BD.18307/3	**Screw**, Set, securing Bracket to Scuttle		2	
C.724	**Washer**, Shakeproof, on Setscrews		2	
BD.19730	**EXTENSION ASSEMBLY AT REAR OF BONNET DUCT FOR HEATER AIR INTAKE**	38–38	1	
BD.23657	**Rubber Seal**, for Air Intake	38–39	1	
BD.16839/3	**Screw**, Self-Tapping, securing Extension to Bonnet		6	
FG.104/X	**Washer**, Spring, on Self-Tapping Screws		6	
BD.542/3	**Special Washer**, under Spring Washers		6	
BD.20816/1	**Rubber Seal**, between Bonnet L.H. Valance and Frame Side Member (9½" long)	38–40	1	
BD.20735	**Fixing Strip**, for Rubber Seal	38–41	1	
BD.20816/2	**Rubber Seal**, between Bonnet L.H. Rear Diaphragm and Frame Side Member (4" long)	38–42	1	
BD.20736	**Fixing Strip**, for Rubber Seal	38–43	1	
BD.1814/2	**Pop Rivet**, securing Fixing Strips		8	
BD.16015	**LOCK ASSEMBLY AT R.H. SIDE OF BONNET (WB.3/10894)**	38–44	1	
BD.16016	**LOCK ASSEMBLY AT L.H. SIDE OF BONNET (WB.3/10893)**	38–45	1	
UCS.419/4H	**Screw**, Set, securing Locks to Bonnet		8	
AG.102/X	**Washer**, Spring, on Setscrews		8	Fitted from Chassis No. 850001 to 850091. 875001 to 875385.
BD.2551	**ESCUTCHEON FOR BONNET LOCKS (WB.16049/B)**	38–46	2	
BD.540/9	**Screw**, Self-Tapping, securing Escutcheons to Bonnet		4	
BD.16012	**BRACKET ASSEMBLY ENGAGING BONNET LOCKS**	38–47	2	
UFS.119/6R	**Screw**, Set, securing Brackets to Body		4	
C.723/A	**Washer**, Shakeproof, on Setscrews		4	
AW.102/T	**Washer**, Plain, under Shakeproof Washers		4	
BD.16013	**Shim**, under Brackets		As req'd	

Part No.	Description	Plate No.	No. per Unit	Remarks
BD.19890	**R.H. LOCKING HOOK ASSEMBLY FOR BONNET**		1	
BD.19891	**L.H. LOCKING HOOK ASSEMBLY FOR BONNET**		1	
BD.19894	**Lever,** on Locking Hook Shafts		2	
C.8737/1	**Nut,** securing Levers to Shafts		2	
BD.19883	**BRACKET ASSEMBLY MOUNTING LOCKING HOOKS**		2	
BD.18307/2	**Screw,** Set, securing Brackets to Dash		6	
C.724	**Washer,** Shakeproof, on Setscrews		6	
BD.19977	**HANDLE AND ROD ASSEMBLY FOR R.H. LOCKING HOOK**		1	
BD.19978	**HANDLE AND ROD ASSEMBLY FOR L.H. LOCKING HOOK**		1	Fitted to Chassis No. 850092 and subs. 875386 and subs.
BD.19903	**Handle** only		2	
BD.19904	**Escutcheon**		2	
BD.19895	**Neoprene Seal,** on Rods		2	
BD.19013/2	**Screw,** Self-Tapping, securing Escutcheons to Body		4	
BD.8633/8	**Speed Nut,** on Self-Tapping Screws (SNU.1686)		4	
C.13806	**Linkage Clip,** securing **Operating Rods** to **Locking Hooks**		2	
BD.19905	**BRACKET ASSEMBLY ON BONNET SIDE PANEL, ENGAGING R.H. HOOK**		1	
BD.19906	**BRACKET ASSEMBLY ON BONNET SIDE PANEL, ENGAGING L.H. HOOK**		1	
BD.18307/2	**Screw,** Set, securing Brackets to Bonnet		4	
C.724	**Washer,** Shakeproof, on Setscrews		4	
BD.541/6	**Special Washer,** under Shakeproof Washers		4	
BD.19896	**Locating Peg,** on Brackets		2	
UFN.231/L	**Nut,** securing Locating Pegs		4	
BD.19936	**Rubber Buffer,** on Locating Pegs		2	
BD.19917	**Bracket,** receiving Locating Pegs		2	
BD.8291/2	**Screw,** Set, securing Brackets to Dash		4	
C.724	**Washer,** Shakeproof, on Setscrews		4	
BD.20903/1	**REST RUBBER FOR REAR EDGE OF BONNET (68″ LONG)**	38–48	1	

BODY FITTINGS
FOR OPEN CARS ONLY

Part No.	Description	Plate No.	No. per Unit	Remarks
BD.10224	**RUBBER BUFFER CUSHIONING BONNET SIDES IN CLOSED POSITION**	38–49	2	Fitted from Chassis No. 850001 to 850091. 875001 to 875385.
UFS.131/8R	**Screw,** Set, securing Rubber Buffers to Dash		2	
UFN.231/L	**Locknut,** on Setscrews		2	
BD.15165	**CARRIER BRACKET FOR BATTERY TRAY**	38–50	1	
UFS.125/4R	**Screw,** Set, securing Carrier Bracket to L.H. Sill		5	
FG.104/X	**Washer,** Spring, on Setscrews		5	
FW.104/T	**Washer,** Plain, under Spring Washers		5	
UFN.125/L	**Nut,** on Setscrews		5	
BD.20048	**R.H. UNDERSHIELD FOR FRONT FRAME**	38–51	1	
BD.20047	**L.H. UNDERSHIELD FOR FRONT FRAME**	38–52	1	
BD.20049	**Bracket,** for fixing of Undershields to Frame		4	
UFS.125/4R	**Screw,** Set, securing Brackets and Undershields to Front Frame		4	
UFN.125/L	**Nut,** on Setscrews		4	
C.724	**Washer,** Shakeproof, under Nuts		4	
FW.104/T	**Washer,** Plain, on Setscrews		4	
BD.8633/6	**Spire Nut,** for fixing of Undershields to Sills and Mudshields		8	
BD.8691/1	**Screw,** Self-Tapping, securing Undershields to Sills and Mudshields		8	
AW.102/T	**Washer,** Plain, on Self-Tapping Screws		8	
BD.25541	**Seal** (Canvas/Rubber) for L.H. Front Frame Undershield		1	Fitted to Chassis No. 850681 and subs. 879160 and subs. **May be fitted to cars prior to above Chassis numbers, if desired.**
BD.19522	**R.H. MUDSHIELD ASSEMBLY**	38–53	1	
BD.20425	**Bracket,** upper, for fixing of R.H. Mudshield		1	
BD.20426	**Bracket,** lower, for fixing of R.H. Mudshield		1	
BD.11712/2	**Pop Rivet,** securing Mudshield		2	
BD.20434/1	**Rubber Seal,** for R.H. Mudshield (27½" long)		1	
BD.20429	**Fixing Strip,** securing Seal to R.H. Mudshield		1	
BD.20427	**Fixing Strip,** securing Seal to R.H. Sill		1	
BD.1814/6	**Pop Rivet,** securing Fixing Strips through Seal		11	

Part No.	Description	Plate No.	No. per Unit	Remarks
BD.19521	**L.H. MUDSHIELD ASSEMBLY**	38–54	1	
BD.20426	**Bracket**, for fixing of L.H. Mudshield		1	
BD.20434/2	**Rubber Seal**, for L.H. Mudshield (14½″ long)		1	
BD.20428	**Fixing Strip**, securing Seal to L.H. Mudshield		1	
BD.20427	**Fixing Strip**, securing Seal to L.H. Sill		1	
BD.1814/6	**Pop Rivet**, securing Fixing Strips through Seal		8	
UFS.125/4R	**Screw**, Set, securing Mudshields to Front Frame and Sills		10	
BD.541/20	**Washer**, Special, on Setscrews		10	
UFN.125/L	**Nut**, on Setscrews		10	
C.724	**Washer**, Shakeproof, under Nuts		10	
BD.19714	**SEAL HOUSING FOR LOWER STEERING COLUMN THROUGH DASH**	38–55	1	
BD.20589	**Sealing Ring**	38–56	1	Fitted from Chassis No. 850001 to 850547.
C.20488	**Sealing Ring**	38–56	1	Fitted to Chassis No. 850548 and subs.
BD.19710	**Retainer**, for Sealing Ring	38–57	1	
BD.19716/1	**Screw**, Self-Tapping, securing Retainer		3	
BD.19707	**Gasket**, under Steering Column Seal	38–58	1	
UFS.125/5R	**Screw**, Set, securing Seal to Dash		4	
FW.104/T	**Washer**, Plain, on Setscrews		4	
UFN.125/L	**Nut**, on Setscrews		4	
C.724	**Washer**, Shakeproof, under Nuts		4	R.H. DRIVE CARS ONLY
BD.19712	**COVER ASSEMBLY, SEALING REDUNDANT BRAKE PEDAL HOUSING APERTURE IN DASH**		1	
BD.19707	**Gasket**, under Cover		1	
UFN.125/L	**Nut**, securing Cover to Dash		4	
C.724	**Washer**, Shakeproof, under Nuts		4	
FW.104/T	**Washer**, Plain, under Shakeproof Washers		4	R.H. DRIVE CARS ONLY.
BD.19713	**COVER ASSEMBLY, SEALING REDUNDANT ACCELERATOR PEDAL HOUSING APERTURE IN DASH**		1	
BD.19708	**Gasket**, under Cover		1	
UFN.125/L	**Nut**, securing Cover to Dash		4	
C.724	**Washer**, Shakeproof, under Nuts		4	
FW.104/T	**Washer**, Plain, under Shakeproof Washers		4	R.H. DRIVE CARS ONLY.

BODY FITTINGS
FOR OPEN CARS ONLY

Part No.	Description	Plate No.	No. per Unit	Remarks
BD.19712	**COVER ASSEMBLY, SEALING REDUNDANT BRAKE PEDAL AND STEERING COLUMN APERTURES IN DASH**		2	
BD.19707	**Gasket,** under Covers		2	L.H. DRIVE CARS ONLY.
UFN.125/L	**Nut,** securing Covers to Dash		8	
C.724	**Washer,** Shakeproof, under Nuts		8	
FW.104/T	**Washer,** Plain, under Nuts		8	
BD.19711	**COVER ASSEMBLY, SEALING REDUNDANT ACCELERATOR PEDAL HOUSING APERTURE IN DASH**		1	
BD.19706	**Gasket,** under Cover		1	L.H. DRIVE CARS ONLY.
UFN.125/L	**Nut,** securing Cover to Dash		3	
C.724	**Washer,** Shakeproof, under Nuts		3	
FW.104/T	**Washer,** Plain, under Shakeproof Washers		3	
BD.20589	**SEAL, IN ACCELERATOR PEDAL HOUSING, FOR LOWER STEERING COLUMN**		1	Fitted from Chassis No. 875001 to 877487.
C.20488	**SEAL, IN ACCELERATOR PEDAL HOUSING, FOR LOWER STEERING COLUMN**		1	Fitted to Chassis No. 877488 and subs.
BD.19710	**Retainer, for Seal**		1	L.H. DRIVE CARS ONLY.
UCS.413/3H	**Screw,** Set, securing Retainer		3	
C.721	**Washer,** Shakeproof, on Setscrews		3	
BD.19717	**PLUG (BLACK P.V.C.) SEALING REDUNDANT HOLES IN DASH**		3	
BD.15501	**WINDSCREEN GLASS**	38–59	1	
BD.15514	**Rubber Seal,** around Windscreen Glass	38–60	1	
BD.17573	**Rubber Insert,** for Seal	38–61	1	
BD.20856	**Chrome Finisher,** at top edge of Windscreen	38–62	1	
BD.17380/7	**Rubber Seal,** under Finisher	38–63	1	
BD.17702	**Chrome Finisher** at R.H. side of Windscreen	38–64	1	Fitted from Chassis No. 850001 to 850087. 875001 to 875309.
BD.17701	**Chrome Finisher** at L.H. side of Windscreen	38–65	1	
BD.17703	**Chrome Finisher** at bottom edge of Windscreen	38–66	1	
BD.17704	**Joint Piece,** for side and bottom Finishers	38–67	2	
BD.20881	**Chrome Finisher** at R.H. side of Windscreen		1	Fitted to Chassis No. 850088 and subs. 875310 and subs.
BD.20882	**Chrome Finisher** at L.H. side of Windscreen		1	
BD.20562	**Chrome Finisher** at bottom edge of Windscreen		1	
BD.540/1	**Screw,** Self-Tapping, securing Side Finishers		2	
BD.1814/4	**Pop Rivet,** securing Side Finishers		4	

Part No.	Description	Plate No.	No. per Unit	Remarks
BD.15508	**CHROME CAPPING AT TOP OF R.H. WINDSCREEN PILLAR**	38–68	1	
BD.15509	**CHROME CAPPING AT TOP OF L.H. WINDSCREEN PILLAR**	38–69	1	
BD.15534/3	**Screw,** Set, securing Cappings to side of Windscreen Pillars		2	
BD.16940/2	**Screw,** Set, securing Cappings to top of Windscreen Pillars		2	
BD.20456	**TRIM PANEL ASSEMBLY ON R.H. SCREEN PILLAR**	38–70	1	
BD.20457	**TRIM PANEL ASSEMBLY ON L.H. SCREEN PILLAR**	38–71	1	
BD.21133	**Spring Clip,** securing Trim Panels	38–72	4	
BD.21181	**LICENCE HOLDER ON WINDSCREEN**		1	
BD.19752	**SCREEN RAIL FACIA ASSEMBLY, COMPLETE**	39– 1	1	FOR SPARES REPLACEMENTS USE BD.22732 TOGETHER WITH BD.23077.
BD.20590	**Bezel,** for centre Demister Slot		1	
BD.20591	**Bezel,** for intermediate Demister Slots		2	
BD.20592	**Bezel,** for outer Demister Slots		2	
BD.539/22	**Screw,** Self-Tapping, securing Bezels		10	
BD.22732	**SCREEN RAIL FACIA ASSEMBLY, COMPLETE**		1	MAY BE USED TO REPLACE BD.19752.
	All items are as for Screen Rail Facia Assembly BD.19752.			
BD.23077	**"Y" Piece,** for Air Duct Hoses		2	
UFN.119/L	**Nut,** securing Screen Rail Facia		4	
C.723/A	**Washer,** Shakeproof, under Nuts		4	
AW.102/T	**Washer,** Plain, under Shakeproof Washers		4	
BD.21182	**Bracket,** for R.H. outer fixing of Screen Rail Facia		1	
BD.21183	**Bracket,** for L.H. outer fixing of Screen Rail Facia		1	
BD.1814/2	**Pop Rivet,** securing Brackets to Dash		4	
BD.20565	**Bracket,** for R.H. inner fixing of Screen Rail Facia		1	
BD.20566	**Bracket,** for L.H. inner fixing of Screen Rail Facia		1	

BODY FITTINGS
FOR OPEN CARS ONLY

Part No.	Description	Plate No.	No. per Unit	Remarks
BD.19643	**L.H. FACIA PANEL ASSEMBLY**	39– 2	1	**R.H. DRIVE CARS ONLY.**
BD.19699	**Cubby Box,** in L.H. Facia		1	
BD.20605	**Fixing Strip,** securing Cubby Box at top		1	
UFN.119/L	**Nut,** securing Fixing Strip		3	
C.723/A	**Washer,** Shakeproof, on Setscrews		3	
BD.1229/16	**Screw,** Self-Tapping, securing Cubby Box at bottom		3	
C.1094	**Distance Piece,** on Self-Tapping Screws		3	
BD.20633/1	**Spire Nut,** on Self-Tapping Screws		3	
BD.19644	**R.H. FACIA PANEL ASSEMBLY**	39– 3	1	**R.H. DRIVE CARS ONLY.**
BD.19645	**L.H. FACIA PANEL ASSEMBLY**		1	**L.H. DRIVE CARS ONLY, BUT NOT REQUIRED FOR ITALY.**
BD.20812	**L.H. FACIA PANEL ASSEMBLY**		1	**REQUIRED ONLY FOR L.H. DRIVE CARS EXPORTED TO ITALY.**
BD.19646	**R.H. FACIA PANEL ASSEMBLY**		1	**L.H. DRIVE CARS ONLY.**
BD.19698	**Cubby Box,** in R.H. Facia		1	
BD.20605	**Fixing Strip,** securing Cubby Box at top		1	
UFN.119/L	**Nut,** securing Fixing Strip		3	
C.723/A	**Washer,** Shakeproof, under Nuts		3	
BD.1229/16	**Screw,** Self-Tapping, securing Cubby Box at bottom		3	
C.1094	**Distance Piece,** on Self-Tapping Screws		3	
BD.20633/1	**Spire Nut,** on Self-Tapping Screws		3	
BD.20861/1	**Screw,** Set, Pan Head, securing Facia Panels at centre		4	
UFS.119/3R	**Screw,** Set, securing Facia Panels at centre		2	
C.723/A	**Washer,** Shakeproof, on Setscrews		4	
AW.102/T	**Washer,** Plain, under Shakeproof Washers		6	
BD.19241	**Bracket,** for fixing of L.H. Facia to Dash side		1	
BD.19242	**Bracket,** for fixing of R.H. Facia to Dash side		1	
BD.1814/2	**Pop Rivet,** securing Brackets		4	
UFN.119/L	**Nut,** securing Facias to Brackets		4	
C.723/A	**Washer,** Shakeproof, under Nuts		4	
BD.20636	**GRAB HANDLE ASSEMBLY AT R.H. SIDE OF DASH**		1	**L.H. DRIVE CARS ONLY.**

Part No.	Description	Plate No.	No. per Unit	Remarks
BD.20637	**GRAB HANDLE ASSEMBLY AT L.H. SIDE OF DASH**	39– 4	1	**R.H. DRIVE CARS ONLY.**
UCS.119/3R	**Screw,** Set, securing Grab Handle to Facia Panel		2	
C.723/A	**Washer,** Shakeproof, on Setscrews		2	
BD.20640	**Bracket,** for fixing of Grab Handle to Dash side		1	
BD.540/19	**Screw,** Self-Tapping, securing Bracket		2	
BD.20639	**Special Bolt,** securing Grab Handle to Bracket		1	
C.739	**Washer,** Shakeproof, on Special Bolt		1	
BD.20462	**CASING ASSEMBLY, UNDER R.H. SIDE OF SCUTTLE**	39– 5	1	
BD.20463	**CASING ASSEMBLY, UNDER L.H. SIDE OF SCUTTLE**	39– 6	1	**R.H. DRIVE CARS ONLY.**
BD.20470	**CASING ASSEMBLY, UNDER CENTRE OF SCUTTLE**	39– 7	1	
BD.20728	**COVER ASSEMBLY, PROTECTING WIRING HARNESS AT L.H. SIDE OF DASH**	39– 8	1	
BD.20464	**CASING ASSEMBLY, UNDER R.H. SIDE OF SCUTTLE**		1	
BD.20465	**CASING ASSEMBLY, UNDER L.H. SIDE OF SCUTTLE**		1	**L.H. DRIVE CARS ONLY.**
BD.20471	**CASING ASSEMBLY, UNDER CENTRE OF SCUTTLE**		1	
BD.21136	**Fixing Bracket,** for Scuttle Casings		4	
BD.8537/1	**Screw,** Self-Tapping, securing Casings		2	
BD.532/2	**Cup Washer,** on Self-Tapping Screws		2	
BD.8536/6	**Spire Nut,** on Self-Tapping Screws		2	

BODY FITTINGS
FOR OPEN CARS ONLY

Part No.	Description	Plate No.	No. per Unit	Remarks
BD.20035	**FRONT FINISHER PANEL ASSEMBLY ABOVE GEARBOX TUNNEL**	39– 9	1	
BD.19967	**Face Panel,** for Front Finisher		1	
BD.19984	**Grille Assembly,** in Loudspeaker Apertures		2	
UCN.113/L	**Nut,** securing Grilles to Front Finisher Panel		8	Fitted from Chassis No.
C.721	**Washer,** Shakeproof, under Nuts		8	850001 to 850609.
AW.104/T	**Washer,** Plain, under Shakeproof Washers		8	875001 to 878301.
BD.20409	**Ash Tray and Panel Assembly**		1	
BD.22669	**Tapped Plate,** securing Ash Tray Panel to Front Finisher Panel		2	
BD.13713/2	**Screw,** Set, securing Ash Tray Panel to Front Finisher Panel		4	
C.2017/1	**Washer,** Special, on Setscrews		4	
BD.23648	**FRONT FINISHER PANEL ASSEMBLY ABOVE GEARBOX TUNNEL**		1	
				Fitted to Chassis No.
BD.23649	**Face Panel,** for Front Finisher		1	850610 and subs.
				878302 and subs.
	All other items are as for Front Finisher Assembly BD.20035.			
BD.19049	**Bracket Assembly,** L.H., for fixing of Front Finisher Panel		1	
BD.19050	**Bracket Assembly,** R.H., for fixing of Front Finisher Panel		1	
UFS.419/4H	**Screw,** Set, securing Brackets to Dash		4	
C.723/A	**Washer,** Shakeproof, on Setscrews		4	
BD.17589	**Knob,** securing Front Finisher Panel		4	
BD.541/32	**Washer,** Special, behind Knobs		4	
BD.20409	**ASH TRAY AND PANEL ASSEMBLY**		1	
BD.20403	**Panel Assembly**	39–10	1	
BD.20410	**Ash Tray Assembly,** complete	39–11	1	
BD.20412	**Motif only,** on Ash Tray		1	
AN.106/K	**Nut,** securing Motif		1	
C.720	**Washer,** Shakeproof, under Nut		1	
BD.24393	**Light Shield** (Rubber Strip $\frac{1}{16}'' \times \frac{1}{4}'' \times 10''$)		1	
BD.24394	**Retainer,** for Light Shield		1	
BD.540/19	**Self-Tapping Screw,** securing Retainer		2	
BD.711/9	**Self-Tapping Screw,** securing Retainer		2	
BD.20722	**FINISHER PANEL ASSEMBLY IN RADIO CONTROL UNIT APERTURE**	39–12	1	
UFN.119/L	**Nut,** securing Finisher to Front Finisher Panel		2	**NOT REQUIRED WHEN RADIO IS FITTED.**
C.723/A	**Washer,** Shakeproof, under Nuts		2	
BD.541/13	**Washer,** Plain, under Shakeproof Washers		2	
BD.17354	**BASE PLATE AND SURROUND (CHROME PLATED) FOR RADIO APERTURE FINISHER PANEL**	39–13	1	**NOT REQUIRED WHEN RADIO IS FITTED.**

Part No.	Description	Plate No.	No. per Unit	Remarks
BD.15488	**GEARBOX COVER**	39–14	1	SUPERSEDED BY BD.24129.
BD.8691/7	**Screw,** Self-Tapping, securing Gearbox Cover		12	
BD.542/3	**Washer,** Plain, on Self-Tapping Screws		12	
BD.24129	**GEARBOX COVER**		1	SUPERSEDES BD.15488.
BD.8691/7	**Screw,** Self-Tapping, securing Gearbox Cover		12	
BD.542/3	**Washer,** Plain, on Self-Tapping Screws		12	
BD.10821	**RUBBER PLUG, SEALING GEARBOX ACCESS APERTURES**		2	
BD.20031	**FINISHER PANEL ASSEMBLY ON GEARBOX COVER AND PROPELLER SHAFT TUNNEL**	39–15	1	Fitted from Chassis No. 850001 to 850609. 875001 to 878301.
BD.19979	**Top Face Panel**		1	
BD.19971	**Gauntlet Face Panel**		1	
BD.19981	**Chrome Bezel,** at top of Gauntlet Panel		1	
BD.22385	**Rivet,** securing Bezel to Gauntlet Panel		14	
BD.23650	**FINISHER PANEL ASSEMBLY ON GEARBOX COVER AND PROPELLER SHAFT TUNNEL**		1	Fitted to Chassis No. 850610 and subs. 878302 and subs.
BD.23651	**Top Face Panel**		1	
BD.23652	**Gauntlet Face Panel**		1	
BD.19981	**Chrome Bezel,** at top of Gauntlet Panel		1	
BD.22385	**Rivet,** securing Bezel to Gauntlet Panel		14	
BD.20469	**Seal,** for Handbrake Lever Aperture (Rubber Strip $\frac{1}{16}'' \times 2\frac{1}{2}'' \times 6''$)		1	
BD.19728	**Chrome Ferrule,** at top of Gear Lever Gauntlet		1	
BD.19729	**Ferrule Base** (Nylon)		1	
BD.17546/1	**Screw,** Set, securing Finisher Panel to Tunnel		3	
BD.541/32	**Special Washer,** on Setscrews		3	
BD.20820	**SEAT SQUAB FRAME ASSEMBLY (TRIMMED)**	39–16	2	
BD.20148	**SEAT CUSHION ASSEMBLY**	39–17	2	

BODY FITTINGS
FOR OPEN CARS ONLY

Part No.	Description	Plate No.	No. per Unit	Remarks
BD.18958	**LOCKING SLIDE FOR R.H. SEAT**		1	Fitted from Chassis No. 850001 to 850526. 875001 to 877355.
BD.18959	**LOCKING SLIDE FOR L.H. SEAT**	39–18	1	
BD.22810	**LOCKING SLIDE FOR L.H. SEAT**		1	Fitted to Chassis No. 850527 and subs. 877356 and subs.
BD.22811	**LOCKING SLIDE FOR R.H. SEAT**		1	
BD.18960	**SEAT SLIDE (PLAIN)**	39–19	2	Fitted from Chassis No. 850001 to 850526. 875001 to 877355.
BD.22812	**SEAT SLIDE (PLAIN)**		2	Fitted to Chassis No. 850527 and subs. 877356 and subs.
BD.18117/4	**Screw,** Set, securing Slides to Floor		8	
BD.17648	**Packing,** between Slides and Floor		8	
UFN.125/L	**Nut,** securing Slides to Seats		8	
BD.542/3	**Washer,** Special, under Nuts		8	
C.724	**Washer,** Shakeproof, on Setscrews and under Nuts		16	
C.18698	**Distance Piece,** at fixings of Slides to Seats		4	
BD.19378	**Support Strap,** for Adjusting Levers		2	
UFS.519/4H	**Screw,** Set, securing Support Straps		4	
UFN.119/L	**Nut,** on Setscrews		4	
C.723/A	**Washer,** Shakeproof, under Nuts		4	
C.5203/1	**Washer,** Special, under Shakeproof Washers		4	
BD.20216	**MAT ASSEMBLY, ON FLOOR, BEHIND SEATS**		2	Fitted from Chassis No. 850001 to 850526. 875001 to 877355.
BD.23624	**MAT ASSEMBLY, ON FLOOR, BEHIND SEATS**		2	Fitted to Chassis No. 850527 and subs. 877356 and subs.
BD.20436	**SHIELD ASSEMBLY, FRONT, FOR HEAT INSULATION FROM EXHAUST SYSTEM**	39–20	1	Fitted from Chassis No. 850001 to 850648. 875001 to 878888.

Part No.	Description	Plate No.	No. per Unit	Remarks
BD.25237	**SHIELD ASSEMBLY, FRONT, FOR HEAT INSULATION FROM EXHAUST SYSTEM**		1	Fitted to Chassis No. 850649 and subs. 878889 and subs. **See note below.**
BD.711/23	**Screw,** Self-Tapping, securing Shield to Floor		2	
UFS.125/3R	**Screw,** Set, securing Shield to Floor		1	
C.724	**Washer,** Shakeproof, on Setscrews		1	
BD.19059/1	**Screw,** Self-Tapping, securing Shield to gearbox side panel		1	
BD.18545	**Cup Washer,** on Self-Tapping Screw		1	
BD.8633/2	**Spire Nut,** on Self-Tapping Screw		1	
BD.20439	**SHIELD ASSEMBLY, REAR, FOR HEAT INSULATION FROM EXHAUST SYSTEM**	39–21	1	
BD.1814/5	**Pop Rivet,** securing Shield to Body		8	
BD.20452	**TRIM PANEL ASSEMBLY ON R.H. SHUT PILLAR**	39–22	1	
BD.20453	**TRIM PANEL ASSEMBLY ON L.H. SHUT PILLAR**		1	
BD.20379	**TRIM PANEL ASSEMBLY BETWEEN R.H. REAR WHEEL ARCH AND SHUT PILLAR**	39–23	1	
BD.2703	**Clip,** for fixing of Trim Panel		5	
BD.20380	**TRIM PANEL ASSEMBLY BETWEEN L.H. REAR WHEEL ARCH AND SHUT PILLAR**		1	
BD.2703	**Clip,** for fixing of Trim Panel		5	
BD.539/4	**Screw,** Self-Tapping, securing Trim Panels to Body		2	
BD.532/1	**Cup Washer,** on Self-Tapping Screws		2	
BD.711/3	**Screw,** Self-Tapping, securing Trim Panels to Body		8	

NOTE: The following cars were fitted with Heat Shield BD.20436:
R.H. Drive 850653, 850654.
L.H. Drive 878895, 878900, 878907, 878908, 878913, 878914, 878915, 878926, 878936, 878937, 878939, 878958, 878986, 879005, 879024, 879049.

BODY FITTINGS
FOR OPEN CARS ONLY

Part No.	Description	Plate No.	No. per Unit	Remarks
BD.20383	**QUARTER TRIM PANEL ASSEMBLY ABOVE R.H. REAR WHEEL ARCH**	39–24	1	
BD.20384	**QUARTER TRIM PANEL ASSEMBLY ABOVE L.H. REAR WHEEL ARCH**		1	
BD.1749	**Stud**, on Quarter Trim Panels, for "Lift the Dot" Fasteners		2	
AN.102/L	**Nut**, securing Studs		2	
C.723	**Washer**, Shakeproof, under Nuts		2	
AW.102/T	**Washer**, Plain, under Shakeproof Washers		2	
BD.20532	**TRIM PANEL ASSEMBLY, R.H., ON TONNEAU, BELOW BACKLIGHT**	39-25	1	
BD.20533	**TRIM PANEL ASSEMBLY, L.H., ON TONNEAU, BELOW BACKLIGHT**	39-26	1	
BD.539/1	**Screw**, Self-Tapping, securing Quarter and Tonneau Trims ($\frac{7}{8}$" long)		2	
BD.539/4	**Screw**, Self-Tapping, securing Quarter and Tonneau Trims ($\frac{1}{2}$" long)		4	
BD.532/1	**Cup Washer**, on Self-Tapping Screws		6	
BD.20343	**MAT ASSEMBLY ON REAR BULKHEAD PANEL**	39–27	1	Fitted from Chassis No. 850001 to 850526. 875001 to 877355.
BD.23625	**MAT ASSEMBLY ON REAR BULKHEAD PANEL**		1	Fitted to Chassis No. 850527 and subs. 877356 and subs.
BD.21484	**R.H. DOOR ASSEMBLY, COMPLETE (INCLUDING GLASS, TRIM, LOCK AND HANDLES, ETC.)**		1	

Part No.	Description	Plate No.	No. per Unit	Remarks
BD.21485	**L.H. DOOR ASSEMBLY, COMPLETE (INCLUDING GLASS, TRIM, LOCK AND HANDLES, ETC.)**		1	
BD.20095	**LOCK ASSEMBLY ON R.H. DOOR (WB.3/11289)**		1	
BD.20096	**LOCK ASSEMBLY ON L.H. DOOR (WB.3/11290)**	40- 1	1	
BD.19445	**Link,** between Locks and Outside Handle (WB.1/8881)	40- 2	2	
BD.23473	**Clip,** retaining Links (WB.3/6928)	40- 3	4	
BD.1708/9	**Spring Washer,** for Link fixing at Lock		2	
UFS.419/3H	**Screw,** Set, securing Lock to Doors		6	
C.723/A	**Washer,** Shakeproof, on Setscrews		6	
BD.20780/3	**Shakeproof Screw,** securing Lock to Doors		2	
BD.19245	**OUTSIDE HANDLE ON R.H. DOOR (1/8871)**		1	
7903	**Operating Lever Assembly** for R.H. Door Handle (1/6491)		1	
9601	**Housing,** for Tension Spring in R.H. Door Handle (1/8868)		1	
BD.21486	**Locking Barrel,** for "F" Series Key, in Handle		1	
BD.19246	**OUTSIDE HANDLE ON L.H. DOOR (1/8870)**	40- 4	1	
7904	**Operating Lever Assembly** for L.H. Door Handle (1/6492)		1	
9602	**Housing,** for Tension Spring in L.H. Door Handle (1/8869)		1	
BD.21486	**Locking Barrel,** for "F" Series Key, in handle		1	
UFN.119/L	**Nut,** securing Outside Handles		4	
C.723/A	**Washer,** Shakeproof, under Nuts		4	
AW.102/T	**Washer,** Plain, under Shakeproof Washers		4	
BD.20098	**REMOTE CONTROL AND LINK ASSEMBLY, FOR OPERATION OF R.H. DOOR LOCK (3/16347)**		1	

BODY FITTINGS
FOR OPEN CARS ONLY

Part No.	Description	Plate No.	No. per Unit	Remarks
BD.20097	**REMOTE CONTROL AND LINK ASSEMBLY, FOR OPERATION OF L.H. DOOR LOCK (3/16349)**	40– 5	1	
BD.19575	**Wavy Washer,** at connection of Link to Lock	40– 6	2	
BD.23743	**Spring Clip,** securing Link to Lock	40– 7	2	
BD.19574	**Washer,** Special, behind Spring Clips		2	
UFS.419/3H	**Screw,** Set, securing Remote Controls to Doors		6	
C.723/A	**Washer,** Shakeproof, on Setscrews		6	
BD.10728	**INSIDE HANDLE FOR DOORS (WB.1/3858)**	40– 8	2	
BD.10729	**HANDLE OPERATING WINDOW REGULATORS (WB.1/6671)**	40– 9	2	
BD.10730	**OUTER ESCUTCHEON BEHIND REGULATOR AND INSIDE DOOR HANDLES (W.128)**	40–10	4	
BD.10731	**INNER ESCUTCHEON BEHIND REGULATOR AND INSIDE DOOR HANDLES (W.129)**	40–11	4	
BD.10732	**SPRING BEHIND ESCUTCHEONS (41/379)**	40–12	4	
BD.10734	**Rubber Plug,** behind Handles (16-10)	40–13	4	
BD.10733	**Peg,** securing Handles to Remote Controls and Regulators	40–14	4	
BD.20522	**REGULATOR ASSEMBLY FOR WINDOW IN R.H. DOOR**		1	

Part No.	Description	Plate No.	No. per Unit	Remarks
BD.20523	**REGULATOR ASSEMBLY FOR WINDOW IN L.H. DOOR**	40–15	1	
UFS.425/3H	**Screw,** Set, securing Regulator to Doors		8	
UFN.125/L	**Nut,** securing Regulator to Doors		8	
C.724	**Washer,** Shakeproof, on Setscrews and under Nuts		16	
BD.20997	**FIXED FRAME ASSEMBLY FOR WINDOW IN R.H. DOOR**		1	
BD.20998	**FIXED FRAME ASSEMBLY FOR WINDOW IN L.H. DOOR**	40–16	1	
BD.10099	**Felt,** in forward channel of Fixed Frames	40–17	2	
BD.16465	**Bracket,** for forward mounting of Fixed Frames	40–18	2	
BD.20668	**Bracket,** for rear mounting of Fixed Frames	40–19	2	
UFN.125/L	**Nut,** securing Brackets to Doors and Fixed Frames to Brackets		6	
UFS.125/4R	**Screw,** Set, securing Brackets to Doors and Fixed Frames to Brackets		2	
C.724	**Washer,** Shakeproof, under Nuts and on Setscrews		8	
FW.104/T	**Washer,** Plain, under Shakeproof Washers		8	
BD.17622/1	**Screw,** Self-Tapping, securing Fixed Frames to Doors at top		6	
BD.17621	**Spire Nut,** on Self-Tapping Screws		6	
BD.540/8	**Screw,** Self-Tapping (Countersunk Head) securing Frames to Doors		4	
BD 17623/2	**Screw,** Self-Tapping (Pan Head) securing Frames to Doors		6	
BD.20873/1	**Packing Washer** (18 S.W.G.) at Fixed Frame mountings		As req'd	
BD.20873/2	**Packing Washer** (10 S.W.G.) at Fixed Frame mountings		As req'd	
BD.19397/2	**Rubber Seal,** for front Channel of Window Frames	40–20	2	
BD.15975	**GLASS ASSEMBLY, FOR WINDOW IN R.H. DOOR**		1	
BD.15976	**GLASS ASSEMBLY, FOR WINDOW IN L.H. DOOR**	40–21	1	
BD.5440/6	**Square Nut,** limiting downward movement of Glasses		2	
BD.13819/1	**Screw,** Set, securing Square Nuts		2	

BODY FITTINGS
FOR OPEN CARS ONLY

Part No.	Description	Plate No.	No. per Unit	Remarks
BD.16997	**CHROME FINISHER ASSEMBLY AT TOP OF R.H. DOOR**		1	
BD.16700	**Outer Seal,** for Door Glass		1	
BD.10413	**Clip,** securing Outer Seal		7	
				Fitted from Chassis No. 850001 to 850506. 875001 to 877201.
BD.16998	**CHROME FINISHER ASSEMBLY AT TOP OF L.H. DOOR**	40–22	1	
BD.16700	**Outer Seal,** for Door Glass		1	
BD.10413	**Clip,** securing Outer Seal		7	
BD.540/9	**Screw,** Self-Tapping, securing Chrome Finishers		4	
BD.21333	**CHROME FINISHER ASSEMBLY AT TOP OF R.H. DOOR**		1	
BD.16700	**Outer Seal,** for Door Glass		1	
BD.10413	**Clip,** securing Outer Seal		7	
				Fitted to Chassis No. 850507 and subs. 877202 and subs.
BD.21334	**CHROME FINISHER ASSEMBLY AT TOP OF L.H. DOOR**		1	
BD.16700	**Outer Seal,** for Door Glass		1	
BD.10413	**Clip,** securing Outer Seal		7	
BD.540/9	**Screw,** Self-Tapping, securing Chrome Finishers		4	
BD.19070	**STRIKER FOR MAP LIGHT DOOR SWITCHES**	40–23	4	
BD.539/15	**Screw,** Self-Tapping, securing Strikers		4	
BD.19223	**FILLER BLOCK, ON SHUT FACE OF R.H. DOOR, SEATING RUBBER SEAL**		1	
BD.19224	**FILLER BLOCK, ON SHUT FACE OF L.H. DOOR, SEATING RUBBER SEAL**	40–24	1	
UCS.516/3H	**Screw,** Set, securing Filler Blocks		2	

Part No.	Description	Plate No.	No. per Unit	Remarks
BD.15504	**UPPER TRIM PANEL ASSEMBLY ON R.H. DOOR**		1	
BD.20010/3	**Weatherstrip,** for Door Glass		1	
BD.20082	**Clip,** securing Weatherstrip		5	
BD.15505	**UPPER TRIM PANEL ASSEMBLY ON L.H. DOOR**	40–25	1	
BD.20010/3	**Weatherstrip,** for Door Glass		1	
BD.20082	**Clip,** securing Weatherstrip		5	
BD.540/12	**Screw,** Self-Tapping, securing Upper Trim Panels		4	
BD.20190	**CHROME FINISHER ON UPPER TRIM PANELS**	40–26	2	
BD.17497	**Clip,** securing Chrome Finishers		10	
BD.711/1	**Screw,** Self-Tapping, securing Clips		10	
BD.15510	**CASING ASSEMBLY ON R.H. DOOR**		1	
BD.15511	**CASING ASSEMBLY ON L.H. DOOR**	40–27	1	
BD.18068	**Clip,** for fixing of Casings		38	
BD.21133	**Clip,** for fixing of Casings at front edge		4	
BD.20503	**CHROME FINISHER ON DOOR CASINGS**	40–28	2	
BD.11546	**Clip,** securing Chrome Finishers		10	
BD.25376	**SEALING RUBBER AND RETAINER ASSEMBLY, LOWER, FOR R.H. "A" POST**		1	
BD.25308	**Sealing Rubber** only		1	

BODY FITTINGS
FOR OPEN CARS ONLY

Part No.	Description	Plate No.	No. per Unit	Remarks
BD.25377	**SEALING RUBBER AND RETAINER ASSEMBLY, LOWER, FOR L.H. "A" POST**	40–29	1	
BD.25309	**Sealing Rubber only**		1	
BD.21202	**SEALING RUBBER, UPPER, FOR "A" POSTS**	40–30	2	
BD.21197	**SEALING RUBBER, FOR DOOR SILLS**	40–31	2	**SUPERSEDED BY BD.24789.**
BD.24789	**SEALING RUBBER, FOR DOOR SILLS**		2	**SUPERSEDES BD.21197.**
BD.21196	**SEALING RUBBER, FOR BODY SHUT PILLARS**	40–32	2	
BD.19295	**STRIKER FOR R.H. DOOR LOCK (WB.3/8994)**		1	
BD.19296	**STRIKER FOR L.H. DOOR LOCK (WB.3/8995)**	40–33	1	
BD.19297	**Shakeproof Shim,** under Strikers (WB.3/9586)		2	
BD.19298	**Shim,** packing Strikers (20 S.W.G.)		As req'd	
BD.17821/7	**Screw,** Set, securing Strikers		6	
BD.19129	**CHROME FINISHER AT EDGE OF DOOR SILLS**	40–34	2	
BD.16794	**Clip,** securing Finishers	40–35	14	

Part No.	Description	Plate No.	No. per Unit	Remarks
BD.15898	**LOCK ASSEMBLY FOR BOOT LID** (WB.3/10875)	41– 1	1	
UFS.319/4H	**Screw,** Set, securing Lock to Bracket		4	
C.723/A	**Washer,** Shakeproof, on Setscrews		4	
AW.102/T	**Washer,** Plain, under Shakeproof Washers		4	
UFN.119/L	**Nut,** securing Lock		2	
BD.16202	**BRACKET, FOR MOUNTING OF BOOT LID LOCK**	41– 2	1	
UFN.119 L	**Nut,** securing Bracket		4	
C.723/A	**Washer,** Shakeproof, under Nuts		4	
AW.102 T	**Washer,** Plain, under Shakeproof Washers		4	
BD.15899	**CONTROL CABLE ASSEMBLY FOR RELEASE OF BOOT LID LOCK**	41– 3	1	
BD.16213	**Clamp,** for Outer Cable	41– 4	1	
UFS.119/3R	**Screw,** Set, securing Outer Cable to Clamp		1	
UFN.119/L	**Nut,** securing Clamp to Bracket		1	
C.723/A	**Washer,** Shakeproof, under Nut		1	
C.18461	**Clip,** for Outer Cable		1	
BD.15489	**STRIKER FOR BOOT LID LOCK** (371/130)	41– 5	1	
BD.8291/1	**Screw,** Set, securing Striker to Boot Lid		4	
C.724	**Washer,** Shakeproof, on Setscrews		4	
FW.104/T	**Washer,** Plain, under Shakeproof Washers		4	
BD.11321	**Shim** (.036" thick) for Striker		As req'd	
BD.17726	**"JAGUAR" MOTIF ON BOOT LID**	41– 6	1	
BD.10735	**Spire Nut,** securing Motif		3	
BD.15293	**Rubber Washer,** under Spire Nuts		3	
BD.18055/1	**RUBBER SEAL FOR BOOT LID**	41– 7	1	
BD.659/10	**DRAIN TUBE FOR BOOT LID APERTURE**		1	Fitted from Chassis No. 850001 to 850117. 875001 to 875520.

BODY FITTINGS
FOR OPEN CARS ONLY

Part No.	Description	Plate No.	No. per Unit	Remarks
BD.23335	**DRAIN TUBE AT R.H. SIDE OF BOOT LID APERTURE**		1	
				Fitted to Chassis No. 850118 and subs. 875521 and subs.
BD.659/12	**DRAIN TUBE AT L.H. SIDE OF BOOT LID APERTURE**		1	
BD.22536	**RUBBER BUFFER CUSHIONING PETROL FILLER LID**		2	
BD.18492	**COVER PLATE, IN BOOT FLOOR TOP PANEL, OVER REAR SUSPENSION UNIT**		1	
BD.18493	**Rubber Seal,** under Cover Plate		1	
BD.8691/6	**Screw,** Self-Tapping, securing Cover Plate		7	
BD.19053	**Spring Latch,** in Top Panel, for Boot R.H. Floorboard fixing	41– 8	1	
BD.1814/1	**Pop Rivet,** securing Spring Latch		2	
BD.19051	**R.H. FLOORBOARD ASSEMBLY, IN BOOT**	41– 9	1	
BD.10958	**Stud,** for Floorboard fixing		1	
BD.9909/5	**Tee Nut,** receiving Stud		1	
C.723	**Washer,** Shakeproof, under Nut		1	
BD.19054	**Spring Clip,** on Number Plate Panel, retaining R.H. Floorboard		1	
BD.1814/1	**Pop Rivet,** securing Spring Clip		3	
BD.19052	**L.H. FLOORBOARD ASSEMBLY, IN BOOT**	41–10	1	
BD.19059/2	**Screw,** Set, securing L.H. Floorboard		2	
BD.18545	**Cup Washer,** on Setscrews		2	
BD.20641/2	**Screw,** Self-Tapping, securing L.H. Floorboard		1	
BD.541/34	**Washer,** Special, on Self-Tapping Screw		1	
BD.4321	**Rubber Buffer,** in Support Strip		3	

Part No.	Description	Plate No.	No. per Unit	Remarks
BD.11007/1	**SPARE WHEEL CLAMP ASSEMBLY**	41–11	1	
BD.10637	**Handle,** operating Spare Wheel Clamp		1	
BD.11008/1	**Screw**		1	
BD.10639	**Plate,** on Screw, holding Spare Wheel		1	
C.704/1	**Mills Pin,** securing Handle to Screw		1	
BD.3438	**Clip,** on Boot Floor, carrying Jack Handle		2	} **NOT REQUIRED FOR JACK**
BD.711/8	**Self-Tapping Screw,** securing Clip		2	} **WITH INTEGRAL HANDLE**
BD.659/9	**DRAIN TUBE FOR PETROL FILLER BOX (20″ LONG)**		1	
C.2905/2	**Clip,** securing Drain Tube		2	
BD.19637	**TRIM BOARD ON BOOT FORWARD BULKHEAD**	41–12	1	
BD.19394	**TRIM BOARD AT R.H. SIDE OF BOOT**	41–13	1	
BD.19395	**TRIM BOARD AT L.H. SIDE OF BOOT**	41–14	1	
BD.539/4	**Screw,** Self-Tapping, securing Side Trim Boards		8	
BD.532/1	**Cup Washer,** on Self-Tapping Screws		8	
BD.20335	**MAT ASSEMBLY ON BOOT FLOOR**		1	
BD.1286/1	**Button,** for fixing of Mat to Boot Floor		4	
BD.1286/2	**Socket,** securing Buttons to Mat		4	
BD.1286/3	**Stud,** receiving Buttons		4	
BD.540/1	**Screw,** Self-Tapping, securing Studs to Boot Floor		4	
C.18921	**REAR NUMBER PLATE**		1	
BD.1229/13	**Screw,** Self-Tapping, securing Rear Number Plate		4	
BD.6581	**Rubber Plug,** in Rear Number Plate Panel		4	

BODY FITTINGS
FOR OPEN CARS ONLY

Part No.	Description	Plate No.	No. per Unit	Remarks
BD.19092/1	**CHROME BEADING AT R.H. SIDE OF REAR NUMBER PLATE**	41–15	1	
BD.19092/2	**CHROME BEADING AT L.H. SIDE OF REAR NUMBER PLATE**	41–16	1	
BD.24183	**JOINT PIECE FOR BEADINGS**	41–17	1	
BD.711/6	**Screw,** Self-Tapping, securing Joint Piece		1	
BD.15891	**SEAL ASSEMBLY AT FRONT OF R.H. REAR WHEEL ARCH**	41–18	1	
BD.15892	**SEAL ASSEMBLY AT FRONT OF L.H. REAR WHEEL ARCH**	41–19	1	
BD.15893	**Rubber Strip,** on Seals		2	
				Fitted from Chassis No. 850001 to 850655. 875001 to 879023.
BD.15894	**SEAL ASSEMBLY AT REAR OF R.H. REAR WHEEL ARCH**	41–20	1	
BD.15895	**SEAL ASSEMBLY AT REAR OF L.H. REAR WHEEL ARCH**	41–21	1	
BD.15896	**Rubber Strip,** on Seals		2	
BD.1814/2	**Pop Rivet,** securing Wheel Arch Seals to Body		16	

Part No.	Description	Plate No.	No. per Unit	Remarks
BD.25200	**SEALING PLATE AT FRONT OF R.H. REAR WHEEL ARCH**		1	
BD.25201	**SEALING PLATE AT FRONT OF L.H. REAR WHEEL ARCH**		1	
BD.25198	**SEALING PLATE AT REAR OF R.H. REAR WHEEL ARCH**		1	
BD.25199	**SEALING PLATE AT REAR OF L.H. REAR WHEEL ARCH**		1	Fitted to Chassis No. 850656 and subs. 879024 and subs.
BD.25363	**SEALING PLATE, UPPER, FOR R.H. REAR WHEEL ARCH**		1	
BD.25364	**SEALING PLATE, UPPER, FOR L.H. REAR WHEEL ARCH**		1	
BD.11712/1	**Pop Rivet,** securing Sealing Plates		22	

INTERIOR TRIMMING

Part No.	Description	Plate No.	No. per Unit	Remarks
BD.23626	**Face Piece** (Moquette) for Bulkhead lower (15″ × 50″)		1	Fitted to Chassis No. 850527 and subs. 877356 and subs.
BD.20345	**Face Piece** (Moquette) on R.H. Rear Wheel Arch (17″×19″)		1	
BD.20346	**Face Piece** (Moquette) on L.H. Rear Wheel Arch (17″×19″)		1	
BD.20344	**Felt Backing,** for Rear Wheel Arches (12″×15″)		2	
BD.20375	**Face Piece** (Vynide) on R.H. side of Floor Cross Member (9″×24″)		1	
BD.20376	**Face Piece** (Vynide) on L.H. side of Floor Cross Member (9″×24″)		1	
BD.20541	**Face Piece** (Vynide) on Door Sills (14″×36″)		2	
BD.20913	**Backing** (Polyurethane) for Sills		2	
BD.20456/2	**Face Piece** (Rexine) on Screen Pillars, at side of Facias (3″×5″)		2	
BD.21185	**Face Piece** (Rexine) behind Boot Lid Lock Control (3″×3″)		1	
BD.20377	**Face Piece** (Vynide) at R.H. mounting for Hoodsticks (9″×14″)		1	
BD.20378	**Face Piece** (Vynide) at L.H. mounting for Hoodsticks (9″×14″)		1	
BD.20906	**Face Piece** (Vynide) on Tonneau Tacking Strips (2″×66″)		1	
BD.20728	**Cover Assembly,** protecting Wiring Harness at L.H. side of Scuttle		1	
BD.1814/6	**Pop Rivet,** securing Cover		2	
BD.20209	**Mat Assembly** (Hardura) for R.H. side of Scuttle		1	
BD.20210	**Mat Assembly** (Hardura) for L.H. side of Scuttle		1	
BD.539/4	**Screw,** Self-Tapping, securing Mats		10	
BD.532/1	**Cup Washer,** on Self-Tapping Screws		10	

BODY FITTINGS
FOR OPEN CARS ONLY

Part No.	Description	Plate No.	No. per Unit	Remarks
	SEALING RUBBERS			
BD.18559	**Sealing Rubber,** lower, for R.H. "A" Post	42– 1	1	
BD.18560	**Sealing Rubber,** lower, for L.H. "A" Post	42– 2	1	
BD.21202	**Sealing Rubber,** Upper, for "A" Posts (13¾" long)	42– 3	2	
BD.21197	**Sealing Rubber,** for Door Sills	42– 4	2	SUPERSEDED BY BD.24789.
BD.24789	**Sealing Rubber,** for Door Sills		2	SUPERSEDES BD.21197.
BD.21196	**Sealing Rubber,** for Body Shut Pillars	42– 5	2	
BD.20413	**Sealing Rubber,** for front of Cantrails (4⅛" long)	42– 6	2	
BD.20414	**Sealing Rubber,** for centre of Cantrails (8 9/16" long)	42– 7	2	
BD.20415	**Sealing Rubber,** for rear of Cantrails (4" long)	42– 8	2	Fitted from Chassis No. 850001 to 850091. 875001 to 875373.
BD.20416	**Sealing Rubber,** for Hood Pillars	42– 9	2	
BD.21799/1	**Sealing Rubber,** for front of R.H. Cantrail (4⅛" long)		1	
BD.21800/1	**Sealing Rubber,** for front of L.H. Cantrail (4⅛" long)		1	
BD.21799/2	**Sealing Rubber,** for centre of R.H. Cantrail (8 9/16" long)		1	
BD.21800/2	**Sealing Rubber,** for centre of L.H. Cantrail (8 9/16" long)		1	Fitted to Chassis No. 850092 and subs. 875374 and subs.
BD.21799/3	**Sealing Rubber,** for rear of R.H. Cantrail (4" long)		1	
BD.21800/3	**Sealing Rubber,** for rear of L.H. Cantrail (4" long)		1	
BD.21799/4	**Sealing Rubber,** for R.H. Hood Pillar		1	
BD.21800/4	**Sealing Rubber,** for L.H. Hood Pillar		1	
BD.18055/1	**Sealing Rubber,** for Boot Lid (121" long)	42–10	1	
BD.17413	**Sealing Rubber,** for Canopy Panel to top of Windscreen (55" long)	42–11	1	NOT REQUIRED WHEN GLASS FIBRE CANOPY IS FITTED.
BD.22392/1	**Sealing Rubber,** for Canopy Panel to top of Windscreen (49½" long)		1	REQUIRED WHEN GLASS FIBRE CANOPY IS FITTED.
BD.20903/1	**Sealing Rubber,** for rear edge of Bonnet (68" long)	42–12	1	
	ANTI-DRUM MATERIAL			
BD.20272	**Flintkote,** on Door Panels (9" × 24")		2	
BD.20273	**Flintkote,** on Door Bottom Rails (2" × 18")		2	
BD.20211	**Flintkote,** for R.H. side of Scuttle (15" × 13")		1	
BD.20212	**Flintkote,** for L.H. side of Scuttle (15" × 13")		1	
BD.20217	**Flintkote,** on Front Floors (27" × 19½")		2	Fitted from Chassis No. 850001 to 850357. 875001 to 876581.
BD.22965	**Flintkote,** on R.H. Front Floor		1	Fitted to Chassis No. 850358 and subs.
BD.22966	**Flintkote,** on L.H. Front Floor		1	
BD.22965	**Flintkote,** on R.H. Front Floor		1	Fitted to Chassis No. 876582 and subs.
BD.22967	**Flintkote,** on L.H. Front Floor		1	
BD.20422	**Flintkote,** at top front of Gearbox Cover (7" × 8")		1	
BD.20902	**Flintkote,** on Tunnel (16" × 18")		1	
BD.20215	**Flintkote,** on Floor Panel, behind Seats (21" × 18¼")		2	
BD.20340	**Flintkote,** Top, for Rear Bulkhead Panel (15" × 36")		1	
BD.20341	**Flintkote,** Centre, for Rear Bulkhead Panel (14" × 48")		1	
BD.20342	**Flintkote,** Lower, for Rear Bulkhead Panel (8" × 24")		2	

Part No.	Description	Plate No.	No. per Unit	Remarks

CARPETS FOR R.H. DRIVE CARS

Part No.	Description	Plate No.	No. per Unit	Remarks
BD.20347	**Carpet Assembly,** on R.H. Front Floor	42–13	1	} Fitted from Chassis No.
BD.20348	**Carpet Assembly,** on L.H. Front Floor	42–14	1	850001 to 850357.
BD.22962	**Carpet Assembly,** on R.H. Front Floor		1	Fitted to Chassis No.
BD.22963	**Carpet Assembly,** on L.H. Front Floor		1	850358 and subs.
BD.20350	**Carpet Assembly,** on Toeboards	42–15	2	
BD.20352	**Carpet Assembly,** at front R.H. side of Tunnel	42–16	1	
BD.20353	**Carpet Assembly,** at front L.H. side of Tunnel	42–17	1	
BD.20354	**Carpet Assembly,** at rear R.H. side of Tunnel	42–18	1	
BD.20355	**Carpet Assembly,** at rear L.H. side of Tunnel	42–19	1	

CARPETS FOR L.H. DRIVE CARS

Part No.	Description	Plate No.	No. per Unit	Remarks
BD.20347	**Carpet Assembly,** on R.H. Front Floor		1	} Fitted from Chassis No.
BD.20349	**Carpet Assembly,** on L.H. Front Floor		1	875001 to 876581.
BD.22962	**Carpet Assembly,** on R.H. Front Floor		1	Fitted to Chassis No.
BD.22964	**Carpet Assembly,** on L.H. Front Floor		1	876582 and subs.
BD.20350	**Carpet Assembly,** on Toeboards		2	
BD.20352	**Carpet Assembly,** at front R.H. side of Tunnel		1	
BD.20353	**Carpet Assembly,** at front L.H. side of Tunnel		1	
BD.20354	**Carpet Assembly,** at rear R.H. side of Tunnel		1	
BD.20355	**Carpet Assembly,** at rear L.H. side of Tunnel		1	

INSULATING FELTS FOR R.H. DRIVE CARS

Part No.	Description	No. per Unit
BD.20218	**Rubberised Felt,** on R.H. Front Floor ($28'' \times 19\frac{1}{2}'' \times \frac{1}{2}''$)	1
BD.20230	**Rubberised Felt,** on L.H. Front Floor ($28'' \times 19\frac{1}{2}'' \times \frac{1}{2}''$)	1
BD.20220	**Rubberised Felt,** on R.H. Toe Board ($13'' \times 10'' \times \frac{1}{2}''$)	1
BD.20221	**Rubberised Felt,** on L.H. Toe Board ($14'' \times 10'' \times \frac{1}{2}''$)	1
BD.20235	**Rubberised Felt,** under R.H. side of Scuttle ($19'' \times 19'' \times \frac{1}{2}''$)	1
BD.20236	**Rubberised Felt,** under R.H. side of Scuttle ($18\frac{1}{2}'' \times 10\frac{1}{2}'' \times \frac{1}{2}''$)	1
BD.20237	**Rubberised Felt,** under L.H. side of Scuttle ($15'' \times 8\frac{1}{2}'' \times \frac{1}{2}''$)	1
BD.20227	**Rubberised Felt,** Gearbox Cover to Scuttle ($10'' \times 7'' \times \frac{1}{2}''$)	1
BD.21233	**Rubberised Felt,** at top of Gearbox Cover ($7'' \times 7'' \times \frac{1}{2}''$)	1
BD.20205	**Rubberised Felt,** at front R.H. side of Tunnel ($15'' \times 11'' \times \frac{1}{2}''$)	1
BD.20206	**Rubberised Felt,** at front L.H. side of Tunnel ($15'' \times 11'' \times \frac{1}{2}''$)	1
BD.20207	**Rubberised Felt,** at R.H. side of Tunnel ($17'' \times 8'' \times \frac{1}{2}''$)	1
BD.20208	**Rubberised Felt,** at L.H. side of Tunnel ($17'' \times 8'' \times \frac{1}{4}''$)	1
BD.20339	**Rubberised Felt,** under Petrol Tank ($6'' \times 1'' \times \frac{1}{2}''$)	1
BD.20672	**Rubberised Felt,** at centre of Rear Bulkhead Panel ($48'' \times 13\frac{1}{2}'' \times \frac{1}{2}''$)	1
BD.20222	**Hardura,** on R.H. Toe Board ($14'' \times 10'' \times \frac{1}{2}''$)	1
BD.20223	**Hardura,** on L.H. Toe Board ($14'' \times 10'' \times \frac{1}{2}''$)	1
BD.20336	**Hardura,** for Scuttle Top, L.H. ($17'' \times 18'' \times \frac{1}{4}''$)	1
BD.20337	**Hardura,** for Scuttle Top, R.H. ($10'' \times 19'' \times \frac{1}{4}''$)	1
BD.20338	**Hardura,** for Scuttle Top, Centre ($7'' \times 8'' \times \frac{1}{4}''$)	1

BODY FITTINGS
FOR OPEN CARS ONLY

Part No.	Description	Plate No.	No. per Unit	Remarks
	INSULATING FELTS FOR L.H. DRIVE CARS			
BD.20218	**Rubberised Felt,** on R.H. Front Floor (28″×19½″×½″)		1	
BD.20219	**Rubberised Felt,** on L.H. Front Floor (28″×19½″×½″)		1	
BD.20220	**Rubberised Felt,** on R.H. Toe Board (13″×10″×½″)		1	
BD.20221	**Rubberised Felt,** on L.H. Toe Board (14″×10″×½″)		1	
BD.20224	**Rubberised Felt,** under R.H. side of Scuttle (19″×19″×½″)		1	
BD.20225	**Rubberised Felt,** under L.H. side of Scuttle (18½″×10½″×½″)		1	
BD.20226	**Rubberised Felt,** under L.H. side of Scuttle (15″×8½″×½″)		1	
BD.20227	**Rubberised Felt,** Gearbox Cover to Scuttle (10″×7″×½″)		1	
BD.21233	**Rubberised Felt,** at top of Gearbox Cover (7″×7″×½″)		1	
BD.20205	**Rubberised Felt,** at front R.H. side of Tunnel (15″×11″×½″)		1	
BD.20206	**Rubberised Felt,** at front L.H. side of Tunnel (15″×11″×½″)		1	
BD.20207	**Rubberised Felt,** at R.H. side of Tunnel (17″×8″×½″)		1	
BD.20208	**Rubberised Felt,** at L.H. side of Tunnel (17″×8″×¼″)		1	
BD.20672	**Rubberised Felt,** at centre of Rear Bulkhead Panel (48″×13½″×½″)		1	
BD.20339	**Rubberised Felt,** under Petrol Tank (6″×7″×½″)		1	
BD.20222	**Hardura,** on R.H. Toe Board (14″×10″×¼″)		1	
BD.20223	**Hardura,** on L.H. Toe Board (14″×10″×¼″)		1	
BD.20231	**Hardura,** for Scuttle Top, R.H. (17″×18″×¼″)		1	
BD.20232	**Hardura,** for Scuttle Top, L.H. (10″×19″×¼″)		1	
BD.20233	**Hardura,** for Scuttle Top, centre (7″×8″×¼″)		1	
BD.19464	**HOOD STICKS ASSEMBLY**	43– 1	1	
BD.19492	**Stop Stud,** in No. 2 Links		2	
UFN.225/L	**Locknut,** on Stop Studs		2	
BD.20359	**Pivot Bolt,** securing Link No. 1 to Link No. 2		2	
BD.19259	**Dome Nut,** on Pivot Bolts		2	
BD.19193	**Pivot Bolt,** joining Link No. 3 to Main Stick		2	
BD.21193	**Pivot Bolt,** joining Link No. 6 to Main Stick		2	
BD.541/22	**Brass Washer,** on Pivot Bolts		2	
BD.541/23	**Brass Washer,** on Pivot Bolts		6	
BD.19302	**Bolt,** securing Link No. 1 to Canopy Rail		4	
BD.541/32	**Washer,** Special, on Bolts		4	
UFN.125/L	**Nut,** on Bolts		4	
C.724	**Washer,** Shakeproof, under Nuts		4	
BD.19249	**Cantrail Channel,** L.H. Front	43– 2	1	
BD.19250	**Cantrail Channel,** R.H. Front		1	
BD.19249/1	**Cantrail Channel,** L.H. Rear	43– 3	1	
BD.19250/1	**Cantrail Channel,** R.H. Rear		1	
UFS.519/4H	**Screw,** Set, securing Cantrail Channels to Hoodstick Links		6	
UFS.119/4R	**Screw,** Set, securing Cantrail Channels to Hoodstick Links		4	
BD.541/28	**Special Washer,** on Setscrews		10	
AW.102/T	**Washer,** Plain, on Setscrews		4	
UFN.119/L	**Nut,** on Setscrews		10	
C.723/A	**Washer,** Shakeproof, under Nuts		10	
BD.19367	**Main Head Pillar Assembly,** L.H.	43– 4	1	
BD.19368	**Main Head Pillar Assembly,** R.H.		1	
UCS.513/4H	**Screw,** Set, securing Pillars to Main Stick		4	
BD.532/1	**Washer,** Cupped, under Shakeproof Washer		As req'd.	
UFS.419/3H	**Screw,** Set, securing Pillars to Main Stick		4	
C.723/A	**Washer,** Shakeproof, on Setscrews		4	
AW.102/T	**Washer,** Plain, under Shakeproof Washer		4	

Part No.	Description	Plate No.	No. per Unit	Remarks
BD.20657	**PIVOT BRACKET ASSEMBLY, R.H., FOR MAIN STICK**		1	
BD.19458	**PIVOT BRACKET ASSEMBLY, L.H., FOR MAIN STICK**	43– 5	1	
UFN.131/L	**Nut,** securing Pivot Brackets to Wheel Arches		4	
C.725	**Washer,** Shakeproof, under Nuts		4	
FW.105/T	**Washer,** Plain, under Shakeproof Washers		4	
BD.23469	**Shim,** for Pivot Bracket adjustment		As req'd	
BD.19160	**Bolt,** Special, pivoting Main Stick		2	
BD.19393	**Bolt,** Special, securing Control Link to Body		2	
BD.541/30	**Brass Washer,** on Special Bolts		6	
BD.17413	**SEALING RUBBER FOR CANOPY PANEL TO TOP OF WINDSCREEN (55″ LONG)**		1	NOT REQUIRED WHEN GLASS FIBRE CANOPY IS FITTED.
BD.22392/1	**SEALING RUBBER FOR CANOPY PANEL TO TOP OF WINDSCREEN (49½″ LONG)**		1	REQUIRED WHEN GLASS FIBRE CANOPY IS FITTED.
BD.20413	**SEALING RUBBER FOR FRONT OF CANTRAILS (4⅛″ LONG)**		2	Fitted from Chassis No. 850001 to 850091. 875001 to 875373.
BD.21799/1	**SEALING RUBBER FOR FRONT OF R.H. CANTRAIL (4⅛″ LONG)**		1	Fitted to Chassis No. 850092 and subs. 875374 and subs.
BD.21800/1	**SEALING RUBBER FOR FRONT OF L.H. CANTRAIL (4⅛″ LONG)**		1	
BD.20414	**SEALING RUBBER FOR CENTRE OF CANTRAILS (8 9/16″ LONG)**		2	Fitted from Chassis No. 850001 to 850091. 875001 to 875373.
BD.21799/2	**SEALING RUBBER FOR CENTRE OF R.H. CANTRAIL (8 9/16″ LONG)**		1	Fitted to Chassis No. 850092 and subs. 875374 and subs.
BD.21800/2	**SEALING RUBBER FOR CENTRE OF L.H. CANTRAIL (8 9/16″ LONG)**		1	

BODY FITTINGS
FOR OPEN CARS ONLY

Part No.	Description	Plate No.	No. per Unit	Remarks
BD.20415	**SEALING RUBBER FOR REAR OF CANTRAILS (4″ LONG)**		2	Fitted from Chassis No. 850001 to 850091. 875001 to 875373.
BD.21799/3	**SEALING RUBBER FOR REAR OF R.H. CANTRAIL (4″ LONG)**		1	Fitted to Chassis No. 850092 and subs. 875374 and subs.
BD.21800/3	**SEALING RUBBER FOR REAR OF L.H. CANTRAIL (4″ LONG)**		1	

SEAL RETAINERS

Part No.	Description	Plate No.	No. per Unit	Remarks
BD.19254	**Retainer Assembly,** on L.H. Front Cantrail		1	NOT REQUIRED WHEN GLASS FIBRE CANOPY IS FITTED.
BD.19255	**Retainer Assembly,** on R.H. Front Cantrail		1	
BD.19256	**Retainer Assembly,** on L.H. Rear Cantrail		1	
BD.19257	**Retainer Assembly,** on R.H. Rear Cantrail		1	
BD.1814/2	**Pop Rivet,** securing Retainers		14	
BD.23734	**Retainer Assembly,** on L.H. Front Cantrail		1	REQUIRED WHEN GLASS FIBRE CANOPY IS FITTED.
BD.23733	**Retainer Assembly,** on R.H. Front Cantrail		1	
BD.23736	**Retainer Assembly,** on L.H. Rear Cantrail		1	
BD.23735	**Retainer Assembly,** on R.H. Rear Cantrail		1	
BD.1814/2	**Pop Rivet,** securing Retainers		24	
BD.20416	**SEALING RUBBER FOR HOOD PILLARS**		2	Fitted from Chassis No. 850001 to 850091. 875001 to 875373.
BD.21799/4	**SEALING RUBBER FOR R.H. HOOD PILLAR**		1	Fitted to Chassis No. 850092 and subs. 875374 and subs.
BD.21800/4	**SEALING RUBBER FOR L.H. HOOD PILLAR**		1	
BD.19293	**DRIP MOULDING 'L.H.' AT REAR OF HOOD OPENING**	43–6	1	

Part No.	Description	Plate No.	No. per Unit	Remarks
BD.19294	**DRIP MOULDING 'R.H.' AT REAR OF HOOD OPENING**		1	
BD.711/18	**Screw**, Self-Tapping, securing Drip Mouldings		10	
BD.20582	**HOOD CLOTH ASSEMBLY, COMPLETE**	43– 7	1	
BD.568/1	**Socket**, on Hood Cloth, for "Lift the Dot" Fasteners		2	
BD.568/2	**Clinch Plate**, securing Sockets		2	
	TACKING STRIPS			
BD.20140	**Tacking Strip**, L.H., for Hood Cloth fixing		1	
BD.20141	**Tacking Strip**, R.H., for Hood Cloth fixing		1	
BD.20142	**Tacking Strip**, Centre, for Hood Cloth fixing		1	
BD.711/1	**Screw**, Self-Tapping, securing Tacking Strips		14	
BD.20460	**Fillet** (Hardwood) for Tonneau Side, R.H. inner		1	
BD.20461	**Fillet** (Hardwood) for Tonneau Side, L.H. inner		1	
BD.540/14	**Screw**, Self-Tapping, securing Fillets		6	
BD.20099	**CHROME BEADING ON CANOPY RAIL**	43– 8	1	} NOT REQUIRED WHEN GLASS FIBRE CANOPY IS FITTED.
BD.16794	**Clip**, securing Beading	43– 9	20	
BD.24649	**CHROME BEADING ON CANOPY RAIL**		1	} REQUIRED WHEN GLASS FIBRE CANOPY IS FITTED.
BD.17497	**Clip**, securing Beading		13	
BD.540/24	**Screw**, Self-Tapping, securing Beading		13	
BD.19683	**CHROME BEADING ON TONNEAU**	43–10	1	
BD.11719	**Clip**, securing Beading		14	
BD.711/3	**Screw**, Self-Tapping, securing Clips		14	} USE BD.21397 FOR ALL REPLACEMENTS
BD.9248	**Special Bolt**, securing Chrome Beading		2	
UCN.116/L	**Nut**, on Special Bolts		2	
C.722	**Washer**, Shakeproof, under Nuts		2	
BD.21397	**CHROME BEADING ON TONNEAU**		1	} SUPERSEDES BD.19683
BD.539/10	**Screw**, Self.Tapping, securing Chrome Beading		8	
BD.539/16	**Screw**, Self-Tapping, securing Chrome Beading		2	
BD.20658	**HOOK PLATE, UNDER TONNEAU BEADING, FOR FIXING OF HOOD ENVELOPE**	43–11	4	
BD.540/1	**Screw**, Self-Tapping, securing Hook Plates		8	

BODY FITTINGS
FOR OPEN CARS ONLY

Part No.	Description	Plate No.	No. per Unit	Remarks
BD.15907	**TOGGLE CLAMP ASSEMBLY, OUTER, SECURING HOOD WHEN RAISED**	43–12	2	
BD.15912	**Hook only,** for Toggle Clamps		2	
BD.20892	**Locknut,** for Hooks		2	NOT REQUIRED WHEN GLASS FIBRE CANOPY IS FITTED.
BD.17546/2	**Screw,** Set, securing Toggle Clamps to Canopy Rail		4	
C.724	**Washer,** Shakeproof, on Setscrews		4	
BD.541/32	**Washer,** Special, under Shakeproof Washers		4	
BD.23581/1	**Anti Rattle Tube,** for Toggle Clamps		2	
BD.22678	**TOGGLE CLAMP ASSEMBLY, OUTER, SECURING HOOD WHEN RAISED**		2	
BD.15912	**Hook only,** for Toggle Clamps		2	REQUIRED WHEN GLASS FIBRE CANOPY IS FITTED.
BD.20892	**Locknut,** for Hooks		2	
BD.13713/2	**Screw,** Set, securing Toggle Clamps to Canopy Rail		4	
BD.21516/5	**Washer,** Shakeproof, on Setscrews		4	
BD.541/27	**Washer,** Special, under Shakeproof Washers		4	
BD.15508	**CHROME SOCKET, AT TOP OF R.H. SCREEN PILLAR, RECEIVING HOOK**		1	
BD.15509	**CHROME SOCKET, AT TOP OF L.H. SCREEN PILLAR, RECEIVING HOOK**	43–13	1	
BD.15534/3	**Screw,** Set, securing Cappings to side of Screen Pillars		2	
BD.16940/2	**Screw,** Set, securing Cappings to top of Screen Pillars		2	
BD.21098	**RUBBER SEALING PAD AT TOP OF R.H. SCREEN PILLAR**		1	
BD.21099	**RUBBER SEALING PAD AT TOP OF L.H. SCREEN PILLAR**		1	
BD.540/12	**Screw,** Self-Tapping, securing Sealing Pads		2	
BD.19515	**TOGGLE CLAMP ASSEMBLY, CENTRE, SECURING HOOD WHEN RAISED**	43–14	1	
BD.15912	**Hook only,** for Toggle Clamp		1	
BD.20892	**Locknut,** for Hook		1	
BD.13713/2	**Screw,** Set, securing Toggle Clamp to Canopy Rail ($\frac{1}{2}$" long)		2	
BD.13713/6	**Screw,** Set, securing Toggle Clamp to Canopy Rail (1" long)		2	
BD.541/27	**Special Washers,** on Setscrews		4	
BD.23581/1	**Anti Rattle Tube,** for Toggle Clamps		1	

Part No.	Description	Plate No.	No. per Unit	Remarks
BD.20857	**CHROME SOCKET, AT TOP OF WINDSCREEN, RECEIVING CENTRE TOGGLE**	43–15	1	
BD.20861/1	**Screw,** Set, Self-Locking, securing Boss to Screen Top Finisher		2	
BD.19517	**TENSION ROD, BETWEEN SOCKET AND SCREEN RAIL**	43–16	1	
BD.19518	**Nut,** securing Tension Rod to Bracket on Dash		2	
FW.104/T	**Washer,** Plain, under Nuts		2	
BD.23138	**Bracket Assembly,** on Dash, receiving lower end of Tension Rod		1	
BD.1229/14	**Screw,** Self-Tapping, securing Bracket to Dash		4	
BD.8633/6	**Spire Nut,** on Self-Tapping Screws		4	
BD.20660	**STRAP ASSEMBLY, ON CANOPY RAIL, FOR FIXING OF HOOD WHEN FOLDED**	43–17	2	
BD.20674	**Socket,** on Straps, for "Lift the Dot" Fasteners		2	
BD.568/2	**Clinch Plate,** securing Sockets		2	
BD.20659	**Chrome Bezel,** in Canopy Panel, for Straps	43–18	2	
BD.13713/7	**Screw,** Set, securing Straps to Canopy Rail		2	NOT REQUIRED WHEN GLASS FIBRE CANOPY IS FITTED.
C.2017/2	**Washer,** Special, on Setscrews		2	
BD.20781	**Spacer,** on Setscrews		2	
BD.1750	**"Lift the Dot"** Stud, securing end of Straps when not in use		2	
BD.23610	**Chrome Bezel,** in Canopy Panel, for Straps		2	
BD.13713/3	**Screw,** Set, securing Straps to Canopy Rail		2	REQUIRED WHEN GLASS FIBRE CANOPY IS FITTED.
C.2017/2	**Washer,** Special, on Setscrews		2	
BD.20781	**Spacer,** on Setscrews		2	
BD.1749	**"Lift the Dot"** Stud, securing end of Straps when not in use		2	
BD.20721	**ENVELOPE ASSEMBLY, ENCLOSING HOOD WHEN FOLDED**	43–19	1	
BD.568/1	**Socket,** on Envelope, for "Lift the Dot" Fasteners		3	
BD.568/2	**Clinch Plate,** securing Sockets		3	
BD.3822	**"Tenax" Fastener Assembly,** for fixing of Hood Envelope		2	
BD.1749	**Stud** (Short) on Rear Floor Panel, receiving "Lift the Dot" Fasteners		1	
BD.4076	**Stud** (Long) on Rear Floor Panel, receiving "Lift the Dot" Fasteners		2	
AN.102/L	**Nut,** securing Studs		3	
C.723	**Washer,** Shakeproof, under Nuts		3	
BD.3822	**"TENAX" FASTENER ASSEMBLY, COMPLETE**		2	
BD.3822/1	**Button only** (Tenax No. 31)		2	
BD.3822/2	**Nut,** securing Buttons (Tenax No. 32)		2	
BD.23608	**Stud,** receiving Buttons		2	
C.723A	**Washer,** Shakeproof, on Stud		2	

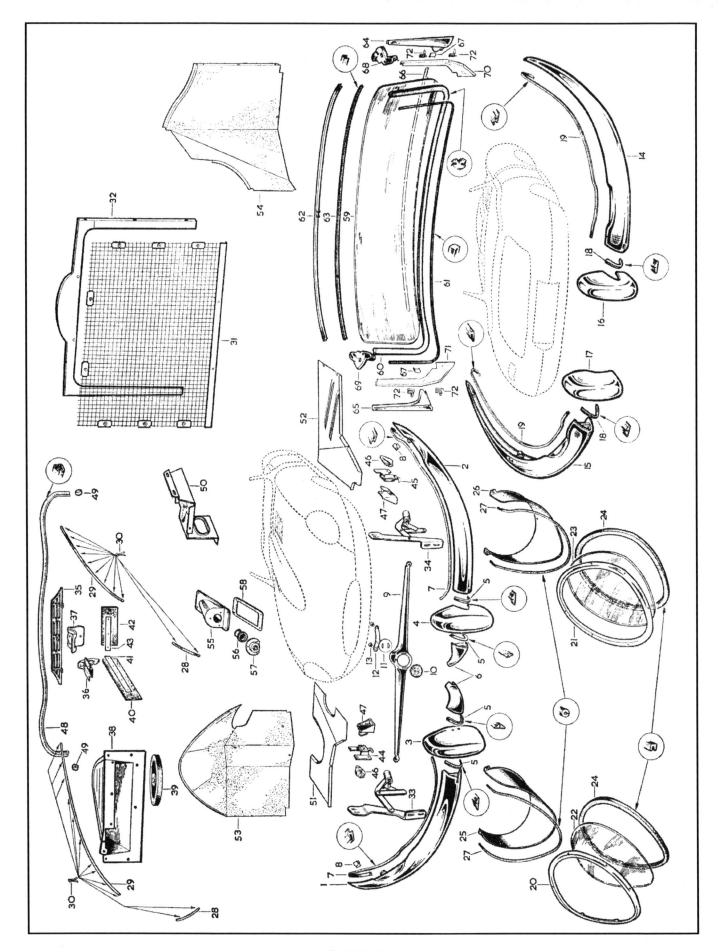

PLATE 38

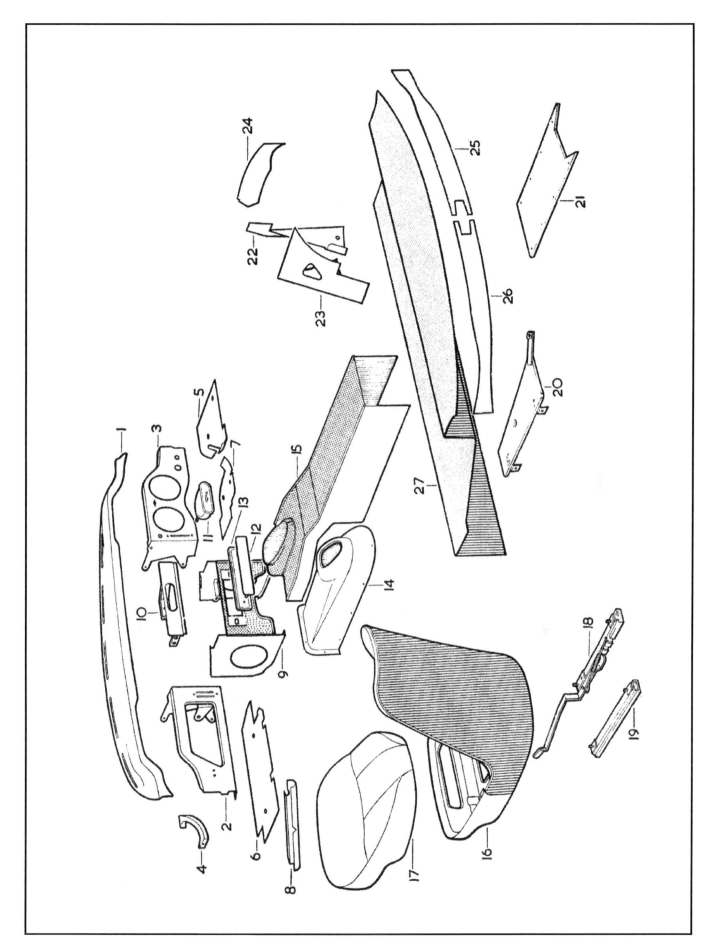

PLATE 39

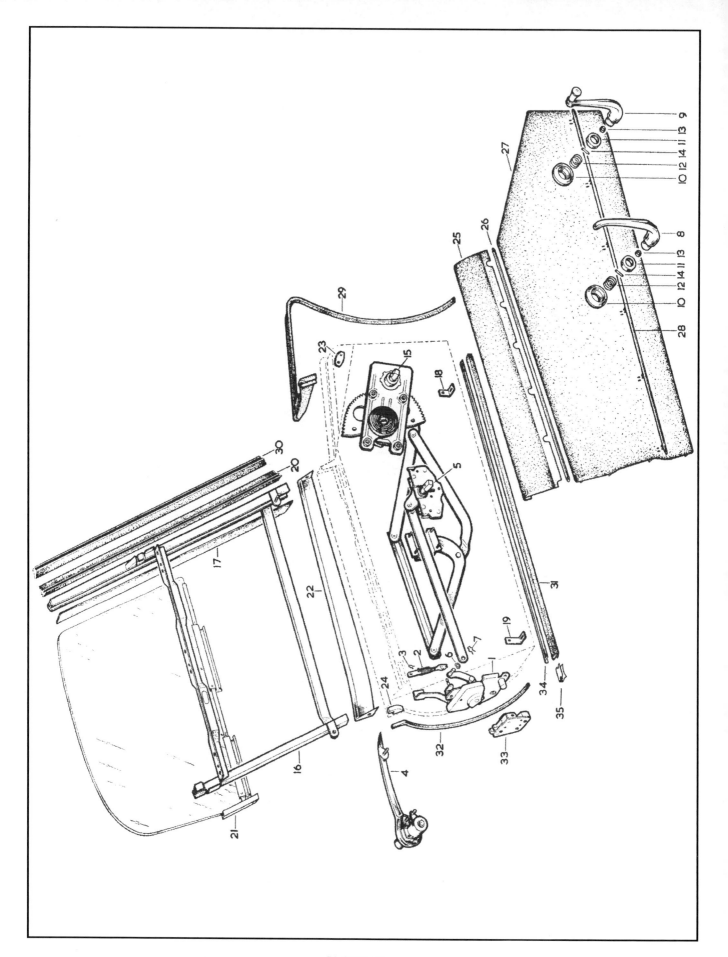

PLATE 40

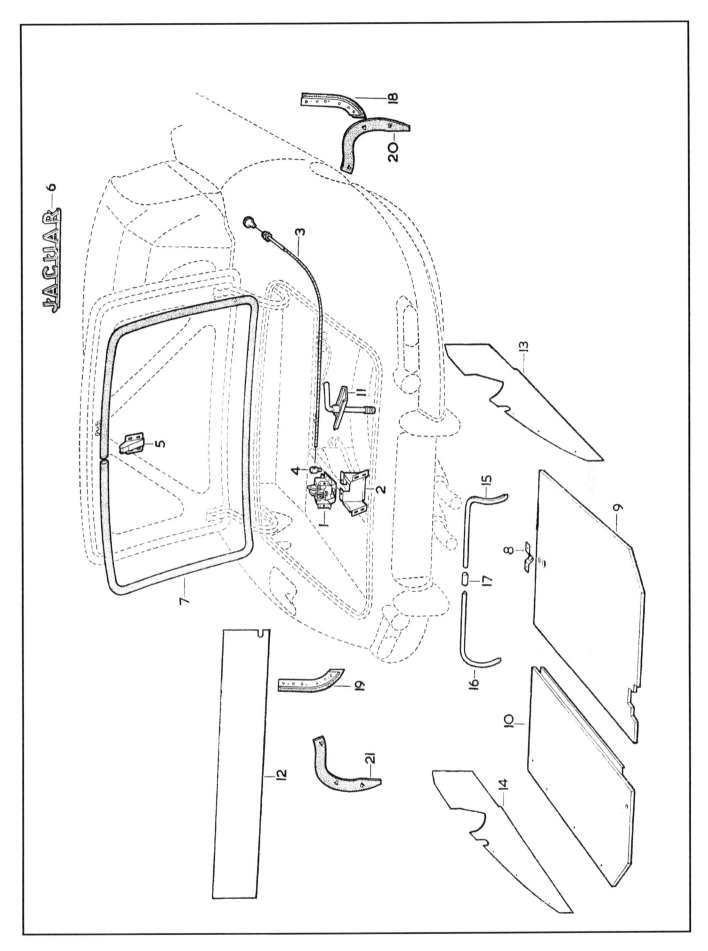

PLATE 41

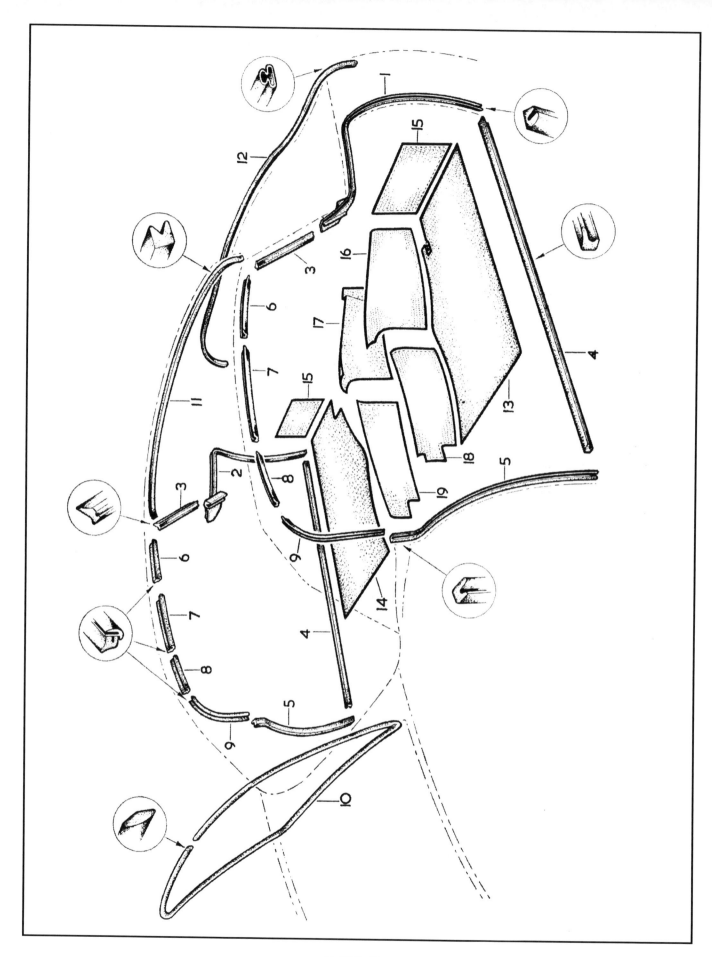

PLATE 42

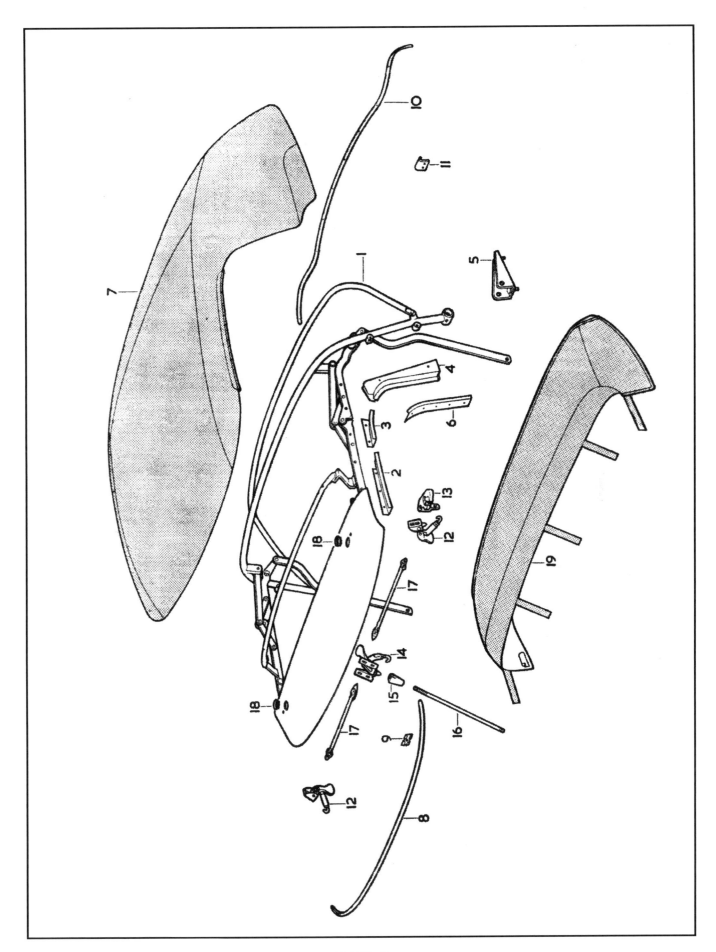

PLATE 43

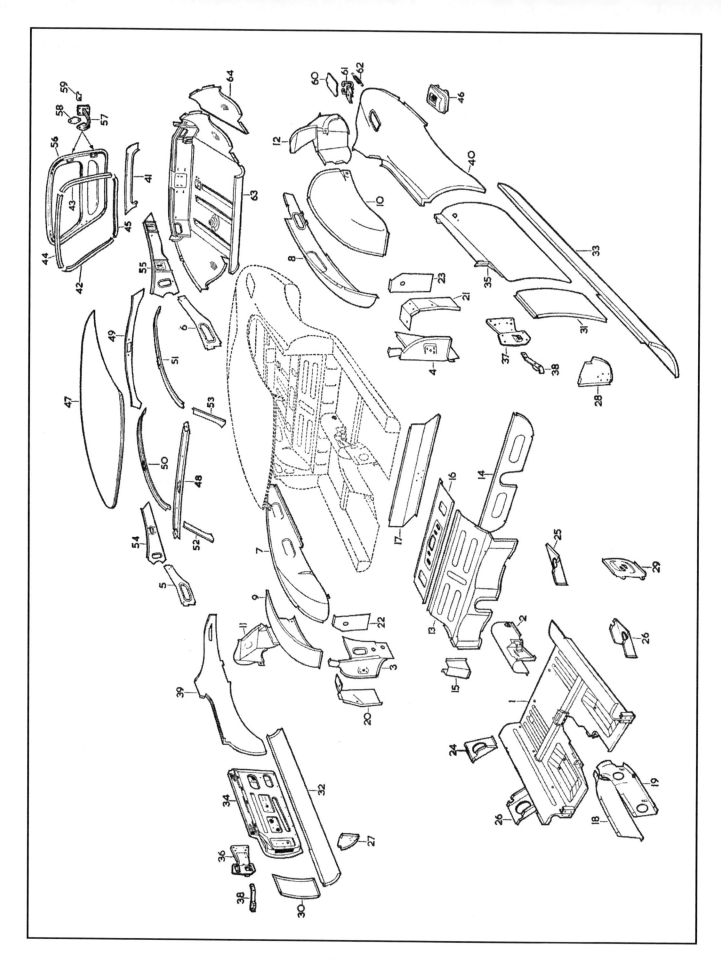

PLATE 44

FITTED FROM CHASSIS No. 860001 TO 860478, 885001 TO 886013

Part No.	Description	Plate No.	No. per Unit	Remarks
BD.19350	**BODY SHELL ASSEMBLY, COMPLETE**		1	
BD.19334	**Underframe Assembly**		1	
BD.16550	**Bonnet and Front Wings Assembly**		1	Fitted from Chassis No. 860001 to 860004. 885001 to 885020.
BD.19929	**Bonnet and Front Wings Assembly**		1	Fitted from Chassis No. 860005 to 860478. 885021 to 886013.
C.16942	**Front Sub-Frame Assembly**		1	Fitted from Chassis No. 860001 to 860138. 885001 to 885384.
C.19339	**Front Sub-Frame Assembly**		1	Fitted from Chassis No. 860139 to 860478. 885385 to 886013.
C.15014	**Front Cross Member Assembly**		1	
C.15029	**R.H. Side Member Assembly**		1	
C.15030	**L.H. Side Member Assembly**		1	
C.16803	**Hinge,** for Bonnet		2	Fitted from Chassis No. 860001 to 860138. 885001 to 885384.
C.19326	**Hinge,** for Bonnet		2	Fitted from Chassis No. 860139 to 860478. 885385 to 886013.
BD.19739	**Door Shell Assembly, R.H.**		1	
BD.19740	**Door Shell Assembly, L.H.**		1	
BD.15495	**Hinge Assembly,** for R.H. Door		1	
BD.15496	**Hinge Assembly,** for L.H. Door		1	
BD.20957	**Scuttle Top Panel Assembly**		1	
BD.19341	**R.H. Windscreen Pillar Assembly**		1	
BD.19342	**L.H. Windscreen Pillar Assembly**		1	
BD.15217	**Filler Panel** between R.H. Screen Pillar and Scuttle Top Panel		1	
BD.15218	**Filler Panel** between L.H. Screen Pillar and Scuttle Top Panel		1	
BD.15467	**Closing Panel,** under R.H. Screen Pillar		1	
BD.15468	**Closing Panel,** under L.H. Screen Pillar		1	
BD.17069	**Corner Panel,** Dash to Scuttle Top, R.H.		1	
BD.17070	**Corner Panel,** Dash to Scuttle Top, L.H.		1	
BD.15180	**Exterior Panel Assembly,** R.H. Dash Side		1	
BD.15181	**Exterior Panel Assembly,** L.H. Dash Side		1	
BD.15133	**R.H. Sill Outer Panel**		1	
BD.15134	**L.H. Sill Outer Panel**		1	
BD.15184	**End Plate,** at front of R.H. Sill		1	
BD.15187	**Bracket Assembly,** at front of R.H. Sill, mounting Air Cleaner		1	
BD.15185	**End Plate Assembly,** at front of L.H. Sill		1	
BD.15186	**Bracket Assembly,** at front of L.H. Sill, mounting Battery Tray		1	
BD.19586	**Bracket Assembly,** for Jack location		2	
BD.19338	**Panel Assembly,** lower rear		1	
BD.20310	**Rear Wing Panel Assembly, R.H.**		1	
BD.20311	**Rear Wing Panel Assembly, L.H.**		1	
BD.19340/4	**Tail Panel,** below Boot Lid		1	
BD.19340/1	**Roof Panel Assembly**		1	
BD.19617	**Cantrail Panel Assembly, R.H.**		1	
BD.19618	**Cantrail Panel Assembly, L.H.**		1	
BD.20809	**Support Panel Assembly** at R.H. side of Boot Lid aperture		1	
BD.20810	**Support Panel Assembly** at L.H. side of Boot Lid aperture		1	
BD.19550	**Boot Lid Shell Assembly**		1	
BD.20306	**Hinge Assembly,** upper, for Boot Lid		1	
BD.20307	**Hinge Assembly,** lower, for Boot Lid		1	
BD.19355	**Lid Assembly,** for Petrol Filler Box		1	
BD.19532	**Fixing Bracket,** outer, for R.H. Stop/Tail Lamp		1	
BD.19533	**Fixing Bracket,** outer, for L.H. Stop/Tail Lamp		1	
BD.19534	**Fixing Bracket,** inner, for R.H. Stop/Tail Lamp		1	
BD.19535	**Fixing Bracket,** inner, for L.H. Stop/Tail Lamp		1	
BD.19869	**Reinforcement Channel,** at top of R.H. Windscreen Pillar		1	
BD.19870	**Reinforcement Channel,** at top of L.H. Windscreen Pillar		1	

For Fixings to Main Body Portion, please refer to Section for Front Frame.

BODY SHELL
FOR FIXED HEAD COUPE ONLY

FITTED FROM CHASSIS No. 860479 TO 860580, 886014 TO 886092

Part No.	Description	Plate No.	No. per Unit	Remarks
BD.20748	**BODY SHELL ASSEMBLY, COMPLETE**		1	
BD.19334	**Underframe Assembly**		1	
BD.19929	**Bonnet and Front Wings Assembly**		1	
C.19339	**Front Sub-Frame Assembly**		1	
C.15014	**Front Cross Member Assembly**		1	
C.15029	**R.H. Side Member Assembly**		1	
C.15030	**L.H. Side Member Assembly**		1	
C.19326	**Hinge,** for Bonnet		2	
BD.19739	**Door Shell Assembly,** R.H.		1	
BD.19740	**Door Shell Assembly,** L.H.		1	
BD.15495	**Hinge Assembly,** for R.H. Door		1	
BD.15496	**Hinge Assembly,** for L.H. Door		1	
BD.20957	**Scuttle Top Panel Assembly**		1	
BD.23913	**R.H. Windscreen Pillar Assembly**		1	
BD.23914	**L.H. Windscreen Pillar Assembly**		1	
BD.15217	**Filler Panel,** between R.H. Screen Pillar and Scuttle Top Panel		1	
BD.15218	**Filler Panel,** between L.H. Screen Pillar and Scuttle Top Panel		1	
BD.15467	**Closing Panel,** under R.H. Screen Pillar		1	
BD.15468	**Closing Panel,** under L.H. Screen Pillar		1	
BD.17069	**Corner Panel,** Dash to Scuttle Top, R.H.		1	
BD.17070	**Corner Panel,** Dash to Scuttle Top, L.H.		1	
BD.15180	**Exterior Panel Assembly,** R.H. Dash Side		1	
BD.15181	**Exterior Panel Assembly,** L.H. Dash Side		1	
BD.15133	**R.H. Sill Outer Panel**		1	
BD.15134	**L.H. Sill Outer Panel**		1	
BD.15184	**End Plate,** at front of R.H. Sill		1	
BD.15187	**Bracket Assembly,** at front of R.H. Sill, mounting Air Cleaner		1	
BD.15185	**End Plate Assembly,** at front of L.H. Sill		1	
BD.15186	**Bracket Assembly,** at front of L.H. Sill, mounting Battery Tray		1	
BD.19586	**Bracket Assembly,** for Jack Location		2	
BD.19338	**Panel Assembly,** Lower Rear		1	
BD.23180	**Roof Panel and Rear Wings Assembly**		1	
BD.19635	**Drain Tube,** for Boot Lid Aperture		1	
BD.19532	**Fixing Bracket,** outer, for R.H. Stop/Tail Lamp		1	
BD.19533	**Fixing Bracket,** outer, for L.H. Stop/Tail Lamp		1	
BD.19534	**Fixing Bracket,** inner, for R.H. Stop/Tail Lamp		1	
BD.19535	**Fixing Bracket,** inner, for L.H. Stop/Tail Lamp		1	
BD.20203	**Reinforcement Channel,** at top of R.H. Windscreen Pillar		1	
BD.20202	**Reinforcement Channel,** at top of L.H. Windscreen Pillar		1	
BD.21448	**Drip Bead Extension,** on R.H. Windscreen Pillar		1	
BD.21449	**Drip Bead Extension,** on L.H. Windscreen Pillar		1	
BD.19544	**Boot Lid Shell Assembly**		1	
BD.19626	**Support Panel Assembly,** at R.H. Side of Boot Lid Aperture		1	
BD.19627	**Support Panel Assembly,** at L.H. Side of Boot Lid Aperture		1	
BD.20261	**Hinge Assembly,** for Boot Lid		2	
BD.22242	**Lid Assembly,** for Petrol Filler Box		1	
BD.19552	**Hinge Assembly,** for Petrol Filler Lid		1	

FITTED FROM CHASSIS No. 860581 AND SUBS., 886093 AND SUBS.

Part No.	Description	Plate No.	No. per Unit	Remarks
BD.22941	**BODY SHELL ASSEMBLY, COMPLETE**		1	
BD.22936	**Underframe Assembly**		1	

All other items are as for **Body Shell Assembly BD.20748.**

BODY UNDERFRAME AND PANELS
FOR FIXED HEAD COUPE ONLY

Part No.	Description	Plate No.	No. per Unit	Remarks
BD.19334	**BODY UNDERFRAME ASSEMBLY**		1	Fitted from Chassis No. 860001 to 860580. 885001 to 886092.
BD.15171	**Floor Assembly**		1	Fitted from Chassis No. 860001 to 860175. 885001 to 885503.
BD.23141	**Floor Assembly** (Complete with Heel Wells)		1	Fitted from Chassis No. 860176 to 860580. 885504 to 886092.
BD.19337	**Rear End Assembly**		1	
BD.22936	**BODY UNDERFRAME ASSEMBLY**		1	Fitted to Chassis No. 860581 and subs. 886093 and subs.
BD.22819	**Floor Assembly**	44– 1	1	
BD.23100	**Rear End Assembly**		1	
BD.15171	**FLOOR ASSEMBLY**		1	Fitted from Chassis No. 860001 to 860175. 885001 to 885503.
BD.19238	**Bracket Assembly,** for Exhaust Silencer Mounting		4	
BD.23141	**FLOOR ASSEMBLY (COMPLETE WITH HEEL WELLS)**		1	Fitted from Chassis No. 860176 to 860580. 885504 to 886092.
BD.15131/2	**Heel Well,** only		2	
BD.19238	**Bracket Assembly,** for Exhaust Silencer Mounting		4	
BD.22819	**FLOOR ASSEMBLY (COMPLETE WITH HEEL WELLS)**	44– 1	1	Fitted to Chassis No. 860581 and subs. 886093 and subs.
BD.15131/2	**Heel Well,** only		2	
BD.19238	**Bracket Assembly,** for Exhaust Silencer Mounting		4	
BD.15588/1	**Plastic Plug,** in Floor ($\frac{3}{8}$" dia.)		26	
BD.15588/2	**Plastic Plug,** in Floor ($\frac{1}{2}$" dia.)		2	**R.H. DRIVE CARS ONLY.**
BD.15588/4	**Plastic Plug,** in Floor ($\frac{3}{4}$" dia.)		2	
BD.15588/5	**Plastic Plug,** in Floor ($\frac{7}{8}$" dia.)		10	
BD.19902	**Plastic Plug,** in Floor		1	
BD.22756	**Plastic Plug,** in Floor (Safety Harness)		4	
BD.19337	**REAR END ASSEMBLY**		1	
BD.16650	**Tunnel Assembly**	44– 2	1	
BD.19322	**Shut Pillar Assembly,** R.H.	44– 3	1	
BD.19323	**Shut Pillar Assembly,** L.H.	44– 4	1	
BD.19322/3	**Support Panel,** for R.H. Inner Quarter	44– 5	1	
BD.19323/3	**Support Panel,** for L.H. Inner Quarter	44– 6	1	
BD.20544	**Wheel Arch Panel Assembly,** R.H. Inner forward	44– 7	1	
BD.20545	**Wheel Arch Panel Assembly,** L.H. Inner forward	44– 8	1	
BD.19628	**Wheel Arch Panel Assembly,** R.H. Outer forward	44– 9	1	
BD.19629	**Wheel Arch Panel Assembly,** L.H. Outer forward	44–10	1	
BD.19545	**Wheel Arch Panel Assembly,** R.H. rear	44–11	1	Fitted from Chassis No. 860001 to 860580. 885001 to 886092.
BD.19546	**Wheel Arch Panel Assembly,** L.H. rear	44–12	1	
BD.15985	**Floor Panel,** rear	44–13	1	
BD.20162	**Cross Member Assembly,** for Rear Floor	44–14	1	
BD.17445	**Stiffening Bracket,** at sides of Rear Floor Cross Member	44–15	2	
BD.19077	**Bracket Assembly,** R.H., for mounting of Rear Suspension Cross Member		1	
BD.19078	**Bracket Assembly,** L.H., for mounting of Rear Suspension Cross Member		1	
BD.17442	**Top Panel Assembly,** above Rear Floor	44–16	1	
BD.15228	**Panel Assembly,** for front of Petrol Tank and Spare Wheel Compartment	44–17	1	
BD.15238	**Reinforcement Angle,** between Tank Compartment Panel and Top Panel		1	

Part No.	Description	Plate No.	No. per Unit	Remarks
BD.23100	**REAR END ASSEMBLY**		1	
BD.22809	**Floor Panel Assembly**		1	Fitted to Chassis No. 860581 and subs. 886093 and subs.
BD.22816	**Stiffening Bracket,** at R.H. side of Rear Cross Member		1	
BD.22817	**Stiffening Bracket,** at L.H. side of Rear Cross Member		1	
	All other items are as for Rear End Assembly BD.19337.			
BD.19132	**Bracket Assembly,** for mounting of Rear Suspension Bump Stop Rubbers		2	
BD.15137	**Panel Assembly,** at R.H. side of Gearbox	44–18	1	
BD.15138	**Panel Assembly,** at L.H. side of Gearbox	44–19	1	
BD.15198	**Reinforcement Panel,** for R.H. Shut Pillar	44–20	1	
BD.15199	**Reinforcement Panel,** for L.H. Shut Pillar	44–21	1	
BD.19897	**Closing Panel Assembly,** for R.H. Shut Pillar	44–22	1	
BD.19898	**Closing Panel Assembly,** for L.H. Shut Pillar	44–23	1	
BD.17456	**Support Panel,** for Shut Pillars		2	
BD.18368	**Reinforcement Panel,** lower rear, for Propeller Shaft Tunnel		1	
BD.15982	**Reinforcement Panel,** at rear of R.H. Sill	44–24	1	
BD.15983	**Reinforcement Panel,** at rear of L.H. Sill	44–25	1	
BD.16488	**Reinforcement Panel,** at front of Sills	44–26	2	
BD.15202	**Closing Panel,** for front of R.H. Sill	44–27	1	
BD.15203	**Closing Panel,** for front of L.H. Sill	44–28	1	
BD.14918	**Reinforcement Panel,** for R.H. Dash side		1	
BD.14919	**Reinforcement Panel,** for L.H. Dash side	44–29	1	
BD.16942	**Closing Panel Assembly,** R.H. lower Dash front		1	
BD.16943	**Closing Panel,** L.H. lower Dash, front		1	
BD.15180	**EXTERIOR PANEL ASSEMBLY, R.H. DASH SIDE**	44–30	1	
BD.15181	**EXTERIOR PANEL ASSEMBLY, L.H. DASH SIDE**	44–31	1	
BD.15133	**R.H. SILL OUTER PANEL**	44–32	1	
BD.15184	**End Plate,** at front of R.H. Sill		1	
BD.15187	**Bracket Assembly,** at side of R.H. Sill for Mounting Air Cleaner		1	
BD.15134	**L.H. SILL OUTER PANEL**	44–33	1	
BD.15185	**End Plate Assembly,** at front of L.H. Sill		1	
BD.15186	**Bracket Assembly,** at side of L.H. Sill for Mounting Battery Tray		1	
BD.19586	**BRACKET, UNDER SILLS, FOR JACK LOCATION**		2	
BD.19739	**DOOR SHELL ASSEMBLY, R.H.**	44–34	1	
BD.19741	**Outer Panel Assembly,** for R.H. Door		1	
BD.15453	**Inner Panel Assembly,** for R.H. Door		1	
BD.21030	**Drain Tray,** at top of R.H. Door		1	
BD.11712/1	**Pop Rivet,** securing Drain Tray		2	
BD.20878	**Shroud,** for Drain Holes at bottom of Door		2	
BD.1814/1	**Pop Rivet,** securing Shrouds		6	
BD.21180	**Drain Tube Rubber,** for Tray		1	
BD.20978	**Shroud,** for Drain Holes, at front of Door		1	
BD.20979	**Shroud,** for Drain Holes, at rear of Door		1	
BD.1814/2	**Pop Rivet,** securing Shrouds at front and rear of Door		7	

Part No.	Description	Plate No.	No. per Unit	Remarks
BD.19740	**DOOR SHELL ASSEMBLY, L.H.**	44–35	1	
BD.19742	**Outer Panel Assembly,** for L.H. Door		1	
BD.15454	**Inner Panel Assembly,** for L.H. Door		1	
BD.21031	**Drain Tray,** at top of L.H. Door		1	
	All other items are as for Door Shell Assembly BD.19739.			
BD.15495	**HINGE ASSEMBLY, FOR R.H. DOOR**	44–36	1	
BD.15496	**HINGE ASSEMBLY, FOR L.H. DOOR**	44–37	1	
C.16168	**Grease Nipple,** on Door Hinges (Tec.YH.109)		2	
BD.22662	**CHECK ARM ASSEMBLY FOR DOORS**	44–38	2	
BD.22661	**Brass Cam,** for Check Arms		2	**Self-Tapping Screw BD.17503/1 may be required for some cars.**
UCS.519/4H	**Screw,** Set, Csk. Hd., securing Cam to Check Arms		4	
UFS.425/5H	**Screw,** Set, securing Check Arm to Door Hinges		4	
C.724	**Washer,** Shakeproof, on Setscrews		4	
BD.17034/5	**Screw,** Set, securing Hinge to Doors		8	
BD.711/20	**Screw,** Self-Tapping, securing Hinge to Doors		4	
BD.13565/3	**Screw,** Set, securing Hinges to Body		8	
FG.105/X	**Washer,** Spring, on Setscrews		8	
BD.20310	**REAR WING ASSEMBLY, R.H.**	44–39	1	Fitted from Chassis No. 860001 to 860478. 875001 to 886013.
BD.20311	**REAR WING ASSEMBLY, L.H.**	44–40	1	
BD.24830	**REAR WING ASSEMBLY, R.H.**		1	Fitted to Chassis No. 860479 and subs. 886014 and subs.
BD.24831	**REAR WING ASSEMBLY, L.H.**		1	
BD.19340/4	**TAIL PANEL, BELOW BOOT LID**	44–41	1	Fitted from Chassis No. 860001 to 860478. 875001 to 886013.
BD.19878/1	**GUTTER AT R.H. SIDE OF BOOT LID APERTURE**	44–42	1	
BD.19878/2	**GUTTER AT L.H. SIDE OF BOOT LID APERTURE**	44–43	1	
BD.19878/3	**GUTTER AT TOP OF BOOT LID APERTURE**	44–44	1	Fitted from Chassis No. 860001 to 860478. 875001 to 886013.
BD.19878/4	**GUTTER AT BOTTOM OF BOOT LID APERTURE**	44–45	1	

Part No.	Description	Plate No.	No. per Unit	Remarks
BD.21386	**PETROL FILLER BOX ASSEMBLY IN L.H. WING**		1	Fitted from Chassis No. 860001 to 860478. 875001 to 886013.
BD.19339	**PETROL FILLER BOX ASSEMBLY IN L.H. WING**	44–46	1	Fitted to Chassis No. 860479 and subs. 886014 and subs.
BD.19340/1	**ROOF PANEL ASSEMBLY**		1	
BD.19619	**Windscreen Header Panel Assembly**		1	Fitted from Chassis No. 860001 to 860478. 875001 to 886013.
BD.19672	**Reinforcement Rail Assembly,** at rear of Roof		1	
BD.19617	**R.H. Cantrail Panel Assembly**		1	
BD.19618	**L.H. Cantrail Panel Assembly**		1	
BD.19540/1	**ROOF PANEL ASSEMBLY**	44–47	1	
BD.20106	**Windscreen Header Panel Assembly**		1	Fitted to Chassis No. 860479 and subs. 886014 and subs.
BD.20119	**Reinforcement Rail Assembly,** at rear of Roof		1	
BD.20115	**R.H. Cantrail Panel Assembly**		1	
BD.20116	**L.H. Cantrail Panel Assembly**		1	
BD.19619	**WINDSCREEN HEADER PANEL ASSEMBLY**		1	Fitted from Chassis No. 860001 to 860478. 885001 to 886013.
BD.19762	**Reinforcement Rail Assembly,** for Roof		1	
BD.20106	**WINDSCREEN HEADER PANEL**	44–48	1	Fitted to Chassis No. 860479 and subs. 886014 and subs.
BD.20119	**Reinforcement Rail Assembly,** for Roof	44–49	1	
BD.19617	**R.H. CANTRAIL PANEL ASSEMBLY**		1	Fitted from Chassis No. 860001 to 860478. 885001 to 886013.
BD.19618	**L.H. CANTRAIL PANEL ASSEMBLY**		1	
BD.20115	**R.H. CANTRAIL PANEL ASSEMBLY**	44–50	1	Fitted to Chassis No. 860479 and subs. 886014 and subs.
BD.20116	**L.H. CANTRAIL PANEL ASSEMBLY**	44–51	1	
BD.21354	**DRIP BEAD EXTENSION ON R.H. CANTRAIL PANEL**		1	Fitted from Chassis No. 860001 to 860478. 885001 to 886013.
BD.21355	**DRIP BEAD EXTENSION ON L.H. CANTRAIL PANEL**		1	

BODY UNDERFRAME AND PANELS
FOR FIXED HEAD COUPE ONLY

Part No.	Description	Plate No.	No. per Unit	Remarks
BD.21448	**DRIP BEAD EXTENSION ON R.H. CANTRAIL PANEL**	44–52	1	Fitted to Chassis No. 860479 and subs. 886014 and subs.
BD.21449	**DRIP BEAD EXTENSION ON L.H. CANTRAIL PANEL**	44–53	1	
BD.20809	**SUPPORT PANEL ASSEMBLY, AT R.H. SIDE OF BOOT LID APERTURE**		1	Fitted from Chassis No. 860001 to 860478. 885001 to 886013.
BD.20810	**SUPPORT PANEL ASSEMBLY, AT L.H. SIDE OF BOOT LID APERTURE**		1	
BD.19626	**SUPPORT PANEL ASSEMBLY, AT R.H. SIDE OF BOOT LID APERTURE**	44–54	1	Fitted to Chassis No. 860479 and subs. 886014 and subs.
BD.19627	**SUPPORT PANEL ASSEMBLY, AT L.H. SIDE OF BOOT LID APERTURE**	44–55	1	
BD.19550	**BOOT LID SHELL ASSEMBLY**		1	Fitted from Chassis No. 860001 to 860478. 885001 to 886013.
BD.19544	**BOOT LID SHELL ASSEMBLY**	44–56	1	Fitted to Chassis No. 860479 and subs. 886014 and subs.
BD.20306	**HINGE ASSEMBLY, UPPER, FOR BOOT LID**		1	
BD.20307	**HINGE ASSEMBLY, LOWER, FOR BOOT LID**		1	Fitted from Chassis No. 860001 to 860478. 885001 to 886013.
UFS.125/4R	**Screw**, Set, securing Hinges to Boot Lid		4	
C.724	**Washer**, Shakeproof, on Setscrews		4	
BD.541/20	**Special Washer**, under Shakeproof Washers		4	
UFS.425/3H	**Screw**, Set, securing Hinges to Body		8	
C.724	**Washer**, Shakeproof, on Setscrews		8	
BD.20261	**HINGE ASSEMBLY, FOR BOOT LID**	44–57	2	Fitted to Chassis No. 860479 and subs. 886014 and subs.
BD.17034/3	**Screw**, Set, securing Hinges to Boot Lid		4	
BD.2906/6	**Washer**, Shakeproof, Csk., on Setscrews		4	
BD.23163	**Shim**, between Hinges and Boot Lid	44–58	As req'd	
UFS.125/5R	**Screw**, Set, securing Hinges to Body		8	
C.724	**Washer**, Shakeproof, on Setscrews		8	
BD.23164	**Shim**, between Hinges and Body	44–59	As req'd	
BD.19355	**LID ASSEMBLY, FOR PETROL FILLER BOX**		1	Fitted from Chassis No. 860001 to 860478. 885001 to 886013.

Part No.	Description	Plate No.	No. per Unit	Remarks
BD.22242	**LID ASSEMBLY, FOR PETROL FILLER BOX**	44–60	1	Fitted to Chassis No. 860479 and subs. 886014 and subs.
BD.19552	**HINGE ASSEMBLY FOR PETROL FILLER LID**	44–61	1	
BD.8291/1	**Screw,** Set, securing Hinge to Lid, and to Body		4	
C.724	**Washer,** Shakeproof, on Setscrews		4	
FW.104/T	**Washer,** Plain, under Shakeproof Washers		4	
BD.15930	**SPRING, BETWEEN LID AND HINGE**	44–62	1	
BD.19338	**PANEL ASSEMBLY, LOWER REAR**	44–63	1	
BD.18837	**Lower Panel,** R.H. Outer		1	
BD.18838	**Lower Panel,** L.H. Outer	44–64	1	
BD.19532	**Fixing Bracket,** outer, for R.H. Stop/Tail Lamp		1	
BD.19533	**Fixing Bracket,** outer, for L.H. Stop/Tail Lamp		1	
BD.19534	**Fixing Bracket,** inner, for R.H. Stop/Tail Lamp		1	
BD.19535	**Fixing Bracket,** inner, for L.H. Stop/Tail Lamp		1	
BD.19970	**PANEL ASSEMBLY FOR REAR NUMBER PLATE**		1	
BD.16550	**BONNET AND FRONT WINGS ASSEMBLY**		1	
BD.15174	**Centre Panel Assembly,** for Bonnet	45– 1	1	
BD.15175	**Front Under Panel Assembly**	45– 2	1	
BD.16557	**Air Duct Lower Panel Assembly**	45– 3	1	
BD.16839/3	**Screw,** Self-Tapping, securing Air Duct Panel to Valances		6	
UCS.125/5R	**Screw,** Set, securing Front Under Panel to Valances, Centre Panel and Wings		14	
UCN.125/L	**Nut,** on Setscrews		14	
FG.104/X	**Washer,** Spring, under Nuts and on Self-Tapping Screws		20	
BD.542/3	**Washer,** Special, on Setscrews and Self-Tapping Screws		34	
BD.15176	**Front Wing Assembly,** R.H.	45– 4	1	Fitted from Chassis No. 860001 to 860004. 885001 to 885020.
BD.15177	**Front Wing Assembly,** L.H.	45– 5	1	
UCS.125/5R	**Screw,** Set, securing Wings to Centre Panel		18	
UCN.125/L	**Nut,** on Setscrews		18	
FG.104/X	**Washer,** Spring, under Nuts		18	
BD.542/3	**Washer,** Special, on Setscrews		36	
BD.19021	**R.H. Valance and Air Duct Assembly**	45– 6	1	
BD.19022	**L.H. Valance and Air Duct Assembly**	45– 7	1	
BD.16839/2	**Screw,** Self-Tapping, securing Valance and Duct Assemblies to Centre Panel and Front Under Panel		23	
FG.104/X	**Washer,** Spring, on Self-Tapping Screws		23	
BD.542/3	**Washer,** Special, under Spring Washers		23	
BD.16422	**R.H. Front Diaphragm Assembly,** mounting Headlamp	45– 8	1	
BD.16423	**L.H. Front Diaphragm Assembly,** mounting Headlamp	45– 9	1	
UCS.125/5R	**Screw,** Set, securing Diaphragms to Wings		8	
UCN.125/L	**Nut,** on Setscrews		8	
BD.16839/2	**Screw,** Self-Tapping, securing Diaphragms to Valances, Wings and Front Under Panel		26	

Part No.	Description	Plate No.	No. per Unit	Remarks
	BONNET AND FRONT WINGS **ASSEMBLY** (continued)			
FG.104/X	**Washer,** Spring, on Setscrews, and Self-Tapping Screws		34	
BD.542/3	**Washer,** Special, on Setscrews and Self-Tapping Screws		42	
BD.22749	**Sealing Panel,** for R.H. Headlamp Diaphragm		1	
BD.22750	**Sealing Panel,** for L.H. Headlamp Diaphragm		1	
BD.22749/1	**Felt,** on Sealing Panel		4	
BD.1328/2	**Rivet,** securing Felt to Panel		8	
UFS.419/3H	**Screw,** Set, securing Sealing Panel		2	
UFN.119/L	**Nut,** on Setscrews		2	
C.723/A	**Washer,** Shakeproof, on Setscrews		2	
AW.102/T	**Washer,** Plain, under Shakeproof Washers		2	Fitted from Chassis No.
BD.16381	**R.H. Diaphragm Assembly,** at rear of Bonnet	45–10	1	860001 to 860004.
BD.16382	**L.H. Diaphragm Assembly,** at rear of Bonnet	45–11	1	885001 to 885020.
UCS.125/5R	**Screw,** Set, securing Rear Diaphragms to Wings, Valances, and Centre Panel		18	
UCN.125/L	**Nut,** on Setscrews		18	
BD.16839/2	**Screw,** Self-Tapping, securing Rear Diaphragms to Centre Panel		7	
FG.104/X	**Washer,** Spring, on Setscrews and Self-Tapping Screws		25	
BD.542/3	**Washer,** Special, on Setscrews and Self-Tapping Screws		43	
BD.18767	**Reinforcing Angle,** between Wings and Centre Panel at rear		2	
UFS.125/4R	**Screw,** Set, securing Reinforcing Angles		8	
FG.104/X	**Washer,** Spring, on Setscrews		8	
FW.104/T	**Washer,** Plain, under Spring Washers		8	
BD.19929	**BONNET AND FRONT WINGS** **ASSEMBLY**		1	
BD.19930	**Front Wing Assembly,** R.H.		1	Fitted to Chassis No.
BD.19931	**Front Wing Assembly,** L.H.		1	860005 and subs.
	All other items are as for Bonnet and Front Wing Assembly BD.16550.			885021 and subs.
C.16803	**BONNET HINGE**	45–12	2	
C.16804	**Nylon Bush,** in Hinges	45–13	4	Fitted from Chassis No.
C.8667/5	**Nut,** Self-Locking, retaining Hinges on Sub-Frame Cross Bar		2	860001 to 860138.
C.8676	**Washer,** Plain, under Nuts		2	885001 to 885384.
C.19326	**BONNET HINGE**		2	
C.16804	**Nylon Bush,** in Bonnet Hinges		4	Fitted to Chassis No.
C.19330	**Bearing** (Steel) for Bonnet Hinges		2	860139 and subs.
UFB.137/18R	**Bolt,** retaining Bonnet Hinges to Front Sub-Frame		2	885385 and subs.
FG.106/X	**Washer,** Spring, on Bolts		2	
BD.13565/6	**Screw,** Set, securing Hinges to Bonnet		4	
BD.13565/8	**Screw,** Set, securing Hinges to Bonnet		4	
C.725	**Washer,** Shakeproof, on Setscrews		8	
C.985	**Washer,** Plain, under Shakeproof Washers		8	
BD.18951	**Shim** (.064″ thick) for Bonnet Hinges		As req'd	
BD.18951/1	**Shim** (.036″ thick) for Bonnet Hinges		As req'd	
BD.20950/1	**Special Shim** (Slotted) (.036″ thick) for Bonnet Hinges		As req'd	
BD.20950/2	**Special Shim** (Slotted) (.128″ thick) for Bonnet Hinges		As req'd	

BODY UNDERFRAME AND PANELS
FOR FIXED HEAD COUPE ONLY

Part No.	Description	Plate No.	No. per Unit	Remarks
BD.20957	**SCUTTLE TOP PANEL ASSEMBLY**	45–14	1	
BD.19341	**R.H. WINDSCREEN PILLAR ASSEMBLY**	45–15	1	
BD.19342	**L.H. WINDSCREEN PILLAR ASSEMBLY**	45–16	1	Fitted from Chassis No. 860001 to 860478. 885001 to 886013.
BD.19869	**Reinforcement Channel,** at top of R.H. Pillar	45–15A	1	
BD.19870	**Reinforcement Channel,** at top of L.H. Pillar	45–16A	1	
BD.15217	**Filler Panel,** between R.H. Windscreen Pillar and Scuttle Top Panel	45–17	1	
BD.15218	**Filler Panel,** between L.H. Windscreen Pillar and Scuttle Top Panel	45–18	1	
BD.23913	**R.H. WINDSCREEN PILLAR ASSEMBLY**		1	
BD.23914	**L.H. WINDSCREEN PILLAR ASSEMBLY**		1	Fitted to Chassis No. 860479 and subs. 886014 and subs.
BD.20203	**Reinforcement Channel,** at top of R.H. Pillar		1	
BD.20202	**Reinforcement Channel,** at top of L.H. Pillar		1	
BD.15217	**Filler Panel,** between R.H. Windscreen Pillar and Scuttle Top Panel		1	
BD.15218	**Filler Panel,** between L.H. Windscreen Pillar and Scuttle Top Panel		1	
BD.17069	**CORNER PANEL, DASH TO SCUTTLE TOP, R.H.**	45–19	1	
BD.17070	**CORNER PANEL, DASH TO SCUTTLE TOP, L.H.**	45–20	1	
BD.15467	**CLOSING PANEL, UNDER R.H. WINDSCREEN PILLAR**	45–21	1	
BD.15468	**CLOSING PANEL, UNDER L.H. WINDSCREEN PILLAR**	45–22	1	
BD.18710	**FRAME ASSEMBLY MOUNTING STONEGUARD**	45–23	1	

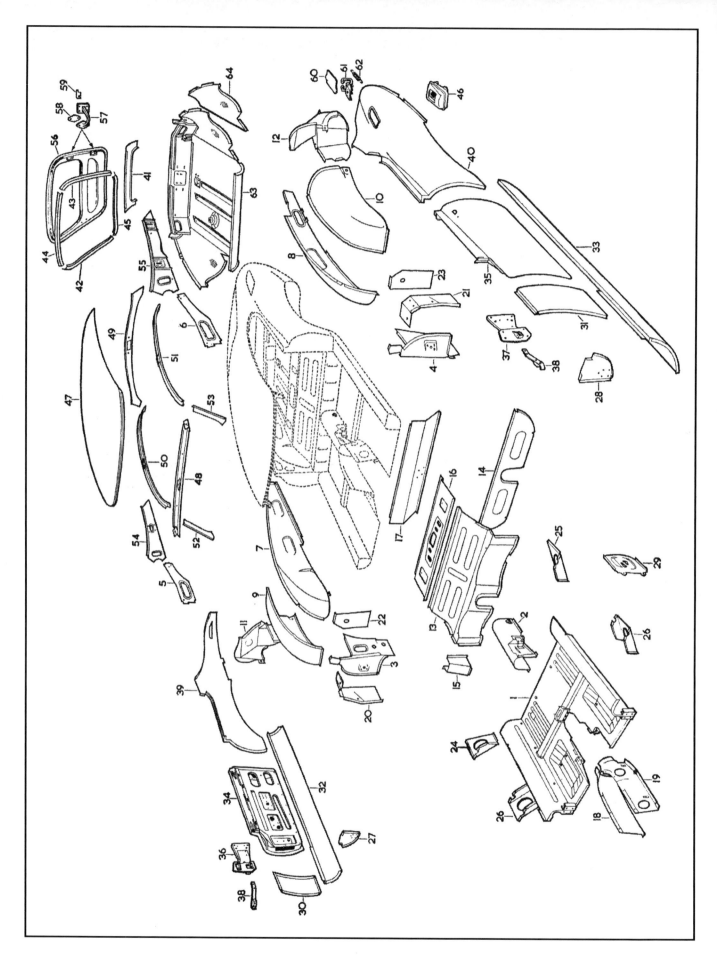

PLATE 44

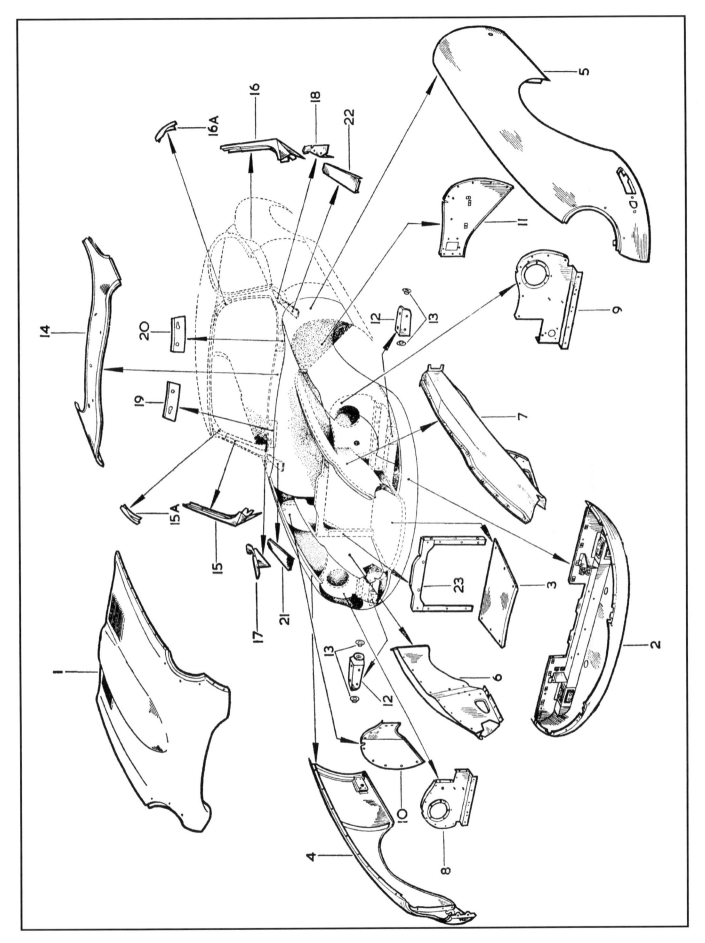

PLATE 45

BODY FITTINGS
FOR FIXED HEAD COUPE ONLY

Part No.	Description	Plate No.	No. per Unit	Remarks
BD.19145	**R.H. FRONT BUMPER ASSEMBLY**		1	
BD.19146	**L.H. FRONT BUMPER ASSEMBLY**		1	
BD.15533	**Bar Assembly only,** for R.H. Front Bumper	46– 1	1	
BD.15532	**Bar Assembly only,** for L.H. Front Bumper	46– 2	1	
BD.19111	**Over Rider Assembly,** on R.H. Front Bumper	46– 3	1	
BD.19112	**Over Rider Assembly,** on L.H. Front Bumper	46– 4	1	
BD.19149	**Beading,** between Over Rider and Front Bumpers	46– 5	4	
UFN.137/L	**Nut,** securing Over Rider to Front Bumpers		2	
FG.106/X	**Washer,** Spring, under Nuts		2	
FW.106/T	**Washer,** Plain, under Spring Washers		2	
BD.19113	**Extension Assembly,** for fixing of Motif Bar	46– 6	2	
UFS.125/6R	**Screw,** Set, securing Extension Bracket to Over Riders		4	
C.724	**Washer,** Shakeproof, on Setscrews		4	
FW.104/T	**Washer,** Plain, under Shakeproof Washers		4	
BD.19119	**Distance Piece,** on Setscrews		4	
UFS.137/10R	**Screw,** Set, securing Front Bumpers to Bonnet		4	
FG.106/X	**Washer,** Spring, on Setscrews		4	
C.410	**Washer,** Plain, under Spring Washers		4	
BD.20893	**Spacer,** on Setscrews at side fixings		2	
BD.20663	**Spacer,** on Setscrews at front fixings		2	
BD.18947/2	**Rubber Seal,** between Front Bumpers and Bonnet	46– 7	2	
BD.10313	**Clip,** securing Seal	46– 8	2	
BD.17700	**MOTIF BAR IN AIR INTAKE APERTURE**	46– 9	1	
C.16336	**MOTIF**	46–10	1	
BD.19033	**Backing Piece,** behind Motif	46–11	1	
BD.19034	**Spring Clip,** retaining Motif	46–12	1	
BD.11501	**Screw,** Self-Tapping, securing Spring Clip	46–13	2	
UFS.125/5R	**Screw,** Set, securing Motif Bar		2	
FG.104/X	**Washer,** Spring, on Setscrews		2	
BD.19147	**R.H. REAR BUMPER ASSEMBLY**		1	
BD.19148	**L.H. REAR BUMPER ASSEMBLY**		1	
BD.15887	**Bar Assembly only,** for R.H. Rear Bumper	46–14	1	
BD.15888	**Bar Assembly only,** for L.H. Rear Bumper	46–15	1	
BD.19135	**Over Rider Assembly,** on R.H. Rear Bumper	46–16	1	
BD.19136	**Over Rider Assembly,** on L.H. Rear Bumper	46–17	1	
UFN.137/L	**Nut,** securing Over Rider to Rear Bumpers		2	
FG.106/X	**Washer,** Spring, under Nuts		2	
FW.106/T	**Washer,** Plain, under Spring Washers		2	
BD.19149	**Beading,** between Over Rider and Rear Bumpers	46–18	2	
UFS.131/6R	**Screw,** Set, securing Rear Bumpers to Body		2	
FG.105/X	**Washer,** Spring, on Setscrews		2	
FW.105/T	**Washer,** Plain, under Spring Washers		2	
UFS.137/10R	**Screw,** Set, securing Rear Bumpers to Body		2	
UFN.137/L	**Nut,** securing Rear Bumpers to Body		2	
FG.106/X	**Washer,** Spring, on Setscrews and under Nuts		4	
FW.106/T	**Washer,** Plain, under Spring Washers		4	
BD.20893	**Nylon Spacer,** at Rear Bumper mountings		4	
BD.18947/1	**Rubber Seal,** between Rear Bumpers and Body	46–19	2	

Part No.	Description	Plate No.	No. per Unit	Remarks
BD.16789	**CHROME FINISHER ASSEMBLY, AROUND R.H. HEADLAMP APERTURE**	46–20	1	
BD.16790	**CHROME FINISHER ASSEMBLY, AROUND L.H. HEADLAMP APERTURE**	46–21	1	
BD.16786	**GLASS IN R.H. HEADLAMP APERTURE**	46–22	1	
BD.16787	**GLASS IN L.H. HEADLAMP APERTURE**	46–23	1	
BD.16788	**RUBBER SEAL AROUND HEADLAMP GLASSES**	46–24	2	
BD.19013/2	**Screw,** Self-Tapping, securing Headlamp Finishers and Glasses to Bonnet		12	} FOR USE ONLY WITH SPIRE NUT FIXING.
BD.8633/2	**Spire Nut,** on Self-Tapping Screws		12	
BD.22780/4	**Screw,** Set, securing Finishers and Headlamp Glasses to Bonnet		12	FOR USE ONLY WITH TAPPED PLATE FIXING.
BD.17651	**FINISHING PANEL ASSEMBLY IN R.H. HEADLAMP RECESS**	46–25	1	
BD.17652	**FINISHING PANEL ASSEMBLY IN L.H. HEADLAMP RECESS**	46–26	1	
BD.20543/1	**Rubber Seal,** for forward edge of Panels	46–27	2	
UFS.119/6R	**Screw,** Set, securing Panels to Headlamp Diaphragms		2	
UFS.119/8R	**Screw,** Set, securing Panels to Headlamp Diaphragms		4	
AG.102/X	**Washer,** Spring, on Setscrews		6	
AW.102/T	**Washer,** Plain, under Spring Washers		6	
UFN.119/L	**Nut,** on Setscrews		6	
C.1094	**Distance Piece,** for Panels		As req'd	
BD.19029/2	**CHROME BEADING FORWARD OF HEADLAMP APERTURES**	46–28	2	
BD.19029/1	**CHROME BEADING, AT REAR OF HEADLAMP APERTURES**	46–29	2	
BD.19030	**Brass Clip,** securing Chrome Beads	46–30	22	

BODY FITTINGS
FOR FIXED HEAD COUPE ONLY

Part No.	Description	Plate No.	No. per Unit	Remarks
BD.20989	**RUBBER PLUG SEALING APERTURE IN BONNET FRONT UNDER PANEL**		1	NOT REQUIRED WHEN FRONT NUMBER PLATE CARRIER IS FITTED.
BD.20934	**PIVOTED CARRIER BRACKET ASSEMBLY FOR FRONT NUMBER PLATE**		1	
UFN.125/L	**Nut,** securing Carrier Bracket to Bonnet Front Under Panel		2	
C.724	**Washer,** Shakeproof, under Nuts		2	
BD.20939	**Packing Block** (Aluminium) at Carrier Bracket fixings		2	
				TO BE FITTED ONLY AS REQUIRED.
BD.20936	**CONTROL ROD, OPERATING CARRIER BRACKET PIVOT WHEN BONNET IS MOVED**		1	
C.13806	**Clip,** securing Control Rod to Carrier Bracket		1	
C.4548	**GROMMET, IN BONNET FRONT UNDER PANEL, FOR CONTROL ROD**		1	
BD.20937	**FORK END FOR CONNECTION OF CONTROL ROD TO BRACKET ON FRONT SUB-FRAME**		1	TO BE FITTED ONLY AS REQUIRED.
UFN.125/L	**Nut,** locking Fork End to Control Rod		1	
J.103/10S	**Clevis Pin,** securing Fork End to Bracket on Front Sub-Frame		1	
L.102/4U	**Split Pin,** retaining Clevis Pin		1	
AW.102/T	**Washer,** Plain, behind Split Pin		1	
BD.20093	**STONE GUARD ASSEMBLY AT REAR OF BONNET AIR INTAKE APERTURE**	46–31	1	
BD.20150/3	**Screw,** Set, securing Stone Guard to Bonnet		8	
C.723/A	**Washer,** Shakeproof, on Setscrews		8	
BD.541/34	**Special Washer,** under Shakeproof Washers, at side fixings		6	
AW.102/T	**Washer,** Plain, under Shakeproof Washers at top fixings		2	
BD.20579	**Bracket,** for lower fixing of Stone Guard		2	
UFS.125/4R	**Screw,** Set, securing Brackets and Stone Guard		4	
UFN.125/L	**Nut,** on Setscrews		4	
C.724	**Washer,** Shakeproof, under Nuts		4	
FW.104/T	**Washer,** Plain, under Shakeproof Washers		4	

Part No.	Description	Plate No.	No. per Unit	Remarks
BD.18710	**FRAME ASSEMBLY FOR FIXING OF STONE GUARD**	46–32	1	
BD.19031	**Felt Strip,** at top of Frame ($\frac{1}{4}'' \times \frac{5}{8}'' \times 23''$)		1	
BD.16839/2	**Screw,** Self-Tapping, securing Frame to Bonnet		6	
BD.542/3	**Special Washer,** on Self-Tapping Screws		6	
BD.20014	**BONNET BALANCE LINK ASSEMBLY, R.H.**	46–33	1	
BD.20015	**BONNET BALANCE LINK ASSEMBLY, L.H.**	46–34	1	
BD.19972	**Spring,** on Bonnet Balance Links		4	
BD.20013/4	**Brass Washer,** at each side of spring "eyes"		16	
L.102/6U	**Split Pin,** retaining Springs		8	
BD.8291/2	**Screw,** Set, securing Balance Links to Bonnet		8	
C.724	**Washer,** Shakeproof, on Setscrews		8	
BD.541/20	**Special Washer,** under Shakeproof Washers		8	
BD.19736	**Bolt** (Shouldered) securing Balance Links to Front Frame		2	
BD.20013/1	**Brass Washer,** on Bolts		2	
BD.20013/2	**Brass Washer,** on Bolts		2	
C.8667/1	**Nut,** Self-Locking, on Bolts		2	
BD.19178	**GRILLE AT REAR OF BONNET**	46–35	1	
BD.17290	**Thread Cutting Fix,** securing Grille to Bonnet		2	
UFS.419/4H	**Screw,** Set, securing Grille to Bonnet		2	
C.723/A	**Washer,** Shakeproof, on Setscrews		2	
BD.20315	**BONNET SAFETY CATCH ASSEMBLY**	46–36	1	
BD.20318	**Spring,** on Safety Catch		1	
J.103/15S	**Clevis Pin,** through Safety Catch		1	
L.102/4U	**Split Pin,** retaining Clevis Pin		1	
BD.541/28	**Special Washer,** behind Split Pin		1	
BD.20319	**Tapped Plate,** for fixing of Safety Catch		1	
UFS.419/3H	**Screw,** Set, securing Safety Catch to Bonnet		4	
C.723/A	**Washer,** Shakeproof, on Setscrews		4	
BD.20320	**BRACKET, RECEIVING SAFETY CATCH**	46–37	1	
BD.18307/3	**Screw,** Set, securing Bracket to Scuttle		2	
C.724	**Washer,** Shakeproof, on Setscrews		2	

BODY FITTINGS
FOR FIXED HEAD COUPE ONLY

Part No.	Description	Plate No.	No. per Unit	Remarks
BD.19730	**EXTENSION ASSEMBLY, AT REAR OF L.H. BONNET DUCT, FOR HEATER AIR INTAKE**	46–38	1	
BD.23657	**Rubber Seal,** for Air Intake Extension	46–39	1	
BD.16839/3	**Screw,** Self-Tapping, securing Extension to Bonnet		6	
FG.104/X	**Washer,** Spring, on Self-Tapping Screws		6	
BD.542/3	**Special Washer,** under Spring Washers		6	
BD.20816/1	**Rubber Seal,** between Bonnet L.H. Valance and Frame Side Member ($\frac{3}{32}'' \times 1\frac{3}{4}'' \times 9\frac{1}{2}''$)	46–40	1	
BD.20735	**Fixing Strip,** for Rubber Seal	46–41	1	
BD.20816/2	**Rubber Seal,** between Bonnet L.H. Rear Diaphragm and Frame Side Member ($\frac{3}{32}'' \times 1\frac{3}{4}'' \times 4''$)	46–42	1	
BD.20736	**Fixing Strip,** for Rubber Seal	46–43	1	
BD.1814/2	**Pop Rivet,** securing Fixing Strips		8	
BD.16015	**LOCK ASSEMBLY AT R.H. SIDE OF BONNET (WB.3/10894)**	46–44	1	
BD.16016	**LOCK ASSEMBLY AT L.H. SIDE OF BONNET (WB.3/10893)**	46–45	1	
UCS.419/4H	**Screw,** Set, securing Locks to Bonnet		8	
AG.102/X	**Washer,** Spring, on Setscrews		8	Fitted from Chassis No. 860001 to 860004. 885001 to 885020.
BD.2551	**ESCUTCHEON FOR BONNET LOCKS (WB.16049/B)**	46–46	2	
BD.540/9	**Screw,** Self-Tapping, securing Escutcheons		4	
BD.16012	**BRACKET ASSEMBLY ENGAGING BONNET LOCKS**	46–47	2	
UFS.119/6R	**Screw,** Set, securing Brackets to Body		4	
C.723/A	**Washer,** Shakeproof, on Setscrews		4	
AW.102/T	**Washer,** Plain, under Shakeproof Washers		4	
BD.16013	**Shim,** under Brackets		As req'd	

Part No.	Description	Plate No.	No. per Unit	Remarks
BD.19890	**R.H. LOCKING HOOK ASSEMBLY FOR BONNET**		1	
BD.19891	**L.H. LOCKING HOOK ASSEMBLY FOR BONNET**		1	
BD.19894	**Lever,** on Locking Hook Shafts		2	
C.8737/1	**Nut,** securing Levers to Shafts		2	
BD.19883	**BRACKET ASSEMBLY, MOUNTING LOCKING HOOKS**		2	
BD.18307/2	**Screw,** Set, securing Brackets to Dash		6	
C.724	**Washer,** Shakeproof, on Setscrews		6	
BD.19977	**HANDLE AND ROD ASSEMBLY FOR R.H. LOCKING HOOK**		1	
BD.19978	**HANDLE AND ROD ASSEMBLY FOR L.H. LOCKING HOOK**		1	Fitted to Chassis No. 860005 and subs. 885021 and subs.
BD.19903	**Handle** only		2	
BD.19904	**Escutcheon**		2	
BD.19895	**Neoprene Seal,** on Rods		2	
BD.19013/2	**Screw,** Self-Tapping, securing Escutcheons to Body		4	
BD.8633/8	**Speed Nut,** on Self-Tapping Screws (5NU.1686)		4	
C.13806	**Linkage Clip,** securing Operating Rods to Locking Hooks		2	
BD.19905	**BRACKET ASSEMBLY, ON BONNET SIDE PANEL, ENGAGING R.H. HOOK**		1	
BD.19906	**BRACKET ASSEMBLY, ON BONNET SIDE PANEL, ENGAGING L.H. HOOK**		1	
BD.18307/2	**Screw,** Set, securing Brackets to Bonnet		4	
C.724	**Washer,** Shakeproof, on Setscrews		4	
BD.541/6	**Special Washer,** under Shakeproof Washers		4	
BD.19896	**Locating Peg,** on Brackets		2	
UFN.231/L	**Nut,** securing Locating Pegs		4	
BD.19936	**Rubber Buffer,** on Locating Pegs		2	
BD.19917	**Bracket,** receiving Locating Pegs		2	
BD.8291/2	**Screw,** Set, securing Brackets to Dash		4	
C.724	**Washer,** Shakeproof, on Setscrews		4	

BODY FITTINGS
FOR FIXED HEAD COUPE ONLY

Part No.	Description	Plate No.	No. per Unit	Remarks
BD.20903/1	**REST RUBBER FOR REAR EDGE OF BONNET**	46—48	1	
BD.10224	**RUBBER BUFFER, CUSHIONING BONNET SIDES IN CLOSED POSITION**	46—49	2	Fitted from Chassis No. 860001 to 860004. 885001 to 885020.
UFS.131/8R	**Screw,** Set, securing Rubber Buffers to Dash		2	
UFN.231/L	**Nut,** on Setscrews		2	
BD.15165	**CARRIER BRACKET, FOR BATTERY TRAY**	46—50	1	
UFS.125/4R	**Screw,** Set, securing Carrier Bracket to L.H. Sill		5	
FG.104/X	**Washer,** Spring, on Setscrews		5	
FW.104/T	**Washer,** Plain, under Spring Washers		5	
UFN.125/L	**Nut,** on Setscrews		5	
BD.20048	**R.H. UNDERSHIELD FOR FRONT FRAME**	46—51	1	
BD.20047	**L.H. UNDERSHIELD FOR FRONT FRAME**	46—52	1	
BD.20049	**Bracket,** for fixing of Undershields to Front Frame		4	
UFS.125/4R	**Screw,** Set, securing Brackets and Undershields to Front Frame		4	
UFN.125/L	**Nut,** on Setscrews		4	
C.724	**Washer,** Shakeproof, under Nuts		4	
FW.104/T	**Washer,** Plain, under Shakeproof Washers		4	
BD.8633/6	**Spire Nut,** for fixing of Undershields to Sills and Mudshields		8	
BD.8691/1	**Screw,** Self-Tapping, securing Undershields to Sills and Mudshields		8	
AW.102/T	**Washer,** Plain, on Self-Tapping Screws		8	
BD.25541	**Seal** (Canvas/Rubber) for L.H. Front Frame Undershield		1	Fitted to Chassis No. 861121 and subs. 888353 and subs. **May be fitted to cars prior to above Chassis numbers, if desired.**
BD.19522	**R.H. MUDSHIELD ASSEMBLY**	46—53	1	
BD.20425	**Bracket,** upper, for fixing of R.H. Mudshield		1	
BD.20426	**Bracket,** lower, for fixing of R.H. Mudshield		1	
BD.11712/2	**Pop Rivet,** securing Mudshield		2	
BD.20434/1	**Rubber Seal** (27½″ long) for R.H. Mudshield		1	
BD.20429	**Fixing Strip,** securing Seal to R.H. Mudshield		1	
BD.20427	**Fixing Strip,** securing Seal to R.H. Sill		1	
BD.1814/6	**Pop Rivet,** securing Fixing Strips and Seal		11	

Part No.	Description	Plate No.	No. per Unit	Remarks
BD.19521	**L.H. MUDSHIELD ASSEMBLY**	46–54	1	
BD.20426	**Bracket,** for fixing of L.H. Mudshield		1	
BD.20434/2	**Rubber Seal** (14¾″ long) for L.H. Mudshield		1	
BD.20428	**Fixing Strip,** securing Seal to L.H. Mudshield		1	
BD.20427	**Fixing Strip,** securing Seal to L.H. Sill		1	
BD.1814/6	**Pop Rivet,** securing Fixing Strips and Seal		8	
UFS.125/4R	**Screw,** Set, securing Mudshields to Front Frame and Sills		10	
BD.541/20	**Washer,** Special, on Setscrews		10	
UFN.125/L	**Nut,** on Setscrews		10	
C.724	**Washer,** Shakeproof, under Nuts		10	
BD.19714	**SEAL HOUSING FOR LOWER STEERING COLUMN THROUGH DASH**	46–55	1	
BD.20589	**Sealing Ring** (P.V.C.)	46–56	1	Fitted from Chassis No. 860001 to 860646.
C.20488	**Sealing Ring**		1	Fitted to Chassis No. 860647 and subs.
BD.19710	**Retainer,** for Sealing Ring	46–57	1	R.H. DRIVE CARS ONLY.
BD.19716/1	**Screw,** Self-Tapping, securing Retainer		3	
BD.19707	**Gasket,** under Steering Column Seal	46–58	1	
UFS.125/5R	**Screw,** Set, securing Seal to Dash		4	
FW.104/T	**Washer,** Plain, on Setscrews		4	
UFN.125/L	**Nut,** on Setscrews		4	
C.724	**Washer,** Shakeproof, under Nuts		4	
BD.19712	**COVER ASSEMBLY, SEALING REDUNDANT BRAKE PEDAL HOUSING APERTURE IN DASH**		1	R.H. DRIVE CARS ONLY.
BD.19707	**Gasket,** under Cover		1	
UFN.125/L	**Nut,** securing Cover to Dash		4	
C.724	**Washer,** Shakeproof, under Nuts		4	
FW.104/T	**Washer,** Plain, under Shakeproof Washers		4	
BD.19713	**COVER ASSEMBLY, SEALING REDUNDANT ACCELERATOR PEDAL HOUSING APERTURE IN DASH**		1	R.H. DRIVE CARS ONLY.
BD.19708	**Gasket,** under Cover		1	
UFN.125/L	**Nut,** securing Cover to Dash		4	
C.724	**Washer,** Shakeproof, under Nuts		4	
FW.104/T	**Washer,** Plain, under Shakeproof Washers		4	
BD.19712	**COVER ASSEMBLY, SEALING REDUNDANT BRAKE PEDAL AND STEERING COLUMN APERTURES IN DASH**		2	L.H. DRIVE CARS ONLY.
BD.19707	**Gasket,** under Covers		2	
UFN.125/L	**Nut,** securing Covers to Dash		8	
C.724	**Washer,** Shakeproof, under Nuts		8	
FW.104/T	**Washer,** Plain, under Shakeproof Washers		8	

BODY FITTINGS
FOR FIXED HEAD COUPE ONLY

Part No.	Description	Plate No.	No. per Unit	Remarks
BD.19711	**COVER ASSEMBLY, SEALING REDUNDANT ACCELERATOR PEDAL HOUSING APERTURE IN DASH**		1	
BD.19706	**Gasket,** under Cover		1	L.H. DRIVE CARS ONLY.
UFN.125/L	**Nut,** securing Cover to Dash		3	
C.724	**Washer,** Shakeproof, under Nuts		3	
FW.104/T	**Washer,** Plain, under Shakeproof Washers		3	
BD.20589	**SEAL, IN ACCELERATOR PEDAL HOUSING, FOR LOWER STEERING COLUMN**		1	Fitted from Chassis No. 885001 to 886213.
C.20488	**SEAL, IN ACCELERATOR PEDAL HOUSING, FOR LOWER STEERING COLUMN**		1	Fitted to Chassis No. 886214 and subs.
				L.H. DRIVE CARS ONLY.
BD.19710	**Retainer,** for Seal		1	
UCS.413/3H	**Screw,** Set, securing Retainer		3	
C.721	**Washer,** Shakeproof, on Setscrews		3	
BD.19717	**PLUG (BLACK P.V.C.) SEALING REDUNDANT HOLES IN DASH**		3	
BD.19360	**WINDSCREEN GLASS**	46–59	1	
BD.20499	**Rubber Seal,** around Windscreen Glass	46–60	1	
BD.19359	**Rubber Insert,** for Seal	46–61	1	
BD.20562	**Chrome Finisher,** at bottom edge of Windscreen	46–62	1	
BD.20563	**Chrome Finisher,** at top edge of Windscreen	46–63	1	
BD.19561	**Chrome Finisher,** at R.H. side of Windscreen	46–64	1	
BD.19562	**Chrome Finisher,** at L.H. side of Windscreen	46–65	1	
BD.21365	**R.H. SUN VISOR ASSEMBLY, COMPLETE**		1	
BD.21366	**L.H. SUN VISOR ASSEMBLY, COMPLETE**		1	
BD.13642/5	**Screw,** Set, securing Sun Visors to Body		1	
BD.21181	**LICENCE HOLDER ON WINDSCREEN**		1	

Part No.	Description	Plate No.	No. per Unit	Remarks
BD.20634	**SCREEN RAIL FACIA ASSEMBLY, COMPLETE**	47– 1	1	FOR SPARES REPLACEMENTS USE BD.23832 TOGETHER WITH BD.25214.
BD.20632	**Bezel,** for centre Demister Slot		1	
BD.20591	**Bezel,** for intermediate Demister Slots		2	
BD.20592	**Bezel,** for outer Demister Slots		2	
BD.539/22	**Screw,** Self-Tapping, securing Bezels		10	
BD.23832	**SCREEN RAIL FACIA ASSEMBLY, COMPLETE**		1	MAY BE USED TO REPLACE BD.20634.
	All items are as for Screen Rail Facia Assembly BD.20634.		2	
BD.25214	**"Y" Piece,** for Air Duct Hoses			
UFN.119/L	**Nut,** securing Screen Rail Facia		4	
C.723/A	**Washer,** Shakeproof, under Nuts		4	
AW.102/T	**Washer,** Plain, under Shakeproof Washers		4	
			4	
BD.21182	**Bracket,** for R.H. outer fixing of Screen Rail Facia		1	
BD.21183	**Bracket,** for L.H. outer fixing of Screen Rail Facia		1	
BD.1814/2	**Pop Rivet,** securing Brackets to Dash		4	
BD.20565	**Bracket,** for R.H. inner fixing of Screen Rail Facia		1	
BD.20566	**Bracket,** for L.H. inner fixing of Screen Rail Facia		1	
BD.19643	**L.H. FACIA PANEL ASSEMBLY**	47– 2	1	R.H. DRIVE CARS ONLY.
BD.19699	**Cubby Box** in L.H. Facia		1	
BD.20605	**Fixing Strip,** securing Cubby Box at top		1	
UFN.119/L	**Nut,** securing Fixing Strip		3	
C.723/A	**Washer,** Shakeproof, under Nuts		3	
BD.1229/16	**Screw,** Self-Tapping, securing Cubby Box at bottom		3	
C.1094	**Distance Piece,** on Self-Tapping Screws		3	
BD.20633/1	**Spire Nut,** on Self-Tapping Screws		3	
BD.19644	**R.H. FACIA PANEL ASSEMBLY**	47– 3	1	R.H. DRIVE CARS ONLY.
BD.19645	**L.H. FACIA PANEL ASSEMBLY**		1	L.H. DRIVE CARS ONLY, BUT NOT REQUIRED FOR ITALY.
BD.20812	**L.H. FACIA PANEL ASSEMBLY**		1	REQUIRED ONLY FOR L.H. DRIVE CARS EXPORTED TO ITALY.

BODY FITTINGS
FOR FIXED HEAD COUPE ONLY

Part No.	Description	Plate No.	No. per Unit	Remarks
BD.19646	**R.H. FACIA PANEL ASSEMBLY**		1	**L.H. DRIVE CARS ONLY.**
BD.19698	**Cubby Box** in R.H. Facia		1	
BD.20605	**Fixing Strip,** securing Cubby Box at top		1	
UFN.119/L	**Nut,** securing Fixing Strip		3	
C.723/A	**Washer,** Shakeproof, under Nuts		3	
BD.1229/16	**Screw,** Self-Tapping, securing Cubby Box at bottom		3	
C.1094	**Distance Piece,** on Self-Tapping Screws		3	
BD.20633/1	**Spire Nut,** on Self-Tapping Screws		3	
BD.20861/1	**Screw,** Set, Pan Head, securing Facia Panels at centre		4	
UFS.119/3R	**Screw,** Set, securing Facia Panels at centre		2	
C.723/A	**Washer,** Shakeproof, on Setscrews		4	
AW.102/T	**Washer,** Plain, under Shakeproof Washers		6	
BD.19241	**Bracket,** for fixing of L.H. Facia to Dash side		1	
BD.19242	**Bracket,** for fixing of R.H. Facia to Dash side		1	
BD.1814/2	**Pop Rivet,** securing Brackets		4	
UFN.119/L	**Nut,** securing Facias to Brackets		4	
C.723/A	**Washer,** Shakeproof, under Nuts		4	
BD.20636	**GRAB HANDLE ASSEMBLY AT R.H. SIDE OF DASH**		1	**L.H. DRIVE CARS ONLY.**
BD.20637	**GRAB HANDLE ASSEMBLY AT L.H. SIDE OF DASH**	47– 4	1	**R.H. DRIVE CARS ONLY.**
UCS.119/3R	**Screw,** Set, securing Grab Handle to Facia Panel		2	
C.723/A	**Washer,** Shakeproof, on Setscrews		2	
BD.20640	**Bracket,** for fixing of Grab Handle to Dash Side		1	
BD.540/19	**Screw,** Self-Tapping, securing Bracket		2	
BD.20639	**Special Bolt,** securing Grab Handle to Bracket		1	
C.739	**Washer,** Shakeproof, on Special Bolt		1	
BD.20462	**SCUTTLE TOP CASING ASSEMBLY, R.H.**	47– 5	1	
BD.20463	**SCUTTLE TOP CASING ASSEMBLY, L.H.**	47– 6	1	**R.H. DRIVE CARS ONLY.**
BD.20470	**SCUTTLE TOP CASING ASSEMBLY, CENTRE**	47– 7	1	
BD.20728	**COVER ASSEMBLY, PROTECTING WIRING HARNESS AT L.H. SIDE OF DASH**	47– 8	1	

Part No.	Description	Plate No.	No. per Unit	Remarks
BD.20464	**SCUTTLE TOP CASING ASSEMBLY, R.H.**		1	
BD.20465	**SCUTTLE TOP CASING ASSEMBLY, L.H.**		1	L.H. DRIVE CARS ONLY.
BD.20471	**SCUTTLE TOP CASING ASSEMBLY, CENTRE**		1	
BD.21136	**Fixing Bracket,** for Scuttle Casings		4	
BD.8537/1	**Screw,** Self-Tapping, securing Casings		2	
BD.532/2	**Cup Washer,** on Self-Tapping Screws		2	
BD.8536/6	**Spire Nut,** on Self-Tapping Screws		2	
BD.20035	**FRONT FINISHER PANEL ASSEMBLY ABOVE GEARBOX TUNNEL**	47– 9	1	
BD.19967	**Face Panel,** for Front Finisher		1	
BD.19984	**Grille Assembly** in Loudspeaker Apertures		2	
UCN.113/L	**Nut,** securing Grilles to Front Finisher Panel		8	Fitted from Chassis No. 860001 to 860912. 885001 to 887131.
C.721	**Washer,** Shakeproof, under Nuts		8	
AW.104/T	**Washer,** Plain, under Shakeproof Washers		8	
BD.20409	**Ash Tray and Panel Assembly**		1	
BD.22669	**Tapped Plate,** securing Ash Tray Panel to Front Finisher Panel		2	
BD.13713/2	**Screw,** Set, securing Ash Tray Panel to Front Finisher Panel		4	
C.2017/1	**Washer,** Special, on Setscrews		4	
BD.23648	**FRONT FINISHER PANEL ASSEMBLY ABOVE GEARBOX TUNNEL**		1	
BD.23649	**Face Panel,** for Front Finisher		1	Fitted to Chassis No. 860913 and subs. 887132 and subs.
	All other items are as for Front Finisher Assembly BD.20035.			
BD.19049	**Bracket Assembly,** L.H., for fixing of Front Finisher Panel		1	
BD.19050	**Bracket Assembly,** R.H., for fixing of Front Finisher Panel		1	
UFS.419/4H	**Screw,** Set, securing Brackets to Door		4	
C.723/A	**Washer,** Shakeproof, on Setscrews		4	
BD.17589	**Knob,** securing Front Finisher Panel		4	
BD.541/32	**Special Washer,** behind Knobs		4	
BD.20409	**ASH TRAY AND PANEL ASSEMBLY**		1	
BD.20403	**Panel Assembly**	47–10	1	
BD.20410	**Ash Tray Assembly,** complete	47–11	1	
BD.20412	**Motif only,** on Ash Tray		1	
AN.106/K	**Nut,** securing Motif		1	
C.720	**Washer,** Shakeproof, under Nut		1	
BD.24393	**Light Shield** (Rubber Strip $\frac{1}{16}'' \times \frac{1}{4}'' \times 10''$)		1	
BD.24394	**Retainer,** for Light Shield		1	
BD.540/19	**Self-Tapping Screw,** securing Retainer		2	
BD.711/9	**Self-Tapping Screw,** securing Retainer		2	

BODY FITTINGS
FOR FIXED HEAD COUPE ONLY

Part No.	Description	Plate No.	No. per Unit	Remarks
BD.20722	**FINISHER PANEL ASSEMBLY IN RADIO CONTROL UNIT APERTURE**	47–12	1	NOT REQUIRED WHEN RADIO IS FITTED.
UFN.119/L	**Nut,** securing Finisher to Front Finisher Panel		2	
C.723/A	**Washer,** Shakeproof, under Nuts		2	
BD.541/13	**Special Washer,** under Shakeproof Washers		2	
BD.17354	**BASE PLATE AND SURROUND (CHROME PLATED) FOR RADIO APERTURE FINISHER PANEL**	47–13	1	NOT REQUIRED WHEN RADIO IS FITTED.
BD.15488	**GEARBOX COVER**	47–14	1	SUPERSEDED BY BD.24129.
BD.8691/7	**Screw,** Self-Tapping, securing Gearbox Cover		12	
BD.542/3	**Washer,** Plain, on Self-Tapping Screws		12	
BD.24129	**GEARBOX COVER**		1	SUPERSEDES BD.15488.
BD.8691/7	**Screw,** Self-Tapping, securing Gearbox Cover		12	
BD.542/3	**Washer,** Plain, on Self-Tapping Screws		12	
BD.10821	**RUBBER PLUG, SEALING GEARBOX ACCESS APERTURES**		2	
BD.20031	**FINISHER PANEL ASSEMBLY ON GEARBOX COVER AND PROPELLER SHAFT TUNNEL**	47–15	1	Fitted from Chassis No. 860001 to 860912. 885001 to 887131.
BD.19979	**Top Face Panel**		1	
BD.19971	**Gauntlet Face Panel**		1	
BD.19981	**Chrome Bezel,** at top of Gauntlet Panel		1	
BD.22385	**Rivet,** securing Bezel to Gauntlet Panel		14	
BD.23650	**FINISHER PANEL ASSEMBLY ON GEARBOX COVER AND PROPELLER SHAFT TUNNEL**		1	Fitted to Chassis No. 860913 and subs. 887132 and subs.
BD.23651	**Top Face Panel**		1	
BD.23652	**Gauntlet Face Panel**		1	
BD.19981	**Chrome Bezel,** at top of Gauntlet Panel		1	
BD.22385	**Rivet,** securing Bezel to Gauntlet Panel		14	
BD.20469	**Seal,** for Handbrake Lever Aperture (Rubber Strip $\frac{1}{16}'' \times 2\frac{1}{2}'' \times 6''$)		1	
BD.19728	**Chrome Ferrule,** at top of Gear Lever Gauntlet		1	
BD.19729	**Ferrule Base** (Nylon)		1	
BD.17546/1	**Screw,** Set, securing Finisher Panel to Tunnel		3	
BD.541/32	**Special Washer,** on Setscrews		3	
BD.24175	**SEAT SQUAB FRAME ASSEMBLY (TRIMMED)**	47–16	2	

Part No.	Description	Plate No.	No. per Unit	Remarks
BD.20148	**SEAT CUSHION ASSEMBLY**	47–17	2	
BD.18958	**LOCKING SLIDE FOR R.H. SEAT**	47–18	1	Fitted from Chassis No. 860001 to 860580. 885001 to 886092.
BD.18959	**LOCKING SLIDE FOR L.H. SEAT**		1	
BD.22810	**LOCKING SLIDE FOR L.H. SEAT**		1	Fitted to Chassis No. 860581 and subs. 886093 and subs.
BD.22811	**LOCKING SLIDE FOR R.H. SEAT**		1	
BD.18960	**SEAT SLIDE (PLAIN)**	47–19	2	Fitted from Chassis No. 860001 to 860580. 885001 to 886092.
BD.22812	**SEAT SLIDE (PLAIN)**		2	Fitted to Chassis No. 860581 and subs. 886093 and subs.
BD.18117/4	**Screw**, Set, securing Slides to Floor		8	
BD.17648	**Packing**, between Slides and Floor		8	
UFN.125/L	**Nut**, securing Slides to Seats		8	
BD.542/3	**Washer**, Special, under Nuts		8	
C.724	**Washer**, Shakeproof, on Setscrews and under Nuts		16	
C.18698	**Distance Piece**, at fixings of Slides to Seats		4	
BD.19378	**Support Strap**, for Adjusting Levers		2	
UFS.519/4H	**Screw**, Set, securing Support Straps		4	
UFN.119/L	**Nut**, on Setscrews		4	
C.723/A	**Washer**, Shakeproof, under Nuts		4	
C.5203/1	**Washer**, Plain, under Shakeproof Washers		4	
BD.20436	**SHIELD ASSEMBLY, FRONT, FOR HEAT INSULATION FROM EXHAUST SYSTEM**	47–20	1	Fitted from Chassis No. 860001 to 861061. 885001 to 888081.
BD.25237	**SHIELD ASSEMBLY, FRONT, FOR HEAT INSULATION FROM EXHAUST SYSTEM**		1	Fitted to Chassis No. 861062 and subs. 888082 and subs. **See note below.**
BD.711/23	**Screw**, Self-Tapping, securing Shield to Floor		2	
UFS.125/3R	**Screw**, Set, securing Shield to Floor		1	
C.724	**Washer**, Shakeproof, on Setscrews		1	
BD.19059/1	**Screw**, Self-Tapping, securing Shield to Gearbox Side Panel		1	
BD.18545	**Cup Washer**, on Self-Tapping Screw		1	
BD.8633/2	**Spire Nut**, on Self-Tapping Screw		1	

NOTE: The following cars were fitted with **BD.20436** Heat Shield:
R.H. Drive   861087.
L.H. Drive   888086, 888096, 888101, 888103, 888109, 888113, 888117, 888118, 888120, 888134, 888157, 888178, 888238.

BODY FITTINGS
FOR FIXED HEAD COUPE ONLY

Part No.	Description	Plate No.	No. per Unit	Remarks
BD.20439	**SHIELD ASSEMBLY, REAR, FOR HEAT INSULATION FROM EXHAUST SYSTEM**	47–21	**1**	
BD.1814/5	**Pop Rivet,** securing Shield to Body		**8**	
BD.20268	**TRIM PANEL ASSEMBLY, FOR SHUT PILLAR, AT R.H. QUARTER**	47–22	**1**	Fitted from Chassis No. 860001 to 861098. 885001 to 888301.
BD.20269	**TRIM PANEL ASSEMBLY, FOR SHUT PILLAR, AT L.H. QUARTER**		**1**	
BD.24463	**TRIM PANEL ASSEMBLY, FOR SHUT PILLAR, AT R.H. QUARTER**		**1**	Fitted to Chassis No. 861099 and subs. 888302 and subs.
BD.24464	**TRIM PANEL ASSEMBLY, FOR SHUT PILLAR, AT L.H. QUARTER**		**1**	
BD.21068/5	**DRAUGHT PIPING ON SHUT PILLARS**		**2**	
BD.20266	**TRIM PANEL, REAR, ABOVE R.H. CANTRAIL**	47–23	**1**	
BD.20267	**TRIM PANEL, REAR, ABOVE L.H. CANTRAIL**		**1**	
BD.20216	**MAT ASSEMBLY, ON FLOOR BEHIND SEATS**	47–24	**2**	Fitted from Chassis No. 860001 to 860580. 885001 to 886092.
BD.23624	**MAT ASSEMBLY, ON FLOOR BEHIND SEATS**		**2**	Fitted to Chassis No. 860581 and subs. 886093 and subs.

Part No.	Description	Plate No.	No. per Unit	Remarks
BD.20751	**R.H. DOOR ASSEMBLY, COMPLETE (INCLUDING GLASS, TRIM, LOCK AND HANDLES, ETC.)**		1	Fitted from Chassis No. 860001 to 860478. 885001 to 886013.
BD.20752	**L.H. DOOR ASSEMBLY, COMPLETE (INCLUDING GLASS, TRIM, LOCK AND HANDLES, ETC.)**		1	
BD.22351	**R.H. DOOR ASSEMBLY, COMPLETE (INCLUDING GLASS, TRIM, LOCK AND HANDLES, ETC.)**		1	Fitted to Chassis No. 860479 and subs. 886014 and subs.
BD.22352	**L.H. DOOR ASSEMBLY, COMPLETE (INCLUDING GLASS, TRIM, LOCK AND HANDLES, ETC.)**		1	
BD.20095	**LOCK ASSEMBLY ON R.H. DOOR (WB.3/11289)**		1	
BD.20096	**LOCK ASSEMBLY ON L.H. DOOR (WB.3/11290)**	48– 1	1	
BD.19445	**Link,** between Lock and Outside Handle (WB.1/8881)	48– 2	2	
BD.23473	**Clip,** retaining Links (WB.3/6928)	48– 3	4	
BD.1708/9	**Spring Washer,** for Link fixing at Lock		2	
UFS.419/3H	**Screw,** Set, securing Lock to Doors		6	
C.723/A	**Washer,** Shakeproof, on Setscrews		6	
BD.20780/3	**Shakeproof Screw,** securing Lock to Doors		2	
BD.19245	**OUTSIDE HANDLE ON R.H. DOOR (WB.1/8871)**		1	
7903	**Operating Lever Assembly,** for R.H. Door Handle (1/6491)		1	
9601	**Housing,** for Tension Spring in R.H. Handle (1/8868)		1	
BD.21486	**Locking Barrel,** for "F" series Key, in Handle		1	
BD.19246	**OUTSIDE HANDLE ON L.H. DOOR (WB.1/8870)**	48– 4	1	
7904	**Operating Lever Assembly,** for L.H. Door Handle (1/6492)		1	
9602	**Housing,** for Tension Spring, in L.H. Handle (1/8869)		1	
BD.21486	**Locking Barrel** for "F" series Key, in Handle		1	
UFN.119/L	**Nut,** securing Outside Handles		4	
C.723/A	**Washer,** Shakeproof, under Nuts		4	
AW.102/T	**Washer,** Plain, under Shakeproof Washers		4	

BODY FITTINGS
FOR FIXED HEAD COUPE ONLY

Part No.	Description	Plate No.	No. per Unit	Remarks
BD.20098	**REMOTE CONTROL AND LINK ASSEMBLY, FOR OPERATION OF R.H. DOOR LOCK (WB.3/16347)**		1	
BD.20097	**REMOTE CONTROL AND LINK ASSEMBLY, FOR OPERATION OF L.H. DOOR LOCK (WB.3/16348)**	48– 5	1	
BD.19575	**Wavy Washer,** at connection of Link to Lock	48– 6	2	
BD.23473	**Spring Clip,** securing Link to Lock	48– 7	2	
BD.19574	**Washer,** Special, behind Spring Clips		2	
UFS.419/3H	**Screw,** Set, securing Remote Control to Doors		6	
C.723/A	**Washer,** Shakeproof, on Setscrews		6	
BD.10728	**INSIDE HANDLE FOR DOORS (WB.1/3858)**	48– 8	2	
BD.10729	**HANDLE OPERATING WINDOW REGULATORS (WB.1/6671)**	48– 9	2	
BD.10730	**OUTER ESCUTCHEON BEHIND REGULATOR AND INSIDE DOOR HANDLES (W.128)**	48–10	4	
BD.10731	**INNER ESCUTCHEON BEHIND REGULATOR AND INSIDE DOOR HANDLES (W.129)**	48–11	4	
BD.10732	**SPRING BEHIND ESCUTCHEONS (41/379)**	48–12	4	
BD.10734	**Rubber Plug,** behind Handles (16-10)	48–13	4	
BD.10733	**Peg,** securing Handles to Remote Controls and Regulators	48–14	4	
BD.20522	**REGULATOR ASSEMBLY, FOR WINDOW IN R.H. DOOR**		1	
BD.20523	**REGULATOR ASSEMBLY, FOR WINDOW IN L.H. DOOR**	48–15	1	
UFS.425/3H	**Screw,** Set, securing Regulator to Doors		8	
UFN.125/L	**Nut,** securing Regulator to Doors		8	
C.724	**Washer,** Shakeproof, on Setscrews and under Nuts		16	

Part No.	Description	Plate No.	No. per Unit	Remarks
BD.20511	**FRAME ASSEMBLY, FOR WINDOW IN R.H. DOOR**		1	
BD.20512	**FRAME ASSEMBLY, FOR WINDOW IN L.H. DOOR**	48–16	1	Fitted from Chassis No. 860001 to 860478. 885001 to 886013.
BD.20773	**FRAME ASSEMBLY, FOR WINDOW IN R.H. DOOR**		1	
BD.20774	**FRAME ASSEMBLY, FOR WINDOW IN L.H. DOOR**		1	Fitted to Chassis No. 860479 and subs. 886014 and subs.
BD.16465	**Bracket,** for forward fixing of Window Frames	48–17	2	
BD.20668	**Bracket,** for rear fixing of Window Frames	48–18	2	
UFN.125/L	**Nut.** securing Brackets to Doors and Frames to Brackets		8	
C.724	**Washer,** Shakeproof, under Nuts		8	
FW.104/T	**Washer,** Plain, under Shakeproof Washers		8	
BD.17622/1	**Screw,** Self-Tapping, securing Window Frames to Doors at top		6	
BD.17621	**Spire Nut,** on Self-Tapping Screws		6	
BD.20517	**GLASS ASSEMBLY, FOR WINDOW IN R.H. DOOR**		1	
BD.20518	**GLASS ASSEMBLY, FOR WINDOW IN L.H. DOOR**	48–19	1	
BD.23361	**FELT IN FORWARD AND TOP CHANNELS OF WINDOW FRAMES** ($\frac{3}{32}$" × 1" × 49")	48–20	2	
BD.10099	**FELT IN REAR CHANNEL OF WINDOW FRAMES** ($\frac{3}{32}$" × 1" × 28")	48–21	2	
BD.16700	**OUTER SEAL FOR DOOR GLASS**	48–22	2	
BD.10413	**Clip,** securing Outer Seals	48–23	14	
BD.19070	**STRIKER FOR MAP LIGHT DOOR SWITCHES**	48–24	4	
BD.539/15	**Screw,** Self-Tapping, securing Strikers		4	

BODY FITTINGS
FOR FIXED HEAD COUPE ONLY

Part No.	Description	Plate No.	No. per Unit	Remarks
BD.19611	**UPPER TRIM PANEL ASSEMBLY ON R.H. DOOR**		1	
BD.20010/3	**Weather Strip,** for Door Glass		1	
BD.20399	**Clip,** securing Inner Seal		5	
BD.19612	**UPPER TRIM PANEL ASSEMBLY ON L.H. DOOR**	48–25	1	
BD.20010/3	**Weather Strip,** for Door Glass		1	
BD.20399	**Clip,** securing Inner Seal		5	
BD.20190	**CHROME FINISHER ON UPPER TRIM PANELS**	48–26	2	
BD.17497	**Clip,** securing Finishers		10	
BD.711/1	**Screw,** Self-Tapping, securing Clips		10	
BD.20567	**CASING ASSEMBLY ON R.H. DOOR**		1	
BD.20568	**CASING ASSEMBLY ON L.H. DOOR**	48–27	1	
BD.18068	**Clip,** for fixing of Casings		42	
BD.711/3	**Screw,** Self-Tapping, securing Casing to Doors		4	
BD.20503	**CHROME FINISHER ON DOOR CASINGS**	48–28	2	
BD.11546	**Clip,** securing Chrome Finishers		10	
BD.19295	**STRIKER FOR R.H. DOOR LOCK (WB.3/8994)**		1	
BD.19296	**STRIKER FOR L.H. DOOR LOCK (WB.3/8995)**	48–29	1	
BD.19297	**Shakeproof Shim,** under Strikers (WB.3/9586)		2	
BD.19298	**Shim,** packing Strikers (20 S.W.G.)		As req'd	
BD.17821/7	**Screw,** Set, securing Strikers		6	
BD.19129	**CHROME FINISHER AT EDGE OF DOOR SILLS**	48–30	2	
BD.16794	**Clip,** securing Finishers		14	

Part No.	Description	Plate No.	No. per Unit	Remarks
BD.25376	**SEALING RUBBER AND RETAINER ASSEMBLY, LOWER, FOR R.H. "A" POST**		1	
BD.25308	**Sealing Rubber only**		1	
BD.25377	**SEALING RUBBER AND RETAINER ASSEMBLY, LOWER, FOR L.H. "A" POST**	48–31	1	
BD.25309	**Sealing Rubber only**		1	
BD.21197	**SEALING RUBBER FOR DOOR SILLS**	48–32	2	**SUPERSEDED BY BD.24789.**
BD.24789	**SEALING RUBBER FOR DOOR SILLS**		2	**SUPERSEDES BD.21197.**
BD.21196	**SEALING RUBBER FOR BODY SHUT PILLARS**	48–33	2	
BD.19397/1	**SEALING RUBBER, IN TOP CHANNEL OF DOOR LIGHT FRAMES**	48–34	2	
BD.19622	**GLASS ASSEMBLY FOR R.H. QUARTER LIGHT**		1	⎫
BD.19623	**GLASS ASSEMBLY FOR L.H. QUARTER LIGHT**	48–35	1	⎬ Fitted from Chassis No. 860001 to 860194. 885001 to 885584.
BD.20494	**Hinge Plate,** for Quarter Lights	48–36	2	
BD.4899/1	**Screw,** Set, securing Hinge Plates to Hinge Pillars		10	⎭
BD.22462	**GLASS ASSEMBLY, FOR R.H. QUARTER LIGHT**		1	⎫
BD.22463	**GLASS ASSEMBLY FOR L.H. QUARTER LIGHT**		1	⎬ Fitted from Chassis No. 860195 to 860478. 885585 to 886013.
BD.21230	**Attachment Block,** for Quarter Light Catch Arm		2	**MAY BE USED TO REPLACE BD.19622 AND BD.19623.**
BD.17276/1	**Screw,** Set, securing Attachment Blocks to Quarter Light Frames		4	
BD.20494	**Hinge Plate,** for Quarter Lights		2	
BD.4899/1	**Screw,** Set, securing Hinge Plates to Hinge Pillars		10	⎭

BODY FITTINGS
FOR FIXED HEAD COUPE ONLY

Part No.	Description	Plate No.	No. per Unit	Remarks
BD.20757	**GLASS ASSEMBLY FOR R.H. QUARTER LIGHT**		1	
BD.20758	**GLASS ASSEMBLY FOR L.H. QUARTER LIGHT**		1	Fitted to Chassis No. 860479 and subs. 886014 and subs.
BD.21230	**Attachment Block,** for Quarter Light Catch Arm		2	
BD.17276/1	**Screw,** Set, securing Attachment Blocks to Quarter Light Frames		4	
BD.22515	**Hinge Plate,** for Quarter Lights		2	
BD.4899/1	**Screw,** Set, securing Hinge Plates to Hinge Pillars		10	
BD.20367	**HINGE PILLAR ASSEMBLY FOR R.H. QUARTER LIGHT**		1	
BD.20368	**HINGE PILLAR ASSEMBLY FOR L.H. QUARTER LIGHT**	48–37	1	Fitted from Chassis No. 860001 to 860478. 885001 to 886013.
BD.22331	**Screw,** Shakeproof Thread, securing Hinge Pillars to Body (Top)		4	
UCS.516/4H	**Screw,** Set, securing Hinge Pillars to Body (Top)		4	
BD.22332	**Tapped Plate Fixing** (Bottom)		2	
BD.20766	**HINGE PILLAR ASSEMBLY FOR R.H. QUARTER LIGHT**		1	
BD.20767	**HINGE PILLAR ASSEMBLY FOR L.H. QUARTER LIGHT**		1	Fitted to Chassis No. 860479 and subs. 886014 and subs.
BD.22728/4	**Screw,** Set, securing Hinge Pillars to Body		8	
BD.22726	**Shim,** at top of Hinge Pillars		As req'd	
BD.22727	**Shim,** at bottom of Hinge Pillars		As req'd	
BD.17071/2	**SEALING RUBBER ON QUARTER LIGHT HINGE PILLARS**	48–38	2	
BD.17071/2	**SEALING RUBBER ON STANDING PILLAR OF DOOR LIGHT FRAME**	48–39	2	

Part No.	Description	Plate No.	No. per Unit	Remarks
BD.21307	**CATCH ASSEMBLY OPERATING R.H. QUARTER LIGHT**		1	
BD.21308	**CATCH ASSEMBLY OPERATING L.H. QUARTER LIGHT**	48—40	1	Fitted from Chassis No. 860001 to 860194. 885001 to 885584.
BD.21232	**Hinge Pin,** securing Catch Arm to Quarter Light Frame	48—41	2	
BD.4863/2	**Screw,** Set, securing Catches to Body		4	
BD.21127	**CATCH ASSEMBLY OPERATING R.H. QUARTER LIGHT**		1	
BD.21128	**CATCH ASSEMBLY OPERATING L.H. QUARTER LIGHT**		1	Fitted from Chassis No. 860195 to 860478. 885585 to 886013.
BD.22297	**Reinforcing Plate,** for Catch Assembly		2	
BD.1814/2	**Pop Rivet,** securing Reinforcing Plate		4	
BD.21232	**Hinge Pin,** securing Catch Arm to Quarter Light Frame		2	
BD.22296	**Screw,** Special, securing Catches to Body		4	
BD.20467	**CATCH ASSEMBLY OPERATING R.H. QUARTER LIGHT**		1	
BD.20468	**CATCH ASSEMBLY OPERATING L.H. QUARTER LIGHT**		1	Fitted from Chassis No. 860479 to 861098. 886014 to 888301.
BD.21232	**Hinge Pin,** securing Catch Arm to Quarter Light Frame		2	
BD.539/23	**Screw,** Self-Tapping, securing Catches to Body		4	
BD.24406	**CATCH ASSEMBLY OPERATING R.H. QUARTER LIGHT**		1	
BD.24407	**CATCH ASSEMBLY OPERATING L.H. QUARTER LIGHT**		1	Fitted to Chassis No. 861099 and subs. 888302 and subs.
BD.25722	**Shim,** for Catch adjustment		As req'd	
BD.21232	**Hinge Pin,** securing Catch Arm to Quarter Light Frame		2	
BD.539/23	**Screw,** Self-Tapping, securing Catches to Body		4	
BD.20500/2	**SEALING RUBBER FOR CANTRAILS**	48—42	2	Fitted from Chassis No. 860001 to 860478. 885001 to 886013.
BD.20497	**Retainer,** for Seal, on R.H. Cantrail		1	
BD.20498	**Retainer,** for Seal, on L.H. Cantrail	48—43	1	
BD.1814/2	**Pop Rivet,** securing Retainers		32	

BODY FITTINGS
FOR FIXED HEAD COUPE ONLY

Part No.	Description	Plate No.	No. per Unit	Remarks
BD.20500/2	**SEALING RUBBER FOR CANTRAILS**		2	Fitted to Chassis No. 860479 and subs. 886014 and subs.
BD.20803	**Retainer,** for Seal, on R.H. Cantrail		1	
BD.20804	**Retainer,** for Seal, on L.H. Cantrail		1	
BD.1814/2	**Pop Rivet,** securing Retainers		32	
BD.21577	**FACING ASSEMBLY (HEADLINING) ON R.H. CANTRAIL AND REAR TRIM PANEL**		1	Fitted from Chassis No. 860001 to 860478. 885001 to 886013.
BD.21578	**FACING ASSEMBLY (HEADLINING) ON L.H. CANTRAIL AND REAR TRIM PANEL**		1	
BD.21340	**Pad** (Polyurethane) behind Facings		2	
BD.23515	**FACING ASSEMBLY (HEADLINING) ON R.H. CANTRAIL AND REAR TRIM PANEL**		1	Fitted to Chassis No. 860479 and subs. 886014 and subs.
BD.23516	**FACING ASSEMBLY (HEADLINING) ON L.H. CANTRAIL AND REAR TRIM PANEL**		1	
BD.23517	**Pad** (Polyurethane) behind Facings		2	
BD.20860	**HEAD LINING**		1	Fitted from Chassis No. 860001 to 860478. 885001 to 886013.
BD.23514	**HEAD LINING**		1	Fitted to Chassis No. 860479 and subs. 886014 and subs.
BD.21078	**PANEL ASSEMBLY FOR TRIMMING WINDSCREEN HEADER RAIL**		1	Fitted from Chassis No. 860001 to 860478. 885001 to 886013.
BD.21339	**Pad** (Polyurethane) on Panel		1	
BD.24086	**TRIM PANEL ASSEMBLY FOR WINDSCREEN HEADER RAIL**		1	Fitted to Chassis No. 860479 and subs. 886014 and subs.
BD.1814/1	**Pop Rivet,** securing Panel Assembly		5	
BD.1814/7	**Pop Rivet,** securing Panel Assembly		6	

Part No.	Description	Plate No.	No. per Unit	Remarks
BD.20191	**CRASH PADDING ASSEMBLY ON R.H. CANTRAIL**		1	Fitted from Chassis No. 860001 to 860478. 885001 to 886013.
BD.20192	**CRASH PADDING ASSEMBLY ON L.H. CANTRAIL**	48–44	1	
BD.23508	**CRASH PADDING ASSEMBLY ON R.H. CANTRAIL**		1	Fitted from Chassis No. 860479 to 861098. 886014 to 888301.
BD.23509	**CRASH PADDING ASSEMBLY ON L.H. CANTRAIL**		1	
BD.24457	**CRASH PADDING ASSEMBLY ON R.H. CANTRAIL**		1	Fitted to Chassis No. 861099 and subs. 888302 and subs.
BD.24458	**CRASH PADDING ASSEMBLY ON L.H. CANTRAIL**		1	
BD.24414	**Finisher Bead,** on Crash Padding		2	
BD.711/1	**Screw,** Self-Tapping, securing Crash Padding		18	
BD.21356	**CHROME BEAD ABOVE CANTRAIL PADDING**		2	
BD.20174	**CASING ASSEMBLY, BELOW R.H. QUARTER LIGHT**		1	Fitted from Chassis No. 860001 to 860580. 885001 to 886092.
BD.20175	**CASING ASSEMBLY, BELOW L.H. QUARTER LIGHT**	48–45	1	
BD.18068	**Clip,** for fixing of Casings		16	
BD.23552	**CASING ASSEMBLY, BELOW R.H. QUARTER LIGHT**		1	Fitted from Chassis No. 860581 to 861098. 886093 to 888301.
BD.23553	**CASING ASSEMBLY, BELOW L.H. QUARTER LIGHT**		1	
BD.18068	**Clip,** securing Casings		18	

BODY FITTINGS
FOR FIXED HEAD COUPE ONLY

Part No.	Description	Plate No.	No. per Unit	Remarks
B.D.24467	**CASING ASSEMBLY, BELOW R.H. QUARTER LIGHT**		1	Fitted to Chassis No. 861099 and subs. 888302 and subs.
BD.24468	**CASING ASSEMBLY, BELOW L.H. QUARTER LIGHT**		1	
BD.18068	**Clip,** securing Casings		18	
BD.711/3	**Screw,** Self-Tapping, securing Casings		12	
BD.24418	**CRASH PADDING ASSEMBLY AT TOP OF R.H. QUARTER CASING**		1	Fitted to Chassis No. 861099 and subs. 888302 and subs.
BD.24419	**CRASH PADDING ASSEMBLY AT TOP OF L.H. QUARTER CASING**		1	
BD.24486	**Finisher Bead,** forward, on Crash Padding		2	
BD.24415	**Finisher Bead,** rear, on Crash Padding		2	
BD.711/7	**Screw,** Self-Tapping, securing Crash Padding to Quarters		12	
BD.24834	**CHROME FINISHER AT FORWARD END OF R.H. CRASH PADDING**		1	Fitted to Chassis No. 861099 and subs. 888302 and subs.
BD.24835	**CHROME FINISHER AT FORWARD END OF L.H. CRASH PADDING**		1	
BD.711/3	**Screw,** Self-Tapping, securing Finishers		2	
BD.20777	**POCKET ASSEMBLY IN CASING BELOW R.H. QUARTER LIGHT**		1	
BD.20778	**POCKET ASSEMBLY IN CASING BELOW L.H. QUARTER LIGHT**	48—46	1	
BD.24411	**CHROME ESCUTCHEON FOR SAFETY HARNESS ATTACHMENT POINTS AT REAR QUARTERS**		2	Fitted to Chassis No. 861099 and subs. 888302 and subs.
BD.24484	**Screw,** securing Escutcheons		2	

Part No.	Description	Plate No.	No. per Unit	Remarks
BD.20184	**CASING ASSEMBLY, R.H. REAR, AT SIDE OF LUGGAGE COMPARTMENT FLOOR**	49– 1	1	
BD.20185	**CASING ASSEMBLY, L.H. REAR, AT SIDE OF LUGGAGE COMPARTMENT FLOOR**	49– 2	1	Fitted from Chassis No. 860001 to 860478. 885001 to 886013.
BD.18068	**Clip,** securing Casings		32	
BD.20786	**CASING ASSEMBLY, R.H. REAR, AT SIDE OF LUGGAGE COMPARTMENT FLOOR**		1	
BD.20787	**CASING ASSEMBLY, L.H. REAR, AT SIDE OF LUGGAGE COMPARTMENT FLOOR**		1	Fitted from Chassis No. 860479 to 861098. 886014 to 888301.
BD.18068	**Clip,** securing Casings		17	
BD.24476	**CASING ASSEMBLY, R.H. REAR, AT SIDE OF LUGGAGE COMPARTMENT FLOOR**		1	
BD.24477	**CASING ASSEMBLY, L.H. REAR, AT SIDE OF LUGGAGE COMPARTMENT FLOOR**		1	Fitted to Chassis No. 861099 and subs. 888302 and subs.
BD.18068	**Clip,** securing Casings		17	
BD.20246	**COVER ASSEMBLY, SEALING APERTURE IN L.H. REAR CASING**	49– 3	1	
BD.539/20	**Screw,** Self-Tapping, securing Cover		2	
BD.543/3	**Cup Washer,** on Self-Tapping Screws		2	
BD.8536/4	**Spire Nut,** on Self-Tapping Screws		2	
BD.20167	**TRIM PANEL ASSEMBLY, BELOW BOOT LID APERTURE**	49– 4	1	

BODY FITTINGS
FOR FIXED HEAD COUPE ONLY

Part No.	Description	Plate No.	No. per Unit	Remarks
BD.20501	**CHROME FINISHER ON R.H. ROOF GUTTER**	49– 5	1	Fitted from Chassis No. 860001 to 860478. 885001 to 886013.
BD.20502	**CHROME FINISHER ON L.H. ROOF GUTTER**	49– 6	1	
BD.20745	**CHROME FINISHER ON R.H. ROOF GUTTER**		1	Fitted to Chassis No. 860479 and subs. 886014 and subs.
BD.20746	**CHROME FINISHER ON L.H. ROOF GUTTER**		1	
BD.19543	**BOOT LID ASSEMBLY, COMPLETE** (COMPRISING BOOT LID SHELL, GLASS, SEAL, FINISHERS, MOTIF, CASING, LOCK-STRIKER, PROP AND REST-RUBBER)		1	Fitted from Chassis No. 860001 to 860478. 885001 to 886013.
BD.19555	**BOOT LID ASSEMBLY, COMPLETE** (COMPRISING BOOT LID SHELL, GLASS, SEAL, FINISHERS, MOTIF, CASING, LOCK-STRIKER, PROP AND REST-RUBBER)		1	Fitted to Chassis No. 860479 and subs. 886014 and subs.
BD.19362	**GLASS IN BOOT LID**	49– 7	1	Fitted from Chassis No. 860001 to 860478. 885001 to 886013.
BD.19650	**GLASS IN BOOT LID**		1	Fitted to Chassis No. 860479 and subs. 886014 and subs.
BD.20309	**RUBBER SEAL AROUND BOOT LID GLASS**	49– 8	1	
BD.20201	**Insert,** for Rubber Seal	49– 9	1	
BD.20158/1	**CHROME FINISHER AT TOP OF RUBBER SEAL**	49–10	1	Fitted from Chassis No. 860001 to 860478. 885001 to 886013.
BD.20158/2	**CHROME FINISHER AT BOTTOM OF RUBBER SEAL**	49–11	1	

Part No.	Description	Plate No.	No. per Unit	Remarks
BD.20159/1	**CHROME FINISHER AT TOP OF RUBBER SEAL**		1	Fitted to Chassis No. 860479 and subs. 886014 and subs.
BD.20159/2	**CHROME FINISHER AT BOTTOM OF RUBBER SEAL**		1	
BD.5366	**Joint Piece,** for Chrome Finisher	49–12	2	
BD.17726	**"JAGUAR" MOTIF ON BOOT LID**	49–13	1	
BD.10735	**Spire Nut,** securing Motif		3	
BD.15293	**Rubber Washer,** under Spire Nuts		3	
BD.20163/1	**PLASTIC FINISHER AROUND BOOT LID GUTTER**	49–14	1	
BD.20500/1	**SEALING RUBBER AROUND BOOT LID APERTURE**	49–15	1	Fitted from Chassis No. 860001 to 860478. 885001 to 886013.
BD.23347/1	**SEALING RUBBER AROUND BOOT LID APERTURE**		1	Fitted to Chassis No. 860479 and subs. 886014 and subs.
BD.22754	**CASING ASSEMBLY (UPPER) ON BOOT LID, R.H.**	49–16	1	Fitted from Chassis No. 860001 to 860478. 885001 to 886013.
BD.22755	**CASING ASSEMBLY (UPPER) ON BOOT LID, L.H.**	49–17	1	
BD.22725	**CASING ASSEMBLY (UPPER) ON BOOT LID**		1	Fitted to Chassis No. 860479 and subs. 886014 and subs.
BD.23763	**CASING ASSEMBLY AT R.H. SIDE OF BOOT LID, BETWEEN UPPER AND LOWER CASING**		1	Fitted to Chassis No. 860479 and subs. 886014 and subs.
BD.18068	**Clip,** securing Casing		2	

BODY FITTINGS
FOR FIXED HEAD COUPE ONLY

Part No.	Description	Plate No.	No. per Unit	Remarks
BD.20165	**CASING ASSEMBLY (LOWER) ON BOOT LID**	49–18	1	Fitted from Chassis No. 860001 to 860478. 885001 to 886013.
BD.18068	**Clip,** for fixing of Casing		14	
BD.20782	**CASING ASSEMBLY (LOWER) ON BOOT LID**		1	Fitted to Chassis No. 860479 and subs. 886014 and subs.
BD.18068	**Clip,** for fixing of Casing		14	
BD.20683	**LOCK ASSEMBLY, COMPLETE, FOR BOOT LID**	49–19	1	
BD.20061	**Lock Mechanism Assembly** (WB.3/16193)		1	
UFS.419/5H	**Screw,** Set, securing Lock to Housing		4	
BD.20122	**Spring,** assisting Boot Lid opening		1	
BD.20573	**Return Spring,** for Operating Lever		1	
BD.20645	**Clamp,** for Operating Cable		1	
UFS.419/3H	**Screw,** Set, securing Clamp		1	
C.723/A	**Washer,** Shakeproof, on Setscrews		1	
UFS.425/4H	**Screw,** Set, securing Lock Assembly to Body		4	
C.724	**Washer,** Shakeproof, on Setscrews		4	
BD.541/32	**Special Washer,** under Shakeproof Washers		4	
BD.21298	**RELEASE MECHANISM ASSEMBLY FOR BOOT LID LOCK**		1	
BD.21066	**Return Spring,** for Release Mechanism		1	
BD.711/12	**Screw,** Self-Tapping, securing Release Mechanism to R.H. Quarter Panel		6	
BD.20900	**ESCUTCHEON, IN R.H. QUARTER PANEL, AROUND RELEASE MECHANISM**		1	
BD.540/11	**Screw,** Self-Tapping, securing Escutcheon		2	
BD.21299	**CABLE FOR RELEASE OF BOOT LID LOCK**		1	
BD.22643	**Pad,** for Control Cable		1	
BD.20682	**STRIKER AND SAFETY CATCH ASSEMBLY FOR BOOT LID LOCK**	49–20	1	Fitted from Chassis No. 860001 to 860478. 885001 to 886013.
BD.20574	**Spring,** on Safety Catch		1	
UFS.425/4H	**Screw,** Set, securing Striker to Boot Lid		2	
C.724	**Washer,** Shakeproof, on Setscrews		2	
BD.541/9	**Special Washer,** under Shakeproof Washers		2	

Part No.	Description	Plate No.	No. per Unit	Remarks
BD.22596	**STRIKER AND SAFETY CATCH ASSEMBLY FOR BOOT LID LOCK**		1	
BD.20574	**Spring,** on Safety Catch		1	Fitted to Chassis No. 860479 and subs. 886014 and subs.
UNF.425/4H	**Screw,** Set, securing Striker to Boot Lid		2	
C.724	**Washer,** Shakeproof, on Setscrews		2	
BD.541/32	**Special Washer,** under Shakeproof Washers		2	
BD.659/10	**DRAIN TUBE FOR BOOT LID APERTURE (9½" LONG)**		1	
BD.21279	**PROP, SUPPORTING BOOT LID IN OPEN POSITION**	49–21	1	Fitted from Chassis No. 860001 to 860478. 885001 to 886013.
BD.23752	**PROP, SUPPORTING BOOT LID IN OPEN POSITION**		1	Fitted to Chassis No. 860479 and subs. 886014 and subs.
BD.21280	**PIVOT BRACKET ASSEMBLY, ON BOOT LID, FOR PROP**	49–22	1	Fitted from Chassis No. 860001 to 860478. 885001 to 886013.
BD.21287	**PIVOT BRACKET ASSEMBLY, ON BOOT LID, FOR PROP**		1	Fitted to Chassis No. 860479 and subs. 886014 and subs.
BD.13713/2	**Screw,** Set, securing Pivot Bracket		2	
C.723/A	**Washer,** Shakeproof, on Setscrews		2	
C.15542	**Clevis Pin,** securing Prop in Pivot Bracket		1	
BD.1708/4	**Washer,** Double Coil Spring, on Clevis Pin		1	
BD.848/2	**Brass Washer,** on Clevis Pin		2	
L.102/6U	**Split Pin,** retaining Clevis Pin		1	
BD.21281	**BRACKET, ON BODY, RECEIVING PROP**	49–23	1	
BD.13713/2	**Screw,** Set, securing Bracket		2	Fitted from Chassis No. 860001 to 860478. 885001 to 886013.
UFN.119/L	**Nut,** on Setscrews		2	
C.723/A	**Washer,** Shakeproof, under Nuts		2	
BD.21311	**Plate,** reinforcing Bracket		1	
UFS.419/4H	**Screw,** Set, securing Plate to Body		2	
UFN.119/L	**Nut,** on Setscrews		2	
C.723/A	**Washer,** Shakeproof, under Nuts		2	
BD.23712	**BRACKET, ON BODY, RECEIVING PROP**		1	
BD.13713/1	**Screw,** Set, securing Bracket		2	Fitted to Chassis No. 860479 and subs. 886014 and subs.
UFN.119/L	**Nut,** on Setscrews		2	
C.723/A	**Washer,** Shakeproof, under Nuts		2	

BODY FITTINGS
FOR FIXED HEAD COUPE ONLY

Part No.	Description	Plate No.	No. per Unit	Remarks
BD.21282	**REST RUBBER ASSEMBLY, HOLDING PROP WHEN NOT IN USE**	49–24	1	
BD.711/19	**Screw,** Self-Tapping, securing Rest Rubber to Boot Lid		2	
C.18921	**REAR NUMBER PLATE**		1	
BD.1229/13	**Screw,** Self-Tapping, securing Rear Number Plate		4	
BD.6581	**Rubber Plug,** in Rear Number Plate Panel		4	
BD.659/9	**DRAIN TUBE FOR PETROL FILLER BOX (20″ LONG)**		1	
C.2905/2	**Clip,** securing Drain Tube		2	
BD.22536	**RUBBER STOP, CUSHIONING PETROL FILLER LID**		2	
BD.18492	**COVER PLATE, IN FLOOR TOP PANEL OVER REAR SUSPENSION UNIT**		1	
BD.18493	**Rubber Seal,** under Cover Plate		1	
BD.8691/6	**Screw,** Self-Tapping, securing Cover Plate		7	
BD.19053	**Spring Latch,** for fixing of Spare Wheel Cover		1	
BD.1814/1	**Pop Rivet,** securing Spring Latch to Floor		2	
BD.11007/1	**SPARE WHEEL CLAMP ASSEMBLY**	49–25	1	
BD.10637	**Handle,** operating Spare Wheel Clamp		1	
BD.11008/1	**Screw**		1	
BD.10639	**Plate,** on Screw, holding Spare Wheel		1	
C.704/1	**Mills Pin,** securing Handle to Screw		1	
BD.3438	**Clip,** on Boot Floor, carrying Jack Handle		2	} **NOT REQUIRED FOR JACK**
BD.711/18	**Self-Tapping Screw,** securing Clip		2	} **WITH INTEGRAL HANDLE.**
BD.21137	**COVER ASSEMBLY OVER SPARE WHEEL**	49–26	1	
BD.10958	**Stud,** for fixing of Cover		1	
BD.9909/5	**Tee Nut,** receiving Stud		1	
C.723	**Washer,** Shakeproof, under Nut		1	
BD.22797	**Spring Clip,** for Spare Wheel Cover fixing		1	
UCS.511/4H	**Screw,** Set, securing Clip to Cover		3	
UCN.111/L	**Nut,** on Setscrews		3	
C.721	**Washer,** Shakeproof, under Nuts		3	

Part No.	Description	Plate No.	No. per Unit	Remarks
BD.19052	**COVER ASSEMBLY OVER PETROL TANK**	49–27	1	
BD.19059/2	**Screw,** Set, securing Cover		3	
BD.18545	**Cup Washer,** on Setscrews		3	
BD.4321	**Rubber Buffer,** in Support Strip		3	
BD.20214	**MAT ASSEMBLY ON SPARE WHEEL COVER**	49–28	1	Fitted from Chassis No. 860001 to 861092. 885001 to 888256.
BD.1286/1	**Button,** for "Durable Dot" Fastener, securing Mat to Spare Wheel Cover		4	
BD.1286/2	**Socket,** securing Buttons		4	
BD.20213	**MAT ASSEMBLY ON LUGGAGE COMPARTMENT FLOOR**	49–29	1	Fitted from Chassis No. 860001 to 861092. 885001 to 888256.
BD.1286/1	**Button,** for "Durable Dot" Fastener, securing Mat to Floor		7	
BD.1286/2	**Socket,** securing Buttons		7	
BD.1286/3	**Stud,** on Spare Wheel Cover and Luggage Compartment Floor, receiving "Durable Dot" Fasteners		11	
BD.540/1	**Screw,** Self-Tapping, securing Studs		11	
BD.25664	**MAT ASSEMBLY ON LUGGAGE COMPARTMENT FLOOR**		1	Fitted to Chassis No. 861093 and subs. 888257 and subs. **May be fitted to replace two separate Mats BD.20213 and BD.20214, if desired.**
BD.1286/1	**Button,** for "Durable Dot" Fastener, securing Mat to Floor		8	
BD.1286/2	**Socket,** securing Buttons		8	
BD.1286/3	**Stud,** receiving "Durable Dot" Fasteners		8	
BD.540/1	**Screw,** Self-Tapping, securing Studs to Floor		8	
	RUBBER BEADING ON LUGGAGE FLOOR			
BD.604/2	**Rubber Beading** (39½" long)	49–30	1	
BD.604/3	**Rubber Beading** (38" long)	49–31	1	
BD.604/4	**Rubber Beading** (11⅞" long)	49–32	3	
BD.604/5	**Rubber Beading** (28¼" long)	49–33	2	
BD.604/6	**Rubber Beading** (26¾" long)	49–34	1	
	RETAINERS FOR RUBBER BEADING			
BD.332/13	**Retainer,** for Beading (39" long)	49–35	1	
BD.332/14	**Retainer,** for Beading (37½" long)	49–36	1	
BD.20291/1	**Retainer,** for Beading (11¾" long)	49–37	3	
BD.20291/2	**Retainer,** for Beading (27⅝" long)	49–38	2	
BD.20291/3	**Retainer,** for Beading (26¼" long)	49–39	1	
BD.20243	**Spring Clip,** securing Retainers to Mats		32	

Part No.	Description	Plate No.	No. per Unit	Remarks
BD.20795	**HINGED EXTENSION ASSEMBLY FOR LUGGAGE COMPARTMENT FLOOR**		1	
BD.20131	**Hinge,** for Extension		3	
M.108/3R	**Woodscrew,** securing Hinges to Extension		9	
BD.20134	**Stud,** for fixing of Extension in lowered position		2	
BD.9909/5	**Nut,** securing Studs		2	
C.2017/1	**Chromed Washer,** on Studs		2	
BD.20133	**Chrome Strip,** along edge of Extension		1	
BD.711/16	**Screw,** Self-Tapping, securing Chrome Strip		9	Fitted from Chassis No. 860001 to 860580. 885001 to 886092.
BD.17503/2	**Screw,** Self-Tapping, securing Extension Hinges to Body		9	
BD.9395	**Sliding Catch,** securing Hinged Extension in raised position		2	
BD.1499/6	**Woodscrew,** securing Sliding Catches to Extension		12	
BD.9912	**Striker Plate,** engaging Sliding Catches		2	
BD.11712/1	**Pop Rivet,** securing Striker Plates to Wheel Arches		4	
BD.604/1	**Rubber Beading,** on Hinged Extension (8¼" long)		3	
BD.332/12	**Retainer,** for Rubber Beading (8¼" long)		3	
M.104/3R	**Woodscrew,** securing Retainers		12	
C.9743	**Rubber Buffer,** cushioning Hinged Extension in raised position		2	
BD.22913	**HINGED EXTENSION ASSEMBLY FOR LUGGAGE COMPARTMENT FLOOR**	49–40	1	Fitted from Chassis No. 860581 to 861098. 886093 to 888301.
BD.20131	**Hinge,** for Extension		3	
M.108/3R	**Woodscrew,** securing Hinges to Extension		9	
BD.23717	**Stud,** fixing Extension in lowered position		2	
BD.9909/5	**Nut,** securing Studs		2	
BD.22914	**Chrome Strip,** along edge of Extension		1	
BD.711/16	**Screw,** Self-Tapping, securing Chrome Strip		9	
BD.9395	**Sliding Catch,** securing Hinged Extension in raised position	49–41	2	
BD.1499/6	**Woodscrew,** securing Catches to Extension		12	
BD.20135	**Luggage Stop Arm Assembly,** on Extension		2	
BD.21798	**Cover Plate,** over Luggage Stop Apertures		2	
BD.13642/11	**Screw,** Set, securing Luggage Stops and Cover Plates		8	
BD.24398	**HINGED EXTENSION ASSEMBLY FOR LUGGAGE COMPARTMENT FLOOR**		1	Fitted to Chassis No. 861099 and subs. 888302 and subs.
BD.24400	**Hinge,** for Extension		3	
BD.13642/11	**Screw,** Set, securing Hinges to Extension		6	
BD.23717	**Stud,** fixing Extension in lowered position		2	
BD.24403	**Chrome Strip,** along edge of Extension		1	
BD.24404	**Chrome Capping,** at R.H. end of Extension		1	
BD.24405	**Chrome Capping,** at L.H. end of Extension		1	
BD.24402	**Finger Pull,** at centre of Extension		1	
BD.711/16	**Screw,** Self-Tapping, securing Chrome Strip, Cappings and Finger Pull		10	
BD.9395	**Sliding Catch,** securing Extension when raised		2	
BD.1499/6	**Woodscrew,** securing Catches		12	
BD.20135	**Luggage Stop Arm Assembly**		2	
BD.21798	**Cover Plate,** over Luggage Stop Apertures		2	
BD.13642/11	**Screw,** Set, securing Stop Arms and Cover Plates		8	
BD.17503/2	**Screw,** Self-Tapping, securing Extension Hinges to Body		9	
BD.540/22	**Screw,** Self-Tapping, securing Extension Hinges to Floor		9	
BD.23142	**Striker Plate,** on Wheel Arches, receiving Sliding Catches	49–42	2	
BD.11712/1	**Pop Rivet,** securing Striker Plates		4	Fitted to Chassis No. 860581 and subs. 886093 and subs.
BD.604/7	**Rubber Beading,** on Hinged Extension (7½" long)	49–43	3	
BD.332/5	**Retainer,** for Rubber Beading (7" long)	49–44	3	
M.104/3R	**Woodscrew,** securing Retainers		12	
BD.23144	**Rubber Buffer,** cushioning Hinged Extension in raised position		2	

Part No.	Description	Plate No.	No. per Unit	Remarks
BD.22476	**SUPPORT RAIL ASSEMBLY FOR HINGED EXTENSION IN LOWERED POSITION**		1	Fitted from Chassis No. 860001 to 860580. 885001 to 886092.
BD.19053	**Spring Latch**, receiving Studs of Hinged Extension		2	
BD.1814/1	**Pop Rivet**, securing Spring Latches		4	
BD.1814/1	**Pop Rivet**, securing Support Rail to Body		19	
C.9743	**Rubber Plug**, seating Hinged Extension when lowered		4	
BD.22942	**SUPPORT RAIL ASSEMBLY FOR HINGED EXTENSION IN LOWERED POSITION**		1	Fitted to Chassis No. 860581 and subs. 886093 and subs.
BD.23848	**Clip**, receiving Studs of Extension		2	
BD.1814/1	**Pop Rivet**, securing Clips		4	
BD.17503/2	**Screw**, Self-Tapping, securing Support Rail		9	

CARPETS FOR R.H. DRIVE CARS

Part No.	Description	Plate No.	No. per Unit	Remarks
BD.20347	**Carpet Assembly**, on R.H. Front Floor	50– 1	1	Fitted from Chassis No. 860001 to 860175.
BD.20348	**Carpet Assembly**, on L.H. Front Floor	50– 2	1	
BD.22962	**Carpet Assembly**, on R.H. Front Floor		1	Fitted to Chassis No. 860176 and subs.
BD.22963	**Carpet Assembly**, on L.H. Front Floor		1	
BD.20350	**Carpet Assembly**, on Toe Boards	50– 3	2	
BD.20352	**Carpet Assembly**, R.H., for front of Tunnel	50– 4	1	
BD.20353	**Carpet Assembly**, L.H., for front of Tunnel	50– 5	1	
BD.20354	**Carpet Assembly**, R.H., for rear of Tunnel	50– 6	1	
BD.20355	**Carpet Assembly**, L.H., for rear of Tunnel	50– 7	1	

CARPETS FOR L.H. DRIVE CARS

Part No.	Description	Plate No.	No. per Unit	Remarks
BD.20347	**Carpet Assembly**, on R.H. Front Floor		1	Fitted from Chassis No. 885001 to 885503.
BD.20349	**Carpet Assembly**, on L.H. Front Floor		1	
BD.22962	**Carpet Assembly**, on R.H. Front Floor		1	Fitted to Chassis No. 885504 and subs.
BD.22964	**Carpet Assembly**, on L.H. Front Floor		1	
BD.20350	**Carpet Assembly**, on Toe Boards		2	
BD.20352	**Carpet Assembly**, R.H., for front of Tunnel		1	
BD.20353	**Carpet Assembly**, L.H., for front of Tunnel		1	
BD.20354	**Carpet Assembly**, R.H., for rear of Tunnel		1	
BD.20355	**Carpet Assembly**, L.H., for rear of Tunnel		1	

BODY FITTINGS
FOR FIXED HEAD COUPE ONLY

Part No.	Description	Plate No.	No. per Unit	Remarks

INSULATING FELTS FOR R.H. DRIVE CARS

Part No.	Description	Plate No.	No. per Unit	Remarks
BD.20218	**Rubberised Felt,** on R.H. Front Floor ($28'' \times 19\frac{1}{2}'' \times \frac{1}{2}''$)		1	
BD.20230	**Rubberised Felt,** on L.H. Front Floor ($28'' \times 19\frac{1}{2}'' \times \frac{1}{2}''$)		1	
BD.20235	**Rubberised Felt,** under R.H. side of Scuttle ($19'' \times 19'' \times \frac{1}{2}''$)		1	
BD.20236	**Rubberised Felt,** under R.H. side of Scuttle ($18\frac{1}{2}'' \times 10\frac{1}{2}'' \times \frac{1}{2}''$)		1	
BD.20237	**Rubberised Felt,** under L.H. side of Scuttle ($15'' \times 8\frac{1}{2}'' \times \frac{1}{2}''$)		1	
BD.20220	**Rubberised Felt,** on R.H. Toe Board ($14'' \times 10'' \times \frac{1}{2}''$)		1	
BD.20221	**Rubberised Felt,** on L.H. Toe Board ($14'' \times 10'' \times \frac{1}{2}''$)		1	
BD.20205	**Rubberised Felt,** at front R.H. side of Gearbox Tunnel ($15'' \times 11'' \times \frac{1}{2}''$)		1	
BD.20206	**Rubberised Felt,** at front L.H. side of Gearbox Tunnel ($15'' \times 11'' \times \frac{1}{2}''$)		1	
BD.21233	**Rubberised Felt,** at top of Gearbox Cover ($7'' \times 7'' \times \frac{1}{2}''$)		1	
BD.20207	**Rubberised Felt,** at R.H. side of Gearbox Tunnel ($17'' \times 8'' \times \frac{1}{4}''$)		1	
BD.20208	**Rubberised Felt,** at L.H. side of Gearbox Tunnel ($17'' \times 8'' \times \frac{1}{4}''$)		1	
BD.20339	**Rubberised Felt,** under Petrol Tank ($6'' \times 7'' \times \frac{1}{2}''$)		1	
BD.20227	**Rubberised Felt,** Gearbox Cover to Scuttle ($11'' \times 7'' \times \frac{1}{2}''$)		1	
BD.20209	**Hardura,** under R.H. side of Scuttle		1	
BD.20210	**Hardura,** under L.H. side of Scuttle		1	
BD.539/4	**Screw,** Self-Tapping, securing Hardura		10	
BD.532/1	**Cup Washer,** on Self-Tapping Screws		10	
BD.20222	**Hardura,** on R.H. Toe Board ($14'' \times 10'' \times \frac{1}{4}''$)		1	
BD.20223	**Hardura,** on L.H. Toe Board ($14'' \times 10'' \times \frac{1}{4}''$)		1	
BD.20336	**Hardura,** under L.H. side of Scuttle ($17'' \times 18'' \times \frac{1}{4}''$)		1	
BD.20337	**Hardura,** under R.H. side of Scuttle ($10'' \times 19'' \times \frac{1}{4}''$)		1	
BD.20338	**Hardura,** under centre of Scuttle ($7'' \times 8'' \times \frac{1}{4}''$)		1	

INSULATING FELTS FOR L.H. DRIVE CARS

Part No.	Description	Plate No.	No. per Unit	Remarks
BD.20218	**Rubberised Felt,** on R.H. Front Floor ($28'' \times 19\frac{1}{2}'' \times \frac{1}{2}''$)		1	
BD.20219	**Rubberised Felt,** on L.H. Front Floor ($28'' \times 19\frac{1}{2}'' \times \frac{1}{2}''$)		1	
BD.20220	**Rubberised Felt,** on R.H. Toe Board ($14'' \times 10'' \times \frac{1}{2}''$)		1	
BD.20221	**Rubberised Felt,** on L.H. Toe Board ($14'' \times 10'' \times \frac{1}{2}''$)		1	
BD.20224	**Rubberised Felt,** under R.H. side of Scuttle ($19'' \times 19'' \times \frac{1}{2}''$)		1	
BD.20225	**Rubberised Felt,** under L.H. side of Scuttle ($18\frac{1}{2}'' \times 10\frac{1}{2}'' \times \frac{1}{2}''$)		1	
BD.20226	**Rubberised Felt,** under L.H. side of Scuttle ($15'' \times 8\frac{1}{2}'' \times \frac{1}{2}''$)		1	
BD.20227	**Rubberised Felt,** Gearbox Cover to Scuttle ($11'' \times 7'' \times \frac{1}{2}''$)		1	
BD.20205	**Rubberised Felt,** at front R.H. side of Gearbox Tunnel ($15'' \times 11'' \times \frac{1}{2}''$)		1	
BD.20206	**Rubberised Felt,** at front L.H. side of Gearbox Tunnel ($15'' \times 11'' \times \frac{1}{2}''$)		1	
BD.20207	**Rubberised Felt,** at R.H. side of Gearbox Tunnel ($17'' \times 8'' \times \frac{1}{4}''$)		1	
BD.20208	**Rubberised Felt,** at L.H. side of Gearbox Tunnel ($17'' \times 8'' \times \frac{1}{4}''$)		1	
BD.20339	**Rubberised Felt,** under Petrol Tank ($6'' \times 7'' \times \frac{1}{2}''$)		1	
BD.21233	**Rubberised Felt,** at top of Gearbox Cover ($7'' \times 7'' \times \frac{1}{2}''$)		1	
BD.20222	**Hardura,** on R.H. Toe Board ($14'' \times 10'' \times \frac{1}{4}''$)		1	
BD.20223	**Hardura,** on L.H. Toe Board ($14'' \times 10'' \times \frac{1}{4}''$)		1	
BD.20231	**Hardura,** under R.H. side of Scuttle ($17'' \times 18'' \times \frac{1}{4}''$)		1	
BD.20232	**Hardura,** under L.H. side of Scuttle ($10'' \times 19'' \times \frac{1}{4}''$)		1	
BD.20233	**Hardura,** under centre of Scuttle ($7'' \times 9'' \times \frac{1}{4}''$)		1	

Part No.	Description	Plate No.	No. per Unit	Remarks
	ANTI-DRUM MATERIAL			
BD.20272	**Flintkote,** on Door Panels (9″×24″)		2	
BD.20273	**Flintkote,** on Door Bottom Rails (2″×18″)		2	
BD.20351	**Flintkote,** on Boot Lid Panel		1	
BD.20215	**Flintkote,** on Rear Floor Panel (18½″×21″)		2	
BD.20902	**Flintkote,** on Propeller Shaft Tunnel (16″×18″)		1	
BD.20422	**Flintkote,** top front, for Gearbox Cover		1	
BD.20217	**Flintkote,** on Main Floors (19½″ × 27″)		2	Fitted from Chassis No. 860001 to 860175. 885001 to 885503.
BD.22965	**Flintkote,** on R.H. Front Floor		1	Fitted to Chassis No. 860176 and subs.
BD.22966	**Flintkote,** on L.H. Front Floor		1	
BD.22965	**Flintkote,** on R.H. Front Floor		1	Fitted to Chassis No. 885504 and subs.
BD.22967	**Flintkote,** on L.H. Front Floor		1	
BD.20211	**Flintkote,** for R.H. side of Scuttle (13″×15″)		1	
BD.20212	**Flintkote,** for L.H. side of Scuttle (13″×15″)		1	
	INTERIOR TRIMMING			
BD.20456/2	**Face Piece** (Rexine) on Screen Pillars, at side of Facias (3″×5″)		2	
BD.20375	**Face Piece** (Rexine) for R.H. side of Floor Cross Member (9″×24″)		1	
BD.20376	**Face Piece** (Rexine) for L.H. side of Floor Cross Member (9″×24″)		1	
BD.20541	**Face Piece** (Vynide) (14″×36″) for Door Sills		2	
BD.20913	**Pad** (Polyurethane) under Sill Face Pieces		2	
BD.20169	**Face Piece** (Moquette) on R.H. rear Wheel Arch		1	
BD.20170	**Face Piece** (Moquette) on L.H. rear Wheel Arch		1	
BD.20173	**Felt Pad,** on rear Wheel Arches		2	
BD.20209	**Mat Assembly** (Hardura) for R.H. side of Scuttle		1	
BD.20210	**Mat Assembly** (Hardura) for L.H. side of Scuttle		1	
BD.539/4	**Screw,** Self-Tapping, securing Mats		10	
BD.532/1	**Cup Washer,** on Self-Tapping Screws		10	
BD.20216	**Mat Assembly** (Hardura) on Rear Floor Panel		2	
BD.20728	**Cover Assembly,** protecting Wiring Harness at L.H. side of Scuttle		1	
BD.1814/6	**Pop Rivet,** securing Cover		2	
	SEALING RUBBERS			
BD.21197	**Sealing Rubber,** on Door Sills	50–8	2	**SUPERSEDED BY BD.24789.**
BD.24789	**Sealing Rubber,** on Door Sills		2	**SUPERSEDES BD.21197.**
BD.21196	**Sealing Rubber,** for Door Shut Pillars	50–9	2	
BD.18559	**Sealing Rubber,** lower, for R.H. "A" Post	50–10	1	
BD.18560	**Sealing Rubber,** lower, for L.H. "A" Post	50–11	1	
BD.19397/1	**Sealing Rubber,** in top channel of Door Light Frames		2	
BD.17071/2	**Sealing Rubber,** on Quarter Light Hinge Pillars, and Standing Pillar of Door Light Frame	50–12	4	
BD.20500/2	**Sealing Rubber,** for Cantrail (90″ long)	50–13	2	
BD.20500/1	**Sealing Rubber,** around Boot Lid aperture (126″ long)	50–14	1	Fitted from Chassis No. 860001 to 860478. 885001 to 886013.
BD.23347/1	**Sealing Rubber,** around Boot Lid aperture (126″ long)		1	Fitted to Chassis No. 860479 and subs. 886014 and subs.
BD.20309	**Sealing Rubber,** around Boot Lid Glass		1	
BD.20903/1	**Sealing Rubber,** for rear edge of Bonnet (68″ long)	50–15	1	

BODY FITTINGS
FOR FIXED HEAD COUPE ONLY

Part No.	Description	Plate No.	No. per Unit	Remarks
	SEAL RETAINERS			
BD.20497	**Retainer,** for R.H. Cantrail Seal (90″ long)		1	⎫ Fitted from Chassis No.
BD.20498	**Retainer,** for L.H. Cantrail Seal (90″ long)		1	⎬ 860001 to 860478.
				885001 to 886013.
BD.20803	**Retainer,** for R.H. Cantrail Seal (90″ long)		1	⎫ Fitted to Chassis No.
BD.20804	**Retainer,** for L.H. Cantrail Seal (90″ long)		1	⎬ 860479 and subs.
				⎭ 886014 and subs.
BD.23654	**Retainer,** Lower, for R.H. "A" Post Seal		1	
BD.23653	**Retainer,** Lower, for L.H. "A" Post Seal		1	

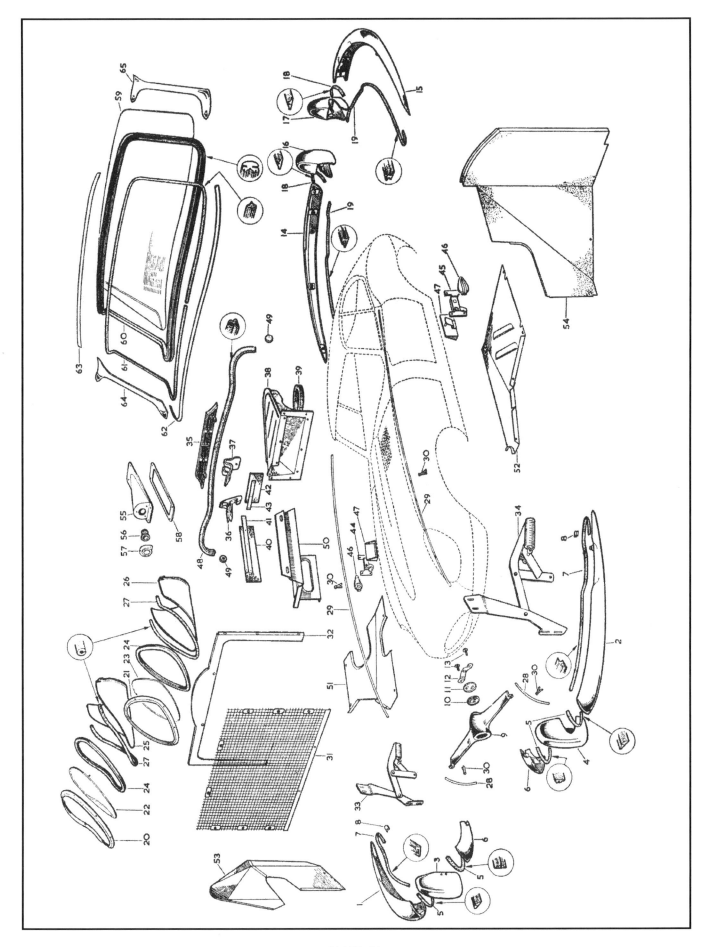

PLATE 46

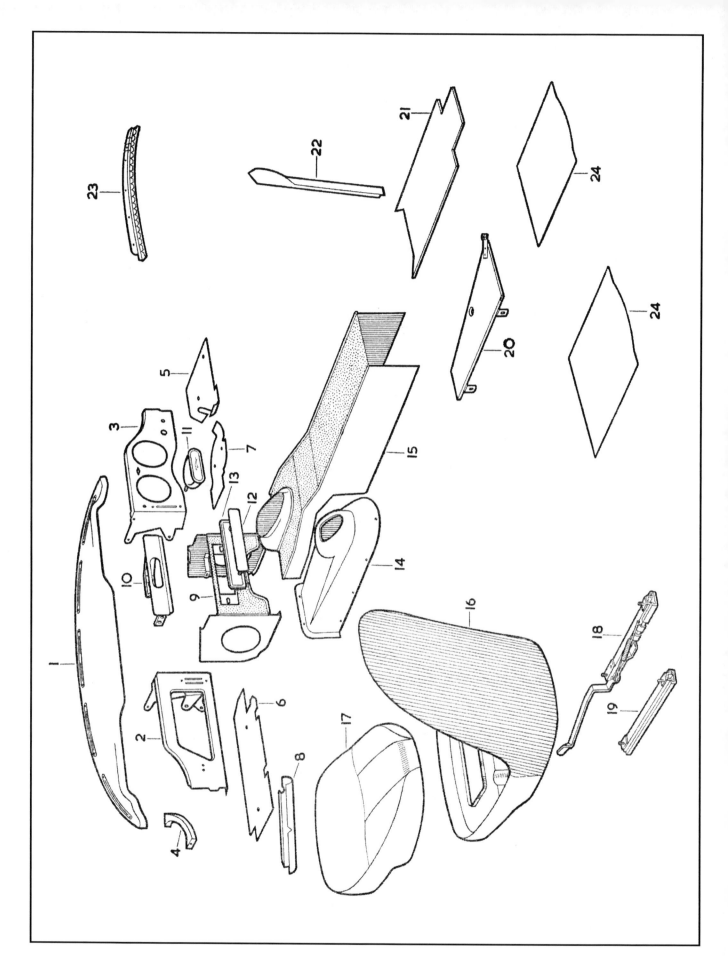

PLATE 47

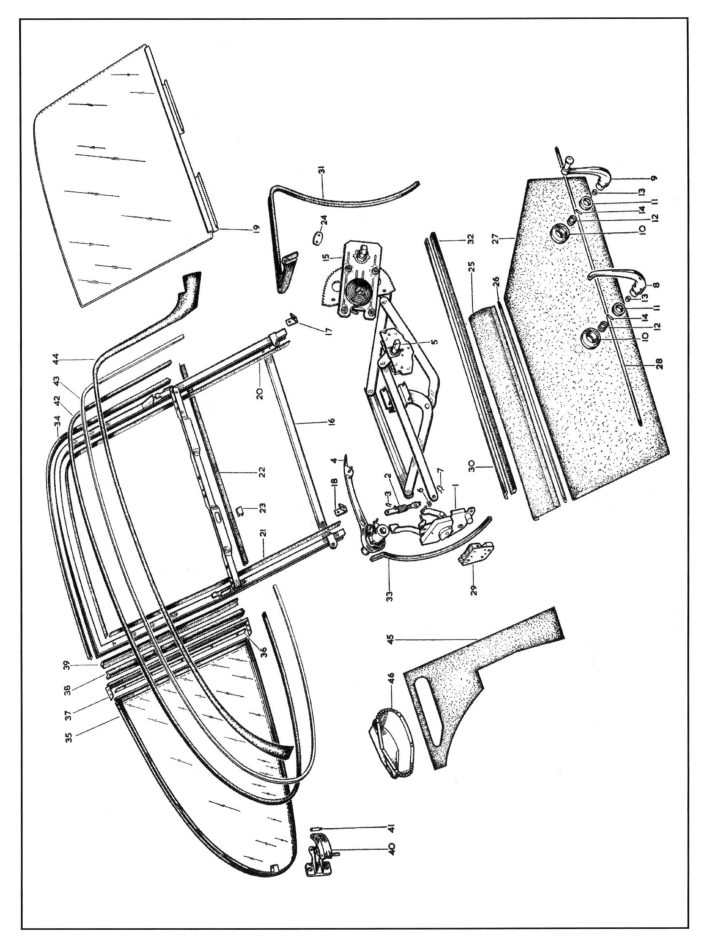

PLATE 48

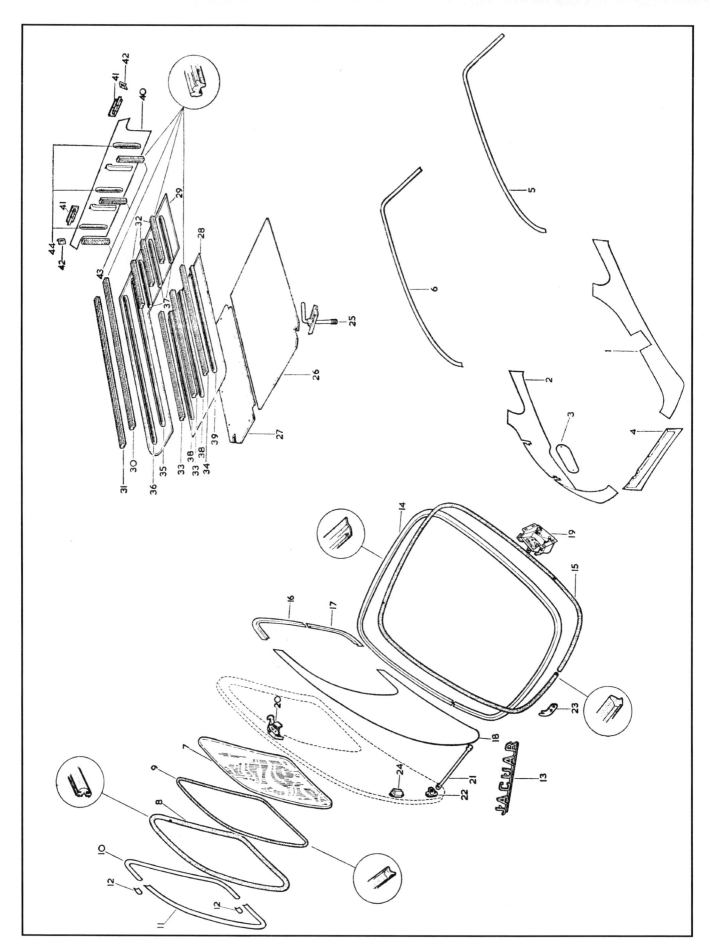

PLATE 49

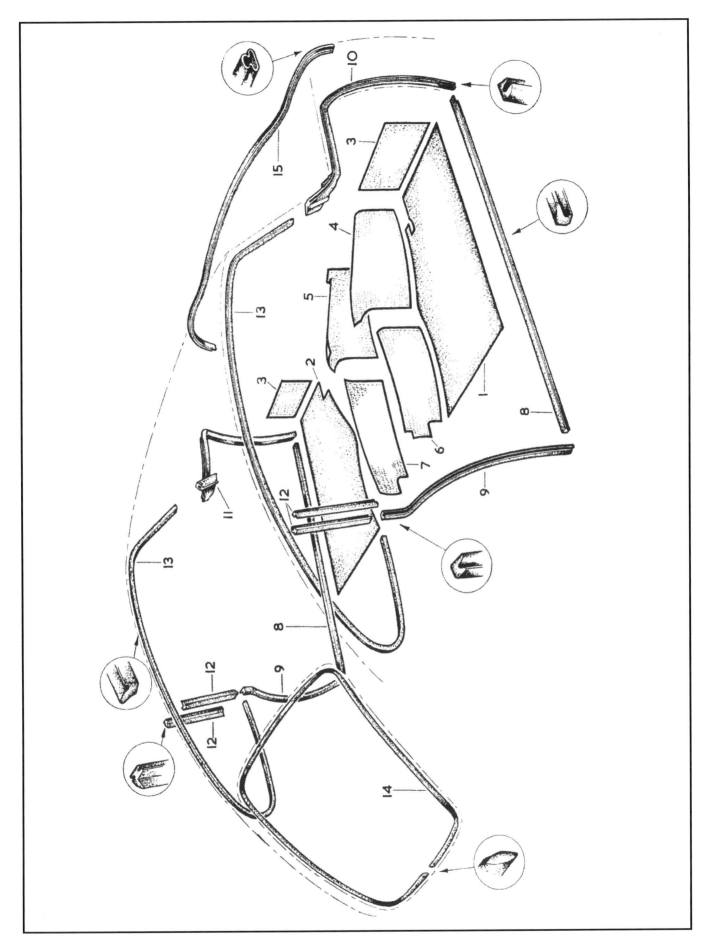

PLATE 50

TOOL KIT

Part No.	Description	Plate No.	No. per Unit	Remarks
C.4651	**Adjustable Spanner**		1	
C.996	**Pliers**		1	
C.11753	**Tyre Pressure Gauge**		1	
C.5444	**Screwdriver,** for adjustment of Contact Breaker Points		1	
C.5587	**Feeler Gauge**		1	
C.993	**Extractor,** for Tyre Valve		1	
C.4585	**Screwdriver**		1	See "Combination Screwdriver" below.
C.10155	**Box Spanner,** for Sparking Plugs and Cylinder Head Nuts		1	
C.4094	**Box Spanner** ($\frac{7}{16}'' \times \frac{1}{2}''$ S.A.E.)		1	
C.4095	**Box Spanner** ($\frac{9}{16}'' \times \frac{5}{8}''$ S.A.E.)		1	
C.4096	**Box Spanner** ($\frac{3}{4}'' \times \frac{7}{8}''$ S.A.E.)		1	
C.2896	**Tommy Bar** (Long) for Box Spanners		1	
C.34	**Tommy Bar** (Short) for Box Spanners		1	
C.4594	**Open Ended Spanner** ($\frac{3}{4}'' \times \frac{7}{8}''$ A.F.)		1	
C.4595	**Open Ended Spanner** ($\frac{9}{16}'' \times \frac{5}{8}''$ A.F.)		1	
C.4596	**Open Ended Spanner** ($\frac{1}{2}'' \times \frac{7}{16}''$ A.F.)		1	
C.4638	**Open Ended Spanner** ($\frac{11}{32}'' \times \frac{3}{8}''$ A.F.)		1	
C.3993	**Valve Timing Gauge**		1	
C.13269	**Grease Gun** (Tecalemit GC.3020)		1	
C.13620	**Bleeder Tube,** in Container (SYN.179)		1	
C.992	**Hammer** (Copper and Rawhide)		1	
2072	**Budget Lock Key**		1	
C.19524	**Fan Belt**		1	
C.18636	**Special Wrench,** for Handbrake adjustment		1	
C.17822	**Jack** (complete with Operating Handle)		1	Fitted from Chassis No. 850001 to 850548. 875001 to 877518. 860001 to 860660. 885001 to 886246.
C.17823	**Handle only,** for Jack Operation		1	
C.20661	**Jack** (complete with Integral Operating Handle)		1	Fitted to Chassis No. 850549 and subs. 877519 and subs. 860661 and subs. 886247 and subs.
BD.23688	**Container for Jack**		1	
C.5578	**Tool Roll**		1	
C.14927	**Tool,** for fitting and removing Hub Caps		1	**FOR CARS EXPORTED TO GERMANY AND SWITZERLAND.**
C.20482	**Combination Screwdriver** (Phillips Head/Conventional)		1	Fitted to Chassis No. 850648 and subs. 878937 and subs. 861071 and subs. 888139 and subs.

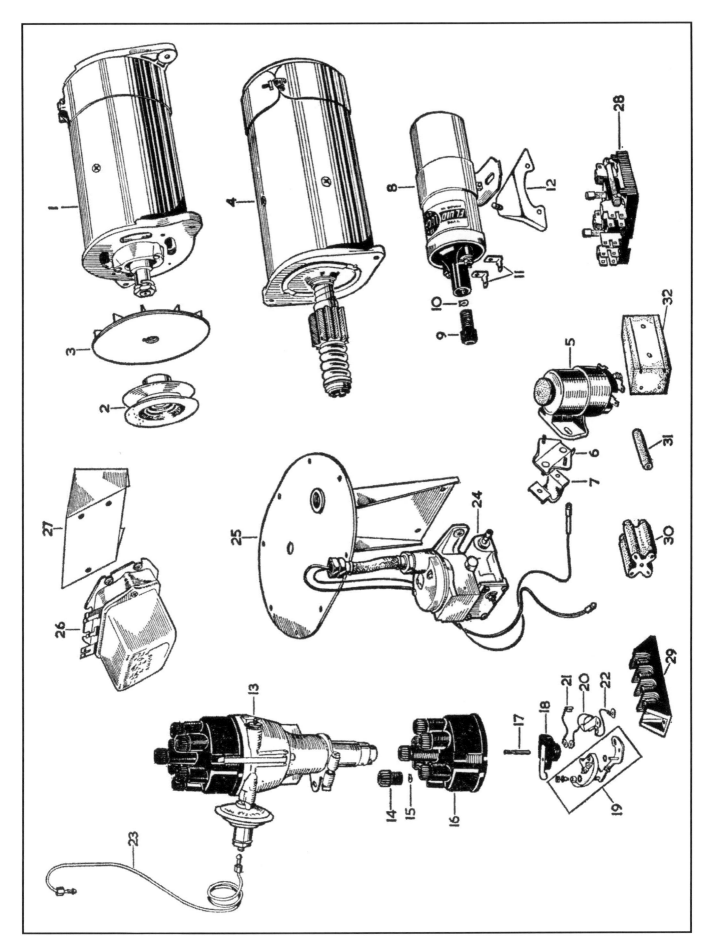

PLATE 51

ELECTRICAL EQUIPMENT

Part No.	Description	Plate No.	No. per Unit	Remarks
C.16054	**DYNAMO (22531/A-C45.PVS/6)**	51– 1	1	Fitted from Chassis No. 850001 to 850091. 875001 to 875385. 860001 to 860004. 885001 to 885020.
6502	**Cover Band** (227015)		1	
7906	**Brush** (54210090)		1 set	
7907	**Spring,** for Brush Tension (54210091)		1 set	
8580	**Bracket,** Commutator End (54211251)		1	
2754	**Bearing,** for C.E. Bracket (189237)		1	
8578	**Thrust Spring,** at Commutator End (238954)		1	
8579	**Thrust Screw,** at Commutator End (238579)		1	
8582	**Distance Collar,** at Commutator End (227532)		1	
2749	**Nut,** on Commutator Shaft (180620)		1	
6508	**Washer,** under Nut (185187)		1	
5919	**Bracket,** Drive End (239012)		1	
2757	**Bearing,** for D.E. Bracket (189308)		1	
8581	**Collar,** for D.E. Bearing (238024)		1	
7514	**Retainer,** for Bearing Ring (238824)		1	
8233	**Armature** (239511)		1	
2789	**Field Coils** (238820)		1 set	
7911	**Bolt,** through fixing (272752)		2	
C.18286	**DYNAMO (22902/A-C42)**		1	Fitted to Chassis No. 850092 and subs. 875386 and subs. 860005 and subs. 885021 and subs.
8583	**Brush** (54213141)		1 set	
9017	**Spring,** for Brush Tension (227542)		1 set	
8584	**Bracket,** Commutator End (54213139)		1	
8881	**Bearing,** for C.E. Bracket (54210144)		1	
9977	**Oiler,** for Bearing (54211097)		1	
9364	**Thrust Washer,** at Commutator End (164746)		1	
8586	**Nut,** on Commutator Shaft (198800)		1	
9365	**Washer,** under Nut (185085)		1	
8585	**Bracket,** Drive End (54213140)		1	
2756	**Bearing,** for D.E. Bracket (189307)		1	
9368	**Plate,** for Bearing (229400)		1	
8582	**Collar,** for D.E. Bearing (227532)		1	
9367	**Retainer,** for Bearing Ring (227631)		1	
8587	**Armature** (54210952)		1	
8588	**Field Coils** (54210950)		1 set	
8590	**Bolt,** through fixing (54210147)		2	
8589	**Terminal Set,** Lucar Connections (54211890)		1	
FW.105/T	**Washer,** Plain, at Dynamo mounting		1	
C.14590	**DYNAMO PULLEY**	51– 2	1	Fitted from Engine No. R.1001 to R.1509.
C.18227	**DYNAMO PULLEY**		1	Fitted from Engine No. R.1510 to R.5249.
C.19520	**DYNAMO PULLEY**		1	Fitted to Engine No. R.5250 and subs.

Part No.	Description	Plate No.	No. per Unit	Remarks
C.7428	**FAN FOR DYNAMO PULLEY**	51– 3	1	Fitted from Engine No. R.1001 to R.1509.
C.18300	**FAN FOR DYNAMO PULLEY**		1	Fitted to Engine No. R.1510 and subs.
UCS.131/10R	**Screw,** Set, securing Dynamo Belt Tension		1	
C.5454	**Nut,** Self-Locking, on Setscrew		1	
FW.105/T	**Washer,** Plain, under Nut		1	
C.12679	**STARTER MOTOR (26140/A-M.45G)**	51– 4	1	
2804	**Brush** (255659)		1 set	
2811	**Spring,** for Brush Tension (270004)		1 set	
6653	**Bracket,** Commutator End (271305)		1	
2801	**Bearing,** for C.E. Bracket (255491)		1	
2813	**Armature** (270482)		1	
2819	**Field Coils** (271306)		1 set	
5923	**Bracket,** Drive End (271458)		1	
2812	**Bearing,** for D.E. Bracket (270038)		1	
2803	**Pinion and Sleeve** (255649)		1	
2806	**Spring,** retaining Pinion (255728)		1	
UFB.137/13R	**Bolt,** securing Starter Motor		2	
UFN.137/L	**Nut,** on Bolts		2	
FG.106/X	**Washer,** Spring, under Nuts		2	
C.19468	**SOLENOID FOR STARTER MOTOR (76464/A.-2ST.)**	51– 5	1	
8710	**Rubber Cap** (760130)		1	
8713	**Lucar Blade** (small cranked connector) for connection of Cable from Starter Switch (54190015)		1	
8711	**Lucar Blade** (small stepped connector) for connection of Cable from Fuse Box (54190013)		1	
8712	**Lucar Blade** (large stepped connector) for connection of Cable from Ammeter (54190014)		1	
C.17106	**Bracket Assembly,** for mounting of Solenoid	51– 6	1	
C.17107	**Clamp,** for Bracket	51– 7	1	
UFN.125/L	**Nut,** securing Bracket to Side Member		2	
C.724	**Washer,** Shakeproof, under Nuts		2	
UFN.119/L	**Nut,** securing Solenoid to Bracket		2	
C.723/A	**Washer,** Shakeproof, under Nuts		2	
C.8749	**IGNITION COIL (45067/D-HA.12)**	51– 8	1	
C.5451	**Nut,** in centre of Coil, for attachment of Ignition Cable (408120)	51– 9	1	
C.5452	**Washer** (Copper) for attachment of Ignition Cable (185015)	51–10	1	
6472	**Terminal Nut** (166043)		2	
C.723/A	**Washer,** Shakeproof, under Nuts		2	
8638	**Lucar Blade,** for connection of Switch and Contact Breaker Cables (54190096)	51–11	2	
C.8047	**BRACKET ASSEMBLY, MOUNTING IGNITION COIL**	51–12	1	
C.6558	**Stud,** in Engine Breather Housing, mounting Coil		1	
UFN.125/L	**Nut,** securing Coil		2	
C.724	**Washer,** Shakeproof, under Nuts		2	
FW.104/T	**Washer,** Plain, under Shakeproof Washers		2	

Part No.	Description	Plate No.	No. per Unit	Remarks
C.18525	**EXTENSION ASSEMBLY FOR COIL BRACKET**		1	Fitted to Chassis No. 850092 and subs. 875386 and subs. 860005 and subs. 885021 and subs.
C.14269	**DISTRIBUTOR (40617A/D-DMBZ.6A)**	51–13	1	Fitted from Engine No. R.1001 to R.9999. RA.1001 to RA.1381. **FOR 8:1 OR 9:1 COMPRESSION RATIO.**
C.11906	**Nut,** for connection of High Tension Cables (410600)	51–14	7	
C.5452	**Washer** (Copper) for end of High Tension Cables (185015)	51–15	7	
6476	**Clamping Plate** (423605)		1	
6477	**Screw** (415087)		1	
6478	**Cap** (418857)	51–16	1	
6479	**Brush and Spring,** inside Cap (418856)	51–17	1	
6060	**Rotor** (418726)	51–18	1	
C.11990	**Contact Set** (420197)	51–19	1	
C.11991	**Condenser** (423871)	51–20	1	
6480	**Base Plate** (419980)		1	
6481	**Bearing,** for Base Plate (420375)		1	
6482	**Star Spring** (496058)		1	
6483	**Circlip,** fixing Base (496059)		1	
6484	**Terminal Pin,** Low Tension (407019)		1	
6485	**Insulating Bush,** Low Tension Terminal (408927)		1	
6486	**Insulating Pin,** Low Tension Terminal (405319)		1	
6487	**Insulating Bush** (419950)		1	
6488	**Lead,** Low Tension (419021)	51–21	1	
6489	**Lead,** Earth (419023)	51–22	1	
6491	**Cam** (496079)		1	
8235	**Springs,** Auto Advance (54410416)		1 set	
6493	**Weight,** Auto Advance (410033/S)		2	
6804	**Shaft and Action Plate** (419741)		1	
6495	**Knurled Nut,** adjusting Vacuum Control (419087)		1	
6496	**Spring Ratchet** (421825)		1	
6497	**Return Spring** (419086)		1	
8236	**Vacuum Unit** (54410415)		1	
2755	**Bearing** (189272)		1	
6499	**Bush** (419673)		1	
7177	**Clip,** securing Cap (421824)		2	
6501	**Oil Seal** (418723)		1	
2943	**Driving Dog** (410601)		1	
C.20679	**DISTRIBUTOR (40887A/B-22.D.6)**		1	Fitted to Engine No. RA.1382 and subs. **FOR 8:1 OR 9:1 COMPRESSION RATIO.**
C.11906	**Nut,** for connection of H.T. Cables (410600)		7	
C.5452	**Copper Washer,** for end of H.T. Cables (185015)		7	
6476	**Clamping Plate** (423605)		1	
6477	**Screw** (415087)		1	
9930	**Cap** (54414989)		1	
6479	**Brush and Spring,** inside Cap (418856)		1	
6060	**Rotor** (418726)		1	
9931	**Contact Set** (423153)		1	
6487	**Insulating Bush,** for Contact Breaker Lever (419950)		1	
C.11991	**Condenser** (423871)		1	
9932	**Terminal Assembly** (54413549)		1	
9933	**Insulating Washer,** for Terminal (161353)		1	
9934	**Earth Lead** (421088)		1	
9967	**Springs,** Auto Advance (54415561)		1 set	
9936	**Weight,** Auto Advance (54413922)		2	
6497	**Return Spring,** for Vacuum Unit (419086)		1	
9969	**Vacuum Unit** (54415894)		1	
9938	**Oil Seal** (188639)		1	
9253	**Driving Dog** (420620)		1	
C.18916	**Lucar Blade,** for connection of "CB" Lead from Coil (199279)		1	
C.2607	**Cable Sleeve,** for Distributor Cables (14965)		7	

Part No.	Description	Plate No.	No. per Unit	Remarks
C.12336	**SUCTION PIPE FOR DISTRIBUTOR VACUUM UNIT**	51–23	1	Fitted from Engine No. R.1001 to R.9999. RA.1001 to RA.1381.
C.21576	**SUCTION PIPE FOR DISTRIBUTOR VACUUM UNIT**		1	Fitted to Engine No. RA.1382 and subs.
C.21573	**Neoprene Elbow,** connecting Suction Pipe to Vacuum Unit		1	
C.17468	**PETROL PUMP ASSEMBLY** (78388/A-2.FP)	51–24	1	
8569	**End Plate** (771373)		1	
8570	**Impeller and Driving Peg** (54713567)		1	
8571	**Valve Cover** (771408)		1	
8572	**Ball,** for Valve (771333)		1	
8573	**Spring,** behind Ball (771387)		1	
8574	**Grommet,** for Pump mounting (771391)		2	
C.17570	**Outlet Union** (771390)		1	
C.18919	**Washer** (Fibre) on Outlet Union		1	Fitted from Chassis No. 850001 to 850091. 875001 to 875385. 860001 to 860004. 885001 to 885020.
8809	**Petroflex Pipe,** around Electrical Cables (54714650)		1	
8811	**Fibre Washer,** at fixings of Petroflex Pipe (54140054)		2	
8810	**Locknut,** securing Petroflex Pipe to Pump Mounting Bracket (54130820)		1	
8812	**Banjo Bolt,** securing Petrol Pipe to Inlet side of Pump (54710343)		1	
8813	**Washer,** at each side of Banjo (54148514)		2	
UFB.125/8R	**Bolt,** securing Petrol Pump to Mounting Bracket		2	
C.8667/1	**Nut,** Self-Locking, on Bolts		2	
FW.104/T	**Washer,** Plain, under Nuts		2	
C.17499	**Bracket Assembly,** for mounting of Petrol Pump	51–25	1	
C.19919	**PETROL PUMP ASSEMBLY** (78387/D-2.FP)		1	
8569	**End Plate** (771373)		1	
8570	**Impeller and Driving Peg** (54713567)		1	
8571	**Valve Cover** (771408)		1	
8572	**Ball,** for Valve (771333)		1	
9978	**Spring,** behind Ball (54714439)		1	
8574	**Grommet,** for Pump Mounting (771391)		2	Fitted to Chassis No. 850092 and subs. 875386 and subs. 860005 and subs. 885021 and subs.
8809	**Petroflex Pipe,** around Electrical Cables (54714610)		1	
8811	**Fibre Washer** at fixing of Petroflex Pipe (54140054)		2	
8810	**Locknut,** securing Petroflex Pipe to Pump Mounting Bracket (54130820)		1	
C.18952	**Special Washer,** for Pump Mounting		2	
C.18953	**Special Washer,** for Pump Mounting		2	
C.8667/1	**Self-Locking Nut,** securing Pump		2	
C.18907	**Bracket Assembly,** for Mounting of Petrol Pump		1	
C.16051	**CONTROL BOX** (37304A/B-RB.310)	51–26	1	
7912	**Cover** (54380178)		1	Fitted from Chassis No. 850001 to 850091. 875001 to 875385. 860001 to 860004. 885001 to 885020.
8554	**Resistance** (54380858)		1	
8555	**Contact Set,** for Cut-out (335766)		1	
8556	**Contact Set,** for Voltage Regulator (335765)		1	
8557	**Contact Set,** for Current Regulator (335764)		1	

ELECTRICAL EQUIPMENT

Part No.	Description	Plate No.	No. per Unit	Remarks
C.18287	**CONTROL BOX (37331A/RB.340)**		1	Fitted to Chassis No.
8558	**Cover** (54381342)		1	850092 and subs.
8559	**Resistance,** Swamp, 55 ohms. (54380438)		1	875386 and subs.
8560	**Resistance,** Points, 40 ohms. (54380673)		1	860005 and subs.
				885021 and subs.
C.17102	**BRACKET ASSEMBLY FOR MOUNTING OF CONTROL BOX**	51–27	1	Fitted from Chassis No.
UFN.119/L	**Nut,** securing Bracket to Body		4	850001 to 850091.
C.723/A	**Washer,** Shakeproof, under Nuts		4	875001 to 875385.
				860001 to 860004.
UFS.125/4R	**Screw,** Set, securing Control Box to Bracket		3	885001 to 885020.
C.724	**Washer,** Shakeproof, on Setscrews		3	
C.18289	**BRACKET ASSEMBLY FOR MOUNTING OF CONTROL BOX**		1	Fitted to Chassis No.
UFN.119/L	**Nut,** securing Bracket to Body		4	850092 and subs.
C.723/A	**Washer,** Shakeproof, under Nuts		4	875386 and subs.
				860005 and subs.
UFS.119/9R	**Screw,** Set, securing Control Box to Bracket		3	885021 and subs.
C.16053	**FUSE BOX (54038032-4.FJ)**	51–28	3	
C.5638	**Fuse,** 35 amp (188218)		6	
8576	**Terminal Screw** (120650)		3	
C.17467	**FUSE BOX (54038010-4.FJ)**	51–28	1	
8577	**Fuse,** 5 amp (188206)		1	
C.13932	**Fuse,** 50 amp (188219)		1	
UFS.319/4H	**Screw,** Set, securing Fuse Boxes to Dash		4	
C.723/A	**Washer,** Shakeproof, on Setscrews		4	
	CONNECTOR AND TERMINAL BLOCKS			
C.2532	**Connector Block** (37082/A-TB.8)	51–29	1	
3571	**Connector Block,** for Screen Wiper Cable (850832)	51–30	1	
3586	**Connector Block,** for Screen Wiper Cable (900288)	51–31	1	
C.18346	**Terminal Block,** for Petrol Pump Harness	51–32	1	
C.17435	**Fixing Strap,** for Screen Wiper Connector Block		1	
BD.711/3	**Screw,** Self-Tapping, securing Strap		2	
C.2796	**Bracket,** for Connector Block fixing		1	
UCN.113/L	**Nut,** securing Bracket and Connector Blocks		4	
C.721	**Washer,** Shakeproof, under Nuts		4	
UCN.119/L	**Nut,** securing Petrol Pump Connector Block		2	
AW.102/T	**Washer,** Plain, under Nuts		2	

Part No.	Description	Plate No.	No. per Unit	Remarks
C.16257	**INSTRUMENT PANEL ASSEMBLY**	52– 1	1	
C.18555	**Face Panel,** for Instrument Panel	52– 2	1	Fitted from Chassis No. 850001 to 850609. 875001 to 878301. 860001 to 860912. 885001 to 887131.
C.20740	**Face Panel,** for Instrument Panel		1	Fitted to Chassis No. 850610 and subs. 878302 and subs. 860913 and subs. 887132 and subs.
UFS.419/2H	**Screw,** Set, for fixing of Cable Clips		3	
C.723/A	**Washer,** Shakeproof, on Setscrews		3	
UCN.116/L	**Nut,** for fixing of Switches, Fuel Indicator Plate and Earth Connections		6	
BD.541/29	**Washer,** Plain, under Nuts		6	
C.722	**Washer,** Shakeproof, under Nuts		6	
C.17473	**Fuse Indicator Plate**		1	
C.15785	**Fixing Screw,** for Instrument Panel		2	
BD.5453	**Fibre Washer,** on Fixing Screws		2	
C.16258	**Pivot Screw,** for Instrument Panel		2	
C.782	**Fibre Washer,** under Head of Pivot Screws		2	
C.16318	**Nylon Bush,** on Pivot Screws		2	
C.15289	**LIGHT FILTER FOR INDICATOR STRIP**	52– 3	1	
C.15916	**CHROME FINISHER AT TOP OF INDICATOR STRIP**	52– 4	1	
C.15609	**INDICATOR STRIP, AT BOTTOM OF INSTRUMENT PANEL, DETAILING SWITCH POSITIONS (54850103)**	52– 5	1	**R.H. DRIVE CARS ONLY.**
C.15610	**INDICATOR STRIP, AT BOTTOM OF INSTRUMENT PANEL, DETAILING SWITCH POSITIONS (54850104)**		1	**L.H. DRIVE CARS ONLY.**
BD.17503/2	**Screw,** Self-Tapping, securing Indicator Strip		4	
C.15787	**Bulb** (2 watt Lilliput) illuminating Indicator Strip		3	
C.15454	**IGNITION SWITCH (31962/A-S.45)**	52– 6	1	
9401	**Locking Ring** (Chrome) (54130301)		1	
BD.10610	**Barrel,** for Ignition Switch (WB.1/6545)	52– 7	1	
C.15667	**Adaptor Plate,** for fixing of Ignition Switch (54332197)	52– 8	1	
C.20239	**LOCK AND IGNITION SWITCH ASSEMBLY (NEIMAN) ON STEERING COLUMN**		1	**EXPORT GERMANY.** Fitted from Chassis No. 876665 to 878036. 885567 to 886753.

ELECTRICAL EQUIPMENT

Part No.	Description	Plate No.	No. per Unit	Remarks
C.20171	**LOCK AND IGNITION SWITCH ASSEMBLY (WASO WERKEN) ON STEERING COLUMN**		1	**EXPORT GERMANY.** Fitted to Chassis No. 878037 and subs. 886754 and subs. **IF REQUIRED MAY BE** Fitted to Chassis No. 850588 and subs. 878037 and subs. 860863 and subs. 886754 and subs. **IRRESPECTIVE OF COUNTRY**
C.18188	**ROAD LIGHTS SWITCH (34382/A-PRS.7)**	52– 9	1	
C.15449	**Escutcheon,** for Road Lights Switch (54850094)	52–10	1	
C.15452	**Hollow Bolt,** securing Escutcheon (54332269)	52–11	1	
C.15451	**Nut,** on Bolt (156574)	52–12	1	
C.15928	**Washer,** under Nut (154604)	52–13	1	
C.15450	**LEVER, OPERATING ROAD LIGHTS SWITCH (54332270)**	52–14	1	
C.17513/1	**Sleeve** (Plastic) for Lever		1	
C.16072	**STARTER SWITCH (34263/A-SS.5)**	52–15	1	
C.15455	**PANEL LIGHTS SWITCH (31963/A-57.SA)**	52–16	1	
C.15589	**HEATER FAN SWITCH (31960/A-57.SA)**	52–17	1	
C.15456	**WINDSCREEN WIPER SWITCH (31966/A-79.SA)**	52–18	1	
C.15759	**WINDSCREEN WASHER SWITCH (31984/A-65.SA)**	52–19	1	
C.15760	**MAP LIGHT SWITCH (31963/A-65.SA)**	52–20	1	

Part No.	Description	Plate No.	No. per Unit	Remarks
C.15760	**INTERIOR LIGHT SWITCH** (31963/A-65.SA)	52–21	1	
C.15457	**AMMETER (36262/A-CZU.60)**	52–22	1	
8057	**Connector** (Lucar "M" Large) (199317)		2	
8058	**Connector** (Lucar "M" Small) (199275)		2	
987	**Bulb,** illuminating Ammeter (987)		1	
C.16897	**Bulb Holder** (54947338)		1	
C.16896	**PETROL GAUGE (BF.2200/01)**	52–23	1	
987	**Bulb,** for illumination of Petrol Gauge (987)		1	
C.16897	**Bulb Holder** (54947338)		1	
C.15473	**OIL PRESSURE GAUGE (PE.2300/01)**	52–24	1	**SUPERSEDED BY C.18641.**
C.18641	**OIL PRESSURE GAUGE (PE.2300/02)**		2	**SUPERSEDES C.15473.**
C.15474	**Electric Element,** for Oil Pressure Gauge (PT.1801/06)	52–25	1	
C.15288	**Lucar Blade,** for cable connection to Oil Pressure Gauge (54190107)	52–26	1	
987	**Bulb,** for illumination of Oil Pressure Gauge (987)		1	
C.16897	**Bulb Holder** (54947338)		1	
C.15471	**WATER TEMPERATURE GAUGE** (BT.2200/00)	52–27	1	**SUPERSEDED BY C.18640.**
C.18640	**WATER TEMPERATURE GAUGE** (BT.2200/01)		1	**SUPERSEDES C.15471.**
C.16895	**Electric Element,** for Water Temperature Gauge (TT.4201/00)	52–28	1	
C.2296/1	**Copper Washer,** under Element	52–29	1	
987	**Bulb,** for illumination of Water Temperature Gauge		1	
C.16897	**Bulb Holder** (54947338)		1	
C.15485	**VOLTAGE CONTROL UNIT AT BACK OF INSTRUMENT PANEL (BR.1300/01)**	52–30	1	

ELECTRICAL EQUIPMENT

Part No.	Description	Plate No.	No. per Unit	Remarks
C.17110	**SPEEDOMETER (SN.6322/00)** (CALIBRATED IN MILES)	52–31	1	**FOR USE WITH 3.31 : 1 FINAL DRIVE RATIO.**
C.17111	**SPEEDOMETER (SN.6322/01)** (CALIBRATED IN KILOS)		1	**FOR USE WITH 3.31 : FINAL DRIVE RATIO. NOT FOR GERMANY OR ITALY.**
C.17112	**SPEEDOMETER (SN.6322/02)** (CALIBRATED IN KILOS)		1	**FOR USE WITH 3.31 : 1 FINAL DRIVE RATIO ON CARS EXPORTED TO GERMANY AND ITALY.**
C.17113	**SPEEDOMETER (SN.6322/03)** (CALIBRATED IN MILES)	52–31	1	**FOR USE WITH 3.54 : 1 FINAL DRIVE RATIO.**
C.17114	**SPEEDOMETER (SN.6322/04)** (CALIBRATED IN KILOS)		1	**FOR USE WITH 3.54 : 1 FINAL DRIVE RATIO. NOT FOR GERMANY OR ITALY.**
C.17115	**SPEEDOMETER (SN.6322/05)** (CALIBRATED IN KILOS)		1	**FOR USE WITH 3.54 : 1 FINAL DRIVE RATIO ON CARS EXPORTED TO GERMANY AND ITALY.**
C.17116	**SPEEDOMETER (SN.6322/06)** (CALIBRATED IN MILES)	52–31	1	**FOR USE WITH 2.93 : 1 FINAL DRIVE RATIO.**
C.17117	**SPEEDOMETER (SN.6322/07)** (CALIBRATED IN KILOS)		1	**FOR USE WITH 2.93 : 1 FINAL DRIVE RATIO. NOT FOR GERMANY OR ITALY.**
C.17118	**SPEEDOMETER (SN.6322/08)** (CALIBRATED IN KILOS)		1	**FOR USE WITH 2.93 : 1 FINAL DRIVE RATIO ON CARS EXPORTED TO GERMANY AND ITALY.**
C.18970	**SPEEDOMETER (SN.6322/09)** (CALIBRATED IN MILES)	52–31	1	**FOR USE WITH 3.07 : 1 FINAL DRIVE RATIO.**
C.18971	**SPEEDOMETER (SN.6322/10)** (CALIBRATED IN KILOS)		1	**FOR USE WITH 3.07 : 1 FINAL DRIVE RATIO. NOT FOR GERMANY OR ITALY.**

NOTE : To ensure that the correct Speedometer is supplied by Jaguar Spares Division IT IS IMPORTANT WHEN ORDERING, to quote the number printed on the dial of the displaced instrument.

On some specially calibrated instruments, the number is printed on the back of the Speedometer casing.

Part No.	Description	Plate No.	No. per Unit	Remarks
C.18972	**SPEEDOMETER (SN.6322/11)** (CALIBRATED IN KILOS)		1	FOR USE WITH 3.07 : 1 FINAL DRIVE RATIO. ON CARS EXPORTED TO GERMANY AND ITALY.
C.15468	**REMOTE CONTROL OPERATING TRIP MILEAGE RECORDER ON SPEEDOMETER (41-741-152-01/9)**	52–32	1	
8409	**Screwed Escutcheon,** securing Remote Control at winding end		1	
987	**BULB (2.2 WATT M.E.S.) FOR ILLUMINATION OF SPEEDOMETER AND FOR IGNITION, LOW FUEL CONTENTS AND HEADLAMP MAIN BEAM WARNING LIGHTS (987)**		5	
C.16898	**Holder,** for Speedometer Illumination Bulbs (54360731)		2	
C.17434	**FLEXIBLE SPEEDOMETER CABLE COMPLETE (DF.1110/00/60)**	52–33	1	
8681	**Inner Cable only (DI.1110/00/60)**		1	
8682	**Outer Cable only (DO.1110/00/60)**		1	
C.17087	**RIGHT ANGLE GEARBOX FOR SPEEDOMETER CABLE DRIVE (BG.2402/02)**	52–34	1	
C.16075	**REV. COUNTER AND CLOCK (RV.7403/02)**	52–35	1	Fitted from Chassis No. 850001 to 850288. 875001 to 876116. 860001 to 860028. 885001 to 885205.
8879	**Rev. Counter less Clock** (RV.7403/03)		1	
8260	**Electric Clock only** (CE.1111/00)		1	
C.20085	**REV. COUNTER AND CLOCK (RV.7413/03)**		1	Fitted to Chassis No. 850289 and subs. 876117 and subs. 860029 and subs. 885206 and subs.
8985	**Rev. Counter less Clock** (RV.7413/04)		1	
8260	**Electric Clock only** (RV.1111/00)		1	
987	**Bulb** (2.2 watt M.E.S.) for illumination of Rev. Counter (987)		2	
C.16898	**Bulb Holder** (54360731)		2	

ELECTRICAL EQUIPMENT

Part No.	Description	Plate No.	No. per Unit	Remarks
C.14996	**GENERATOR FOR ELECTRIC REV. COUNTER (TV.1100/00)**	52–36	1	
9993	**Connector Moulding Assembly** (41-161-105-00)		1	
9994	**Gasket,** under Moulding (31-754-707)		1	
AS.306/2.5H	**Setscrew,** securing Moulding (30-232-089-11)		2	
AG.106/X	**Washer,** Spring, on Setscrews (30-282-010-11)		2	
C.17487	**REMOTE CONTROL FOR CLOCK ON REV. COUNTER (41-741-127-04)**	52–37	1	
8409	**Screwed Escutcheon,** securing Remote Control at winding end		1	
C.16079	**THERMOSTATIC CIGAR LIGHTER COMPLETE (EL.2414/00)**	52–38	1	Fitted from Chassis No. 850001 to 850168. 875001 to 875589.
C.16079/1	**Body only**		1	860001 to 860009.
C.5631/2	**Element**		1	885001 to 885050.
C.18638	**THERMOSTATIC CIGAR LIGHTER COMPLETE**		1	
				Fitted to Chassis No.
C.18638/1	**Body only**		1	850169 and subs.
C.18638/2	**Element**		1	875590 and subs.
C.18638/3	**Clamping Shell,** for Cigar Lighter		1	860010 and subs.
				885051 and subs.
C.15288	**Lucar Blade,** for Cigar Lighter connection (54190107)		1	
C.18916	**Lucar Blade,** for Cigar Lighter connection (199279)		1	
C.16367	**SWITCH, BEHIND DOOR HINGES, OPERATING MAP LIGHT ABOVE INSTRUMENT PANEL**	52–39	2	
C.17337	**HEADLAMP DIPPER SWITCH ON FACIA PANEL (80603/J)**	52–40	1	
C.20305	**ESCUTCHEON FOR HEADLAMP DIPPER SWITCH**	52–41	1	
C.18981	**SIDELAMP WARNING LIGHT (38232/A-WL.13)**		1	**FOR CARS EXPORTED TO ITALY.**
8826	**Shade** (319222)		1	
8827	**Cover and Window Assembly** (54360905)		1	
8828	**Bulbholder** (54360731)		1	
987	**Bulb** (987)		1	

Part No.	Description	Plate No.	No. per Unit	Remarks
C.16927	**DIRECTION INDICATOR WARNING LIGHT ASSEMBLY (38221/A-5.WL)**	52–42	1	
8641	**Window** (54334281)		1	
8642	**Body** (54334280)		1	
987	**Bulb,** for Warning Light (987)		2	
C.16661	**WARNING LIGHT INDICATING HANDBRAKE "ON" POSITION AND LEVEL IN BRAKE FLUID CONTAINERS (38220/A-WL.3/1)**	52–43	1	
8096	**Cover and Window** (318896)		1	
8638	**Lucar Blade,** for Cable connection (54190096)		1	
8639	**Insulator,** for Blade (54360574)		1	
8640	**Lucar Blade,** for Cable connection (54190574)		1	
987	**Bulb** (987)		1	
C.19637	**ESCUTCHEON FOR HANDBRAKE AND FLUID LEVEL WARNING LIGHT**	52–44	1	
C.16660	**SWITCH, OPERATING HANDBRAKE AND FLUID LEVEL WARNING LIGHT (31893/A-12.SA)**	52–45	1	
UFN.125/L	**Nut,** securing Switch		2	
C.11724	**CHOKE CONTROL WARNING LIGHT ASSEMBLY (38147/A-WL.13)**	52–46	1	
6808	**Bulb Holder** (554734)		1	
987	**Bulb** (2.2 watt) (987)		1	
6806	**Cover** (319306)		1	
6807	**Window** (319305)		1	
6809	**Terminal Screw** (100521)		1	
6810	**Washer,** for Terminal Screw (185012)		1	
C.16899	**Distance Piece,** at Choke Warning Light mounting		1	
C.16660	**SWITCH, OPERATING CHOKE CONTROL WARNING LIGHT (31893/A-12.SA)**	52–47	1	
UFN.125/L	**Nut,** securing Switch		2	
C.17328	**ESCUTCHEON FOR CHOKE CONTROL LEVER**	52–48	1	

Part No.	Description	Plate No.	No. per Unit	Remarks
BD.11802	**PLATE ("COLD" "HOT" "RUN") FOR CHOKE CONTROL LEVER**	52–49	1	
UFN.119/L	**Nut,** securing Escutcheon, Plate and Mounting Bracket to Facia		2	
C.723/A	**Washer,** Shakeproof, under Nuts		2	
C.17909	**LEVER, OPERATING CHOKE CONTROL**	52–50	1	
C.17908	**Quadrant Plate,** between Lever and Mounting Bracket	52–51	1	
UFS.125/4R	**Screw,** Set, securing Quadrant Plate to Mounting Bracket		1	
UFN.125/L	**Nut,** on Setscrew		1	
C.724	**Washer,** Shakeproof, under Nut		1	
BD.11489	**Ball Bearing,** between Lever and Quadrant Plate	52–52	1	
C.17910	**Leaf Spring,** applying tension to Ball Bearing	52–53	1	
C.17911	**Pivot Bolt,** for Choke Control Lever		1	
C.8737/2	**Nut,** Self-Locking, on Pivot Bolt		1	
FW.105/T	**Washer,** Plain, under Nut		1	
C.17912	**Knob,** on Control Lever	52–54	1	
UCS.311/2H	**Screw,** Set, securing Knob to Lever		1	
C.17928	**BRACKET, MOUNTING CHOKE CONTROL LEVER**	52–55	1	
UFB.131/12R	**Bolt,** securing Mounting Bracket to Facia Bracket		1	
C.17366	**Distance Piece,** on Bolt		1	
UFN.131/L	**Nut,** on Bolt		1	
FG.105/X	**Washer,** Spring, under Nut		1	
C.18126	**INNER CABLE, OPERATING CHOKE LINKAGE ON CARBURETTERS**	52–56	1	
BD.11721	**Pin,** securing Cable to Operating Lever	52–57	1	
UCS.113/2R	**Screw,** Set, clamping Cable in Pin		1	
C.8667/20	**Nut,** Self-Locking, securing Pin to Operating Lever		1	
AW.104/T	**Washer,** Plain, under Self-Locking Nut		1	
C.18125	**OUTER CASING FOR OPERATING CABLE**	52–58	1	
C.18127	**Insulating Sleeve,** on Outer Casing	52–59	2	
C.15998	**PIVOT FOR OUTER CASING**	52–60	1	
UFS.119/4R	**Screw,** Set, securing Pivot		1	
C.5203/1	**Washer,** Special, on Setscrew		1	
BD.1708/2	**Washer,** Double Coil Spring, on Setscrew		1	
BD.11524	**Grommet,** for Outer Casing through Dash	52–61	1	

Part No.	Description	Plate No.	No. per Unit	Remarks
C.16077	**PETROL TANK ELEMENT UNIT** (TF.1104/051)	52–62	1	
C.937	**Gasket,** for Element Unit	52–63	1	
C.15288	**Lucar Blade,** for Element Unit earth (54190107)		1	
C.16056	**HEADLAMP, COMPLETE** (58662/B-PL.700)		2	**R.H. DRIVE CARS ONLY.**
8077	**Plate,** retaining Light Unit (554179)	53– 1	2	
8595	**Rim,** seating Light Unit (54520552)	53– 2	2	
8173	**Spring,** retaining Seating Rim (554180)	53– 3	6	
8596	**Screw,** securing Light Unit (186194)		6	
8597	**Light Unit** (556599)	53– 4	2	
7765	**Spring,** retaining Bulb (556442)	53– 5	2	
7764	**Bulb Adaptor** (553738)	53– 6	2	
8518	**Bulb** (416) (60/36 watt Clear)	53– 7	2	
8599	**Trimmer Screw,** for beam adjustment (554182)	53– 8	4	
8600	**Spring,** on Trimmer Screw (554202)	53– 9	4	
8598	**Gasket,** for Headlamp Body (554227)	53–10	2	
C.16057	**HEADLAMP, COMPLETE** (58663/B-PL.700)		2	**L.H. DRIVE CARS ONLY, EXCEPT COUNTRIES SPECIALLY LISTED ON PAGES 289 AND 290.**
8610	**Light Unit** (54520293)		2	
8611	**Bulb** (417) (60/36 watt Clear)		2	
	All other items are as for Headlamp **C.16056**			
C.16058	**HEADLAMP, COMPLETE** (58664/B-F.700)		2	**FOR EXPORT TO EUROPE, EXCEPT COUNTRIES SPECIALLY LISTED BELOW.**
7762	**Light Unit** (556452)		2	
7763	**Bulb** (410) (45/40 watt Clear)		2	
	All other items are as for Headlamp **C.16056**			
C.16795	**HEADLAMP, COMPLETE** (58665/B-F.700)		2	**FOR EXPORT TO FRANCE.**
7762	**Light Unit** (556452)		2	
8612	**Bulb** (411) (45/40 watt Yellow)		2	
	All other items are as for Headlamp **C.16056**			
C.16797	**HEADLAMP, COMPLETE** (58667/B-F.700)		2	**FOR EXPORT TO AUSTRIA.**
8613	**Light Unit** (54520883)		2	
7763	**Bulb** (410) (45/40 watt Clear)		2	
	All other items are as for Headlamp **C.16056**			

ELECTRICAL EQUIPMENT

Part No.	Description	Plate No.	No. per Unit	Remarks
C.16796	**HEADLAMP, COMPLETE** (58666/B-F.700)		2	**FOR EXPORT TO SWEDEN.**
8680	**Light Unit** (54520148)		2	
7763	**Bulb** (410) (45/40 watt Clear)		2	
	All other items are as for Headlamp C.16056			
C.16059	**HEADLAMP, COMPLETE** (58439/D-F.700)		2	**FOR EXPORT TO U.S.A.**
	All details are as for Headlamp C.16056, except that LIGHT UNIT, RETAINING SPRING AND BULB ARE NOT SUPPLIED FOR U.S.A.			
UFS.319/3H	**Screw,** Set, securing Headlamps		8	
C.723/A	**Washer,** Shakeproof, on Setscrews		8	
C.16080	**R.H. SIDE/FLASHER LAMP** (WHITE/AMBER) (52517/A-652)		1	**NOT REQUIRED FOR U.S.A.**
8604	**Lens** (54572374)	53–11	1	
8605	**Bezel** (54571889)	53–12	1	
8606	**Screw,** securing Lens (106871)	53–13	3	
6524	**Washer,** retaining Screws (161385)	53–14	3	
8607	**Gasket,** sealing Lens (54571885)	53–15	1	
3455	**Bulbholder,** Sidelamp (553780)		1	
989	**Sidelamp Bulb** (989)	53–16	1	
6538	**Bulbholder,** Flasher (573832)		1	
C.9126	**Flasher Bulb** (382)	53–17	1	
8615	**Base** (54571965)	53–18	1	
8614	**Gasket,** seating Lamp (54572030)	53–19	1	
C.16081	**L.H. SIDE/FLASHER LAMP** (WHITE/AMBER) (52465/A-652)		1	**NOT REQUIRED FOR U.S.A.**
8609	**Base** (54572000)		1	
8608	**Gasket,** seating Lamp (54572031)		1	
	All other items are as for Lamp C.16080			
C.16082	**R.H. SIDE/FLASHER LAMP** (WHITE/WHITE) (52519/A-652)		1	**FOR EXPORT TO U.S.A.**
8616	**Lens** (54572375)		1	
	All other items are as for Lamp C.16080			

Part No.	Description	Plate No.	No. per Unit	Remarks
C.16083	**L.H. SIDE/FLASHER LAMP** **(WHITE/WHITE) (52518/A-652)**		1	**FOR EXPORT TO U.S.A.**
8616	**Lens** (54572375)		1	
8609	**Base** (54572000)		1	
8608	**Gasket,** seating Lamp (54572031)		1	
	All other items are as for Lamp C.16080			
UFS.319/4H	**Screw,** Set, securing Side/Flasher Lamps		2	
UFS.319/7H	**Screw,** Set, securing Side/Flasher Lamps		4	
BD.18957/3	**Distance Piece** (½" long) on Setscrews		4	
AG.102/X	**Washer,** Spring, on Setscrews		4	
C.16084	**R.H. STOP/TAIL/FLASHER LAMP** **(RED/AMBER) (53866/A-651)**		1	**OPEN CARS ONLY.** **NOT REQUIRED FOR U.S.A.**
8617	**Lens** (54572372)	53–20	1	
8619	**Chrome Strip,** over joint in Lens (54571936)	53–21	1	
8606	**Screw,** securing Lens (106871)	53–22	2	
6524	**Washer,** retaining Screws (161385)	53–23	2	
8620	**Gasket,** seating Lens (54571934)	53–24	1	
6538	**Interior Bulb Holder,** Flasher (573832)		1	
C.9126	**Bulb,** Flasher (382)	53–25	1	
5311	**Interior Bulb Holder,** Stop/Tail (573828)		1	
C.9125	**Bulb,** Stop/Tail (380)	53–26	1	
8084	**Reflex Reflector** (574914)	53–27	1	
8621	**Rubber Spacer,** seating Reflector (54572032)	53–28	1	
8622	**Bracket,** supporting Reflector (54571938)	53–29	1	
8623	**Screw,** securing Support Bracket (198946)	53–30	2	
8627	**Base** (54571939)	53–31	1	
8626	**Gasket,** seating Lamp (54571935)	53–32	1	
C.16085	**L.H. STOP/TAIL/FLASHER LAMP** **(RED/AMBER) (53820/A-651)**		1	**OPEN CARS ONLY.** **NOT REQUIRED FOR U.S.A.**
8625	**Base** (54572040)		1	
8624	**Gasket,** seating Lamp (54572062)		1	
	All other items are as for Lamp C.16084			
C.16086	**R.H. STOP/TAIL/FLASHER LAMP** **(RED/RED) (53868/A-651)**		1	**FITTED TO OPEN CARS EXPORTED TO U.S.A.**
8512	**Lens** (54572373)		1	
	All other items are as for Lamp C.16084			

ELECTRICAL EQUIPMENT

Part No.	Description	Plate No.	No. per Unit	Remarks
C.16087	**L.H. STOP/TAIL/FLASHER LAMP (RED/RED)** (53867/A-651)		1	**FITTED TO OPEN CARS EXPORTED TO U.S.A.**
8512	**Lens** (54572373)		1	
8625	**Base** (54572040)		1	
8624	**Gasket,** seating Lamp (54572062)		1	
	All other items are as for Lamp C.16084			
C.17931	**R.H. STOP/TAIL/FLASHER LAMP (RED/AMBER)** (53948/A-651)		1	
8785	**Base** (54572887)		1	
	All other items are as for Lamp C.16084			
				FIXED HEAD MODELS ONLY. NOT REQUIRED FOR U.S.A.
				Fitted from Chassis No. 860001 to 860478. 885001 to 886013.
C.17932	**L.H. STOP/TAIL/FLASHER LAMP (RED/AMBER)** (53947/A-651)		1	
8786	**Base** (54572888)		1	
	All other items are as for Lamp C.16084			
8624	**Gasket,** seating Lamp (54572062)		1	
C.19854	**R.H. STOP/TAIL/FLASHER LAMP (RED/AMBER)** (54128/A-651)		1	
9322	**Reflex Reflector** (54573735)		1	
9325	**Screw,** securing Support Bracket (54102090)		2	
9324	**Base** (54573952)		1	
	All other items are as for Lamp C.16084			
				FIXED HEAD MODELS ONLY. NOT REQUIRED FOR U.S.A.
				Fitted to Chassis No. 860479 and subs. 886014 and subs.
C.19855	**L.H. STOP/TAIL/FLASHER LAMP (RED/AMBER)** (54129/A-651)		1	
9322	**Reflex Reflector** (54573735)		1	
9325	**Screw,** securing Support Bracket (54102090)		2	
9323	**Base** (54573951)		1	
	All other items are as for Lamp C.16084			
8624	**Gasket,** seating Lamp (54572062)		1	

Part No.	Description	Plate No.	No. per Unit	Remarks
C.17933	**R.H. STOP/TAIL/FLASHER LAMP (RED/RED) (53950/A-651)**		1	
8512	**Lens** (54572373)		1	
8785	**Base** (54572887)		1	
	All other items are as for Lamp **C.16084**			
				REQUIRED FOR FIXED HEAD MODELS EXPORTED TO U.S.A.
C.17934	**L.H. STOP/TAIL/FLASHER LAMP (RED/RED) (53949/A-651)**		1	Fitted from Chassis No. 860001 to 860478. 885001 to 886013.
8512	**Lens** (54572373)		1	
8786	**Base** (54572888)		1	
	All other items are as for Lamp **C.16084**			
8624	**Gasket**, seating Lamp (54572062)		1	
C.19856	**R.H. STOP/TAIL/FLASHER LAMP (RED/RED) (54130/A-651)**		1	
8512	**Lens** (54572373)		1	
9322	**Reflex Reflector** (54573735)		1	
9325	**Screw**, securing Support Bracket (54102090)		2	
9324	**Base** (54573952)		1	
	All other items are as for Lamp **C.16084**			
				REQUIRED FOR FIXED HEAD MODELS EXPORTED TO U.S.A.
C.19857	**L.H. STOP/TAIL/FLASHER LAMP (RED/RED) (54131/A-651)**		1	Fitted to Chassis No. 860479 and subs. 886014 and subs.
8512	**Lens** (54572373)		1	
9322	**Reflex Reflector** (54573735)		1	
9325	**Screw**, securing Support Bracket (54102090)		2	
9323	**Base** (54573951)		1	
	All other items are as for Lamp **C.16084**			
8624	**Gasket**, seating Lamp (54572062)		1	
BD.20092/2	**Screw**, Set (½″ long) securing Stop/Tail/Flasher Lamps		2	
BD.20092/6	**Screw**, Set (1″ long) securing Stop/Tail/Flasher Lamps		4	
BD.18957/1	**Spacer**, on Setscrews		2	
AG.102/X	**Washer**, Spring, on Setscrews		6	
C.16063	**FLASHER UNIT (35011/A-FL.5)**	53–33	1	
UCS.313/8H	**Screw**, Set, securing Flasher Socket to Body		1	

ELECTRICAL EQUIPMENT

Part No.	Description	Plate No.	No. per Unit	Remarks
C.18219	**NUMBER PLATE ILLUMINATION LAMP (53993/A-L.705)**		2	
8771	**Body and Bulb Holder Assembly** (54573381)	53–34	2	
BD.1063	**Bulb** (207)	53–35	2	
8772	**Lens** (54570704)	53–36	2	
8773	**Gasket,** under Lens (54570706)	53–37	2	
8774	**Rim** (54570708)	53–38	2	
8775	**Shield** (54570705)	53–39	2	
8776	**Screw,** securing Rim (54111081)	53–40	2	
BD.15746	**Gasket,** under Number Plate Illumination Lamps	53–41	2	
BD.711/23	**Screw,** Self-Tapping, securing Lamps		4	
C.722	**Washer,** Shakeproof, on Self-Tapping Screws		4	
C.18724	**REVERSE LAMP (52567/A-L.549)**		1	**NOT REQUIRED FOR FRANCE.**
8714	**Lens** (576223)	53–42	1	
8715	**Rim,** for Lens (576227)	53–43	1	
8716	**Gasket,** seating Lens (576228)	53–44	1	
8718	**Screw,** securing Lens (54111011)	53–45	2	
6524	**Washer,** retaining Screws (161385)	53–46	2	
6538	**Bulbholder** (573832)		1	
C.9126	**Bulb** (382)	53–47	1	
8064	**Terminal Sleeve** (555910)		1	
8719	**Grommet,** Cable entry (54572247)	53–48	1	
8720	**Body** (54570992)	53–49	1	
8717	**Gasket,** seating Lamp (576229)	53–50	1	
C.18844	**REVERSE LAMP (52570/A-L.595)**		1	**FOR EXPORT TO FRANCE ONLY.**
8721	**Lens** (Amber) (54573097)		1	
	All other items are as for Reverse Lamp C.18724			
UFS.419/3H	**Screw,** Set, securing Reverse Lamp to Housing		2	
C.723/A	**Washer,** Shakeproof, on Setscrews		2	
BD.20754	**HOUSING ASSEMBLY, MOUNTING REVERSE LAMP TO BODY**		1	
BD.711/23	**Screw,** Self-Tapping, securing Housing to Body		2	
BD.8633/3	**Spire Nut,** on Self-Tapping Screws		2	
C.1083	**SWITCH, IN GEARBOX TOP COVER, OPERATING REVERSE LAMP** (31077/E-SS.10/1)	53–51	1	
C.4531	**Gasket,** under Switch (163682)	53–52	1	

Part No.	Description	Plate No.	No. per Unit	Remarks
C.17192	**HORN (LOW NOTE)** **(69087/A-WT.618/U)**	53–53	1	
5326	**Cover** (702575)		1	
8483	**Bracket** (707095)		1	
8484	**Contact Set** (702687)		1	
8485	**Diaphragm** (702836)		1	
				Fitted from Chassis No. 850001 to 850499. 875001 to 877154. 860001 to 860435. 885001 to 885970.
C.17193	**HORN (HIGH NOTE)** **(69090/A-WT.618/U)**	53–53	1	
8486	**Diaphragm** (702851)		1	
	All other items are as for Horn C.17192			
C.19080	**HORN (LOW NOTE)** **(69127/A-WT.618/U)**		1	
9979	**Cover** (54680655)		1	
8483	**Bracket** (707095)		1	
8484	**Contact Set** (702687)		1	
8485	**Diaphragm** (702836)		1	
				Fitted to Chassis No. 850500 and subs. 877155 and subs. 860436 and subs. 885971 and subs.
C.19081	**HORN (HIGH NOTE)** **(69128/A-WT.618/U)**		1	
8486	**Diaphragm** (702851)		1	
	All other items are as for Horn C.19080			
UFN.125/L	**Nut**, securing Horns		4	
C.724	**Washer**, Shakeproof, under Nuts		4	
C.17339	**Grommet**, in Horns, for Cable entry		2	
C.17338	**HORN RELAY (33209/B-6RA)**	53–54	1	
UFS.419/3H	**Screw**, Set, securing Horn Relay to L.H. Mudshield		2	
UFN.119/L	**Nut**, on Setscrews		2	
C.723/A	**Washer**, Shakeproof, on Setscrews		2	
AW.102/T	**Washer**, Plain, under Shakeproof Washers		2	
C.16070	**STEERING COLUMN HORN PUSH** **(33570A/B-CC.5)**	53–55	1	
8631	**Ring**, Knob retaining (54300576)		1	
8632	**Plate**, upper contact (54300575)		1	
8895	**Cover and Lower Contact Plate** **Assembly** (54300754)		1	
8633	**Medallion** (54300574)		1	

ELECTRICAL EQUIPMENT

Part No.	Description	Plate No.	No. per Unit	Remarks
C.16069	**DIRECTION INDICATOR/HEADLAMP FLASHER SWITCH (34361/A-37.SA)**	53–56	1	
8634	**Contact,** Warning Light (54333162)		1	
8635	**Contact Switch** (54332586)		1	
7523	**Spring,** pawl centring (348323)		1	
7521	**Fixing Clip** (54330333)		1	
8637	**Casing** (54333059)		1	
C.14307	**Cover Assembly** (comprising Front and Rear Covers)		1	
C.16451	**STRIKER FOR RETURN OF DIRECTION INDICATOR CONTROL TO NEUTRAL POSITION**		1	
C.14007/1	**Screw,** Set, securing Striker		2	
C.723/A	**Washer,** Shakeproof, on Setscrews		2	
C.3377	**Washer,** Plain, under Shakeproof Washers		2	
C.16452	**ELECTRIC MOTOR, DRIVING RADIATOR FAN (78378/B-3.GM)**	53–57	1	
8643	**Fixing Bolt** (54100606)		4	
8562	**Cover and Bearing,** Commutator End (745768)		1	
8563	**Brush Gear** (54713564)		1	
8564	**Armature** (54711120)		1	
8565	**Field Coil** (54712958)		1	
8566	**Bearing Bracket** (54712325)		1	
8567	**Dust Cover,** for Bearing Bracket (54713890)		1	
C.18110	**Grommet,** for mounting of Fan Motor (748843)	53–58	4	
C.18123	**Washer,** below Grommets (134710)		4	
C.8667/17	**Nut,** Self-Locking, securing Fan Motor		4	
C.18111	**Washer,** under Nuts (131670)		4	
C.18559	**THERMOSTAT, IN HEADER TANK, CONTROLLING FAN MOTOR**		1	
C.2475	**Gasket,** under Thermostat		1	
UFS.419/3H	**Screw,** Set, securing Thermostat		3	
BD.5453	**Fibre Washer,** on Setscrews		3	
C.18916	**Lucar Blade,** for Cable connection to Thermostat (199279)		1	
C.18122	**RELAY FOR FAN MOTOR (33232/A-6.RA)**	53–59	1	Fitted from Chassis No. 850001 to 850273. 875001 to 878020. 860001 to 861186. 885001 to 886748.
UFS.119/3R	**Screw,** Set, securing Relay to Header Tank Bracket		2	
UFN.119/L	**Nut,** on Setscrews		2	
C.723/A	**Washer,** Shakeproof, under Nuts		2	
AW.102/T	**Washer,** Plain, under Shakeproof Washers		2	
C.16062	**SWITCH, FOR OPERATION OF STOP LAMPS (31802/B-HL.2)**	53–60	1	

Part No.	Description	Plate No.	No. per Unit	Remarks
8575	**WINDSCREEN WIPER MOTOR ASSEMBLY (75403D-DL.3)**	53–61	1	**R.H. DRIVE CARS ONLY.**
8644	**Commutator End Cover,** with Bearing (743653)		1	
3509	**Brush Set** (729367)		1	
6551	**Spring,** tensioning Brushes (735631)		1	
7189	**Armature** (743929)		1	
8645	**Coil** (54713957)		1	
8646	**Shaft and Gear** (54713379)		1	
8643	**Bolt,** through fixing (54100606)		2	
8594	**WINDSCREEN WIPER MOTOR ASSEMBLY (75404D-DL.3)**		1	**L.H. DRIVE CARS ONLY.**
	For individual items, refer to Motor 8575			
BD.16718	**Gasket,** at Wiper mounting	53–62	1	
UFS.125/4R	**Screw,** Set, securing Wiper Motor		4	
C.724	**Washer,** Shakeproof, on Setscrews		4	
8660	**Plate,** securing Motor to Link Set (54711590)		1	
8661	**Rubber Seal,** for Plate (54711593)		1	
8670	**Cover,** over Cam Mechanism (54712745)		1	
8636	**WINDSCREEN WIPER LINK SET (54714605-DL.3)**	53–63	1	
8683	**Main Link Assembly** (54710388)		2	
8651	**Spindle Assembly,** L.H. (54710660)		1	
8652	**Spindle Assembly,** R.H. (54710383)		1	
8653	**Spindle Assembly,** centre (with switch) (54712765)		1	
8654	**Contact Switch** (54711260)		1	
5219	**Nut,** securing Spindles (153511)		3	
8655	**Front Bush** (745128)		3	
8656	**Rubber Washer,** under Front Bushes (744551)		3	
8657	**Rear Bush** (54710417)		3	
8658	**Mounting Bracket** (54710460)		3	
8659	**Mounting Strip** (54710461)		1	
8683	**MAIN LINK ASSEMBLY (54710388)**		2	
8684	**Snaplock Joint** (54714167)		2	
8650	**Locknut** (156610)		2	
8647	**ROTARY LINK (54710596)**		1	
8648	**PRIMARY LINK (54711297)**		1	
8684	**Snaplock Joint** (54714167)		1	
8650	**Locknut** (156610)		1	
8663	**ARM FOR WINDSCREEN WIPER (54712032)**	53–64	3	**R.H. DRIVE CARS ONLY.**

ELECTRICAL EQUIPMENT

Part No.	Description	Plate No.	No. per Unit	Remarks
8662	**ARM FOR WINDSCREEN WIPER** (54712033)		3	**L.H. DRIVE CARS ONLY.**
8664	**BLADE FOR WINDSCREEN WIPER ARMS** (54711281)	53–65	3	
C.15486	**MAP LIGHT** (52477/A-481)	53–66	1	
989	**Bulb** (989)		1	
8064	**Terminal Sleeve** (555910)		1	
BD.1814/2	**Pop Rivet,** securing Map Light		2	
C.17436	**Insulator,** for Map Light		1	
C.16498	**INTERIOR LIGHT** (56075/A-674)	53–67	1	
8602	**Lens** (54571954)		1	
8601	**Gasket,** seating Lens (54571955)		1	
8603	**Base** (54571956)		1	**FITTED ONLY TO OPEN MODELS.**
C.9126	**Bulb** (382)		1	
BD.1229/10	**Screw,** Self-Tapping, securing Interior Light		2	
C.1094	**Distance Washer,** on Self-Tapping Screws		2	
C.18347	**INTERIOR LIGHT** (60114)	53–68	1	
BD.14049/1	**Lens** (01601)		1	
8703	**Backplate and Bulbholder** (60114/A)		1	**FITTED ONLY TO FIXED HEAD MODELS.**
989	**Bulb** (6 watt M.B.C.) (01607)		2	
BD.540/3	**Screw,** Self-Tapping, securing Interior Light		2	Fitted from Chassis No. 860001 to 860478. 885001 to 886013.
BD.540/14	**Screw,** Self-Tapping, securing Interior Light		2	Fitted to Chassis No. 860479 and subs.
BD.8633/4	**Spire Nut,** on Self-Tapping Screw		2	886014 and subs.
C.17757	**INTERIOR MIRROR ASSEMBLY**	53–69	1	**REQUIRED ONLY FOR OPEN MODELS.**
C.17757/1	**Mounting Boss,** for Interior Mirror		1	
C.17757/2	**Mirror Head**		1	
C.18343	**INTERIOR MIRROR ASSEMBLY** (62572/A-608)	53–69A	1	**REQUIRED ONLY FOR FIXED HEAD MODELS** from Chassis No. 860001 to 861056.
8722	**Bracket,** for Mirror (59610206)		1	885001 to 888066.
BD.13642/5	**Screw,** Set, securing Interior Mirror		3	

Part No.	Description	Plate No.	No. per Unit	Remarks
C.20697	**INTERIOR MIRROR ASSEMBLY**		1	
C.20697/1	**Base only**		1	**REQUIRED ONLY FOR FIXED HEAD MODELS** at Chassis No.
C.16407/2	**Head only**		1	861057 and subs.
				888067 and subs.
C.20698	**Packing,** under Interior Mirror		1	
BD.13642/5	**Screw,** Set ($\frac{3}{4}$" long) securing Interior Mirror		1	
BD.13642/6	**Screw,** Set ($\frac{7}{8}$" long) securing Interior Mirror		2	
C.16061	**BATTERY (54028639-FRV.11/7A)**	53–70	1	
C.16473	**BATTERY TRAY**	53–71	1	
C.10640/2	**DRAIN TUBE FOR BATTERY TRAY (5" LONG)**	53–72	1	
C.16474	**BATTERY CLAMP**	53–73	1	
C.17083	**Rubber Pad,** under corners of Clamp		4	Fitted from Chassis No. 850001 to 850572. 875001 to 877660. 860001 to 860722. 885001 to 886381.
C.19740	**Rubber Pad,** under end of Clamp		2	Fitted from Chassis No. 850210 to 850572. 875761 to 877660. 860013 to 860722. 885086 to 886381. **May be fitted retrospectively if desired.**
C.19506	**Rubber Pad,** for Battery Clamp		2	Fitted to Chassis No. 850573 and subs. 877661 and subs. 860723 and subs. 886382 and subs.
C.16475	**ROD, THROUGH CLAMP SECURING BATTERY**	53–74	2	
C.17084	**Wing Nut,** on Rods	53–75	2	
FG.204/X	**Washer,** Spring, under Wing Nuts		2	
C.16923	**BATTERY CABLE (POSITIVE TO EARTH) (810707)**		1	**SUPERSEDED BY C.21517.**
C.21517	**BATTERY CABLE (POSITIVE TO EARTH) (810708)**		1	**SUPERSEDES C.16923.**

ELECTRICAL EQUIPMENT

Part No.	Description	Plate No.	No. per Unit	Remarks
C.16924	**BATTERY CABLE (NEGATIVE) (792908)**		1	
C.2609	**Screw,** securing Cables to Battery Posts (186111)		2	
6826	**Screw** (Oversize) securing Cables to Battery Posts (186114)		2	**REQUIRED ONLY WHEN HOLE IN BATTERY POST IS ENLARGED.**
C.16912	**FORWARD HARNESS (54947485)**		1	**R.H. DRIVE CARS ONLY.** Fitted from Chassis No. 850001 to 850273. 860001 to 861186.
C.20650	**FORWARD HARNESS (54932077)**		1	**R.H. DRIVE CARS ONLY.** Fitted to Chassis No. 850274 and subs. 861187 and subs.
C.17375	**FORWARD HARNESS (54948224)**		1	**L.H. DRIVE CARS ONLY.** Fitted from Chassis No. 875001 to 878020. 885001 to 886748.
C.20649	**FORWARD HARNESS (54932078)**		1	**L.H. DRIVE CARS ONLY.** Fitted to Chassis No. 878021 and subs. 886749 and subs.
C.16915	**R.H. BODY HARNESS (54947738)**		1	
C.17433	**L.H. BODY HARNESS (54947737)**		1	

Part No.	Description	Plate No.	No. per Unit	Remarks
C.16913	**INSTRUMENT PANEL HARNESS** (54947484)		1	**R.H. DRIVE CARS ONLY.**
C.16914	**INSTRUMENT PANEL HARNESS** (54948219)		1	**L.H. DRIVE CARS ONLY.**

ELECTRICAL CABLES

Part No.	Description	Plate No.	No. per Unit	Remarks
C.16911	**Cable,** Front Lamp connector (54947487)		1	Fitted from Chassis No. 850001 to 850499. 875001 to 877154. 860001 to 860435. 885001 to 885970.
C.20332	**Cable,** Front Lamp connector (54931440)		1	Fitted to Chassis No. 850500 and subs. 877155 and subs. 860436 and subs. 885971 and subs.
C.16917	**Cable,** Rev. Counter and Instrument Light connector (54947491)		1	
C.16920	**Cable,** Fluid Level Warning Light connector (54947480)		1	**R.H. DRIVE CARS ONLY.**
C.16922	**Cable,** Instrument Link (54947489)		1	
C.16925	**Cable,** Solenoid to Starter (54947496)		1	
C.18121	**Cable,** Radiator Fan Motor connector (54948340)		1	
C.17356	**Cable,** R.H. Sidelamp connector (54947494)		1	
C.17357	**Cable,** L.H. Sidelamp connector (54947495)		1	
C.17376	**Cable,** Heater Motor connector (54947486)		1	
C.17474	**Cable,** Interior Light connector (54948356)		1	**OPEN CARS ONLY.**
C.17475	**Cable,** Interior Light connector (54948216)		1	**FIXED HEAD CARS ONLY.**
C.18725	**Cable,** Reverse Lamp Switch connector (54949135)		1	
C.18728	**Cable,** Reverse Lamp connector (54949136)		1	
C.18982	**Cable,** Sidelamps Warning Light connector (54949797)		1	**REQUIRED FOR ITALY ONLY.**
C.21141	**Cable,** Starter Switch connector (54933183)		1	
C.20241	**Cable,** Steering Column Lock Connector to Instrument Panel Wiring		1	**GERMANY ONLY.** Fitted from Chassis No. 876665 to 878036. 885567 to 886753.
				IF REQUIRED Fitted to Chassis No. 850588 and subs. 878037 and subs. 860863 and subs. 886754 and subs.
C.16921	**CONNECTOR (8-PIN MALE) FOR FRONT LAMP HARNESS** (54947492)		1	
C.16997	**Fixing Plate Assembly,** for Male Connector		1	
UFS.125/3R	**Screw,** Set, securing Connector to Bonnet Diaphragm		3	
C.724	**Washer,** Shakeproof, on Setscrews		3	
C.17003	**Washer** (Sorbo) at Connector mounting		1	
C.18175	**Washer** (Hard Rubber) at Connector mounting		1	

ELECTRICAL EQUIPMENT

Part No.	Description	Plate No.	No. per Unit	Remarks
	EARTH CABLES			
C.16919	**Earth Cable,** from Engine to Body (54947493)		1	
C.16916	**Earth Cable,** for Instrument Panel (54947490)		1	
C.18699	**Earth Cable,** for Cigar Lighter		1	**FOR USE WITH CIGAR LIGHTER C.18638.**
C.18288	**Earth Cable,** for Control Box (54949797)		1	Fitted to Chassis No. 850092 and subs. 875386 and subs. 860005 and subs. 885021 and subs.
	EARTH CONNECTIONS AND FIXINGS			
C.15789	**Lucar Blade,** for Earth connection of Instrument Panel, Screen Washer, Screen Wiper and Brake Fluid Level Warning Light (54190038)		6	
C.5204	**Earth Terminal,** for Front Lamp Harness (860019)		2	
UFS.137/4R	**Screw,** Set, securing Battery Earth Cable		1	
UFN.137/L	**Nut,** on Setscrew		1	
FW.106/T	**Washer,** Plain, at Earth fixing		1	
C.726	**Washer,** Shakeproof, at Earth fixings		2	
UFS.419/3H	**Screw,** Set, securing Wiper Earth Connection		1	
UFS.419/4H	**Screw,** Set, securing Rear Lamp earth		2	
UFN.119/L	**Nut,** on Setscrews		2	
C.723/A	**Washer,** Shakeproof, under Nuts		2	
	CABLE SLEEVES			
C.2783	**Sleeve,** for Headlamp Cables (859300)		1	
C.18718	**Sleeve,** for Petrol Pump Harness		1	
	RUBBER GROMMETS			
C.2706	**Grommet,** for Interior Light Door Switch Cables, Screen Washer Tube, Headlamp Cable, Speedo Cable and Screen Wiper Park Cable (859059)	See remarks		**9 required for L.H. Drive Cars. 7 required for R.H. Drive Cars.**
C.2706	**Grommet,** for Body Harness through Boot Front Panel (859059)		2	**OPEN CARS ONLY.**
C.1426	**Grommet,** for Forward Harness through Dash (858066)		1	
C.2850	**Grommet,** for Heater Control Cables through Bulkhead and Reverse Lamp (859341)		5	
C.975	**Grommet,** for Body Harness and Number Plate Lamp Harness (54190324)		4	**OPEN CARS ONLY.**
C.975	**Grommet,** for Number Plate Lamp Harness (54190324)		2	**FIXED HEAD CARS ONLY.**
C.976	**Grommet,** for Speedo Cable through Inner Dash (858064)		1	**OPEN CARS ONLY.**
C.976	**Grommet,** for Speedo Cable through Inner Dash and for Body Harness in Rear Quarters (858064)		3	**FIXED HEAD CARS ONLY.**
C.977	**Grommet,** for Body Harness through wheel arch Diaphragms (858065)		2	**FIXED HEAD CARS ONLY.**
C.977	**Grommet,** for Number Plate Lamp Harness (858065)		2	**OPEN CARS ONLY.**
C.17432	**Grommet,** for Handbrake and Speedo Cables (836123)	See remarks		**1 required for L.H. Drive Cars. 2 required for R.H. Drive Cars.**
BD.11524	**Grommet,** for Fluid Level Warning Light Harness and Choke Control Cable	See remarks		**2 required for R.H. Drive Cars. 1 required for L.H. Drive Cars.**
C.8016	**Grommet,** for Fan Motor Harness		1	

Part No.	Description	Plate No.	No. per Unit	Remarks
	RUBBER PLUGS AND BOOTS			
C.4650	**Rubber Boot,** on Starter Motor and Solenoid Terminals (858266)		3	
C.5648	**Rubber Plug,** sealing hole for Screen Washer tubing		1	
C.5648	**Rubber Plug,** sealing hole for Speedo Cable		1	**R.H. DRIVE CARS ONLY.**
BD.14771	**Rubber Plug,** sealing hole for Speedo Cable		1	**L.H. DRIVE CARS ONLY.**
BD.4616	**Rubber Plug,** sealing hole for Brake Fluid Level Warning Light Harness		1	**L.H. DRIVE CARS ONLY.**
	CABLE STRAPPING			
C.17001	**Plastic Strapping,** securing Cables, etc., to Front Frame		1	
C.17002	**Stud,** for Strapping		42	
	CABLE CLIPS AND FIXINGS			
C.1040/1	**Clip,** securing Front Lamp Harness to Bonnet Sides (187079)		5	
C.1040/2	**Clip,** securing Forward Harness to Front Frame (187081)		1	
C.1040/2	**Clip,** securing Rear Lamp Harness (187081)		2	**OPEN CARS ONLY.**
C.1040/4	**Clip,** securing Forward Harness and Vacuum Hose (187085)		See remarks	**1 required for R.H. Drive Cars.** **4 required for L.H. Drive Cars.**
C.1040/5	**Clip,** securing Forward Harness at Heater Bracket (187044)		1	
C.1040/8	**Clip,** securing Reversing Lamp Harness and Speedo Cable (187047)		See remarks	**1 required for R.H. Drive Cars.** **2 required for L.H. Drive Cars.**
C.1040/9	**Clip,** securing Petrol Pipe to Frame, Rear Lamp Harness in Boot, Front Lamp Harness to R.H. side of Bonnet and R.H. Body Harness to Pedal Housing (187052)		6	
C.1040/12	**Clip,** securing Petrol Pipe to Reservac Tank (187042)		1	
C.1040/13	**Clip,** securing Hydraulic Pipes to Toe Board (851536)		1	
C.1040/13	**Clip,** securing Brake Fluid Level Warning Light Harness to Bulkhead (851536)		1	**R.H. DRIVE CARS ONLY.**
C.1040/14	**Clip,** securing Screen Washer Harness to Bulkhead and Side Lamp Harness to Bonnet (900402)		6	
C.1040/16	**Clip,** securing Panel Harness to Instrument Panel and Forward Harness to Pedal Housing (187005)		3	
C.1040/17	**Clip,** securing Rear Lamp Harness at L.H. side of Boot (187048)		1	
C.1040/18	**Clip,** securing Headlamp Harness to Bonnet sides (850358)		2	
C.1040/20	**Clip,** securing Radiator Duct Shield to Front Sub-Frame (187034)		3	
C.1040/24	**Clip,** securing Clutch Pipes and Vacuum Flexible Hose		See remarks	**1 required for R.H. Drive Cars.** **2 required for L.H. Drive Cars.**
C.18410	**Clip,** securing Forward Harness to Bonnet		1	
C.18128	**Clip,** securing Speedo Cable		1	**L.H. DRIVE CARS ONLY.**
C.17410	**Clip,** securing Speedo Cable		1	
UFS.131/4R	**Screw,** Set, securing Clip		1	**R.H. DRIVE CARS ONLY.**
UFN.131/L	**Nut,** on Setscrew		1	
C.725	**Washer,** Shakeproof, under Nut		1	

Part No.	Description	Plate No.	No. per Unit	Remarks
	CABLE CLIPS AND FIXINGS (continued)			
UFS.419/4H	**Screw,** Set, securing Harness Clips to Bonnet		8	
UFN.119/L	**Nut,** on Setscrews		8	
C.723/A	**Washer,** Shakeproof, under Nuts		8	
UFS.119/3R	**Screw,** Set, securing Body Harness Clip to Pedal Housing		1	
UFN.119/L	**Nut,** on Setscrew		1	
C.723/A	**Washer,** Shakeproof, under Nut		1	
UFS.413/4H	**Screw,** Set, securing Rear Lamp Harness Clips in Boot		4	
UFN.113/L	**Nut,** on Setscrews		4	
C.721	**Washer,** Shakeproof, under Nuts		4	
BD.711/12	**Screw,** Self-Tapping, securing Fluid Level Warning Light Harness Clips to Bulkhead		1	**R.H. DRIVE CARS ONLY.**

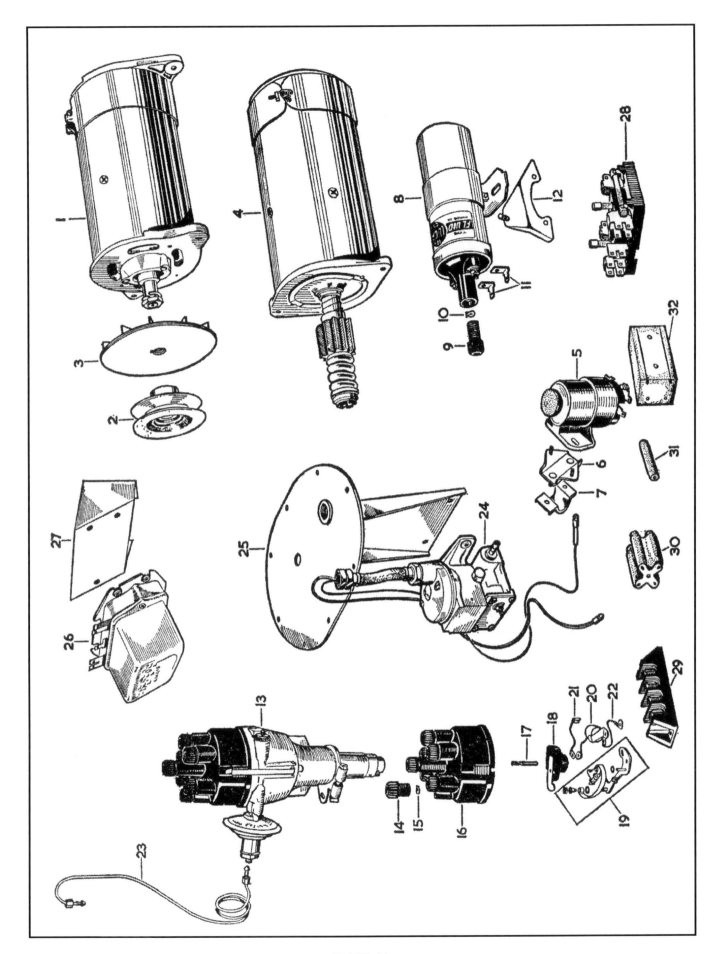

PLATE 51

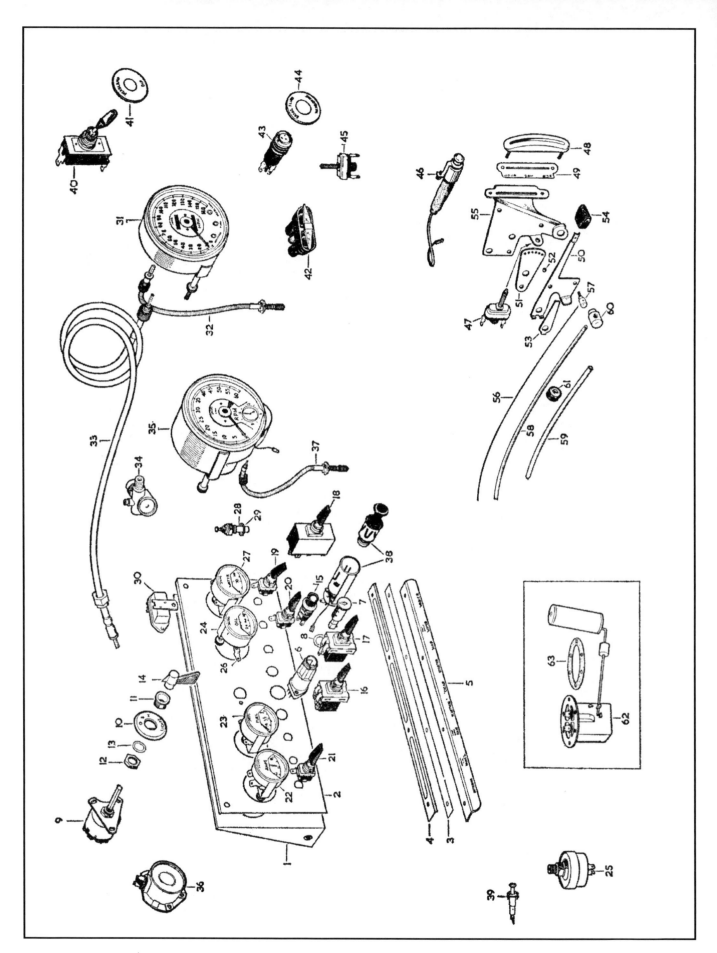

PLATE 52

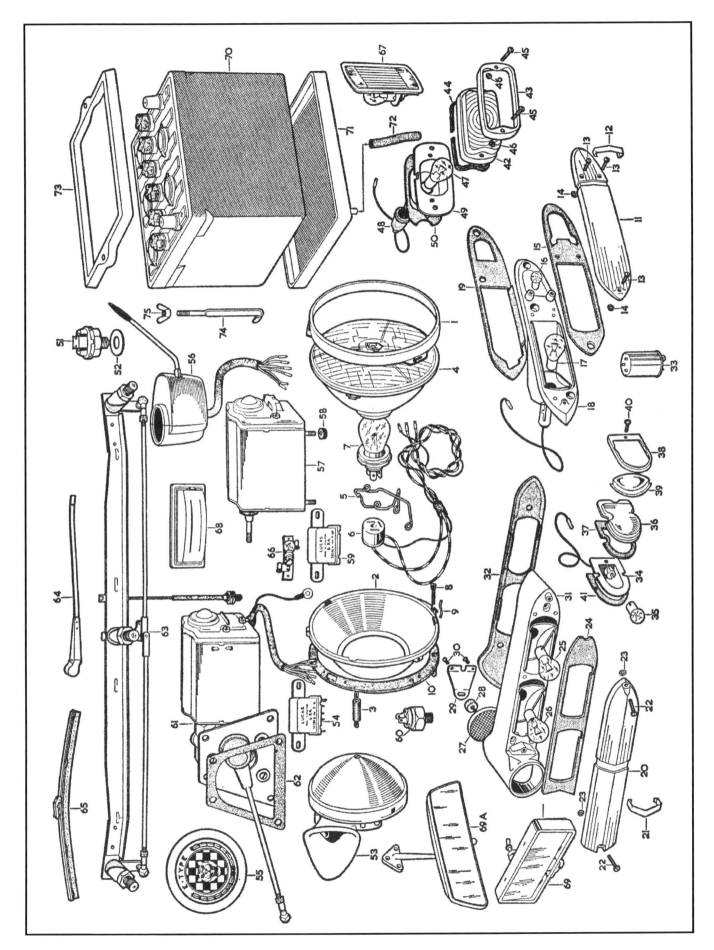

PLATE 53

307

WINDSCREEN WASHER

Part No.	Description	Plate No.	No. per Unit	Remarks
C.17004	**WINDSCREEN WASHER UNIT COMPLETE WITH TUBES, 'T' PIECE AND JETS (54071196-2.SJ)**		1	
8408	**Motor,** complete with Coupling (54711928)	54— 1	1	
8035	**Pump Assembly** (295194)	54— 2	1	
8036	**Moulded Cover,** for Reservoir (295138)	54— 3	1	
8037	**Rubber Gasket,** between Cover and Reservoir (295042)	54— 4	1	
8038	**Rubber Filler Cap,** in Cover (295043)	54— 5	1	
8039	**Union,** securing Motor to Pump (54715154)	54— 6	1	
8040	**Glass Reservoir** (295058)	54— 7	1	
8041	**Bracket,** holding Reservoir (295061)	54— 8	1	
UFS.419/8H	**Screw,** Set, securing Windscreen Washer Bracket to Dash		3	
C.723/A	**Washer,** Shakeproof, on Setscrews		3	
BD.18957/1	**Distance Piece,** on Setscrews		3	
UFS.419/3H	**Screw,** Set, sealing redundant mounting holes		3	
8408	**MOTOR COMPLETE WITH COUPLING (54711928)**	54— 1	1	
8042	**Contact Assembly,** complete with Adjusting Screw		1	
8043	**Brush Set** (295198)		1	
8044	**Armature** (295023)		1	
8990	**Lucar Connector** (54190172)		3	
C.15643/1	**SCREEN WASHER TUBE (70″ LONG)**	54— 9	1	
C.15644	**'T' PIECE AT JUNCTION OF FLUID TUBES (295091)**	54—10	1	
C.15645	**JET ASSEMBLY (54711657)**	54—11	2	

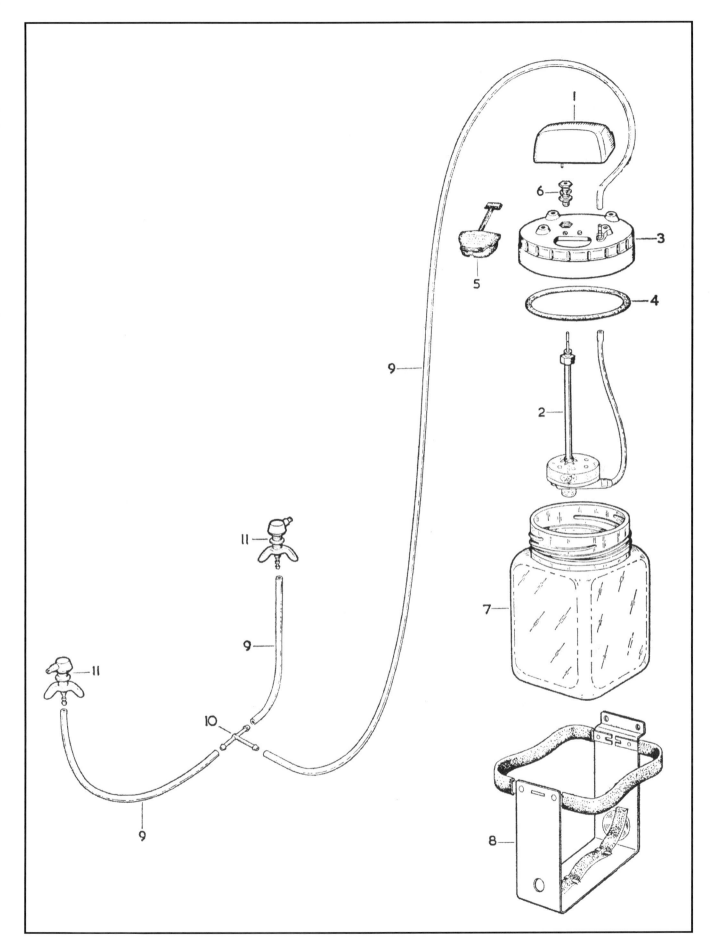

PLATE 54

309

HEATER AND DEMISTER INSTALLATION

Part No.	Description	Plate No.	No. per Unit	Remarks
C.17271	**CASE ASSEMBLY FOR HEATER**	55– 1	1	
C.17300	**Side Panel Assembly,** for Heater Case	55– 2	1	
BD.1229/1	**Screw,** Self-Tapping, securing Side Panel to Case		6	
C.15587	**Spring,** steadying Air Control Flap	55– 3	1	
C.19761	**Lever Assembly,** for connection of Spring to Air Control Flap	55– 4	1	
UFS.119/7R	**Screw,** Set, clamping Lever on Control Flap Shaft		1	
UFN.119/L	**Nut,** on Setscrew		1	
AW.102/T	**Washer,** Plain, under Nut		1	
C.18711	**AIR RELEASE DUCT, ON BOTTOM PANEL, INSIDE HEATER CASE**	55– 5	1	
BD.1814/2	**Pop Rivet,** securing Duct to Heater Case		6	
C.17641	**CLAMP BRACKET FOR MOUNTING OF HEATER CASE TO FRAME SIDE MEMBER**	55– 6	1	
UFS.119/4R	**Screw,** Set, securing Heater Case to Bracket		2	
C.723/A	**Washer,** Shakeproof, on Setscrews		4	
UFN.119/L	**Nut,** on Setscrews		2	
AW.102/T	**Washer,** Plain, on Setscrews		2	
UFS.125/4R	**Screw,** Set, securing Heater Case to Dash		4	
C.724	**Washer,** Shakeproof, on Setscrews		4	
C.17308	**SEAL BETWEEN HEATER CASE AND DASH**	55– 7	1	
C.17092	**WATER RADIATOR FOR HEATER**	55– 8	1	

Part No.	Description	Plate No.	No. per Unit	Remarks
C.17303	**SEAL (FELT) AT TOP AND BOTTOM OF WATER RADIATOR**	55– 9	2	
C.17304	**SEAL (POLYURETHANE) AT L.H. END OF WATER RADIATOR**	55–10	1	
C.17305	**SEAL (POLYURETHANE) AT R.H. END OF WATER RADIATOR**	55–11	1	
C.18514	**SEAL (POLYURETHANE) ON HEATER RADIATOR SEATING AIR CONTROL FLAP WHEN CLOSED**	55–12	1	
C.18107/3	**SEAL (POLYURETHANE) ON HEATER CASE FOR LOWER EDGE OF AIR CONTROL FLAP**	55–13	1	
C.18917	**SEAL (POLYURETHANE) SEATING ENDS OF AIR CONTROL FLAP**	55–14	2	
C.18713	**SEAL (POLYURETHANE) ON AIR CONTROL FLAP, FOR RELEASE DUCT**	55–15	1	

Part No.	Description	Plate No.	No. per Unit	Remarks
C.17427	**HEATER MOTOR ASSEMBLY**	55–16	1	
C.17309	**Adaptor Plate,** for mounting of Heater Motor		1	
C.17352	**Fan,** on Heater Motor	55–17	1	
C.18241	**Spire Nut,** securing Fan	55–18	1	
C.17428	**Resistance,** for Heater Motor (FHE.3103/01)	55–19	1	
BD.1814/1	**Pop Rivet,** securing Resistance to Adaptor Plate		2	
C.17310	**Sealing Ring** (Polyurethane) between Adaptor Plate and Heater Volute	55–20	1	
C.14696	**Grommet,** in motor Adaptor Plate, at fixings to Heater Volute	55–21	4	
UFN.119/L	**Nut,** securing Motor to Volute		4	
AW.102/T	**Washer,** Plain, under Nuts		4	
C.17280	**INTAKE MESH, AT TOP OF HEATER VOLUTE**	55–22	1	
C.18239	**Fixing Ring,** for Intake Mesh	55–23	1	
BD.1229/1	**Screw,** Self-Tapping, securing Fixing Ring to Volute		4	
C.18240	**RUBBER SEAL, BETWEEN BONNET AND HEATER AIR INTAKE**		1	
C.17421	**ADAPTOR, AT REAR OF INLET MANIFOLD, FOR WATER FEED TO HEATER**	55–24	1	
C.2296/1	**Copper Washer,** on Adaptor	55–25	1	
C.18987	**HOSE, BETWEEN ADAPTOR AND R.H. FEED PIPE BEHIND DASH TOP PANEL**	55–26	1	
C.2905/2	**Clip,** securing Hose	55–27	1	

Part No.	Description	Plate No.	No. per Unit	Remarks
C.17771	**R.H. FEED PIPE ASSEMBLY, BEHIND DASH TOP PANEL, BETWEEN HOSE AND WATER CONTROL VALVE**	55–28	1	
C.17314/1	**Fixing Flange,** for Feed Pipe	55–29	2	
BD.1814/2	**Pop Rivet,** securing Feed Pipe to Dash through Fixing Flanges		6	
C.17777	**ELBOW HOSE, BETWEEN R.H. FEED PIPE AND WATER CONTROL VALVE**	55–30	1	
C.2905/1	**Clip,** securing Elbow Hose	55–31	2	
C.17820	**WATER CONTROL VALVE ASSEMBLY (SMITHS FHW.1272/30)**	55–32	1	SUPERSEDED BY C.20820.
C.20820	**WATER CONTROL VALVE ASSEMBLY (SMITHS 011-99. 7109/119)**		1	SUPERSEDES C.17820.
C.17821	**Mounting Block,** under Valve	55–33	1	
C.9928	**Sealing Ring,** for L.H. Feed Pipe	55–34	1	
UFB.119/9R	**Bolt,** securing Control Valve to Dash		2	
AG.102/X	**Washer,** Spring, on Bolts		2	
C.17773	**L.H. FEED PIPE ASSEMBLY, BEHIND DASH TOP PANEL, BETWEEN WATER CONTROL VALVE AND HEATER RADIATOR**	55–35	1	
C.17314/1	**Fixing Flange,** for Feed Pipe	55–36	1	
BD.1814/2	**Pop Rivet,** securing Feed Pipe to Dash through Fixing Flange		3	
C.17778	**ELBOW HOSE, BETWEEN L.H. FEED PIPE AND HEATER RADIATOR INLET**	55–37	1	
C.2905/1	**Clip,** securing Elbow Hose	55–38	2	

Part No.	Description	Plate No.	No. per Unit	Remarks
C.17779	**ELBOW HOSE, BETWEEN HEATER RADIATOR OUTLET AND REAR RETURN PIPE**	55–39	1	
C.2905/1	**Clip,** securing Elbow Hose	55–40	2	
C.17775	**REAR RETURN PIPE ASSEMBLY, BEHIND DASH TOP PANEL, FOR WATER FROM HEATER**	55–41	1	
C.17314/1	**Fixing Flange,** for Rear Return Pipe	55–42	2	
BD.1814/2	**Pop Rivet,** securing Rear Return Pipe to Dash through Fixing Flanges		6	
C.4399	**HOSE BETWEEN REAR AND FRONT RETURN PIPES**	55–43	1	
C.2905/2	**Clip,** securing Hose	55–44	2	
C.16871	**FRONT RETURN PIPE AT R.H. SIDE OF CYLINDER BLOCK**	55–45	1	**SUPERSEDED BY C.19366.**
C.19366	**FRONT RETURN PIPE AT R.H. SIDE OF CYLINDER BLOCK**		1	**SUPERSEDES C.16871.**
C.16963	**Hanger Bracket,** rear, for Front Return Pipe	55–46	1	
C.16964	**Hanger Bracket,** front, for Front Return Pipe	55–47	1	
UFS.119/4R	**Screw,** Set, securing Pipe in Brackets		2	
UFN.119/L	**Nut,** on Setscrews		2	
C.723/A	**Washer,** Shakeproof, under Nuts		2	

Part No.	Description	Plate No.	No. per Unit	Remarks
C.14999/1	**HOSE BETWEEN FRONT RETURN PIPE AND ADAPTOR ON WATER PUMP**	55–48	1	
C.2905/2	**Clip,** securing Hose	55–49	2	
C.17421	**ADAPTOR, IN WATER PUMP, FOR RETURN FROM HEATER**	55–50	1	
C.2296/1	**Copper Washer,** on Adaptor	55–51	1	
C.17872	**L.H. CONTROL LEVER ASSEMBLY OPERATING AIR FLAP IN HEATER CASE**	55–52	1	
C.17873	**R.H. CONTROL LEVER ASSEMBLY OPERATING WATER VALVE**	55–53	1	
UFB.125/10R	**Bolt,** for pivoting of Control Levers		1	
C.18701	**Bush** (Steel) on Bolt		1	
C.17783	**Distance Collar,** between Control Levers		1	
C.18414/1	**Wavy Washer,** between Distance Collar and L.H. Control Lever		1	
BD.541/20	**Special Washer,** outside Control Levers		2	
C.8737/1	**Nut,** Self-Locking, on Bolt		1	
C.18700	**Support Bracket,** on escutcheon fixing studs, for Control Levers	55–54	1	
C.16794/3	**CONTROL CABLE, OPERATING AIR FLAP**	55–55	1	
C.15714/3	**Outer Cable,** on Control Cable	55–56	1	

Part No.	Description	Plate No.	No. per Unit	Remarks
C.16794/1	**CONTROL CABLE, OPERATING WATER VALVE**	55–57	1	
C.15714/2	**Outer Cable**, on Control Cable	55–58	1	
C.17324	**End Fitting**, securing Control Cables to Levers	55–59	2	
C.17874	**Special Screw**, in End Fitting		2	
C.18510	**Bracket**, on L.H. Facia inner mounting Bracket, for Cable Abutment Clamp	55–60	1	
UFS.119/4R	**Screw**, Set, securing Bracket		2	
C.723/A	**Washer**, Shakeproof, on Setscrews		2	
C.18571	**Abutment Clamp**, securing Control Outer Cables to Bracket	55–61	1	
UFS.119/4R	**Screw**, Set, securing Abutment Clamp		1	
UFN.119/L	**Nut**, on Setscrew		1	
C.723/A	**Washer**, Shakeproof, under Nut		1	
C.2850	**Grommet**, for Outer Cables	55–62	See remarks	**4 off required for R.H. Drive Cars.** **5 off required for L.H. Drive Cars.**
C.17801	**ESCUTCHEON FOR HEATER CONTROL LEVERS**	55–63	1	
C.18456	**Plate**, behind Escutcheon, inscribed "OFF-AIR-ON" "COLD-HOT"	55–64	1	
UFN.119/L	**Nut**, securing Escutcheon and Control Lever Support Bracket to L.H. Facia		2	
C.723/A	**Washer**, Shakeproof, under Nuts		2	
C.10351	**TRUNNION FOR CONNECTION OF CONTROL INNER CABLE TO AIR FLAP AND WATER VALVE**	55–65	2	
C.10352	**Screw**, Set, in Trunnions	55–66	2	
C.17287	**Abutment Clamp**, securing Flap Control Outer Cable to Bracket on Heater Case	55–67	1	
UFS.119/4R	**Screw**, Set, through Abutment Clamp		1	
C.723/A	**Washer**, Shakeproof, on Setscrew		1	
BD.19853	**DOOR ASSEMBLY, UNDER SIDES OF DASH, FOR AIR FROM HEATER**	55–68	2	
BD.20506	**Spring**, on Doors		2	
BD.10807	**Knob**, on Doors		2	
UCS.119/3R	**Screw**, Set, securing Knob to Doors		2	
C.723/A	**Washer**, Shakeproof, on Setscrews		2	
BD.19856	**Seal** (Polyurethane) for Doors		2	
UFS.119/3R	**Screw**, Set, securing Doors to Dash		8	
C.723/A	**Washer**, Shakeproof, on Setscrews		8	

Part No.	Description	Plate No.	No. per Unit	Remarks
	DEMISTER CONNECTIONS BEHIND INSTRUMENT PANEL AND FACIAS			
BD.14607	**RUBBER ELBOW, ON HEATER BOX, FOR CONNECTION OF HOSE TO DEMISTER NOZZLES**	55–69	3	**USE IN CONJUNCTION WITH SCREEN RAIL FACIA ASSEMBLIES BD.19752, OPEN CARS, OR BD.23634, FIXED HEAD COUPE.**
BD.14607	**RUBBER ELBOW, ON HEATER BOX, FOR CONNECTION OF HOSE TO DEMISTER NOZZLES**		1	
BD.23569	**RUBBER ELBOW, ON HEATER BOX, FOR CONNECTION OF HOSE TO DEMISTER NOZZLES**		2	**USE IN CONJUNCTION WITH SCREEN RAIL FACIA ASSEMBLIES BD.22732, OPEN CARS, OR BD.23832, FIXED HEAD COUPE.**
BD.5281/10	**FLEXIBLE HOSE BETWEEN RUBBER ELBOW AND CENTRE DEMISTER NOZZLE (7″ LONG)**	55–70	1	
BD.5281/11	**FLEXIBLE HOSE BETWEEN RUBBER ELBOWS AND OUTER DEMISTER NOZZLES (11″ LONG)**	55–71	2	**USE IN CONJUNCTION WITH SCREEN RAIL FACIA ASSEMBLIES BD.19752, OPEN CARS, OR BD.23634, FIXED HEAD COUPE.**
BD.5281/14	**FLEXIBLE HOSE BETWEEN 'Y' PIECES AND INTERMEDIATE DEMISTER NOZZLES AND RUBBER ELBOW TO CENTRE DEMISTER NOZZLE (6″ LONG)**		3	
BD.5281/15	**FLEXIBLE HOSE BETWEEN 'Y' PIECES AND OUTER DEMISTER NOZZLES (14½″ LONG)**		2	**USE IN CONJUNCTION WITH SCREEN RAIL FACIA ASSEMBLIES BD.22732, OPEN CARS, OR BD.23832, FIXED HEAD COUPE.**
BD.25214	**'Y' PIECE FOR FLEXIBLE AIR DUCT HOSES**		2	

HEATER AND DEMISTER INSTALLATION

Part No.	Description	Plate No.	No. per Unit	Remarks
BD.19752	**SCREEN RAIL FACIA ASSEMBLY** **(COMPRISING PANEL, CRASH PAD, FACING, ATTACHMENT BRACKETS AND DEMISTER NOZZLES)**	55–72	1	**OPEN CARS ONLY.** **FOR SPARES REPLACEMENTS USE BD.22732** (See page 185).
BD.22732	**SCREEN RAIL FACIA ASSEMBLY** **(COMPRISING PANEL, CRASH PAD, FACING, ATTACHMENT BRACKETS AND DEMISTER NOZZLES)**		1	**OPEN CARS ONLY.**
BD.20634	**SCREEN RAIL FACIA ASSEMBLY** **(COMPRISING PANEL, CRASH PAD, FACING, ATTACHMENT BRACKETS AND DEMISTER NOZZLES)**		1	**FIXED HEAD COUPE ONLY.** **FOR SPARES REPLACEMENTS USE BD.23832.** (See page 241).
BD.23832	**SCREEN RAIL FACIA ASSEMBLY** **(COMPRISING PANEL, CRASH PAD, FACING, ATTACHMENT BRACKETS AND DEMISTER NOZZLES)**		1	**FIXED HEAD COUPE ONLY.**

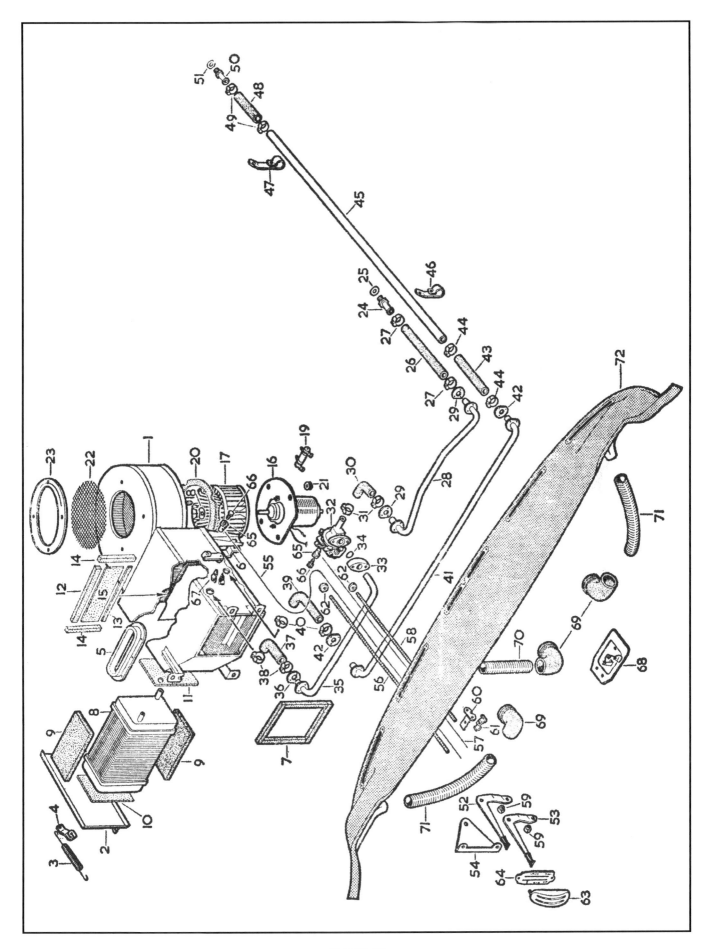

PLATE 55

OPTIONAL EXTRAS

Part No.	Description	Plate No.	No. per Unit	Remarks
C.17632	**CAR RADIO ASSEMBLY** **(MKJA.09-500.TB)**		1	**LONG AND MEDIUM WAVEBANDS ONLY.**
8264	**Control Unit** (500.T)		1	
8267	**Amplifier Unit** (RMH.98200/B)		1	
8673	**Aerial** (AW.606/60)		1	
8519	**Aerial Bracket** (RMO.3449/E)		1	
8674	**Bracket,** mounting Amplifier Unit (RMO.3320/K)		2	
8523	**Loudspeaker** (RMO.3776)		2	
8524	**Loudspeaker Lead** (RMR.2056/12)		1	
8525	**Loudspeaker Lead** (RMR.2081/48)		1	
8675	**Link Cable** (RMR.2010/48)		1	
8542	**Battery Lead** (RMR.2069/6)		1	
8676	**Jumper Lead** (RMR.2033/48)		1	
8677	**Cover,** for Transistor (RMO.3743)		2	
8274	**Fuse** (3 amp.) (RMH.38825/F)		1	
8272	**Sleeve,** for Fuse (RMO.3383)		1	
8628	**Condenser,** for Coil (RMO.1A/T.11)		1	
8629	**Condenser,** for Dynamo (RMO.1A/T.12)		1	
8678	**Condenser,** for Oil Pressure Gauge Electric Element (RMO.1W/T.1)		1	
C.17633	**CAR RADIO ASSEMBLY** **(MKJA.09-502.TB)**		1	**MEDIUM WAVEBAND ONLY**
8265	**Control Unit** (502.T)		1	
	All other items are as for Car Radio C.17632			
C.17634	**CAR RADIO ASSEMBLY** **(MKJA.09-230.RB)**		1	**MEDIUM AND SHORT WAVEBANDS ONLY.**
8266	**Control Unit** (230.R/VCO)		1	
C.12687	**Amplifier Unit** (RMH.92450/RB)		1	
8489	**Bracket,** mounting Amplifier Unit (RMO.3451/BA)		1	
8511	**Cover,** for Amplifier Unit (RMO.3486/BA)		1	
8673	**Aerial** (AW.606/60)		1	
8519	**Aerial Bracket** (RMO.3449/E)		1	
8523	**Loudspeaker** (RMO.3776)		2	
8524	**Loudspeaker Lead** (RMR.2056/12)		1	
C.8525	**Loudspeaker Lead** (RMR.2081/48)		1	
8526	**Loom Assembly** (RMR.3597)		1	
8542	**Battery Lead** (RMR.2069/6)		1	
5241	**Fuse,** 5 amp. (RMH.38825/G)		1	
8272	**Sleeve,** for Fuse (RMO.3383)		1	
8628	**Condenser,** for Coil (RMO.1A/T.11)		1	
8629	**Condenser,** for Dynamo and "D" Terminal on Control Box (RMO.1A/T.12)		2	
C.5367	**Condenser,** for Oil Pressure Gauge Electric Element (RMO.1W/T.1)		1	
C.8630	**Condenser,** for Control Box		1	
C.16114	**WING MIRROR**		2	**SUPERSEDED BY C.19909.**
C.19909	**WING MIRROR (MAGNATEX M2VC/6C)**		2	**SUPERSEDES C.16114.**

Part No.	Description	Plate No.	No. per Unit	Remarks
C.12816	**PETROL FILLER CAP (LOCKING TYPE) (WB.7/8653)**		1	
9212	**FRONT SEAT SAFETY BELT (LAP/DIAGONAL FITTING) COMPLETE WITH ATTACHMENT BOLTS AND EYE BOLTS**		2	Fitted from Chassis No. 850301 and subs. 876359 and subs. 860113 and subs. 885318 and subs.
9213	**REAR SEAT SAFETY BELT (DIAGONAL FITTING) COMPLETE WITH ATTACHMENT BOLTS AND EYE BOLTS**		2	
BD.22629	**GLASS IN BOOT LID (CLEAR GLASS)**		1	**FOR USE WITH ELECTRICALLY HEATED BACK LIGHT FOR FIXED HEAD COUPE CARS** from Chassis No. 860001 to 860478. 885001 to 886013.
BD.22741	**GLASS IN BOOT LID ("SUNDYM" GLASS)** **ALTERNATIVE TO BD.22629.**		1	
BD.22740	**GLASS IN BOOT LID (CLEAR GLASS)**		1	**FOR USE WITH ELECTRICALLY HEATED BACK LIGHT FOR FIXED HEAD COUPE CARS** from Chassis No. 860479 and subs. 886014 and subs.
BD.22744	**GLASS IN BOOT LID ("SUNDYM" GLASS)** **ALTERNATIVE TO BD.22740.**		1	
C.20124	**Fuse Connector**		1	**FOR USE WITH ELECTRICALLY HEATED BACKLIGHT.**
C.20123	**Backlight Connector**		1	
C.15639	**Grommet**		2	
C.18341	**Grommet**		3	
BD.22655	**Clip**, for Fuse Connector		1	
BD.711/5	**Screw**, securing Clip		1	
C.20081	**Sail Eyelet**, and Ring		1	
C.17001	**P.V.C. Strap**, holding Cables (3½" long)		2	
C.17002	**Stud**, for Straps		2	

OPTIONAL EXTRAS

Part No.	Description	Plate No.	No. per Unit	Remarks
5194	**KEY FOB (11/721) (LEATHER) BEARING THE "JAGUAR" WINGS**		1	**PLEASE STATE COLOUR REQUIRED.**
9036	**KEY FOB (11/723) (LEATHER) WITH AN ENAMELLED "JAGUAR" BADGE**		1	
BD.20687	**DETACHABLE HARDTOP ASSEMBLY**		1	**FOR USE WITH OPEN CARS.**
BD.22857	**Attachment Bracket**, R.H.		1	Fitted to Chassis No. 850024 and subs. 875027 and subs.
BD.22856	**Attachment Bracket**, L.H.		1	
BD.20487/3	**Screw**, Set, securing Attachment Brackets to Hardtop		4	
BD.21516/6	**Washer**, Shakeproof, on Setscrews		4	
BD.541/31	**Washer**, Special, under Shakeproof Washers		4	
9222	**HARDTOP FITTING KIT**		1	
BD.23760	**Mounting Bracket**, R.H.		1	
BD.23761	**Mounting Bracket**, L.H.		1	
BD.5552/8	**Screw**, Set (Countersunk Head) securing Mounting Brackets		4	
BD.20092/2	**Screw**, Set (Cheese Head) securing Mounting Brackets		2	Fitted from Chassis No. 850024 to 850091. 875027 to 875385.
C.723/A	**Washer**, Shakeproof, on Setscrews		2	
C.3562	**Washer**, Special, on Setscrews		2	
BD.21191/1	**Tapped Plate**		2	
BD.21191/2	**Retainer**, for Tapped Plate		2	
BD.23469	**Spacer**, for Hoodsticks Mounting		2	
BD.23762	**Bolt**, securing Hardtop		2	
9223	**HARDTOP FITTING KIT**		1	
BD.23760	**Mounting Bracket**, R.H.		1	
BD.23761	**Mounting Bracket**, L.H.		1	
BD.5552/8	**Screw**, Set (Countersunk Head) securing Mounting Brackets		4	Fitted from Chassis No. 850092 to 850455. 875386 to 876974.
BD.20092/2	**Screw**, Set (Cheese Head) securing Mounting Brackets		2	
C.723/A	**Washer**, Shakeproof, on Setscrews		2	
C.3562	**Washer**, Special, on Setscrews		2	
BD.23469	**Spacer**, for Hoodsticks Mounting		2	
BD.23762	**Bolt**, securing Hardtop		2	

INTERPRETATION OF CATALOGUE

Attention is drawn to the lay-out of this catalogue. It will be observed that the heading of each assembly is printed in **BOLD BLOCK LETTERS,** whilst the spares relevant to each assembly are **printed in small type and inset to the right.**

The fact that certain items (printed in small type) are not "inset" indicates that they do not form part of any assembly and must, therefore, be ordered as individual items.

ILLUSTRATIONS

To aid identification of spares, "exploded" illustrations are incorporated in this catalogue.

These illustrations may be used in the following manner:—

(a) If a Flywheel is required, the index shows that the details for the item are printed on page 5 and that it is illustrated on Plate 1. Turning to page 5, the necessary information for the ordering of the part is given, whilst the column headed "Plate No." indicates that reference to item number 44 on plate 1 will give a photographic view of the component required.

(b) The details for each illustrated item are printed in the script in numerical Plate number order. An item may therefore be first identified photographically. For example if Friction Pads are required for the Front Brake, a picture of the part may be found on Plate No. 22, together with the Plate reference number. It is now an easy matter to find Plate number "22—2" in the script and the Part No. and Technical Description are at once apparent.

ORDERING

Customers are advised to make themselves familiar with the method of ordering spare parts in accordance with the explanatory notes which follow.

PUBLICATION J.30

FIRST PUBLISHED AUGUST, 1961
REPRINTED JUNE, 1963 (A.L.1.)

INSTRUCTIONS FOR ORDERING SPARE PARTS

To avoid delay through inaccurate interpretation, it is of great importance that the information detailed in the following paragraphs be strictly adhered to when placing orders.

CAR TYPE

Always quote the engine and chassis numbers except when Stock Orders are placed, in which case the Year and Model must be indicated.

If Gearbox components are required it is necessary to quote on the order the **serial number** of the Gearbox, together with any **prefix or suffix letters** which may be indicated.

The Serial numbers are stamped on a brass plate which is fitted on the right-hand side of the Engine Compartment and also on the Units referred to above.

DETAILS OF PARTS REQUIRED

When ordering, the most complete information should be given to enable us to deal with your requirements expeditiously and to minimise delay in the despatch of the goods. Therefore we strongly recommend that the following procedure be adopted:—

(1) Identify part with technical description in catalogue.

(2) On order, quote (a) part number, (b) technical description.

Note: In no case should the illustration plate number be given.

(3) If doubt exists as to the part number or technical description, a dimensioned sketch will assist in the interpretation of the order, or, alternatively, the old part should accompany the order as a pattern. When patterns are sent, it is **most important** that they be labelled, indicating the name and address of the sender, together with any reference such as order number, etc. Patterns will not be returned unless instructions to that effect accompany the order. In the absence of such instructions, patterns will be scrapped after retention for a period of ONE WEEK.

(4) To order in "sets" is misleading. Please, therefore, **state the specific quantity required.**

SPECIAL ATTENTION

Particular attention is drawn to the fact that when such items as wings, doors, door glasses, etc., are required, care should be taken to indicate whether they are located on the left-hand or right-hand side of the car. The position is determined by the driver's own left or right hand when seated in the car.

Orders for any coloured parts such as carpets, casings, etc., should clearly state the precise colour required.

DESPATCH INSTRUCTIONS

The full address of the destination to which the goods are to be sent, together with that of the customer, should be clearly defined.

Whilst every effort will be made to observe customers' wishes as to the mode of transport, it is the normal custom to utilize the quickest possible method, whether it be post, passenger train or road transport, this being dependent upon the size and weight of the package and the destination to which it is to be sent.

PRICES

Current retail prices shown in the Jaguar Parts Master Price List are subject to alteration without notice, and are for delivery at Works. Postage, carriage and packing will be charged extra.

DAMAGE BY FIRE OR ACCIDENT

Whilst every precaution is taken, we do not accept liability for damage which may be caused by fire to any motor car or part thereof entrusted to us for any purpose whatsoever. Nor is liability accepted for accidental damage.

INDEX TO PARTS

INDEX TO PARTS

INDEX TO PARTS

INDEX TO PARTS

INDEX TO PARTS

INDEX TO PARTS

Printed and distributed by Brooklands Books Ltd., PO Box 904,
Amersham, Bucks, HP6 9JA, England

Pub No. J.30

ISBN: 9781869826314   Ref: J32PH   9W4/2389

OFFICIAL TECHNICAL BOOKS

Brooklands Technical Books has been formed to supply owners,
restorers and professional repairers with
official factory literature.

Workshop Manuals

Jaguar Service Manual 1946-1948		9781855207844
Jaguar XK 120 140 150 150S & Mk 7, 8 & 9		9781870642279
Jaguar Mk 2 (2.4 3.4 3.8 240 340)	E121/7	9781870642958
Jaguar Mk 10 (3.8 & 4.2) & 420G	E136/2	9781855200814
Jaguar 'S' Type 3.4 & 3.8	E133/3	9781870642095
Jaguar E-Type 3.8 & 4.2 Series 1 & 2		
E123/8, E123 B/3 & E156/1		9781855200203
Jaguar E-Type V12 Series 3	E165/3	9781855200012
Jaguar 420	E143/2	9781855201712
Jaguar XJ6 2.8 & 4.2 Series 1		9781855200562
Jaguar XJ6 3.4 & 4.2 Series	E188/4	9781855200302
Jaguar XJ12 Series 1		9781783180417
Jaguar XJ12 Series 2 / DD6 Series 2	E190/4	9781855201408
Jaguar XJ6 & XJ12 Series 3	AKM9006	9781855204010
Jaguar XJ6 OWM (XJ40) 1986-94		9781855207851
Jaguar XJS V12 5.3 & 6.0 Litre	AKM3455	9781855202627
Jaguar XJS 6 Cylinder 3.6 & 4.0 Litre	AKM9063	9781855204638

Owners Workshop Manuals

Jaguar E-Type V12 1971-1974	9781783181162
Jaguar XJ, Sovereign 1968-1982	9781783811179
Jaguar XJ6 Workshop Manual 1986-1994	9781855207851
Jaguar XJ12, XJ5.3 Double Six 1972-1979	9781783181186

Parts Catalogues

Jaguar Mk 2 3.4	J20	9781855201569
Jaguar Mk 2 (3.4, 3.8 & 340)	J34	9781855209084
Jaguar Series 3 12 Cyl. Saloons		9781783180592
Jaguar E-Type 3.8	J30	9781869826314
Jaguar E-Type 4.2 Series 1	J37	9781870642118
Jaguar E-Type Series 2	J37 & J38	9781855201705
Jaguar E-Type V12 Ser. 3 Open 2 Seater	RTC9014	9781869826840
Jaguar XJ6 Series 1		9781855200043
Jaguar XJ6 & Daimler Sovereign Ser. 2	RTC9883CA	9781855200579
Jaguar XJ6 & Daimler Sovereign Ser. 3	RTC9885CF	9781855202771
Jaguar XJ12 Series 2 / DD6 Series 2		9781783180585
Jaguar 2.9 & 3.6 Litre Saloons 1986-89	RTC9893CB	9781855202993
Jaguar XJ-S 3.6 & 5.3 Jan 1987 on	RTC9900CA	9781855204003

Owners Handbooks

Jaguar XK120		9781855200432
Jaguar XK140	E101/2	9781855200401
Jaguar XK150	E111/2	9781855200395
Jaguar Mk 2 (3.4)	E116/10	9781855201682
Jaguar Mk 2 (3.8)	E115/10	9781869826765
Jaguar E-Type (Tuning & prep. for competition)		9781855207905
Jaguar E-Type 3.8 Series 1	E122/7	9781870642927
Jaguar E-Type 4.2 2+2 Series 1	E131/6	9781869826383
Jaguar E-Type 4.2 Series	E154/5	9781869826499
Jaguar E-Type V12 Series 3	E160/2	9781855200029
Jaguar E-Type V12 Series 3 (US)	A181/2	9781855200036
Jaguar XJ (3.4 & 4.2) Series 2	E200/8	9781855201200
Jaguar XJ6C Series 2	E184/1	9781855207875
Jaguar XJ12 Series 3	AKM4181	9781855207868

Carburetters

SU Carburetters Tuning Tips & Techniques	9781855202559
Solex Carburetters Tuning Tips & Techniques	9781855209770
Weber Carburettors Tuning Tips and Techniques	9781855207592

Jaguar - Road Test Books

Jaguar and SS Gold Portfolio 1931-1951	9781855200630
Jaguar XK120 XK140 XK150 Gold Port. 1948-60	9781870642415
Jaguar Mk 7, 8, 9, 10 & 420G	9781855208674
Jaguar Mk 1 & Mk 2 1955-1969	9781855208599
Jaguar E-Type	9781855208360
Jaguar XJ6 1968-79 (Series 1 & 2)	9781855202641
Jaguar XJ12 XJ5.3 V12 Gold Portfolio 1972-1990	9781855200838
Jaguar XJS Gold Portfolio 1975-1988	9781855202719
Jaguar XJ-S V12 1988-1996	9781855204249
Jaguar XK8 & XKR 1996-2005	9781855207578
Road & Track on Jaguar 1950-1960	9780946489695
Road & Track on Jaguar 1968-1974	9780946489374
Road & Track On Jaguar XJ-S-XK8-XK	9781855206298

Available from Amazon and Jaguar specialists

Brooklands Books Ltd., PO Box 904,
Amersham, Bucks, HP6 9JA, England

Printed in Great Britain
by Amazon

57184833R00185